Jossey-Bass Teacher

Jossey-Bass Teacher provides educators with practical knowledge and tools to create a positive and lifelong impact on student learning. We offer classroom-tested and research-based teaching resources for a variety of grade levels and subject areas. Whether you are an aspiring, new, or veteran teacher, we want to help you make every teaching day your best.

From ready-to-use classroom activities to the latest teaching framework, our value-packed books provide insightful, practical, and comprehensive materials on the topics that matter most to K–12 teachers. We hope to become your trusted source for the best ideas from the most experienced and respected experts in the field.

Inspiring Teachers is a teacher-created organization dedicated to empowering and inspiring educators. Our vision is to help teachers create quality learner-centered classrooms and improve student success. To meet this vision, we offer a variety of print and free online resources including our Web site, www. inspiringteachers.com; a free weekly teaching tips newsletter; Ask a Mentor service; practical guides for teachers; and staff development workshops. Each element of our support system can be used individually or in conjunction with other parts. We are here to let educators know they are not alone. We've been there! We understand the daily life of a classroom teacher—stressful, overwhelming, and often lonely. We are here to help ease the stress, offer a listening ear, and lend a helpful hand to any teacher in need. You can contact us at info@inspiringteachers.com.

Classrooms that Spark!

Recharge and Revive Your Teaching

SECOND EDITION

Emma S. McDonald
Dyan M. Hershman

Published in partnership with
Inspiring Teachers

JOSSEY-BASS
A Wiley Imprint
www.josseybass.com

Published by Jossey-Bass
A Wiley Imprint
989 Market Street, San Francisco, CA 94103-1741—www.josseybass.com

Jossey-Bass books and products are available through most bookstores. To contact Jossey-Bass directly call our Customer Care Department within the U.S. at 800-956-7739, outside the U.S. at 317-572-3986, or fax 317-572-4002.

Jossey-Bass also publishes its books in a variety of electronic formats. Some content that appears in print may not be available in electronic books.

Library of Congress Cataloging-in-Publication Data

McDonald, Emma S. (Emma Suzanne), 1970
    Classrooms that spark! : recharge and revive your teaching / Emma S. McDonald and Dyan
M. Hershman. — 2nd ed.
        p. cm.
    Includes bibliographical references and index.
    ISBN 978-0-470-49727-2 (pbk.)
        1. Teaching—Philosophy. 2. Teaching—Handbooks, manuals, etc. I. Hershman, Dyan
M. (Dyan Melissa), 1971- II. Title.
LB1025.3.M348 2010
371.102—dc22
                                                                                        2009044806

Printed in the United States of America
SECOND EDITION
PB Printing   10 9 8 7 6 5 4 3 2 1

The Authors

Emma S. McDonald is a veteran teacher with experience teaching preschool, fifth through eleventh grades in public school, and adults. She received her master's degree in education in 2000 and began working with new teachers as a mentor and advocate. In addition to teaching in the classroom, she has worked as a consultant with the Region 10 Teacher Preparation and Certification program in Richardson, Texas, helping new teacher interns obtain certification. McDonald is the coauthor of several other books, including *Survival Kit for New Teachers, Survival Kit for New Secondary Teachers*, and *ABC's of Effective Parent Communication* with Dyan Hershman. She is also a featured columnist for *Education World* and has published many articles for practical teaching strategies in *Instructor, Classroom Connect, Teachers of Color*, and the Kappa Delta Pi *New Teacher Advocate*. In addition to writing, she conducts professional development workshops for teachers across the United States and continues to mentor new teachers and encourage veteran teachers through the Inspiring Teachers Web site (http://www.inspiringteachers.com).

Dyan M. Hershman is a veteran teacher with experience teaching third, fourth, and fifth grades. In addition to teaching in the classroom, she has worked as a consultant with the Region 10 Teacher Preparation and Certification program in Richardson, Texas, helping new teacher interns obtain certification. She is the coauthor of several books, including *Survival Kit for New Teachers, Survival Kit for New Secondary Teachers*, and *ABC's of Effective Parent Communication* with Emma McDonald. She also works with teachers through professional development workshops offered across the United States and continues to provide helpful guidance and advice to new teachers.

This book is dedicated to our loving husbands, Sean and Matt, and our children, Joshua, James, Mason, and Kylie. Without their unfailing support and help, this book would not have been possible.

We also dedicate this book to our parents, Captain and Mrs. Charles O. Barker and Lieutenant Colonel and Mrs. Michael J. Ferguson. They have given us the drive and discipline to tackle any task with enthusiasm and determination. Without their love and support, we would not be the teachers we are today! We dedicate this book as well to our beloved students.

Finally, we dedicate this book to our great friend and constant supporter, Rita Bukin. Although she is no longer with us, her constant sense of purpose and boundless energy continue to inspire and sustain us in our quest to help other teacher.

Contents

Acknowledgments

We thank the following people for sharing experiences and ideas or offering to review and provide feedback on *Classrooms that Spark*:

Dodie Ainslie, New York
Jeri Asaro, New Jersey
Trina Cochrane, Waco, Texas
Marci Davis, Davenport, Iowa
Marie Fischer, Houston, Texas
Shirley Ann Fukumoto, Kamuela, Hawaii
Angela Hall, North Ogden, Utah
Patti Hanlon, Scottsdale, Arizona
Nada Itani, Beirut, Lebanon
Erica Kruckenberg, Prosper, Texas
Dahkine Lee, Hinesville, Georgia
Carol Loper, Prosper, Texas
Alice McDuffy, Richardson, Texas
Debbie Meadows, Stevenson Ranch, California
Tamora Mennenga, Mansfield, Texas
Karen Morris, Plano, Texas
Barb O'Brien, Ashland, Wisconsin
Tracy Paul, Australia
Terri Richards, Plano, Texas
Suzanne Ryals, Marathon, Florida
Alice Schnepf, Chandler, Arizona
Connie Skipper, Garland, Texas
Juddson Smith, Plano, Texas
Vicki Thompson, Mesquite, Texas
Michelle Vaughn, Frisco, Texas
Grace Yohannan, Orlando, Florida

Introduction

Fire, so primitive and primeval, is at once both fearsome and friendly. It can offer security and warmth from a cold, unfriendly night, and yet if it gets out of hand, it can become a raging inferno that consumes everything in its path. Each of us looks at fire from a different perspective. We bring in our own memories of fire that color our attitude toward it.

While in college, my friends and I would gather at the beach for a bonfire every month or so. The beauty was the way we came together and became a community. Although those days are long past, the memories of that fire are still rich and vibrant in my mind. I can feel the heat of it against the cool ocean breeze and smell the sweetness of toasted marshmallows. I can feel the warmth of good friends surrounding me and the security of the bright orange light on the dark beach. Each of these is a vivid memory.

Fires can conjure up passionate and provoking thoughts for some, while providing peace and relaxation for others. A fire, so vast in its existence and ways it is used, is a perfect metaphor for teaching. Teaching is complex and varied because we each bring to it our own experiences. We add new ideas and remove old ones, we have calm years and tumultuous years, and we feel the ebb and flow for the passion of learning in ourselves and our students. And yet through everything, we continually fight to keep this fire of teaching burning in our hearts because we know it makes a difference in our own lives and the lives of our students.

This book is divided into three parts to build the analogy between teaching and learning and building a strong fire. Part One is "Preparing for the Fire," because, as we all know, preparation is one of the keys to a successful classroom. Part Two offers ideas and strategies for "Lighting the Fire," helping us spark the love of learning in our students. Finally, Part Three, "Fanning the Flames," offers a variety of strategies for maintaining that love of teaching within us and the love of learning within our students. The ideas in each part will also help you integrate technology into your daily classroom life. The purpose of this book, then, is to use these ideas and strategies in unison to create a classroom that is passionate and motivating to students.

For your benefit, reproducible pages are included at the end of each chapter for use in the classroom. Additionally, online and book resources for further reading and study are listed at the end of the chapter. These will assist you in developing a deeper understanding of the ideas and strategies presented in the chapter.

Classrooms that Spark!

Part One

Preparing for the Fire

For the resolute and determined there is time and opportunity.

—Ralph Waldo Emerson

He who dares to teach must never cease to learn.

—John Cotton Dana

Preparations

Organization and More

Just as we need to find firewood and stack it neatly to build a good fire, so we need to organize and prepare for each school year. Many of us begin the year just as harried and frazzled as new teachers because we've just spent a summer either working at another job or relaxing and trying to forget about everything. It sometimes feels as if we are starting all over. Do you find yourself sitting and staring at your pile of books, supplies, files, and notebooks, trying to absorb everything that must be done? This doesn't even begin to describe the nightmare associated with anyone who has had to change classrooms or pack up everything while the school is under renovation. What to do? The obvious choice is to begin with organization. (See the "Before-School Checklist" at the end of the chapter.)

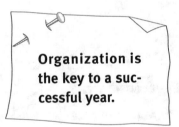

Organization is the key to a successful year.

Organize Your Files

The best place to start organizing is by looking at each of your hard copy files. Are you still using that particular handout or resource? If so, hang on to it. If it is something with which you are loathe to part, put it in a special pile of "keepers," but do not keep it in a separate file folder.

Sort through your files of handouts. Will you remember you have fifty copies of this already? Most likely not. If you are honest with yourself, you'll admit that when it is time to use the handout, you'll have another class set printed or copied. So keep one master, and throw the rest in the recycling bin. There is no need to take up precious filing space with extra copies.

If you have a digital copy of the handout, there is no need to keep a hard copy as well in your filing cabinet. If you do not have a digital copy, think about scanning it into your computer as a .pdf file. Adobe Acrobat is a program you can then use to modify the text and graphics of the file. Be sure to set your scan settings to Document, not Picture. Another option is retyping the document using Microsoft Word or another word processing program.

Organizing Electronic Files

It is no use to have electronic files which help save paper and money, unless you can find what you need. The computer has systems in place to help you organize your files similar to a filing cabinet. Even better, you can organize into deeper levels. Figure 1.1 is one example of how you might organize digital files.

Name ▲	Size	Type
Form1.doc	26 KB	Microsoft Office Word 97 - 2003 Document
Handout.doc	26 KB	Microsoft Office Word 97 - 2003 Document
Lesson Plans_Week of xxxx.doc	26 KB	Microsoft Office Word 97 - 2003 Document
Notes to Self.doc	26 KB	Microsoft Office Word 97 - 2003 Document
Website Resource List.doc	26 KB	Microsoft Office Word 97 - 2003 Document
Presentation1.ppt	99 KB	Microsoft Office PowerPoint 97-2003 Presentation
Video.flv	4,500 KB	Flash video file

Address: C:\Desktop\Grading Period\UNIT NAME

File and Folder Tasks

Other Places

Details

Figure 1.1   Model File Structure

Moment of Reflection

Take some time to think about an organization structure for your digital files. This structure should be logical and make it easy to find each file. How would you label the top folder? What folders and files would be included? What subfolders would you use beneath each?

When organizing digital copies of resource materials such as handouts from workshops attended, magazine articles, forms for classroom management, and so on, separate the files into categories or themes (see example themes in "Setting Up Binders" following). Again, think about scanning handouts and papers you may not use daily and organizing them into files by topic. Also, bear in mind that you may move or transfer to a new school, so keeping reference files on a separate storage system may be useful if you need to transfer files from one computer to another. When considering a digital storage system, keep in mind the capacity (how much it can store), the portability (how easy it is to move), and the accessibility (how easy it is to find and use). One type of digital storage system is a portable external back-up drive or hard drive. This is a drive you connect to your computer through a USB cable. You can get an external hard drive in a variety of storage levels from 250 GB to 500 GB. Another storage system you might consider is a read/rewrite CD. These typically have less storage available, 650 MB or less. A third storage unit is the USB flash drive. The flash drive can hold 280 MB to 250 GB depending on the unit purchased. Below we list some of the pros and cons for each storage system to help you determine which would best meet your needs.

Portable External Backup Drive or Hard Drive

Pros: Large storage capacity

Cons: Can be fragile. If the drive is not disconnected and moved properly, problems can occur with the computer recognizing the drive.

All files kept in one location

If the drive crashes, it can be costly to recover all data stored on it.

R/RW CD

Pros: Smaller, more portable

Cons: Depending on type can only be written to once

Easily stored and organized

Can be broken if not careful

Portable External Backup Drive or Hard Drive (*Continued*)

Easy to label

Can be used on any compatible computer

Can store data pertaining to one topic (ex: classroom management) on each disk

Smaller disk space capacity

Flash Drive

Pros: Small, easily portable

Easy to move between computers

Can easily transfer files and folders between computer and drive (no waiting for files to be "written")

Acts as an external drive

Larger storage space available than a CD

Cons: Harder to label

Easy to misplace

Idea Share

If your preference is to use flash drives, consider using a plastic craft box with separate storage compartments inside. Each compartment can be labeled with the contents of the flash drive. This is a great way to keep these smaller drives organized. Use a small mailing or file folder sticker to label each drive.

Setting Up Binders

If you have more hard copy files than you have room for, consider using a set of binders to hold your materials and masters of handouts or transparencies.

Take the pile of "keepers," and separate them into categories by themes—for example:

- Subject areas
- English as a Second Language/English Language Learners
- Classroom management
- Childhood development
- Assessment tools
- Learning and thinking centers
- Thematic units
- Bulletin boards

- Special needs strategies
- Administrative (for memos, policies, and so on)
- Strategies for gifted and talented students

Place your masters into the appropriate section. Now you can easily find the handout you need.

Setting Up a Teacher Binder

An excellent way to organize yourself and the units you will be teaching is to create a binder that contains your classroom information, lesson plans, and handouts organized for each six-week period. The teacher binder is a useful resource: you can carry it with you throughout the school, it provides a reference when the computer cannot be accessed readily, and it is a good resource for substitute teachers to turn to.

The binder should be organized with tab dividers and contain the following sections:

1. Student information
   - Seating chart
   - Student list for your classes
   - Textbook records
   - Lists and schedules for English as a Second Language and English Language Learners and special education students
   - Student locker and class job information
2. Calendars and schedules
   - Lunch schedules
   - Library daily classroom schedule
   - Counseling
   - A calendar with important district, school, grade information, and personal dates marked
   - Computer lab level
   - Elective and special areas
   - Classroom management procedures
3. Team planning
   - Notes taken during team planning
   - Parent conferences held as a team
   - Detailed records
4. Extra forms
   - Hard copies of forms used frequently, such as parent communication, bonus points, certificates, free homework coupons, and positive notes

5. Six-week unit
   - Planning calendar that shows an overview of the six weeks
   - Six-week lesson plans and daily handouts

Keep everything in the binder in chronological order to make planning easier the following year, and attach transparencies through a hole-punched clear plastic cover.

Moment of Reflection

How might a teacher binder help you stay organized on a daily basis? What sections would you include? What do you see as the pros and cons of this strategy?

You can set up course binders as well, with one binder for each course you'll be planning. In the front of each, insert a planning calendar that shows an overview of the grading period. Keep everything, including transparencies and handouts, in chronological order, and use tabs for easy reference.

Idea Share

At the end of the grading period, transport the material for it into another three-ring binder and clearly label it for future reference with the name of the unit.

If you are planning units in themes that last less than the grading period, move the unit into a new binder as soon as you have completed it.

Many teachers prefer to plan at home rather than in the classroom. If you have a binder, this will cut down on the number of manila files you will have to carry back and forth between school and home. It will also simplify your preparation for the next year.

A flash drive provides an easy way to use and review digital files for a particular unit between school and home. In your lesson plans, reference the label of the correct drive to use so you know which one to take home.

Dealing with Paperwork

Have you ever seen the cartoon drawing showing a desk piled high with paperwork and a tiny hand waving above it as though someone were drowning? Maybe this is how you feel: overwhelmed by the tons of papers put in your box throughout the year. Here are some strategies for dealing with paperwork:

- As soon as you check your mailbox, take five or ten minutes to file, respond to, or recycle each item. Record the dates from memos, bulletins, and other material in your calendar, along with any other pertinent information. Once this information is in your calendar, you can file it or recycle it.

- Handle your e-mail similarly. Scan for junk mail, and delete these first. Next, prioritize messages as high, medium, or low. Use the flags on your e-mail program, and choose a different color to represent each level. Next, set appointments and due dates from e-mails onto your computer calendar program.

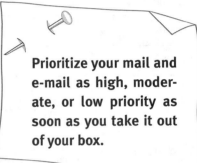

Prioritize your mail and e-mail as high, moderate, or low priority as soon as you take it out of your box.

- If something needs a response, do this right away. Procrastinating will merely ensure it never gets done. You will end up with a huge pile on your desk and people demanding the information they need from you. If the memo or request requires a lengthy response, schedule a time on your calendar to respond to it during your planning time or after school. Put this item in a special folder so you don't forget it.

File memos and other papers as soon as you read them.

- Respond to e-mails by priority from high to low. Not sure how to prioritize? Here are a few examples of each level.

High	Medium	Low
Parent communications	School or district e-news	Ads and sales notices
Tasks or requests due this week	Tasks or requests due next week	Forwards from friends
Principal memos	Teacher requests from other schools	Newsletters
Teacher requests within the school		

- Put due dates on your calendar program, and make appointments for yourself to complete tasks.
- Use your system for filing paperwork. Whether you use manila folders or a three-ring binder with tabbed sections, go ahead and use it! The school's teacher manual is another great place to store memos, newsletters, or other paperwork you receive from the school. Create an additional tabbed section in the notebook if necessary.
- Organize digital files received and e-mails. E-mail attachments can be "saved as" and moved to the appropriate unit or topic folder on the computer. Most e-mail programs have a way to create new folders to hold e-mails. Drag and drop or move individual e-mails into appropriate folders. Some examples of e-mail folders might include:

Principal memos	Team/department	Programs bought/subscribed
District news	Education newsletters	Organizations
District-level supervisor	Parent e-mails	Special education
Professional trainings	Products, wish list	Fun/inspirational stories

- Use subfolders within each main category to help you further organize e-mails.

The most important thing to remember when dealing with paperwork and e-mails is to get everything sorted, prioritized, and handled as soon as possible. If you ignore it or procrastinate, it will pile up on you. Although you may find it hard to devote fifteen minutes to respond to notes, memos, e-mails, and so on, you will save hours in the long run. Set aside time to do this during your planning period or after school. Put all of your daily mail in a letter tray or plastic bin devoted to this. Keep e-mails in bold in your inbox so you know they need to be addressed.

For help staying organized, we strongly recommend FlyLady.com (www.flylady.com), a Web site dedicated to helping people get and stay organized. Although the ideas are mostly for the home, this site does have strategies applicable to the classroom as well. FlyLady stresses the importance of taking baby steps and building good habits. A few FlyLady-like tips from us would be:

- Set a timer for fifteen minutes each morning to work through your paperwork and e-mail.
- Handle today's mail and e-mail before you deal with past correspondence.
- Respond to as much of the past correspondence in those fifteen minutes as you can.
- When the timer goes off, stop and put all the past mail in a large container on the floor. Mark e-mails as "unread" so they appear bold in the inbox.

Classrooms that Spark!

- Repeat this same process in the afternoon, and continue until you have responded to or recycled all your past mail and e-mail.

If you try to do too much at once, you'll get burned out. That is why small steps are so important.

Moment of Reflection

Do you receive more items in your mailbox or in your in-box? How often do you find yourself with mail or e-mail piled up waiting to be addressed? What has helped you deal with this backup in the past? What strategies might you use to help stay on top of this issue? How much time do you typically spend catching up on mail and e-mail?

Getting Students Organized

Organization is an important life skill that should be taught and reinforced throughout a student's academic career. Spending time on training students in organizational skills using binders, folders, lockers, and desks is time well spent. You can't assume students have learned this skill prior to entering your classroom, even the older ones. Use the beginning of the school year to make student organization a focus not only during homeroom or advisory time but also in your lessons.

Organization is a key element of classroom management.

Idea Share

Use plastic shoe boxes with lids to store scissors, crayons, tape, math manipulatives, and other materials. They also make great storage places for supplies for student groups. Label each box with the table number or name so that students can easily locate the supply box for their group.

Student Binder

It is important for students to begin the year in an organized fashion. You can help them do this by requiring them to set up a binder. Here are a few tips on creating an organized binder:

- Place the assignment calendar at the front of the binder.
- Place class or school rules, procedures, and syllabus after the calendar.

- Use tabbed sections. The best way is to organize them in the order you teach each subject. Middle and high school students should order their section according to their class schedule.
- Have students keep graded work in the appropriate subject area. You might encourage students to use pocket dividers, and place graded work in these.
- Pocket dividers can also be used to organize homework and work to be turned in to the teacher.

It is important to check the binders regularly (every six weeks will work). Sometimes it is helpful to give a grade for an organized binder. This will motivate students to continue using it correctly.

One year I had an assistant principal at our middle school who helped us keep the students accountable for their binders staying organized. She would dress up, every couple of weeks or so, as the 'Binder Fairy' and do snap inspections on everyone's binder. You never knew what she would be dressed in—army fatigues, a ballerina tutu, a clown outfit, biker clothes, a poodle skirt—but always with a pair of fairy wings and a wand. She would present a gift certificate of some sort to everyone who had a neat and organized binder. The kids loved it, and it really kept many of them motivated to stay organized with their binder. I would often say to my kids, 'I wonder if the Binder Fairy will come to class today,' and they would all scramble to make sure their binder was in order.

Pocket Folders

In addition to the binder, it is helpful for students to keep and use separate pocket folders that stay in the classroom. Color-coding these folders will help with quick access for each activity or subject area. Here we look at different ways folders can be used:

- *Writing journal.* Students place paper in the middle of the folder using the brads. Have students date and write their daily journal entry on these pages. In order not to waste paper, encourage students to use an entire page before beginning a new one. There could be several entries on a page.
- *Writing workshop folder.* Students keep notes for writing workshop in the middle of the folder, prewriting and drafts in the front pocket, and works in progress in the back pocket (Atwell, 1992). The final copy will go in the writing portfolio. (We discuss writing workshop in greater detail in Chapter Eight.)
- *Test-taking skills folder.* Students place paper in the middle of the folder to keep notes on test-taking strategies covered in class. Practice sheets and answer keys should be kept in the pockets.

- *Reading workshop folder.* Students keep a reading log that includes the title, author, pages read, and a short summary as well as a reading response (Atwell, 1992). Students may also keep their book project work in this folder. (We discuss the reading workshop in Chapter Eight.)

- *Student log.* Students use this pocket folder to turn in major projects. Any data collected and drafts should be placed in the front pocket to show the process of their work. The final copy of the project should be placed in the middle of the folder, with any bulky or odd-sized papers or products placed in the back pocket.

- *Math folder.* Students use this pocket folder to hold math notes, work in progress, and completed work. Have them place paper in the middle of the folder to keep notes taken during class. You might use a spiral notebook as an alternative to the pocket folder. Set aside the first several pages to become a table of contents for the math notes. Each page of notes should be given a page number and title. Students can then enter the title and page number in their table of contents in order to readily locate information at any given time. (This strategy is discussed further in Chapter Nine.)

- *Subject areas.* No matter what subject you teach, a pocket folder is a useful way to contain notes, work in progress, and homework or work completed.

Additional Strategies

Accordion folders would work well instead of multiple pocket folders. Students could use each section within to hold logs, materials, notes, and other material for each subject area.

Middle school teachers can use one pocket folder for their class, with the folders stored in a crate or plastic bin for each class period. Students keep notes, ongoing writing projects, a reading log, or whatever other material is necessary for that class. Place the class set of folders on a table prior to the start of class. When students enter, they take their own folder back to their seat. Call out names of folders left (for those who regularly don't follow instructions); any remaining belong to absent students. This is a way to check for attendance and get folders distributed.

"A few years ago, it was driving me crazy that my students kept losing their writing samples. In my language arts classes, we do several drafts on different topics throughout the semester. Toward the end of the grading period, I have students pick one draft to work into a final copy. Half of my students could never find their previous work! Finally, I insisted that the students leave their writing in the classroom in a writing folder. Then everyone was able to locate their drafts when it came time to choose. This made my life so much less frazzled!"

If you and your school are working toward going green, these folders could also be kept on the computer. This works especially well if every student has access to a computer during class time. Students can journal daily; keep a reading, math, or science log; take notes; and keep ongoing writing projects in separate folders on the computer.

Other Uses for Pocket Folders

You may not have a daily use for the pocket folder in your class. However, a pocket folder is also a way to keep student work throughout the school year for use in a portfolio or to show improvement when meeting with parents. Following are two descriptions for using the pocket folder as a portfolio.

Writing Portfolio Folder

This folder holds student writing pieces. Nancie Atwell, in her book *In the Middle,* describes an excellent way to set up a writing portfolio that also tracks the progress of a student's writing skills throughout the year. A simple portfolio collects student work to be reviewed at the end of the year. Later in the book, we discuss the use of portfolios and give examples (see Chapter Four).

General Portfolio Folder

This folder holds student work of all kinds. Students should have some choice as to the works placed in this folder. Also, when students enter work into this portfolio, they should attach a 3-by-5 index card with comments about their product. They should note to the teacher whether the piece is their best work, a work in progress, or a sample to show how they have improved over time (this can include their "worst" work also). (For more ideas on using the portfolio for assessment purposes, see Chapter Four.)

> In middle school English language arts, we would have students take their portfolio (a binder that was kept in the classroom during the year) home after each quarter to share it with their parents. Students would complete a reflection, and then parents would go over it with their child and add comments or questions. We felt this was a great way to get parents involved, and it also opened up communication between school and home, focusing it on specific projects, writing pieces, or reflections on reading strategies. This portfolio included all graded and commented work for the quarter, offering a full picture of the quarter (and ensuring papers weren't 'eaten up by the locker).

Thinking Folder

This folder holds enrichment work. Students who complete thinking center activities on their own can place the products in their thinking folder to be graded for extra credit.

Absent Folder

This folder is used to collect work and assignments for students who are absent. A student in class can work as a scribe to copy down board assignments, homework, notes, and any other important information and activities done during class on a specific absent form you use consistently all year. (See the "We Missed You" form at the end of the chapter.) The student should place the "We Missed You" form along with any handouts in the absent folder and place it on the absentee's desk. The teacher could be the "scribe" if necessary. This folder offers a way to help students get back on track when they return to school.

Absent work can also be posted on a class Web site or e-mailed directly to older students in order to save paper. When lesson outlines and notes are posted on wiki pages, students can also get important information missed during class in addition to missing assignments.

Student Information

This folder is for teacher purposes. It contains student and parent communication records as well as any other behavior documentation that needs to be kept private. You should use manila folders that will easily fit into your filing cabinet.

Student folders should be kept on the computer as well. These folders can hold parent e-mails, digital forms, samples of student work, and other information sent over the computer. In addition, text files can be created to record tardiness, absences, grades, and disciplinary measures. Keep in mind that you will need to have this information readily accessible for any parent conference. A laptop and flash drive would work.

Digital Folders

Do your students have their own space on the school servers to hold work completed or in progress on the computer? Check to see whether your school has some basic organization already in place. For example, does each teacher or class have a folder where students can place files they have created?

Within your class folder, have students create additional folders to organize their work. This organizational skill will be used by students at home as well as in the workplace. Offer guidance as to the best labels for each folder. Students also need to be able to easily find the files they have created.

Moment of Reflection

In what ways do you encourage student organization? What strategies do you have in place for your classroom? How do you teach and apply organization skills in your classroom? What kind of digital organization do you teach or use? What strategies will you put in place to help students stay organized?

Student Mailboxes and In-Boxes

Each student should have a place to call his or her own in the classroom to keep folders, novels, papers, and personal supplies organized. This "mailbox" doesn't have to be a large tub or box. An inexpensive way to create mailboxes is to use plastic crates and hanging file folders with tabs. This works well for upper-grade teachers as well.

- Mailboxes are handy for storing school supplies on the first day of school before students begin using them.
- They work very nicely for handing out graded papers without taking up class time to do so.
- When students are working on research or group projects, mailboxes are a good place to keep class work so it won't get lost.
- For middle and high school students, set aside a tall filing cabinet with each drawer dedicated to a particular class period. Each student then has a hanging file folder to hold work and materials needed for class.

> "For the longest time, my classroom was in a constant state of chaos, with papers and supplies floating around everywhere. I finally decided to get organized and set up mailboxes. I used hanging file folders and dedicated one for each student in my class. Students keep their journals, books, and unfinished work in their mailbox. I also keep a folder labeled 'graded work' in each. Once a day, my teacher helpers or I file graded student work into these folders. The students can then pull the work out of that folder and put it in their binder to take home. It has really kept the classroom less messy, and I don't feel as if I'm wasting class time every day to pass back student work!"

Creating Materials Ahead of Time

Another way to get organized is to create materials in bulk ahead of time, perhaps on weekends or during school holidays. One resource handy to have available is a stack of positive notes. Students (even high school students) love to get positive notes from their teacher, but what teacher has time to sit and write out a full note at the end of class? One solution is to brainstorm several different "positives," type them out, and copy them on bright paper. Set up a word document with four squares. Type one positive message in each square, using a fun yet easy-to-read font. Copy these on colored card stock paper, and then cut them out and place them in folders on your desk. Other ideas are to use a basket, hanging the folders on the wall or bulletin board, or putting a stack on your overhead or podium. Don't place these in a folder in your filing cabinet because they'll never get used. Put them where you can easily see and remember to use them.

Examples of Positives
- Thank you for participating in class today!
- Thank you for helping another student who needed it!
- Thank you for being such a good helper to me today!
- Thanks for sharing your ideas with us!
- Thanks for being on time!
- Thanks for leading that group!
- Thank you for sharing your materials!
- Thanks for bringing in all your work on time!
- I really liked your thoughts in our discussion about . . .
- You did an amazing job on . . .
- I can tell you did your personal best when . . .
- Thank you for your insights about . . .

Consider other specific positives you want to reinforce in your class, and think about life skills as well: cooperation, teamwork, honesty, integrity, friendship, perseverance, determination, and personal best, for example.

Now choose and sign the note, put a smiley face on it, and hand it to the student in leaving the room. These can also be sent as e-mails to older students in middle and high school or mailed home.

Implementing a New Strategy

Before school starts is the time to think about, plan, and create materials for new strategies you want to implement. Using new teaching ideas and methods helps put that spark back into the classroom. In addition, think about how you can bring your classroom into the twenty-first century. What new technology hardware and programs have you learned lately?

New ways of teaching can invigorate us and motivate our students. When implementing a new strategy

- Sort through new ideas learned during staff development or personal development through classes and reading.
- Choose one that inspires or excites you.
- Determine how the new strategy will fit with the overall vision or mission and curriculum of the school.
- Brainstorm ways you can incorporate this new strategy into your units and lessons. One caution is not to overuse the strategy so that it becomes boring!
- Create any materials needed.

Day-of-the-Week Folders

These folders are an invaluable tool for classroom organization for staying organized on a day-to-day basis. Day-of-the-week folders help manage paperwork and materials in two main ways.

First, it is a place to hold materials. During the week, as you plan for lessons later that week or the following week, you will begin to gather materials such as copies of handouts.

Example: Tuesday during your planning period, you research information, gather materials, and make copies for Thursday's lesson. You immediately place these materials in the Thursday folder so they are ready to be used. Otherwise they end up in piles on your desk, cause clutter, and often are lost when you need them!

You can use these for all sorts of purposes. For example, if you have a special test or form for students to complete on Friday, place these in your Friday folder. If you have a field trip on Wednesday, put all of the necessary information, forms, entrance tickets, and so forth into the Wednesday folder.

The second reason to use these is to relieve stress and promote a professional appearance. Let's say you have a flat tire on the way to work Tuesday morning, and your principal must tend your class for an hour or so until you arrive. Which would he or she appreciate more?

- A mass of papers piled on the desk with your lesson plans somewhere in your room, but she doesn't know where they are.
- A folder labeled "Tuesday" placed neatly on your desk with lesson plans, warm-up activities, materials, copies, and a substitute folder inside all ready to go.

Using day-of-the-week folders not only gives you a more professional appearance, but you will feel calmer and better prepared every morning when you follow these folder guidelines:

- Get everything ready for the next day before you leave the classroom. Set up your chalkboard with the date, agenda, objectives, and warm-up activity.
- Prepare your day-of-the-week folder to be used the following day. Be sure all of your lesson plans and required materials for the day are inside.
- Place it on your desk so that it is the first thing you or anyone else sees when approaching your desk. Put the folder for a substitute in last (on the bottom), just in case.

Strategy for Secondary Teachers

- Create a different folder for each class you teach. For example, if you have two sessions of Rhetoric and three sessions of American literature, you will have two daily folders.
- Label each folder with the title of the class.
- Keep folders not in use in the filing cabinet in a hanging folder for each day. If you use hanging files with a gusset, you'll be able to make copies of handouts ahead of time and store them in the appropriate place.

Creating Day-of-the-Week Folders

Use different colored folders and label for each day of the week. This creates a color-coded system. Then be sure to do the following:

- Laminate the folders so they will last the year.
- Put a stand-up file holder on your desk to hold the folders in an easily accessible place.
- Set aside gusseted hanging files to hold different course folders.
- Put all materials for each day's lesson in the folder: copies, lesson plans, newsletter, activities, and so on.
- Before you leave each day, place your substitute folder inside your day-of-the-week folder in case you are absent.

Substitute Folder

Across the nation there has been a huge shortage of substitute teachers. The biggest reason for this deficit of "guest teachers," according to the National Substitute Teacher Alliance, is the lack of respect and support from school staff and faculty. This includes a lack of prior preparation, communication, and acknowledgment.

One way you can ensure that substitutes will want to come to your classroom is to provide them with detailed plans, instructions, and classroom policies and procedures. If these necessary tools are readily accessible, the substitute teacher will be more comfortable and confident about leading your class through the day. This will more than likely result in a problem-free day for both the substitute and the students. (See the "Checklist for Substitute Folder" form at the end of the chapter.)

When leaving instructions for substitute teachers, be sure to offer detailed explanations of how your classroom management system works. You also want to have alternative plans that can be used at any time during the year.

There are a number of reasons to prepare a substitute folder:

- It identifies school assemblies and other disruptions to scheduled plans.
- Substitute teachers will have an easier time adapting to unexpected disruptions if you have your classroom and school procedures and routines outlined in detail. This information will help the substitute know where to go in emergency situations or for school assemblies.
- Substitute teachers may not understand loosely sketched plans. Leaving detailed plans that identify specific activities in a specific order will help the substitute implement the plans.
- Substitute teachers may not feel qualified to implement a lesson or activity, so having alternate plans will give him or her another option to implement in class.

On the "Substitute Report Form" at the end of the chapter, you will find a place for the substitute teacher to record his or her contact information. When you have had a good substitute you'd like to teach your class again, store this information in your rotating file, personal digital assistance, phone, and computer e-mail or contact program. By having it in a variety of locations, you will be sure to find the information when you need it either at home or school.

Returning to the classroom after an absence can be a pleasure or a pain depending on how prepared you are for having a substitute teacher in your class.

Idea Share

On the computer, type out classroom procedures and other information that will not change much over time. Save this file for future reference and place it in a "class procedures" folder. Next year you can open the file, make the necessary changes, print it out, and you are ready to place the new information into your folder for substitutes.

Create a generic response form using Bloom's taxonomy that can be used with any type of in-class reading, both fiction and nonfiction. A sample page of questions based on Bloom's Taxonomy can be found in Chapter Eight. The substitute can use this form to stimulate discussion or hold students accountable for in-class reading assignments. Have the substitute choose one question starter from each level of Bloom's. Include a class set of this form in your substitute folder ready for use. Be sure to replenish your supply when you return to school. (See Chapter Seven for a description of Bloom's taxonomy and the keywords.)

Moment of Reflection

What is included in your substitute folder? Could you add anything else to make the day easier on the substitute teacher and your students when you are absent?

Setting Up Your Classroom

It is always a good idea to reflect on the effectiveness of your classroom setup each year. Begin this way:

- Make a sketch of your classroom.
- Think about how the layout worked last year. Are there any changes that need to be made? What were the problems? What worked well— and didn't work well?

Classrooms that Spark!

- Think about the flow of your room. Where do you want your students looking? Where is your screen, presentation station, whiteboard, and bulletin board? How do you think your changes will affect these aspects?
- Make necessary changes to your sketch.
- Try the new layout, and see how it works.

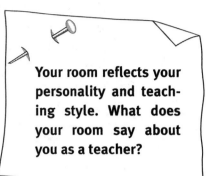

Your room reflects your personality and teaching style. What does your room say about you as a teacher?

Consider these questions to help you decide whether it is time to make a change:

- Is my current setup working? If not, should I change to rows or groups of desks?
- Should I use tables? Would they be more effective with my teaching style or subject area?
- How easily am I able to move between students?
- Can we all get out of the classroom quickly in an emergency?
- Do I have/want a writing center?
- Do I have/want a reading corner?
- Do I have/want learning centers?
- Do I have/want an arts area?
- Do I have/want a time-out or conference area?
- Should I have a computer station? If I do, where will it go?
- How does my teacher area look?
  - Are my desk, filing cabinet, and shelves in the way of the flow?
  - Are my curriculum materials easily accessible?
  - Can I visually monitor students from my desk?

The environment you create for your students is equally as important as the content you teach and the learning strategies you use. This applies to all teachers of all age groups, from preschool to graduate school. The environment encompasses the atmosphere, the traditions you set, the furniture arrangement, the centers or special areas within the room, and the decorations. All of these add up to create either a positive or negative environment for students.

Setting Up Your Digital Classroom

Before school starts is the perfect time for setting up your classroom Web site, blog, twitter account, or wiki space.

Class Web Site

Your district may have a program ready for you to use to upload classroom information. All you need to do now is input the information. Go ahead and put in your class schedule, classroom procedures, frequently asked questions for parents, initial assignments or syllabus, and a welcome letter from you. As the year progresses, you will post announcements, words of praise, assignments, due dates, and upcoming events as well.

If your district does not have a ready-made program, there are several free and paid options available for creating a classroom Web site. Inspiring Teachers (www.inspiringteachers.com) offers both free and paid Web sites for teachers. Free sites often include advertisements, but these are education related. Other options to consult are Classjump.com, Teacherweb.com, Schoolrack.com, Webschoolpro.com, Educatorpages.com, and Teacherwebsite.com.

Class Blog

The word *blog* comes from a combination of the words *web* and *log*. Initially blogs were used as a virtual or online diary or journal for individuals. Since blogs typically use a standard format, they are easier to use and update than a Web site. Individuals can log into their blog account, type in their thoughts, and post the information. It is an easy method for sharing thoughts, ideas, and information with a wide audience. (For additional information on what a blog is, how you can integrate it into your curriculum, and further sources for education blogs, see Chapter Seven.)

You can use a blog to post journal topics or discussion topics for students, keep a diary or reflect on what is happening in your classroom, comment on professional development strategies you've learned, and communicate information and ideas to parents. You can set up several blogs, each with its own purpose.

Take time before school starts to think about the types of blogs you might keep throughout the year. Remember that your blog does not have to be updated daily or even weekly. For example, a blog for parents could be updated monthly or even quarterly. Also keep in mind how you might want students to use blogs as part of your curriculum. This is discussed further in Chapter Seven.

Following are three educator blog sites you might find useful:

- 21classes.com
- Gaggle.net
- Edublogs.org

Twitter

This site allows individuals to post short comments (in a "tweet," which is no more than 140 characters) that are then viewed by those who follow their account. Teachers and students can use Twitter in a number of ways:

- Post short synopses of what is happening in the classroom.
- Set out what students learned during class.
- Offer reminders of forthcoming events and due dates.
- Provide tips for parents.

When using Twitter for middle and high school students, use the class period or course number to identify which class you are posting for.

You can easily set up a Twitter account for free on www.twitter.com. **Warning:** Make sure you set up a separate classroom account from your personal account to avoid having students and parents follow your personal updates.

Decide in advance how you plan to use your class Twitter account. For example, after teaching a lesson, you can have students work together as a class or in groups to develop a tweet summarizing what was learned. You then post the tweet using your phone or a computer, and it will appear on your account. Anyone following you (parents, other teachers, students) will then see the summary.

Encourage parents and students to "follow" your class on Twitter so they can see these regular posts.

Classroom Wiki Space

Some schools and teachers use a classroom wiki space instead of or alongside a classroom Web site. The wiki is a wonderful tool because it is interactive and is also easier to create and update than a Web site. Students go to the teacher's wiki site, which can then be broken into different pages. For example, each lesson may be its own page, or elementary teachers may have a page for each subject taught. This tool could also be used in conjunction with an interactive whiteboard for teaching lessons and completing activities. You could also have a page specifically for parents offering information and updates about the classroom.

The classroom wiki can be used by students to follow preapproved links for research. Students can also read notes provided by the teacher. The wiki can additionally be used for online learning for students. Parents can use the wiki to view information about their child's classroom. The parent page might also include links to school and district resources.

To learn more about educational wikis and creating your own, go to http://www.wikispaces.com/site/for/teachers. Wikispaces for teachers will walk you through step by step to get your wiki space set up and functional. For additional ideas on how you can use the Wikispace in your classroom, go to http://educationalwikis.wikispaces.com/.

Creating a Positive Environment

Students should feel welcomed and inspired to learn from the moment they walk up to your door. Decorate your door with a theme or slogan. Some examples include:

- "Welcome to a Beary Special Place"
- "Blasting Off to Learning"
- "Come Explore Learning in Room 32: Soar the Heights"
- "Learning Is Victory!"
- "Learning = Success!"
- "Using Our Minds to Conquer the World!"

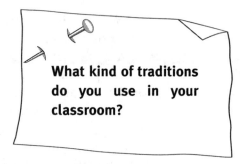

What kind of traditions do you use in your classroom?

Greet students with a smile as they enter the classroom.

Create traditions within your classroom: fun actions or events that students look forward to experiencing each day or week—for example:

- Every Friday we read from our Acts of Kindness box.
- Whenever we read a story, one student gets to introduce the reader.
- Ms. M. always sings a silly song right before the end of class.
- We always have a quote or puzzle of the week.
- The class develops a tweet for the class Twitter account at the end of class.
- A school mascot award is given each week to a student who showed most improvement or a specific character trait emphasized that week.

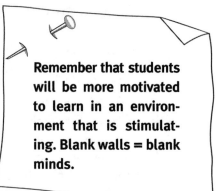

Remember that students will be more motivated to learn in an environment that is stimulating. Blank walls = blank minds.

Classroom walls and bulletin boards are covered with thought-provoking and stimulating material. Materials are age appropriate and include these types:

- Motivational posters
- Posters that are language rich
- Humorous posters
- Manners and character-building posters

Bulletin Board Ideas

You may have some tried-and-true bulletin board ideas you use each year, but it is always refreshing to do something different. The different ideas that follow run the spectrum from pre-K through grade 12, so not every idea will work for your particular classroom. Also, think about additional ways you can use these ideas to get your students involved in locating information and creating their own bulletin boards. This encourages higher-level thinking and creativity. Don't forget about using bulletin boards as thinking centers or learning centers with activities students can complete.

Bulletin Board Topics

- Quotable Quotes
- What's New or In Our World, for posting classroom, school, community, and world events
- Birthday Board, for posting student birthdays or a class birthday graph
- Centers, for posting brain challenges or learning center activities for students to complete
- Manners are Meaningful, for posting manners posters or tips of etiquette
- Famous Authors, for posting information or having students research an author and post their findings on the board.
- Famous Mathematicians, Scientists, Artists, Musicians, Sports Figures, People in History
- Careers
- We Are Learning . . . , to highlight a concept being taught
- See What We're Doing, for posting student work
- Who's Who in Room, for spotlighting students and their work
- Who Am I? which shows a baby picture of one of their classmates and offers clues; students guess who that person is
- Classroom Expectations
- Class slogan
- Theme, which changes with each unit
- Creative writing and journaling, which posts laminated calendar pictures showing landscapes and other types of images to help stimulate student writing

Conclusion

There are so many different tasks to be done before school starts that it can seem overwhelming. Nevertheless, these tasks are necessary to ensure starting the year well prepared. The more prepared you are at the beginning of school, the more effective you are throughout the year. The summer, and especially the few weeks before school starts, is the perfect time for examining new strategies you've learned about or a new technology idea you are ready to try. If you are interested in revitalizing your classroom, now is the time to make that effort.

References

Atwell, Nancie. *In the Middle: Writing, Reading, and Learning with Adolescents.* Upper Montclair, N.J.: Boynton/Cook, 1987.

Gilley, Margaret. *Sink Reflections.* New York: Bantam, 2002.

Web Site Resources

FlyLady, http://www.flylady.com

Scholastic, http://www2.scholastic.com/browse/article.jsp?id=3635

Teacher Vision, http://www.teachervision.fen.com/classroom-management/resource/5803.html

Internet for Classrooms, http://www.internet4classrooms.com/classroom_organization.html.

Before-School Checklist

☐ Laminate supplies.

☐ Set up room.
- Arrange desks and tables.
- Set up reading corner.
- Set up other special areas (for example, writing center, learning centers).
- Post classroom expectations posters.
- Set up bulletin boards.

☐ Set up student mailboxes and cubbies.

☐ Create day-of-the-week folders.

☐ Create individual student folders.

☐ Set up grade book.

☐ Write and mail welcome postcards to students.

☐ Create a class schedule.

☐ Create a substitute folder.

☐ Organize a teacher binder.

☐ Write out lesson plans for the first day.

☐ second day?

☐ third day?

☐ Meet with grade-level or academic department.

☐ Meet with special education and special areas teachers (as needed).

☐ Meet with mentee (as needed).

☐ Create materials for any new strategies to implement.

Name: _____   Date: _____

We Missed You!

You missed these cool activities in class today!	Important assignments
You missed the following quiz/test:	Journal topic/warm-up:
Other:	

Classroms that Spark!

Checklist for Substitute Folder

_____ Seating chart

_____ Class schedule and bell schedule

_____ Administrator and counselor contact information

_____ Easy stable lesson plans

_____ Daily instructions

_____ Class roll

_____ Sponge activities (short activities to focus student learning for a particular topic) and creative writing ideas in case students finish the lesson early (Sponge activities are addressed in more detail in Chapter Five.)

_____ A form for the substitute to report back to you [the "Substitute Report Form" follows]

_____ List of helpful students

_____ Names and room numbers of grade level/team members

_____ A copy of emergency procedures (fire drill, lockdown, hurricane, and so on)

Substitute Report Form

Date: _____

Today we:

Use this space to report what was actually done during class. What activities did you do? How much of the lesson plans did you cover? What else did you do that was not on the original lesson plan? Please include other information that you consider important to report.

The following problems occurred:

Use this space to describe any serious misbehavior or other problems. Be specific and report the facts without emotion.

Problem:	Action taken:
Problem:	Action taken:
Problem:	Action taken:

The following students were exceptionally good and/or helpful:

Contact information (please include phone number and e-mail address):

Creating a Balanced Classroom Environment

In order to have a roaring fire, you must have just the right elements. If the fireplace is too drafty or the firewood is wet, the fire will never start. The same is true in the classroom. It is vital to build a balanced classroom environment where students can learn. In order to do this, you need to nurture certain elements: your surroundings, leadership style, daily procedures, and relationships with your students. Since Chapter One covered the physical aspect of classrooms, we look at the last three in this chapter.

As teachers, we are much more than just babysitters, managers, and timekeepers. We are also leaders, a role that has much more importance than most people realize on the overall classroom climate. A leader guides, shapes, teaches, motivates, corrects, directs, and encourages his or her "platoon." In a teacher's case, the proper leadership style is crucial so that chaos doesn't rule.

We also need to make sure we have routines and procedures in place to begin building healthy habits from the first day of school. We must have clear definitions of these in our own minds in order to communicate them to our students.

Finally, we need to strive for positive relationships with our students, characterized by clear expectations and based on mutual respect, communication, and kindness. Just because we are in control and expect appropriate behavior does not mean we need to be cold or distant. Building positive relationships, in fact, is key to developing a classroom that sparks. Students who feel a personal connection to their teacher are motivated to work and learn.

Throughout this chapter, you will see that you can create a positive and motivating classroom environment by

- Being proactive
- Being organized
- Being well prepared
- Effectively communicating your desires and expectations
- Understanding that students cannot read your mind
- Having a positive and not hurtful sense of humor
- Having a good rapport with students

Classroom Leadership Styles

Teachers use three main leadership styles in the classroom:

- Teacher as dictator
- Teacher as free spirit
- Teachers as balanced leader

Teacher as Dictator

Teachers who act as dictator are often afraid of losing control, so they resort to maintaining a distant and stringent relationship with students that is businesslike, firm, and authoritarian.

Characteristics of a Dictator Leadership Style

- There is no room for lively group discussions or banter of any sort.
- Routines are strictly adhered to.
- Flexibility is not common.
- Tasks are performed in a quiet and efficient manner.
- Students are not encouraged to be individuals and active participants in the lesson.

- Students are required to conform to the teacher's way of learning.
- Creative thinking is not encouraged.
- Memorization and skill and drill are the main learning styles of this classroom.

Although predictability and routine can be positive classroom features, this type of leadership is often boring and squelches creativity. It also promotes a dull and resentful environment instead of one filled with active learning and excitement.

Rarely does a teacher accomplish a smoothly running classroom by resorting to dictatorship. Rather, students are more likely to rebel, complain, and misbehave because they are not intrinsically motivated.

In addition, when student resentment occurs, often parental concerns arise. Is the teacher being fair? Is she too demanding? Is my child's dislike of the teacher justified? What will the teacher think of me as a parent? These concerns can be barriers to a positive parent partnership.

Teacher as Free Spirit

An ingredient in the free spirit recipe is a teacher who is often unorganized and unprepared, which results in a choppy and incomplete presentation or lesson flow. Students are kept waiting while the teacher mentally decides what to do next or takes time to rummage for materials. Students get confused and distracted easily, which results in disruption after disruption and then more breaks because the teacher must stop to deal with unruly behavior.

Characteristics of a Free Spirit Leadership Style

- The teacher wants to be a buddy with the students rather than an authority figure.
- Students end up making most classroom decisions without guidance from the teacher.
- Lesson plans are loosely sketched, and student digressions, rather than the teaching objective, dictate the course of the lesson.
- Students are given maximum freedom to work and move about the classroom.
- The teacher gives the students the responsibility to make the decisions by themselves—in other words, to "be their own boss."
- When students are not actively engaged in learning, this teacher is often quick to anger because he or she feels students are abusing the freedoms they are given.

This leadership style would be perfect in a world where all students had the same set of values: honesty, integrity, responsibility, and determination. We would love for every classroom to be totally student centered, with students always intrinsically motivated. However, this is unrealistic. It is the nature of most children and adolescents to push the limits as far as they can. Therefore, this lax style of leadership is often a recipe for disaster and anarchy.

Parents are apprehensive of this loose classroom environment and wonder what kind of education their child is getting. They might wonder whether their child will be able to keep up academically in future years after a year of fun and games. They wonder as well what learning objectives are being met, and whether the chaos they see has a purpose or simply reflects a lack of preparation on the part of the teacher. These concerns on the part of parents can affect the appearance of the teacher as a professional and can act as a barrier to a positive relationship with both students and parents.

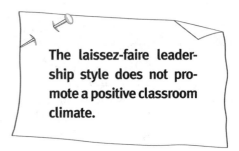

The laissez-faire leadership style does not promote a positive classroom climate.

Teacher as Balanced Leader

This leadership style blends the other two styles and achieves the greatest results. As they say, "Everything in moderation." A teacher using this balanced approach to classroom management will

- Set limits
- Communicate expectations clearly
- Follow routines and procedures
- Provide students with freedoms and responsibilities
- Offer choice
- Value students
- Invite student involvement on a daily basis

Other Characteristics of a Balanced Leadership Style

- It is organized in order to maintain a productive classroom.
- Discipline is a key component to this teacher-student relationship.
- Students are encouraged to be responsible for their own actions and held accountable.
- Students are actively involved in the classroom.
- Clear expectations are explained and reinforced from the first day of school.
- Consequences for inappropriate behavior are consistent.
- Students feel valued and motivated.

- Students are given freedoms and choices in order to discuss, move, and work about the classroom freely.

Students tend to be much more cooperative with this classroom environment because they feel respected, appreciated, and valued. This leads to students who are intrinsically motivated. In addition, parents are more likely to discuss concerns with you knowing that action will be taken and they will not be judged for their home situation.

Idea Share

Discuss the use of choice with parents as a way of motivating and disciplining students at home. Choice is a powerful tool that is not used as often as it should. Parents who use this tool at home are teaching children to make positive decisions in their lives and to self-regulate their behavior.

Moment of Reflection

How would you describe yourself as a leader? Does your style of leadership evoke positive or negative reactions? How does this translate to your relationships with students, colleagues, and parents?

Creating a Balanced Classroom Environment

The balanced leadership style results in a classroom that creates a nonthreatening environment where students and teachers feel safe. This comfort allows students to be better learners.

In providing a balanced classroom, teachers need to be prepared to accept additional roles:

- Mediator
- Tutor
- Leader
- Caregiver
- Listener
- Problem solver
- Disciplinarian

Accepting that you have these roles is vital to positive student relationships. The key to performing all of those roles, as well as the tasks required of us as teachers, is effective time management and organization.

Classrooms are complex, busy places. During a typical day, we are required to perform many tasks:

- Organize learning activities
- Present lessons
- Prepare materials
- Manage student behavior
- Manage classroom equipment
- Handle administrative and housekeeping duties
- Beat the clock!

And all of this must be accomplished while being interrupted for various reasons including assemblies, intercom announcements, office assistants, helping a sick student or getting a brand-new one, and many others.

The challenges you face daily can wear you down over time. The remainder of this chapter is dedicated to providing strategies for recharging your classroom management style so that you can have a balanced and positive classroom environment.

Time Management

Effectively organizing and managing your time is essential for both you and your students. When you feel overwhelmed or stressed by the inordinate number of tasks to be accomplished, your energy is being sapped. That is energy that should be going into your lessons and building relationships with students. If you feel at times that you use up more energy worrying about everything that must be done and less on your students, try some of the following time management ideas.

Portable To-Do List

Keep a small journal or a legal-sized yellow pad with you at all times. On a single page create two to four columns, each to record a to-do list for one aspect of your life. For example, one column may be for your personal or home list, another for paperwork to be completed, another for materials to be gathered, another for people to contact. Or keep it simple with one "home" list and one "work" list.

By keeping the journal or pad with you at all times, you can jot down tasks that occur to you suddenly or are thrust on you in the hallway as you go to lunch. You might also consider setting aside one part of the page to show your appointments for the week as a mini-calendar. This offers a helpful reminder in case you forget to look at your calendar regularly. On Sunday, take the time to create a new set of lists for the upcoming week. Copy down items not completed and add new tasks.

Example

Home	School
Laundry	Lesson plans for next week
Take dry cleaning	Call Mr. Brown re: J.P.
Cat to vet	Set up mtg. with Joan re: H.M.
Grocery store (see list next page)	Grade math unit end exams (Math 101)
Sign up Peter for flag football	Grade math journals (2nd & 4th period)
Appt. for hair cut	Turn in ARD referrals (due by Wed.) Make math foldouts for next unit

- Monday—dry cleaning, staff mtg. @4pm
- Tuesday—soccer practice @5pm; piano recital @7pm
- Wednesday—write lesson plans; referrals due; dr. @4pm
- Thursday—ARD mtg. @8; soccer game @7pm
- Friday—Staff development (all day); ballet recital @7pm
- Saturday—soccer game @11

Once you've listed the tasks to be completed, prioritize from high to low. Which items absolutely must be completed immediately or within a day or two? Those tasks are high priority; mark them with a capital H. Which items must be completed this week? These are medium priority and should be marked with an M. Mark items that are long-term projects you'd like to get done but are optional or have a due date far in the future with an L.

Prioritize all lists. Now you have a plan of which to complete first, second, third, and so on. This helps cut down on indecision and makes the lists more manageable. For some people, a list makes the situation worse because they have no idea where to start. Prioritizing puts tasks into perspective and offers a sense of order.

If you are logical or thorough, you may want to rewrite your tasks in order by priority. If the list still seems overwhelming, try this:

- Ignore everything but the high-priority items.
- Complete the first task, and don't think about the others.
- Once the first task is completed, look at the second task.
- Continue the process one task at a time.

As with anything else in life that seems insurmountable, the best way to tackle it is one step at a time. If two very long lists give you a headache, then try making several smaller lists. You can break up your work list into the different types of tasks that must be accomplished and work on one item from each list, which may give you more a sense of accomplishment. Do whatever works best for you.

Here is the prioritized example from the previous page:

Home	School
(M) Laundry	(M) Lesson plans for next week
(H) Take dry cleaning	(H) Call Mr. Brown re: J.P.
(L) Cat to vet	(H) Set up mtg. with Joan re: H.M.
(H) Grocery story (see list next page)	(M) Grade math unit end exams (Math 101)
(H) Sign up Peter for flag football	(M) Grade math journals (2nd & 4th period)
(M) Appt. for hair cut	(H) Turn in ARD referrals (due by Wed.) (L) Make math foldouts for next unit

Keep Your Calendar

Make checking your calendar and adding appointments part of your daily routine. The calendar is not just for recording meetings, but can be used to schedule your time. If you have a task you know will take a certain amount of time, set an appointment with yourself to complete it when you have an opening.

Your computer can be a huge help here because you can set regular reoccurring appointments for tasks that must be accomplished every day or every week, such as lesson planning. You can also block out segments of time when you are teaching. Make sure you put personal appointments as well as professional appointments on your calendar, which will help you keep track of both aspects of your life. There is nothing worse than making a commitment to help a friend or attend an after-school meeting only to find that you already have a conflicting appointment scheduled at the same time.

Your attitude is equally important. If you schedule an appointment for thirty minutes every day after school to grade papers, then you need to keep that appointment. This consistency will ensure you stay on top of that daily task. Think of these appointments as unbreakable as a meeting with your principal or district supervisor. Discipline yourself to sit at your desk and complete the task at the time you've scheduled. Procrastination will only undermine your efforts at time management.

Tips on Successful Classroom Management

- Read up on brain-based learning. This research clearly shows how a nonthreatening environment increases student learning and leads to open communication between teacher and students. (See the discussion on this topic in Chapter Six.)
- Distinguish between "teacher time" and "student time." A productive classroom allows teachers to instruct without interruptions (the "teacher time") and then gives students opportunities for debriefing, discussing, and assimilating the new information (the "student time").
- When joking with students, be sure to set a limit and end with a phrase such as, "Well, that was fun, but now it's time for us to get back to work. Everyone needs to focus on . . ." Remember that all humor should be free of derogatory references and sarcasm.
- Use eye contact to make sure that everyone has understood the move from play time to work time.
- You'll find that when your lessons are motivating for students they beg to stay in the classroom!
- Post basic classroom procedures so that students and parents know what to expect and can become accustomed to your classroom management style from the very first day.
- When students are actively participating in classroom activities that are meaningful and motivating, they are too focused to misbehave.
- Students crave consistency. Your class will run smoothly if students always know what to expect.
- Consistent behavior builds trust. Trust then builds respect.
- Frustration builds when students are confused. When frustration builds, behavior breaks down. To avoid this, structure your daily routines.
- Personal choice and group discussions are daily occurrences in a classroom that thrives on student involvement.

Being Prepared Every Day

Students can immediately tell when the teacher is not in control due to lack of planning. When this happens, the class quickly becomes rowdy or unmanageable. As we get more and more comfortable with our teaching, it also becomes easier to put off preparing for lessons until the last minute. This can cause extra stress and ultimately results in not being well prepared. The following tips and reminders will help you stay on track.

Planning Lessons

In order to be prepared, stay a little longer after school to plan for the next day. (Use the day-of-the-week folders explained in the previous chapter.)

Never use class time to prepare for the lesson. This includes preparing warm-up assignments and sponge activities (short assignments to focus student attention at the start of class) as well. Write them in your lessons and prepare your board ahead.

Before you start an activity, have all materials organized and ready.

Planning for Transition Times

Don't just let things happen! In your lesson plans. write out specific procedures to follow throughout the class period and give appropriate directions to students. These procedures should include ideas for transitioning between activities and classes, times when chaos can occur. It is helpful to have these procedures or directions written down in the lesson plans or posted in the room so a substitute will know how your classroom operates.

Here are some tips:

Between Activities or When Students Are Finished

- Clapping rhythms, which helps to focus students on you
- Circle time (have primary students meet in a common area)
- Straightening up the classroom or their desk
- Silent reading
- Logic puzzles
- Thinking games
- Identifying colors, numbers, or shapes
- Jigsaw puzzle
- Read-aloud

You might consider putting up a "finished" poster that lists what activities are acceptable for students to do if they finish their class work early.

Primary Idea Share

Tape letters to the floor in your circle-gathering area, and assign each student a specific letter to go to when you meet up during circle time. This provides a clear direction for young students of where each person should sit when gathering.

Between Classes, Lunch, Recess, or Even Activities as a Class

- Quiet game
- Quick questions for particular subject areas including math, science, and geography

- True-or-false facts
- Vocabulary or spelling review, with each student saying one letter as you go down the line
- Other sponge or icebreaker activities

What to Do with an Extra Five Minutes

Although we may try our best to plan lessons that use the entire class period, sometimes we get through the lesson quickly and have an extra five or ten minutes with nothing planned to fill that time. So that doesn't happen, make sure you've provided a closure activity for your lesson. If you have provided closure and still have extra time, what happens next? Unless you have a plan in place, most students will begin talking to their neighbor, doodle on the desk or a notebook, and participate in other off-task behavior. Instead, you need to keep everyone occupied so misbehavior is kept to a minimum. Some teachers may argue that their students need this downtime to relax. It is a nice thought, but we've seen too often how this "R&R" time can turn into major chaos. Following are some ideas to keep primary, intermediate, and upper-level students focused and occupied.

Primary

- Identify items in the room by color, shape, or numbers of sides or identify those that start with a particular letter.
- Count by twos, fives, or tens to a specific number.
- Do jumping jacks or stretching exercises ("Fingers to the sky, fingers to the ground").
- List the ways we use water.
- Name words we know that start with the letter "__."
- Draw or say, "What if?" "What if you were an animal? Say [draw] what you would be." What if you were a car? What if you were in a book? What if you were a plant? What if you were a building? What if you were from a different planet?
- Sing a song.
- Read a picture book.

Intermediate

- Fast facts. Math works especially well with this.
- Quick list—for example: "Quick! List three things that we learned today. Or "three things about plants." Or "three things that cats and elephants have in common."
- Word challenge 1. Go around the room, and have each student say a word starting with the same letter within a time limit.

- Word challenge alternative. Give a category or a set of categories, and have students come up with words for each that start with a specific letter. You might have students work in groups for this.

  Example: "Give me words that start with the letter M. The category is mammals."

- Word challenge 3. Use a starting word from your unit of study. Have each student create a new word using the last letter from the previous word stated. Give one point per word created and bonus points for using another word from your unit of study should be awarded. A time limit to go around the room will challenge students to think quickly.

- Choose a long word from the dictionary, or use a word from a unit of study to have students find as many other words using those letters as they can.

- Twenty questions. Students use twenty questions to guess an object chosen. Use objects in the room or from unit of study.

- Charades. Students use clues acted out by another to guess the phrase, movie, object, or something else. Use ideas and objects from your unit of study.

- Minute mysteries. Students ask yes/no questions to solve the mystery. These are available from MENSA and in bookstores and are short stories with a misleading twist (see www.us.mensa.org). Look for Red Herring books published by The Critical Thinking Company (www.criticalthinking .com). The stories appear to have an obvious conclusion but are misleading. Students must ask yes and no questions to determine the truth of what happened. Students often make assumptions about the main characters and setting of the mini-mystery leading to wrong conclusions. They must question these assumptions to determine the truth of what happened. These types of situation stories can be found online and in situation puzzle books.

- "Ticket out." Students give quick answers that relate to the day's lesson as a way to exit the classroom. If a grammar lesson has focused on studying verbs, for example, each student has to give one vivid verb that describes themselves as their "ticket out" to leave the classroom.

High School

- Pose ethical "what if" questions. Is it ever okay to run a red light? Suppose you buy something and are given more in change than what you are owed? How would you react if someone you think is physically unattractive asks you out on a date? A series of books titled "What Would You Do" poses several of these types of questions along with additional "what-if" scenarios.

- Pyramid. Students pair up, and one person in each pair is given a list of words from the unit of study. They then have to get their partner to say these words within a time limit by shouting out clues. For example, for *atom*, clues of "small particles," "building blocks of everything," and "has protons" would be offered.

- Word challenges. Three are given in the list for intermediate students, and they are also good time fillers for high school students. You might tighten the time limit to make it more challenging.
- What if you were [a historical figure, a main character]? How would you have done things differently?
- What are two positive things that happened to you today?
- How have you helped one person today [or this week]?
- Debate. Have students participate in a two- or three-minute debate of the pros and cons of different elements in your unit of study.
- Minute mysteries. These are very popular with high school students and encourage higher-level thinking. (See the full description in the intermediate section.)

Create a Nonthreatening Environment

A nonthreatening classroom is one in which students feel comfortable participating and interacting with the teacher and other students on a regular basis. Students know what to expect from the teacher and are rarely surprised from one day to the next. Put-downs are not tolerated and students are more likely to participate in class discussions with the knowledge that they will not be insulted or belittled for an incorrect answer.

Maintain Your Composure
Create a classroom climate that is calm by not overreacting to situations or problems that arise. Take notice of students: their emotions, attitudes, and behaviors. Stay alert for behavioral problems, and initiate strategies to dissolve the problem before it gets worse. Saying hello to each student as you check his or her calendar or focus assignment gives you a chance to assess potential issues.

Be Friendly
This does not mean being the buddy of students. It is important to keep the teacher-student relationship intact. Friendly means greeting students with a smile and handshake. It also means offering a pat on the back as needed. This does not mean never using a firm tone of voice or reprimanding students. Instead, it is important to remember to have a pleasant outlook rather than a sour attitude throughout the day. There are times when you will need to show disapproval or disappointment in regard to student misbehavior. Yes, students may get mad at you for a little while, but it will go away.

Have a Sense of Humor

It is important to remember that your students are young and are acting the way most young people do. Rather than getting frustrated with some of their antics, take some time to enjoy these young people. When we can have a sense of humor about what our students do, our lives become less stressful. Sometimes children are just being children. Also, keep in mind that while middle and high school students may look like adults, they are not. Don't take everything quite so seriously, and you'll find yourself having fun each day.

When you are enjoying a funny moment with students, be sure to make a clear transition back into the lesson or activity. It is very easy for students to take that fun moment and turn it into twenty minutes of chaos. Instead, when you feel that the moment is over, say something such as, "You guys are crazy! Okay, now who can tell me the three main principles of . . . " You'll get a bunch of protests, but be firm and start back on the lesson. You'll want to find a way to transition that meshes with your personality. However, if you do not stop and refocus students, they will find a way to stretch out a little bit of fun until it becomes no fun at all.

Avoid Yelling

When you find yourself losing your temper, turn around and count to ten, or take several deep breaths while you close your eyes. This will help you remain calm and focused. Yelling only makes things worse. It upsets students and causes them to lose respect for you. Also, increasing the volume adds to an already chaotic situation.

Use Nonverbal Cues

Use a quiet signal such as "Give Me Five" or put your hand in the air to help students focus on you while you are giving directions. This allows you to use a quiet and deliberate voice. We often have a tendency to want to continue speaking because we are aware of how limited the time is for teaching. However, do not speak until everyone is silent and looking at you. In the long run, this will earn you more teaching time as the year progresses.

Redirect Inappropriate Behavior Immediately

Unnecessary commotion must not rule your classroom. If things get out of control, rely on your nonverbal cues, such as eye contact or a quiet signal, to bring things back to order. Ignoring the situation does not work as effectively as redirection.

Redirect student attention before a problem gets out of control. Ask the student to help you with a task or find a new activity (reading, puzzles, learning center) to occupy his or her attention. Calling a student to help you works wonderfully to pull him or her out of a potential misbehavior or dangerous confrontation with other students.

Maintain a Good Rapport with Students

Get to know your students. Make time each day to talk individually to each one. Greet them at the door. Check their homework calendar at the start or end of class, and use that time to say hello and find out how they are doing. Ask about family, friends, pets, hobbies. If they are involved in sports, ask about the latest game. The more we get to know our students as people and treat them as such, the more they will respect us. It is very easy to get caught up in the day-to-day teaching and forget that we have a group of individuals with us. All of them have their own history, their own stories, their own likes and dislikes that are as important to them as ours are to us. Take some time to get to know those things about your students.

Identify Student Attitudes at the Start of Class

Another benefit to speaking with students before or at the beginning of class is the ability to gauge their mood. If you see a student enter the classroom angry, find out immediately what is wrong and address the problem if possible. At the very least, let the student know you understand there is an issue, and you will work to make time to talk with him or her. If there is an issue between two students, get them to talk out the problem through mediation. Ignoring these issues will lead to inattentive and possibly disruptive students throughout class.

Create an "Australia" Area

This idea is based on the book *Alexander and the Terrible, Horrible, No Good, Very Bad Day,* by Judith Viorst. Everything that can go wrong for Alexander does, making him want to move to Australia.

Many students enter the classroom feeling the same as Alexander. To combat this, have a relaxation area (usually the reading corner) where students can go to calm down when they are upset. Once calm again, the student can then rejoin class. Although this concept may seem as though it is wasting class time for that particular student, the truth is that no learning is occurring while the student is angry or upset. By allowing a five-minute calming period, you are reclaiming the rest of the class time that may have been spent fuming instead of learning. Students also recognize you are working to create a place where they are respected as human beings and individuals.

For older students, if you notice they are having a difficult day, you might privately offer them a few minutes to regroup by going to the restroom or simply letting them know you won't be calling on them for ten minutes or so. This way no one has to know but you and the student.

Moment of Reflection

Why is it important to create a positive climate within the classroom? What are some ways you already work to build this type of climate in your classroom? What are some other strategies you might implement to foster a positive climate?

Keep Students Actively Engaged in Learning

"Busy hands are happy hands," our grandmothers always say. Challenge students, and keep them involved with lessons by planning meaningful activities that have connections to other subject areas and real life.

Give students activities where they must create a product. This can be as simple as a scavenger hunt of important concepts within a chapter or as complex as a diorama and oral presentation. (We offer various strategies for this in Chapters Six through Ten.)

Dealing with your regular classroom duties with efficiency and calmness fosters positive student relationships. Students feel flustered and uneasy when their teacher is in a panicked or unorganized state. Too much unstructured time or too many pauses in instruction result in misbehavior. Also, loss of respect and trust for the teacher can result in additional misconduct. Some tips follow to help you streamline your classroom routines.

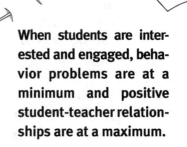

When students are interested and engaged, behavior problems are at a minimum and positive student-teacher relationships are at a maximum.

Using Specific Procedures in the Classroom.

It is important to have procedures ready for students to follow when they arrive in class from the very first day of school. Why? Procedures are an extension of expectations. If you expect students to enter the classroom and complete a series of actions before the bell rings, you need to write these down in a logical order. This then becomes a procedure that provides students with a list of specific actions they are expected to complete.

Many procedures become regular routines within the classroom. It is a good idea to post these in the classroom where students can easily refer to them. Although not all of these require poster-type treatment, you should go ahead and write down all of the procedures for your classroom so you are better able to communicate them (Kovalik, 1997). A few examples of daily routines that need teacher expectations and procedures include the following:

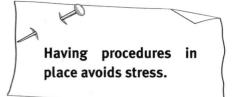

Having procedures in place avoids stress.

- What to do before the bell rings
- Checking attendance
- Giving directions
- Collecting class work and homework
- Distributing materials and papers

- Bathroom breaks during class
- Transition times between lessons and activities
- Working on projects
- Reading workshop
- Writing workshop
- End of the day

Follow your procedures religiously. You may want to post them so that students can see what to do every day. Procedure posters will help students and substitutes throughout the year.

"My first year of teaching fifth grade, I had a horrible feeling at the end of every day! It seemed like chaos as students grabbed their backpacks and began shoving everything inside! Some students were asking me questions about homework, while others were responding to a lesson we had just finished, and most students were excitedly chatting with each other about after-school activities. I felt scattered and disjointed when the bell rang and the students rushed the door. After several weeks of this, I decided to enact an end-of-the-day routine to follow every day. If the procedure wasn't followed, then students didn't get to leave my classroom. This included cleaning up the room, copying homework into their daily planner, packing up their backpacks, and then writing quietly in their journal until the bell rang. I gave them topics that provided closure to my lesson or stimulated interest for the next day. When the bell rang, we all sat in silence until I said, 'Go.' Then they put their journals away, and off they went! I felt so much more collected and relaxed at the end of the day from then on!"

Following are some sample procedures:

Morning Procedure for the Primary Grades

1. Put backpack on hook.
2. Get folders and book.
3. Check cubby.
4. Sit at desk.
5. Begin D.E.A.R. (Drop Everything and Read) time.

Morning Procedure for the Intermediate Grades

1. Check student mailbox, and get out journal, math folder, and graded work.
2. Get supply box and supplies.
3. Sharpen pencils.
4. Copy homework in calendar.
5. Copy word of the day.
6. Write in journal.
7. Complete other morning assignments.

Opening Class Procedure for Secondary School

1. Check student mailbox; retrieve graded work and class materials.
2. Get class or lab supplies if necessary.
3. Sharpen pencils.
4. Copy homework in calendar.
5. Complete focus assignment.

Writing and Reading Workshop Procedure

1. Get your writing folder, reading folder, and novel from your mailbox.
2. Be ready to take notes.
3. When writing, write quietly for the entire twenty minutes.
4. When reading, quietly get your book and reading folder. Find a place to read.
5. When time is up, record your reading in your reading log, and answer the reading response on the board.
6. Put your materials back into your mailbox.

Beginning-of-Class Procedures

- Have the whiteboard, an overhead transparency, your presentation station, or an interactive whiteboard set up with important information and morning assignments. You can create a wiki page with this information that can easily be shown on the whiteboard or presentation station.

- As students enter the classroom, they begin copying important announcements and work on morning assignments.

- Some possible warm-up assignments are a daily journal, daily vocabulary words, daily oral language, daily math, and daily geography activities.

- For forty-five- or fifty-minute classes, warm-ups or sponge activities should not last longer than ten minutes.

- Students should know that as they come to the classroom every day they need to start working on their warm-up activity.

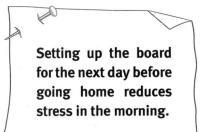

Setting up the board for the next day before going home reduces stress in the morning.

Idea Share

A detailed, well-organized board will keep you and your students on track. It also prevents that pesky question, "What are we doing next?"

A presentation for elementary school could look like this:

Objectives: **Date:**
Homework: Agenda:
Journal: Daily word challenge:

You can adapt this board to fit any grade level. Knowing your objectives is as equally important in kindergarten as in the upper grades.

Teacher Tip

If you are using a thought-provoking introduction and want students to be guided into discovering the objective rather than being told, leave it off the board until after the activity is finished. Then review the objective with students, and write it on the board.

These beginning-of-class guidelines are for secondary school classes:

- Type up a sheet with the date, class objectives, class agenda, any project or homework assignments, due dates, and the focus assignment for the day. Be sure you type up one per course taught.

- Type up this sheet as you make your lesson plans so that everything is ready at the same time. Do not wait until the night before to prepare.

- Copy or print these onto a transparency if you are using an overhead projector.
- Place each sheet in the day-of-the-week folder with the appropriate lesson plans and other materials.

This routine cuts down on having to change board information between class periods. Simply put the new course transparency or printout on the overhead or document camera and you are ready to go.

If you are using an interactive whiteboard or presentation station, create wiki pages for each class period showing this information. These pages can be changed at the end of the day to reflect the following day's lesson. Once you've set up the wiki pages, use them as a template, keeping the same format and changing only the details. This will save you time and energy.

Administrative Routines

These are the daily classroom routines: checking attendance, checking the academic calendar, and completing other housekeeping tasks while students are engaged in a learning activity. A good time to take care of these tasks is while students are completing their focus assignment.

Checking Attendance

One easy way to check attendance is to use a seating chart, check who is missing, and record the information. Another method that works well with teachers who group students together is to call each group and have the students tell you who is missing. One last method is to place student journals or folders out for students to pick up as they enter the room. Folders left on the table belong to absent students.

With secondary classes, an easy way to keep track of attendance is to create a manila folder for each period. Staple the attendance sheet to the right-hand side and a seating chart to the left-hand side. This way you can easily see who is absent and tardy.

Checking Academic Calendars

After roll call, you may want to go around the room, while students are still working on their focus activities, to check that the homework has been copied down correctly. This gives you an excellent way to say hello to each student personally and check on their well-being. It is a positive way to start each class and provides useful information on the emotional state of your students. This procedure also can be used to your benefit during parent conferences, because it shows you have taken a proactive role in teaching students to be responsible. Finally, you can use the academic calendar to encourage two-way communication with parents.

Assigning Class Jobs

Giving students jobs in the classroom makes them feel important and gives them a sense of cohesion in your class. It also helps you build relationships with individual students throughout the year. And assigning jobs to students helps you with the work load. Why not let your students help you take care of routine classroom tasks?

One way to assign jobs for intermediate and secondary classrooms is to have one boy and one girl each week serve as host and hostess, with these responsibilities for the week:

- Line leaders
- Turn lights on and off
- Close and open doors
- Pass out papers
- Serve as teacher helper and errand runner
- Wash transparencies
- Board eraser
- Other miscellaneous jobs

Go down the roll to assign this job, or randomly draw names each Friday for the following week. Once everyone has had a chance to serve, you may assign this job as a privilege to responsible students.

Two other jobs, which are assigned for an entire semester, require an application and letter of interest:

- *Checkers.* At the beginning of class, two students retrieve homework papers from the bins, check who has turned it in on a spreadsheet, make out a list of students who did not turn in assignments and give to the teacher. *Qualifications:* Student must get to class early and finish their morning assignments (or warm-ups), be responsible and neat, have their own homework always done on time, and show upstanding behavior.
- *Filers.* Three students help file graded work in student mailboxes. One student helps the teacher file materials in folders, notebooks, and student information files. *Qualifications:* Students must be responsible and neat, and have upstanding character and behavior.

> Relinquish some of your responsibility, and let the students take part in the class community.

There are many jobs that are easy to assign to children of all ages:

- Board eraser
- Errand runner
- Handout monitor (passes out papers)
- Media person (sets up overhead projector; turns on TV; collects videos, CDs, and other computer programs from librarian)
- Pet monitor
- Lights monitor
- Door monitor
- Table washer
- Transparency washer
- Trash monitor
- Teacher helper
- Line leader

Here are some other methods to sort out and assign class jobs:

- *Student job wheel.* Mark several clothespins with different classroom jobs. Then make a wheel with students' names on it. Clamp the clothespins on different names. You can rotate jobs every week, two weeks, or month.
- *Pocket chart.* Get a clear pocket chart (primary grades use these as calendars), and label each pocket with a different job. Mark each student's name on an index card in bold letters. Place a card in each job pocket. You can rotate jobs as needed.
- *Alphabetically.* Go down your student list and assign jobs alphabetically.

Student Discipline

Student discipline problems will be at a minimum if you keep your students challenged and busy. If students are working and having to think the entire time they are at school, they will be less likely to misbehave. This does not mean that piling worksheets on worksheets will keep your students out of trouble. They need meaningful assignments that are motivating as well as challenging. Meaningful activities

- Show connections between content areas
- Require active student participation
- Offer choices for students

- Relate to the real world and real-world scenarios
- Require thinking rather than regurgitating information

Many teachers confuse the terms *classroom management* and *classroom discipline*. *Classroom management* is the way you organize and manage your daily classroom events, minimizing problems. This includes

- Creating a positive classroom climate
- Implementing classroom procedures
- Organizing both yourself and your students
- Preparing lessons and activities ahead of time

Classroom discipline is behavior modification for students who are not meeting classroom expectations. This can include both rewards and consequences for behavior displayed in the classroom.

Do not confuse classroom discipline with a well-disciplined class. When your students know exactly what to do and when to do it and they meet your expectations every day, you have a well-disciplined class. When students misbehave and do not meet classroom expectations, you will need a classroom discipline plan to help those students modify their behavior.

> **Without effective classroom management, you will never have a well-disciplined class.**

Here is the recipe for a well-disciplined class:

- A teacher who has planned ahead
- Teacher flexibility
- Teacher confidence
- Established routines and procedures
- Positive attitude among students and teacher
- Consistent follow-through
- Brain-based classroom
  - Nonthreatening environment
  - Offers guided choice
  - Teacher as a learning facilitator
  - Relates to real world
  - Motivating
  - Discovery learning
  - Students actively engaged

Establishing Expectations and Consequences

There are a variety of ways to develop classroom expectations that are really classroom rules. Whether you create the list of rules, you use the school's list, or you allow your students to develop their own, expectations go above and beyond basic rules of behavior.

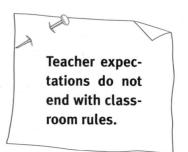

Teacher expectations do not end with classroom rules.

In fact, we can get so caught up in the rules that we forget about our other expectations. This can cause us to feel more disorganized on a daily basis. Instead, it is important to think about what you expect from your students at all times. Don't assume students will know how, when, and where you want homework to be turned in if you don't tell them specifically. If you expect homework to be put in the tray on your desk, explain this to the students. If you don't, then you'll have students handing in their homework throughout the day, often while you are in the middle of something else. Your expectations then become procedures, which then become regular routines in your classroom.

Also, don't forget about the life skills you expect from your students each day. Do you expect honesty, integrity, cooperation, dedication, perseverance, and personal best from your students? Make those expectations clear. Explain to your students exactly what it means to be dedicated or to have perseverance. What does this look like or sound like? Some of the most common life skills taught in classrooms are

honesty	integrity	cooperation	teamwork
friendship	dedication	effort	caring
perseverance	initiative	patience	common sense
curiosity	courage	responsibility	
flexibility	organization	problem solving	

These life skills help us all to have a successful, happy life. Some of these reflect morals and values, while others reflect work habits or attitudes toward others. We will look at some ways in which you might communicate the importance of these skills to your students.

Life Skills That Reflect Morals and Values

Without strong morals and values such as honesty and integrity, we can often fall into the trap of harming ourselves and others emotionally, mentally, and physically with lies and deceptions. Even little white lies can turn around and hurt us later in life. Lack of honesty and integrity can hurt relationships of all kinds, including family, friends, and business associates. When a person is not honest and lacks integrity (doing what is right), others begin to lose respect for that person. Once respect and trust are lost, they are extremely difficult to gain back again.

Life Skills That Reflect Work Habits

Many of the life skills reflect work habits such as effort, perseverance, organization, responsibility, problem solving, and cooperation. These are habits that will lead a person to success in whatever job he or she chooses. These skills also provide a person with the ability to become anything he or she wants. Without these habits, a person is more likely to stay unskilled or mediocre in his or her job and in life, with ramifications for job choice, salary, and upward mobility. A lack of these skills will also affect the ability to get into college or a vocational school.

Idea Share

Ask students to create definitions for certain life skills such as work ethic as it relates to your classroom or a specific subject. This activity offers students a way to relate personally to the skill and provides context for its meaning. Put these up in the classroom and refer to them throughout the year.

Thank you to Dodie Ainslie for sharing this idea with us!

Life Skills That Reflect Attitudes

Our attitude affects our relationships with other people. The attitude life skills include friendship, courage, caring, patience, a sense of humor, and common sense. The more of these skills we exhibit, the more likely we are to have long-lasting relationships with others. Our attitude is generally more positive, and a positive attitude goes a long way toward success in life. When we think positively, positive things begin to happen to us.

The more we talk about life skills in terms of students' lives and their future, the better they will understand why these skills are necessary. It is our job as teachers to encourage and foster these skills within the classroom so they become a habit.

Next, consider the kinds of work behaviors and attitudes you expect from your students. While this is somewhat related to the life skills we explained earlier, it is very important to explain exactly what you want to see and hear from your students every day. Show students a sample of neat and sloppy work so they have a visual image of what is expected.

It is also important to understand that students cannot read our minds. Take some time to brainstorm your pet peeves. What behaviors really annoy you? Often students may hit on one of our pet peeves and never even know it. These behaviors grate on our nerves and affect our attitude, which is not fair to students. They cannot be expected to read our mind. Be sure to communicate clearly what is and is not tolerable in your classroom.

An Analogy for Classroom Expectations

Let's put into perspective this idea of explaining classroom expectations to students. Imagine you are visiting a foreign country where you have never been before. When you arrive, one of the immigration officers gives you a list of cultural guidelines and laws to help you know what is and is not acceptable. You read over these and feel confident you are aware of everything you need to know.

Once you arrive at your hotel, you venture out for dinner. Upon arriving at a restaurant, you enter and wait to be seated. The hostess comes and beckons for you to follow her. You calmly follow her to your table. Suddenly she turns around, looks down at your feet, and begins to yell at you. You are startled and don't understand the problem. The hostess is now quickly ushering you out of the restaurant. As you are being pulled back toward the exit, you realize that everyone else is wearing closed-toed shoes and you are wearing sandals. It is an unwritten rule, or expectation, that everyone wear socks and shoes inside buildings in this country. Unfortunately, this was not in the list of guidelines and no one ever told you about this unwritten rule. Now you are flustered, you feel stupid, and feelings of anger and resentment begin to build because you are being punished for not knowing the expectation.

Think about these questions:

- How do you expect papers to be turned in?
- What are your rules regarding neatness?
- May students write in print versus cursive?

- What type of paper do you want students to use?
- Can they use colored ink pens?
- What are your expectations for bathroom breaks?
- How will students get supplies during class or sharpen pencils?
- What do you expect students to do when they are finished with their work early?
- What are your expectations for students in learning centers, the reading corner, or lab stations?

Idea Share

Have a student stand at the front of the classroom and read a paragraph. As the student is reading, walk around the room talking with other students, sharpening your pencil, doing jumping jacks, and acting the way you wouldn't want your students to act while you are presenting a lesson. Afterward, ask the student to explain how difficult it was to continue reading with all of the distractions.

When going over expectations at the beginning of the year, be sure to

- Maintain eye contact with each student. This type of body language helps keep students focused on you.
- Speak slowly, and pause after each sentence to emphasize the importance of what you are saying.
- Practice procedures over and over until they are habits.
- Have discussions with students to explain why these expectations are important to you.
- Demonstrate some examples of student behavior that would irritate you.

Idea Share

Pausing after an important statement sends a powerful message to students that they had better pay attention to what you are saying. Direct eye contact completes that feeling of seriousness. You'll find that if you pause long enough, everyone will lift his or her head to look at you. In a world where we are bombarded by noise, silence draws attention.

> "I never realized how much my tone of voice influenced the way students responded to me. Although I had gone over the class rules with them several times throughout the year and trained them in my procedures, I was still having trouble with certain students who ignored my directions or acted familiar with me. Then I heard myself on a recording and realized that when I speak, I have a very soft and timid-sounding voice. No wonder they weren't taking me seriously. That summer I practiced using a more forceful voice. I used the tape recorder to help me analyze my voice and could really hear the difference by the end of the summer. The next year, I felt that my students showed me more respect because my tone of voice demanded it."

Have students complete an activity where they demonstrate knowledge and understanding of each expectation (this is a perfect activity for the first day or two of school)—for example:

- Visual presentation. Students work in groups to create a visual poster or skit showing a specific expectation or consequence and present this to the class. All groups should present.
- Is/is not. Students tell or show what each expectation is and is not.
- Looks like, sounds like, feels like. Students tell or show what each expectation would look like, sound like, and feel like if it is properly followed.
- Have students brainstorm and chart behaviors that fall under each expectation.

Simply copying the expectations does not help students internalize the information. This is a passive activity that does not require any higher level of thought and can be easily dismissed.

Moment of Reflection

What kind of expectations do you have for students? How do you communicate and reinforce these in your classroom? Do you feel that your presentation of these expectations is important so that students take you seriously? Why or why not? What could you do differently?

Teaching Polite Behaviors

Many students have not been taught at home how to respond to a greeting such as "good morning." They also have not been taught how to respond respectfully to adults and to each other. These are polite behaviors you might need to teach to your students as a whole class. Simply telling them that you expect everyone to respect adults and each other is not enough. Most students will nod their heads as though they agree without ever really understanding what you mean.

It is important to take some time to think about what you expect from your students in regard to this issue. You set the tone on this subject:

- Brainstorm what polite behaviors you expect from your students. You need to take into account the variety of cultural backgrounds within your classroom and in your geographical area when making this list. Keep in mind that different cultures have different ideas for what constitutes polite behaviors. For example, in some cultures it is not polite for a young person to make direct eye contact with an older person or authority figure when being reprimanded. However, other cultures may see a lack of eye-contact as disrespectful.

- Model these polite behaviors to students, parents, and colleagues within the school.

- Redirect impolite behavior and require students to show the polite behaviors you expect. Just like any other expectation, if impolite behavior is allowed to continue without redirection, no change will occur.

Address How to Greet Another Person

Have a volunteer student help you show what you want to happen when greeting another person. Model it for the students. Then take some time to have everyone practice it with each other—for example:

- When someone greets you with hand held out
  - Grip the person's hand firmly but not squeezing.
  - Look him or her in the eyes.
  - Respond clearly with "Good morning," "Good afternoon," or "Good evening."
- When someone greets you
  - Stop, and look the person in the eyes.
  - Respond clearly with "Good morning" or whatever else is appropriate.

Emma: At my son's school, the director loves to say good-bye to the children. When they leave, he says, "Good-bye, [student's name]. I hope you have a wonderful afternoon." He then teaches them to respond with, "Thank you. You too. I will see you tomorrow." With the younger students, this is also an excellent way to practice their days of the week. They might say, "I will see you on Monday." or "I will see you tomorrow, which is Tuesday."

This ritual teaches students a polite way to leave the school. This custom or something similar might be something you could incorporate as part of your end-of-the-day or end-of-class procedure when students are dismissed.

Accepting No for an Answer

Children who are given no as an answer from an adult should be taught to show respect to the person (model what this looks like) and reply politely (you model a polite response), then walk away calmly. When they get no as an answer from another student, the response for them to learn is to look at the person respectfully, reply, "Okay," and walk away calmly.

Many times students will not be happy about getting no for an answer, and some may even get angry or frustrated. In this case, they have two options. The first is to write their feelings out completely in a correspondence journal to you. They place the journal gently on the teacher's desk or hand it to him or her at an appropriate time. This correspondence journal could have a specific spot in the classroom where students know to find it. Label it clearly. Have students write their feelings as a letter to you that they sign with their name. This response gives them practice in letter-writing skills, offers them a chance to vent their frustrations, and lets you know how the student is feeling. Another option is to allow them time to write in their own personal journal.

The second option is to ask for an honorable appeal. After responding properly to the no answer, students could address the person respectfully and ask for an appeal—for example: "Mrs. McDonald? May I offer an honoring appeal?" or "May I appeal your decision?" They need to ask in a calm and respectful tone of voice, which you should model so they know what this sounds like.

The honoring appeal is outlined in the book, *Say Goodbye to Whining, Complaining, and Bad Attitudes in You and Your Kids* by Scott Turansky and Joanne Miller, and goes something like this: "I understand that you do not want me to . . . [or that you want me to . . .] because . . . However, I [give reason for request and state feelings supporting request]. Could I . . . [rephrase request]?" They could say, for example, "Mrs. McDonald, I understand that you do not want me to leave the class because we are working on an assignment. However, I really have to take this book back to the library before I am fined a late charge. I know that I will not be able to go any other time during the day, and I am afraid that I will forget if I don't take care of it right now. Could I please go quickly to the library? I will return in five minutes." OR "Mrs. McDonald, I understand that you want me to put down my pencil so that I can listen to your directions. May I copy this last part of our homework first? I am almost finished."

If you say yes to the appeal, hold the student accountable to the promise. If Damian says he will be back in five minutes and returns in ten or fifteen minutes, let him know that he may not appeal again for a certain period of time because he did not stick to his word.

Also, just because a student uses the honoring appeal does not mean that you automatically have to agree to the request. Be sure you let him or her know that. If you still say no after the appeal, the student needs to respond politely. Nevertheless, the honoring appeal is a way for students to voice their own opinion, feelings, and needs in a polite manner rather than huffing, rolling their eyes, or storming off.

To be most effective, you need to address the students in your own personality, but with a firm voice that lets them know you are serious about these expectations. We have used these expectations with the students in our classes. They all work as long as you explain, model, practice, and are consistent with expecting this kind of behavior each and every day.

Moment of Reflection

What polite behaviors do you expect from your students? How do you expect students to interact with one another and guests who enter the classroom? Take some time to review your expectations, and brainstorm new ones.

Other Management Issues

Students Leaving the Classroom

A student leaving the classroom to go to the bathroom and for other reasons is a huge issue for intermediate and secondary teachers. Why is this? It is neither right nor fair to subject students to the embarrassment of requesting permission to answer nature's call. As adults we would never stand for that kind of treatment. As long as you discuss your expectations at the beginning of the year, bathroom breaks should not be an issue.

Idea Share

Create a sign-out sheet that includes boxes for date, time left, time returned, destination, reason, and teacher initials. Use a spreadsheet program to help you make this form.

Explain your bathroom policy on the first day of school using the sign-out sheet presented in the Idea Share—for example:

- Students may leave to use the restroom only during "student" time, which is when they are working on assignments. Students may not sign out while the teacher is giving directions or teaching a lesson. This shows respect to the person who is presenting.

- Students must fill out the sign-out sheet completely and fill in the time returned slot when returning. The sign-out sheet must be taken to the teacher before leaving the classroom and initialed on return. Only one student may leave at a time for a particular destination.
- Students are held responsible for completing in-class assignments.

Using a sign-out sheet provides you with documentation when students are not in your classroom for any reason. Should an incident occur within the school during class times, you have a record of which students left, where each student was supposed to be, and how long the student was out of class. Your initials ensure that the student arrived back in class at the time stated on the form.

Student Talking in Class

One of the biggest complaints from teachers is student talking: "They just won't be quiet!" or "I constantly have to ask them to be quiet," and, worst of all, "They don't listen to my lesson."

Appropriate Talking Times

The first thing you need to determine is when they are talking. Are students talking during your instruction, while giving directions, or while working on an assignment? There is nothing wrong in allowing students to talk while they are working. Although students may not always be talking about the subject matter at hand, they will stay on task if you monitor consistently. In addition, students are more likely to talk about their assignment when it is motivating and not a boring worksheet.

Human beings are social creatures by nature. We tend to do a better job when we talk to others about our work. Talking helps us express our thoughts, ideas, and feelings. Students get ideas from one another, judge how well they are doing, and help each other do a good job on the work. Sometimes students are just chatting, but even this helps build a strong community in the classroom.

"My Time" and "Your Time"

Students need to know there will be opportunities to talk and move around while in class. In order to help them understand when it is and is not appropriate, introduce the concept of "my time" and "your time." "My time" is teacher time. This is the time when you are teaching a lesson, giving directions, addressing the class as a whole group, or directly working with a small group. "Your time" is student time. This is the time students are working independently or in groups (excluding testing situations) on classroom activities. This strategy works well if you take the time to explain it logically. During teacher time, students should be quiet and attentive. Then, after about ten to fifteen minutes, students will be given time to work. During this time, they may talk quietly and take care of their needs within reason.

Introduce this concept at the beginning of the year: "Whenever I am giving a lesson, directions, am speaking to the class, or am standing in front of the class as a whole, that is my time. During my time, I expect everyone to be silent, attentive to me, and listen. If you are talking to a neighbor, are you paying attention to me? [No.] If you are rummaging around in your backpack or putting on makeup, are you paying attention to me? [No.] Exactly. Now let's practice what paying attention looks like."

After they have practiced, continue: "Now, if I have given you a class or group assignment and have given you time in class to work, that is your time. You may get supplies, sharpen your pencil, go to the restroom." (These are examples, of course. You do want to be specific in telling student exactly what they are allowed to do. You might allow them to get a drink of water or use the restroom if needed. Keep in mind that students who are thirsty or need to go to the restroom badly are not thinking about their work, but their bodily needs.) "When I put up the quiet signal or ring the bell [a small dinner bell], that is the signal that it is my time again, and I want full attention back on me."

To practice this, tell students to talk and chatter, sing songs, or something else. Then quickly put your hand up in the quiet signal to see how quickly they can come back to order. Practicing this is fun for the students, and it also allows them to internalize your expectations. Having a quiet signal like this is a wonderful way to get students to focus back on you without the need to raise your voice.

> In my classroom, I schedule talking pauses after new or important concepts are introduced. This allows my students to discuss their thoughts on the topic with a neighbor. I don't just stop teaching, but instead say something such as, 'Now I'd like you to turn to a neighbor and discuss what I just presented to you. Write down any new thoughts and ideas you generate so you won't forget them. Be prepared to share some of your ideas with the whole class.'
>
> Then I give everyone several minutes to talk while I walk around listening and engaging in some of the individual discussions.
>
> I got this idea when I went to district training for in-service presenters, but now I find it works beautifully with my sixth graders as well!

Monitoring and Redirect

When you do allow students to talk during their work time, be sure you are walking around monitoring their conversations. Although it is okay for them to get off the assigned topic for a minute or two, too much off-task talking is not appropriate. While you monitor, you are in more of a position to redirect student talking quietly rather than raising your voice to the whole class.

To redirect, walk up behind the students who are talking and say (just to them) something like, "So tell me what you've done so far. I am taking progress checks." The students are immediately back on task, and you haven't singled them out in front of the class or raised your voice. Standing behind a group of students for several minutes while they are working is also effective for redirecting off-task behavior. Ask probing questions to the group to get them focused back on the assignment.

> ## Idea Share
>
> Keep a clipboard with you as you walk around. On the clipboard, have either index cards or a spreadsheet of student names so you can take notes on what is happening: who is on task and who is not, problems, and so on. Another idea is to use blank mailing labels. Jot the student name and observations on the blank label. Then peel and stick it to a sheet in the student's information folder. This makes it easy to have written comments and observations ready to share during a parent conference.

Clipboard Monitoring

The steps for monitoring students during class work using a clipboard follow:

1. Use the computer to create a spreadsheet (see the "Clipboard Monitoring Sheet" at the end of the chapter). Across the top put one expectation or work habit in each box. Leave a couple of boxes blank to write in the concept or skill being taught or practiced that day—for example:

Student Name	Stay in Seat	On Task	Cooperating	Skill
John	1 2 3 4 5	1 2 3 4 5	1 2 3 4 5	1 2 3 4 5
Ashley	1 2 3 4 5	1 2 3 4 5	1 2 3 4 5	1 2 3 4 5

2. Use a system of numbers to help you keep track of infractions, and make sure there is enough space for comments as well if necessary. With rules, each number represents the number of infractions. With concepts or skills, each number represents the level of mastery:

   5 = Excellent   4 = Good   3 = Fair   2 = Poor   1 = No mastery

3. Place a week's worth of spreadsheet forms on the clipboard so you won't have to remember each morning to put on a new sheet.

4. Make enough copies for several weeks (one spreadsheet per day). Label the date at the top of the spreadsheet before using it so you'll know which day to which it refers.

5. Be sure to use the clipboard to record good behavior and make comments about students who go above and beyond what is expected of them. This information will help you when it is time to write progress reports or report card comments. It will also help you if you have been asked to recommend a student for an honor or award.

6. File these sheets in a three-ring binder in chronological order. Use tabbed dividers to separate each six weeks or grading period. The binder keeps all of the papers together in one place with no fear of losing them. Also, it is easier to flip through pages in a binder than it is in a manila folder.

7. Be sure to document behavior disruptions and other problems in the student's folder at the end of the week so you won't have to bring a lot of extra papers to a parent conference. If you are in a hurry, you might just make a copy of the form to put in the student's folder. Just be sure to blank out other student names before putting in a particular folder.

Recording Student Discipline

Clipboard

Some teachers use a clipboard. Attached to the clipboard is a spreadsheet like the one illustrated here. Each time a student does not meet an expectation, a mark is given next to his or her name under the appropriate day of the week. This "mark" could be a circle around the number or a check mark over the number. Each number represents an infraction. For example, if Julie is not prepared with homework and other class materials, the number one would be circled. If, later in class, she is not showing respect to others, the two would also be circled. The clipboard then shows that Julie had two infractions recorded for that day. Consequences are met for marks given that day. Each day starts over fresh. This is an excellent way to hold students accountable while out of your classroom as the clipboard follows the class throughout the school.

Student	Monday	Tuesday	Wednesday	Thursday	Friday
Julie	1 2 3 4 5	1 2 3 4 5	1 2 3 4 5	1 2 3 4 5	1 2 3 4 5
Mark	1 2 3 4 5	1 2 3 4 5	1 2 3 4 5	1 2 3 4 5	1 2 3 4 5
Sandy	1 2 3 4 5	1 2 3 4 5	1 2 3 4 5	1 2 3 4 5	1 2 3 4 5

Mailing Labels

You can mark down the date and the number of the rule/expectation (listed on a poster in the classroom) not followed on a blank mailing label. It is easier and less time-consuming to simply write the number of the rule rather than taking the time to make written comments on the label, although comments are helpful when meeting with parents. Peel and stick the label to a sheet of paper kept in the student's information file. Several sheets can be stapled together as needed. This is helpful when you are contacting parents and want to access a record of student behavior easily.

Teacher Tip

Writing student names on the whiteboard and placing checks next to the names for misbehavior is not an appropriate way to record behavior problems. It serves only to embarrass the student. If it doesn't humiliate the child, it could have the opposite effect, with the student enjoying the negative attention. Either way, this will result in additional rebellious behavior.

Pocket Chart

Place a clear pocket chart on the wall, with one student per pocket. Next to this chart, place your poster of expectations, and attach pockets next to each expectation. Place different colored strips next to each one (for example, expectation 1 has purple strips).

Each time a student does not follow a rule, have him or her pull a colored rule strip and place it in his or her pocket on the chart. Remember to clearly tell the student which expectation was not followed. This is excellent for primary grades because it is so visual. At the end of the day, record each child's infractions in your grade book, on an index card, or on a reward chart. Each day should start fresh.

Using Rewards

Discipline programs based completely on consequences or punishments are not effective in modifying student behavior. However, there is currently a debate about reward-based programs as well. Some researchers contend that rewards can be equally as harmful.

Our belief is that rewards can be used as a motivational tool to help students begin to modify their behavior. As students begin to meet your expectations on a consistent basis, you should rely less and less on rewards as a tool. Remember that students who are actively engaged in their learning do not need outside stimuli such as rewards for motivation. They are motivated by the desire to learn.

In the movie *Dangerous Minds*, Michelle Pfeiffer's character walked into an extremely hostile and volatile classroom situation. She wanted to use positive measures to change student attitudes, and began a reward system for classroom participation. As her students began participating more in class and were more engaged, she slowly reduced the number of rewards passed out until finally students were participating because they were truly interested and were intrinsically motivated to learn.

The same should apply to your situation. If you find yourself in a classroom situation where drastic measures are needed yet you want to foster a positive environment rather than a negative one, a reward-based program is the perfect place to begin. As your students' behavior begins to change, you can wean them off the rewards until they are participating and behaving because they want to, not because you are paying them.

Tips for Using Rewards

- Use rewards sporadically throughout the day, week, month, or year.
- Don't rely on rewards in place of good classroom management.
- Work your way toward having students who are intrinsically motivated through engaging teaching strategies.
- Be fair in giving out rewards: each student should have an equal chance.

Recording Good Behavior

Managing student behavior is not just about recording student infractions, but good behavior as well. The best reward systems encourage students to earn a token of appreciation by consistently making good choices. Below are a few ideas for keeping track of good behavior to help students earn extra privileges and other positive tokens:

An effective teacher seeks to modify student behavior by focusing on positives rather than negatives.

- *Self-manager program.* One discipline program that has been used in Richardson, Texas, is the self-manager program, which uses the clipboard idea for recording student behavior. Students must go ten days without a mark of any kind. When they reach ten days, they are given an application that each teacher must sign. The application is turned in to the librarian (or other faculty member in charge of the program) and the student is given a button with his or her name and picture on it. This self-manager badge gives the student extra privileges. The school and each teacher decides on various rewards to happen weekly, monthly, or each six weeks. A student who receives three marks in a week loses the badge but can earn it back after ten days with no marks.

- *VIP program.* Students in middle school who make the A honor roll or earn all A's in conduct for every class are given VIP badges, which give them extra privileges. They may use their badge as a hall pass, to go to the library or computer lab during lunch, and receive rewards given out by individual teachers.

• *Top ten.* Create a chart for each grading period with student names written down the side and dates written across the top. Each day, record either the number of the rule(s) broken, or place a star or smiley face next to every student's name. When a student acquires ten stars or smiley faces on the chart, the teacher provides a reward. The stars do not have to be ten in a row, just ten total. Once a student has received the reward, the process begins again. A way to publicly honor students receiving the top ten reward is to have a ceremony every Friday for those who earned their top ten that week.

• *Primary idea.* Tape library pockets on each student's desk, and give each student a popsicle or craft stick. Write the student's name on the stick. Every time a student gets a sticker, he or she puts it on the stick. When students have ten stickers, they can "shop" in the treasure chest (a chest of dollar toys, small craft projects, pencils, stickers, and other tokens).

• *Green/Yellow/Red:* To keep track of behavior, paint a yardstick in three sections: green, yellow, and red. When students misbehave, they move the clothespin with their name on it to the next level (yellow or red). If students redeem their behavior throughout the day, the clothespin can be moved back to green. Students who are still on green receive a sticker for that day. At the end of the day students color in the square on their behavior calendar showing the level (green, yellow, red) their clothespin is on. (Thanks to Erica Kruckenberg, first-grade teacher, Prosper ISD, for sharing this idea with us.)

Rather than focusing on individual behavior, you may want instead to focus on the behavior of the class as a whole. Class progress is marked daily or weekly with the goal of earning a class reward. Below are two ideas for keeping track of class behavior:

• *Marbles in a jar.* This method has a jar for each class. As the class earns points for good behavior, following expectations, showing positive life skills, or something else, marbles are added to the jar. When the jar is full, the class participates in a pizza party, gets a movie day, or receives some other reward.

• *Charting progress.* This method requires the use of a bulletin board. Create a theme based on your school mascot, a unit of study, or something motivating to students. As the class earns points for good behavior, move the class marker (a push pin with a symbol or picture attached to the top) along the path. Students can earn rewards for meeting certain goals or get a larger reward for reaching the finish line. This method can be used for individual students as well as for the whole class. It has been used quite successfully in reading programs to encourage student reading on a daily basis, recording pages or minutes spent reading.

With any of these programs, be wary of developing a system that seems reward based but is actually punishment for students. For example, if you offer a reward to students at the end of the week for no marks in their planner, this may seem to be a reward system, but it actually punishes students. If a student gets a mark on Monday or Tuesday, what is to motivate him or her to behave the rest of the week? The one mark has taken away the reward for Friday. A better plan is to have students earn their way toward the reward by collecting stamps for good behavior each day. When five or ten stamps have been received, no matter how long it takes the student to reach that point, the reward is given. Remember that a reward taken away is no reward, but a punishment.

Tokens of Appreciation

Tokens of appreciation are a way of showing students you appreciate their good behavior and are typically given out after a specific period of time (week, month, grading period) rather than daily. Following are a few examples:

- *Weekly top ten.* Every Friday before lunch, announce the names of the students who earned their ten stars or stickers during that week. Students are given a reward during that time.
- *Bonus points.* Create bonus point coupons, and add them onto homework, project, or test grades. Use coupons in denominations of 1s and 5s.
- *Colored tickets.* Buy a roll of brightly colored tickets from a teacher or office supply store. Hand these out for participation, improvement, good deeds, or positive life skills exhibited. Students write their names on the back and put them in a canister for a weekly drawing.
- *Mascot coupons.* Use school "mascot" coupons, or create your own to give to students for the following: first done with morning assignment or sponge activities, parent signatures on binders, life skills shown in class, or best organized binder. Students then redeem these coupons for privileges.

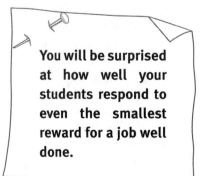

You will be surprised at how well your students respond to even the smallest reward for a job well done.

- *Class leader.* Give this award to the student who has shown the most improvement during the week.
- *Explorer of the month.* Award this to the student who has shown the most effort. Invite the student to eat a special lunch with you. Also, take his or her picture, and post it on a special poster on the bulletin board.

Example Tokens of Appreciation

Special pencils	Children's books
Special lunch with the teacher	Free computer time
Homework passes	Button or badge
Special helper	Small prizes from the dollar store
Treasure chest with goodies	Ice cream bar
Stickers	Free library time
Bookmarks	Coupons for a fun kids' place

Positive Notes

Finding a way to focus on the positive behaviors and attitudes exhibited by students is an excellent way to maintain a positive classroom environment. If you can, spend as much, if not more, time on positive reinforcement such as verbal and written praise to students. This type of praise is an excellent way to reward students for good behavior and will encourage them to continue.

In Chapter One, we discussed making materials in advance to help save time during class. One suggestion was to create a series of positive notes. You can sign these notes and hand them to students prior to leaving class. You can also use these same kinds of positive expressions verbally.

You can use e-mail to send these positive notes to the student and copy the parents as well. Think about posting positive comments about students on your blog or classroom Twitter account. Parents and students will be thrilled to see their name "in lights!"

What are some other specific positives you want to reinforce in your class? Think of the life skills such as cooperation, teamwork, honesty, integrity, friendship, perseverance, determination, and personal best.

Another way to encourage positive attitudes in your class is to allow students to write their own notes of praise and thanks to one another. You could have a special box in your room where students place their notes to be read at the end of class each day. Some students may feel shy about having their name attached to the note, so don't require them to sign it. Find a fun name or phrase for this idea to help students get excited about the idea. For example, if your school mascot is a hound dog, you might use the phrase "Happy Howls" or "The Good Howling Box."

Take a shoe box, cover it with construction paper, and decorate it to match your theme. Make sure you cover the lid separately from the box so that it can be removed easily. Cut a large slit into the box top for students to place their notes. Start the process by putting in your own quick positive notes to students to help them understand what the box is all about. You'll find that students are pleased to hear their name called out for something positive and will begin modifying their behavior in order to hear more.

> ## Moment of Reflection
>
> How do you monitor and record your observations? What methods do you use to record student misbehavior and good behavior? Are these working effectively for you? How might you change these methods to be more effective? What kinds of positive reinforcement do you provide for students? What new strategies might you use to offer praise to students?

Conclusion

A well-disciplined, learner-centered class requires training students in your expectations and procedures. Proactive, not reactive, strategies are required to maintain a classroom where students know what is expected of them at all times. Children need boundaries and structure in order to feel safe in their environment. Although they will test and strain these boundaries, they ultimately want to know that they cannot be broken.

When there is consistency in the classroom, trust is built, and respect follows. If we want students to respect us, we must respect them as well. This includes setting expectations and being consistent in our requirements. When everything changes from day to day, students never know what to expect and can become excitable, unruly, and sometimes angry.

Good classroom management takes time and effort. It is not easy being consistent, and it is not easy to enforce the expectations at all times. However, without consistency, behavior breaks down, and learning falters. Thus, effective learning on the part of the student is the result of your dedication, preparation, and planning.

References

Kovalik, Susan. *Integrated Thematic Instruction: The Model.* (3rd ed.) Village of Oak Creek, Ariz.: Susan Kovalik and Associates, 2003.

Turansky, Scott, and Miller, Joanne. *Say Goodbye to Whining, Complaining, and Bad Attitudes in You and Your Kids.* Colorado Springs, Colo.: Shaw Books, 2000.

Web Site Resources

Teachers Guide to Classroom Management, http://www.theteachersguide.com/ClassManagement.htm.

Teacher Vision Behavior Management Resources, http://www.teachervision.fen.com/classroom-discipline/resource/5806.html.

Education World: Tips from the Pit Crew, http://www.educationworld.com/a_curr/profdev003.shtml.

Clipboard Monitoring Sheet

Date: _____ Class: _____

The numbers indicate which objectives and behaviors the teacher plans to monitor.

Student Names	1	2	3	4	5

Notice of Concern

Date: _____ Student's Name: _____

Student's ID Number: _____ Grade: _____

Subject: _____ Teacher: _____

Counselor: _____

To Parent/Guardian

☐ Your child is having academic difficulties.

☐ Your child is at risk for failure.

☐ Your child's behavioral conduct may result in disciplinary actions.

☐ Your child cannot participate in extracurricular activities due to failure.

☐ Your child is scheduled for tutorial help:

　　　　M　　　　**T**　　　　**W**　　　　**Th**　　　　**F**　　　　**S**　　　　Time: _____

Academic Difficulties

Failure to complete assignments

Failure to bring materials to class

Poor test(s) results

Other

Failure to make up work/ tests

Poor quality of work

Failure to follow directions

Excessive absences

Excessive tardies

Lack of effort

Behavioral Misconduct

Talks excessively

Distracts other students

Other

Ignores correction

Displays negative attitude

Disruptive

Displays disrespect

Parent/Guardian is requested to have a conference with the teacher at one of the conference periods indicated below:

CONFERENCE TIME: First choice _____

Second choice_____

Please Sign and Return

Parent/Guardian Signature: _____

Date:_____

Revisiting Lesson Plans

When building a fire, you need to know whether you plan to have a small campfire or a large bonfire. Prior planning is a must to keep from burning down forests or not getting warm enough on a cold night. The same is true for lesson planning. Without prior planning, lessons smoke and fizzle instead of sparking into a flame. But what kind of planning do you need to do to be effective?

Madeline Hunter (1979) discovered that effective teachers, no matter what their grade level, subject area, or teaching style or the background of their students, all used a similar method of teaching. From these discoveries, she suggested several elements to consider when planning lessons: objectives, standards, anticipatory set, teaching (input, modeling, check for understanding), guided practice, closure, and independent practice. In our teaching courses, this was shown to us as the seven-step lesson design plan. It looked unwieldy and overwhelming. Perhaps at the time you thought, "Well, I'll get around to using that later." But later never came.

Emma: After several years of teaching, I found myself bored with my students, bored with the topics, and bored with teaching. It seemed as if I was doing the same thing day after day. Not until I took a class in curriculum development did I revisit the elements that Hunter had outlined, and I realized I could make my lessons more engaging for both my students and me. There was a way to keep track of what I had taught and have a road map for what I planned to teach next. Nevertheless, the model still seemed somewhat unwieldy in thinking through and writing down each of those elements every day. In a determined effort to do better for my students, I began setting aside one day a week for planning.

Each Wednesday afternoon, I set aside an hour or two after school to do lesson planning for the following week. At first it was difficult, and it took quite a bit of effort on my part to stick with a detailed planning routine. However, the more I planned in this manner, the easier I found the following week to be. At the end of the year, I found the following to be true when writing detailed lesson plans:

- They serve as a way to keep focused and on target with objectives and standards.
- Students see the teacher as well prepared and organized.
- Students and the teacher are excited and engaged in the classroom each day.
- Students are less likely to misbehave and interrupt throughout the class.
- There is no need to write detailed plans for a substitute because they are already done.
- Principals and other staff members view the teacher as efficient and effective.
- The teacher has a smooth day.

Lesson planning affects behavior, motivation, and learning for both the students and the teacher. As we stated in the previous chapter, students can immediately tell when the teacher has not planned and is not in control. In this situation, behavior in the classroom often breaks down. It becomes easier for students to get the teacher off topic, and before you know it, the class is in shambles.

In addition, without effective lesson planning, boredom can set in for everyone. Writing out detailed lesson plans can help us make sure we are varying our activities, meeting different learner needs, and staying on track. Instead of the daily thirty- to forty-minute lecture or textbook reading, we can make sure we are using the different elements that keep student interest and promote learning.

In this chapter, we look at a detailed lesson plan. Although these are not specifically seven steps, they do include Hunter's basic elements including objectives, introduction, direct instruction, practice, application, closure, and assessment.

If you are working for a district that provides a set curriculum and pre-designed lesson plans, you will need to tweak those plans to best meet the needs of your students. You may find that the lesson does not necessarily fit your personality and teaching style. If this is the case, you will want to change some of the procedures and activities to reflect your own personal flair. In fact, you may find some of the lessons to be lacking in terms of motivational and engaging strategies for students. Many of the ideas found within this and other chapters in this book will help you hone that basic lesson plan. You should also make sure it includes the important elements of lesson planning.

Moment of Reflection

What plan or format do you use when planning lessons? Do you feel your lessons sometimes seem boring to both you and your students? Why do you think this is? What elements do you include in every lesson plan? Do you write these out formally or simply perform them through the lesson presentation?

Focus Assignment

When students enter the classroom, they need a focus activity to help them calm down and get ready to start class. It should be easily viewed on the board, the overhead, or the presentation station and must be done every day for every class period in order to maintain consistency. When used only sporadically, students never know what to expect, and this uncertainty has an adverse effect on their behavior. A focus assignment may be called by a different name in your school or district. Some of these names are *bell-ringer, warm-up,* or *sponge activity.*

"My students all copy their homework into an academic calendar as soon as they walk into class. Then, while everyone is working on the warm-up activity, I walk around and check each calendar. I initial each entry that has been copied down correctly. This gives me a chance to say hello to each student and see how everyone is feeling. I can actually diffuse any problems right from the start of class!"

There are lots of focus activities to choose from—for example:

- Writing in journals
- Creative writing activity
- Calendar questions for primary students to review their calendar skills
- Sentence corrections
- Simple review activity
- Name the season, day of the week, or something similar

- Geography questions
- Name the state, scientist, explorer
- Math problems
- Review questions from previous day's lesson
- Vocabulary
- Pop quiz
- Bulletin board activities—current events, calendar, vocabulary, authors, birthdays
- Daily oral language, geography, math, science—short exercises at the beginning of each period that practice or review basic skills
- Quote of the day in which the teacher and students discuss a quote of the day. The quote could be one that relates to the unit of study or the subject matter as a whole.
- Puzzle of the day

While students are completing their focus activity quietly at their desks, use that time to call roll, visit with individual students, and take care of other housekeeping items. This is a great time management skill.

Some quick sponge activities can also be used for transitions when students are finished early, when preparing for lunch or recess, or the end of the class or the day.

Objectives and State Standards

What do you want students to be able to do by the end of the lesson or the day? Your objectives should be written in a manner that can be evaluated and should correlate with your state standards.

Example

- Students will be able to identify the main characters in the story *Charlotte's Web.*
- Students will be able to construct a model of a human cell.

Objectives should not be hard for you to measure student achievement or knowledge.

Example

- Students will understand the main characters.
- Students will learn about cells.

These objectives are not specific enough. Moreover, how will you measure student understanding?

Procedures

What will you do during class time to achieve your objectives? This may include direct instruction, modeling, group practice or application, questioning, lab or learning center activities, individual practice, and possibly even assessment. Your procedures should reflect effective teaching practices such as varying learning activities, making connections to the real world, and application of learning. These are important in developing effective and motivating lessons, and are also discussed in Chapters Six and Seven. Make no mistake: if all you do is list your procedures as lecture, textbook reading, and worksheets, you will not see a change in you or your students.

After writing out your procedures, analyze the activities to determine they meet the following criteria:

- Mostly student centered
- Varied for different learning styles
- Actively engaging for students
- Helping students meet the objectives

Example
Objective: To be able to identify the three layers of the earth.
Procedures:
1. Student groups cut a wedge-shaped slice from the peach, plum, or avocado on their table. (You need to use a fleshy fruit with a large pit for this activity.)
2. Students make observations about the peach and record them on paper or on their laptop as a group.
3. Groups share their observations (they should be noting different layers).
4. Direct instruction: Students take notes about layers of the earth in their notebook.
5. Students draw the planet earth and identify the different layers.
6. Students work in pairs to compare and contrast the earth and the peach in a T-chart or Venn diagram format. (This is an extension activity to be used if there is time.)

Adding Sparkle to Your Introduction

A sparkling introduction (also called an *anticipatory set*) grabs attention, hooks students from the first moment, and provides an opening into direct instruction. Here are ways to achieve this opening:

- *Manipulate objects.* No matter what their age, students love to break, make, color, move, and rearrange stuff. They also love to get their hands dirty. Consider these activities to get students working with objects:
  - Opening a present

- Conducting a simple experiment
- Exploring an everyday object (for example, cutting open a piece of fruit)
- Using objects to sort, count, prioritize, categorize

- *Use humor.* Students love to laugh! Find a way to get everyone laughing and connecting to the lesson.
  - Cartoon (political or satire)
  - Jokes
  - Funny video clip
  - Funny children's book
  - Funny or unique pictures

- *Get students moving.* Get those people up and out of their seats! Nothing is more exciting than moving around—for example:
  - Searching for an object (scavenger hunt)
  - Playing a short game
  - Engaging in a short simulation

- *Presenting interesting facts.* The Internet offers the ability to search for fun, wacky, and little-known facts that directly or indirectly relate to the subject you are teaching.

- *Using a video or sound clip.* Connect a recent movie or new song release to your topic of study. Download one of these from the Internet or your district's streaming video resources, and use it to introduce your lesson.

Lesson Flow

We often think of transitions only in terms of those blank times between classes or activities. However, it is also important to think about the transition from one part of your lesson to the next and incorporate these into your plans. A good flow to your lessons and activities will help students make better connections in their learning. To accomplish this, think through your lesson from start to finish in a logical sequence. Introduce basic concepts first, and then build on them throughout the lesson or day. Then reflect on whether the sequence of the lesson or activity makes sense. Does each part follow one another, or are they mostly unrelated activities that are linked together haphazardly?

The sample elementary lesson that follows, part of a unit about bats and other nocturnal animals, helps to illustrate this point. Note how each part of the lesson flows into the next. Secondary teachers need to look at the flow rather than the lesson itself. How are you creating this kind of flow between the elements of your lessons? No matter what subject area you teach, these transitions are an important part of an effective lesson.

Sample Lesson Plan

1. *Anticipatory set to get students moving.* Blindfold a volunteer student and have him or her try to navigate around the classroom. The rest of the class should be silent. An alternative activity is to blindfold all students and have them navigate a course outside. Discuss the difficulty of navigating without a guide. Next, pair them up with one person guiding a blindfolded partner with verbal instructions.

2. *Reflection, comprehension, and internalization of the activity.* After the activity, ask the student (or students if you did this as a group activity) to describe how he or she was able (or not able) to navigate around the classroom. Since sight is not an option, what other senses did he or she use? (Lead the discussion to the sense of hearing.) With the alternate activity, ask students if it helped having the "navigation guide." If you have a blind student in your class, include this student (if appropriate) in a discussion about how he or she is able to navigate from one place to another. What senses does he or she use? What outside tools does he or she use? The discussion helps students internalize the activity and prepares them to link it to the story and direct instruction.

3. *Relate the student experience to the lesson topic.* What other creatures depend on other senses besides their eyes to help them navigate? [Bats, whales, nocturnal creatures]

4. *Link the activity to a story or other text.* "I'm going to read a story about one creature who was feeling as out of place as [the volunteer student] was earlier."

5. *Story or other text connection.* Read *Stellaluna* by Janell Cannon and discuss how she was out of place. What did she discover about herself throughout the course of the story?

6. *Story or other text discussion.* Connect the story read aloud to direct instruction through prior knowledge of bats and vocabulary—for example:

> Stellaluna learned that she was a bat, not a bird. Let's write down some facts we already know about bats. What are some questions we have about bats?
>
> Before we can really begin to understand bats like Stellaluna, we need to know some important vocabulary words. [Use a wiki page to introduce vocabulary. Students list, copy, and discuss vocabulary words.]
>
> Which of these words would have helped [the volunteer student] if she had this ability? [A student says *sonar.*] Boats use sonar to test the depths of the ocean. Fishermen use sonar to help them find fish. Why do you think *sonar* is one of our vocabulary words for this unit? Think back to Stellaluna. At one point the picture shows her with eyes that look like flashlights. Did she really have flashlights

for eyes? What do you think this picture is trying to tell us? [Lead students through discussion to the concept that when bats use echolocation to navigate in the dark, it is like having a flashlight to help them "see" where they are going.]

7. *Direct instruction.* Ask, "What else do we need to know about bats?" [Answer questions listed earlier.] Use wiki or PowerPoint to deliver information.

8. *Connections between the story or other text, direct instruction, and an upcoming activity:*

Did the birds have echolocation to help them see at night? [No.] Why not? Why does Stellaluna have sonar? [Bats are awake at night.] What vocabulary word is this? [*Nocturnal.*] Are there other differences between Stellaluna and the bird family? [Yes.]

9. *Compare-and-contrast activity connecting story and text, direct instruction, and prior learning about birds:*

Let's use a Venn diagram to help us see the differences and similarities between Stellaluna and the birds. [This can be done on chart paper, on an overhead, or by students in pairs or individually.] Think back to the story. [This is an opportunity to cite the source of information and page numbers where the differences are shown in the pictures or in the story—supporting details. It is never too early to begin introducing students to the concept of supporting their information and opinions from the source.]

10. *Personal connection to the lesson.* Review the differences and similarities shown in the chart. Ask, "If you could be either, would you be a bat or a bird? Draw a picture of the animal you'd choose, and explain why this is your choice." Students then share their pictures and reasons.

11. *Closure.* On a sticky note, students write two or more interesting facts about bats they learned in the lesson. Students can share their responses before the end of class and then hand the note to the teacher before leaving or moving on to a new lesson.

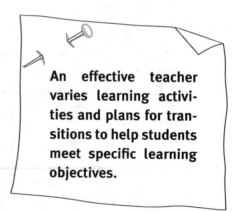

An effective teacher varies learning activities and plans for transitions to help students meet specific learning objectives.

Notice in this introductory lesson how the teacher continues to refer back to the initial activity and the read-aloud story. Each part of the lesson connects to the next part, so there is a flow from one idea to the next. This flow should continue each day, building on what the students learned previously and introducing and expanding on further information until the completion of the unit.

Moment of Reflection

Do your lessons have a logical flow from one part to the next? Is this something that you think about when planning your lessons? How effective are your introductions? Do you find students eager to continue? If not, how might you add a little sparkle?

Closure

Closure to a lesson is one of those elements that is so important and yet misunderstood. In our lives, we often talk about needing some closure before moving onto something new. It is the same with lessons. A teacher who spends time and effort teaching a topic and then immediately switches to a new topic or dismisses students without any kind of a closure leaves the students in the lurch. We all need a conclusion or summary of some sort before moving on. Here are some tips for providing closure:

- Actively involve students.
- Question students about the lesson and what they learned.
- Students reflect in their journal about the lesson and share these in the class.
- Ask students how this lesson or topic relates to the real world or to them personally.
- Use a visual object or catchphrase to sum up the lesson. For example, you might show students a flashlight and ask them to explain how this object relates to the story of Stellaluna and what they just learned about bats.

It is also important that closure be authentic, with students able to analyze, apply, and internalize information in a meaningful manner. This is especially important at the end of a unit. Daily closure may not be as intense, but it should help students add information learned into their personal schema.

If asking the students day after day to review what they learned in class takes on a certain monotony, Chapter Ten offers some ideas—for example:

- Have students write one thing they learned on colored sticky notes, index cards, a chart pad, overhead transparency, or a sentence strip that they share aloud.
- Students work in pairs, groups, or as a class to develop a tweet to post on Twitter. This post should show a clear comprehension of material learned in 140 characters or less.

Materials

It is equally important to plan for all of the materials you will need for the lesson and activities. Be specific, and include the textbook, student notebooks, and any other materials you may need. This will help you know to remind students to bring a particular item that they may not use every day. Planning out materials also helps you stay organized in gathering what you need before you teach a particular lesson. Gathering these materials should show up on your to-do list.

When planning and writing a lesson into your wiki space, be sure to include a list of materials.

Assessment

When you plan, you need to know how you will assess student mastery of the objectives. In order for an assessment to be valid, it must test what the students have learned. Before you plan a lesson, think about how you plan to assess the objective. Will you use a paper-and-pencil test, a class activity, a project or group assignment, or a recitation or application by students?

Once you've decided, you can check your lesson and activities to be sure they appropriately prepare students for the assessment. For example, when looking at the sample objective and lesson for the planet earth, you might decide that an appropriate assessment would be for students to label the layers of the earth on a diagram. This type of assessment would be valid since students learned and applied the information in a similar manner. (Chapter Four on assessment has more ideas.)

Timesaving Tips for Lesson Planning

Lesson planning can be very time-consuming, especially if you create detailed plans. Following are a few ideas to help you save time and energy in your planning and execution of lessons.

Type Lesson Plans on Regular Paper

The lesson-planning books that schools typically provide do not have enough room to adequately plan. The most you can fit into those squares is a brief outline of your plans. While this seems easy enough, it will cause you more grief later on. If you or a family member gets sick unexpectedly, causing you to be absent, you'll need to write out a new set of lesson plans that are more detailed for a substitute to follow. If you write out your lesson plans in more detail from the start, this will be unnecessary. Additionally, you may find it difficult to remember exactly what you planned to do with students if all you've written in the planning box is "Fractions."

You can also type lessons on your wiki space. This provides an opportunity for interactive lessons when used in conjunction with computers or an interactive whiteboard. Wiki lessons allow you to include links to pertinent Web sites as well.

Organize Your Plans on the Computer

On the computer, organize your plans into folders for each six weeks or units (Figure 3.1). Then organize each six weeks into folders for each week. This way you can place typed handouts, tests, newsletters, streamed media, and other material into the folder with your plans. Any handouts not already typed into the computer can be scanned as documents and placed in the file with the rest of your materials. Now go and recycle that piece of paper!

Have a Weekly Planning Day

Choose one day of the week to write lesson plans. Wednesday is a good day because there is plenty of time to gather materials for the next week. Also, many principals request copies of lesson plans on Fridays. If something unexpected happens on Wednesday, you still have one day to finish. Be consistent with this schedule, and plan your time accordingly. Make an appointment in your calendar, and stick with it.

Use a Template

Using a template will help you work out your lesson plans with ease. If you save one week's plans on the computer, you can copy them onto a new file and change as necessary. This saves time since you won't have to change every item. Also, it takes much less time to highlight and change information on a template than to write it over and over for each day's lesson. (See the sample templates at the end of this chapter.)

Back ▾ ○ ▾ 📁	🔍 Search 📁 Folders	▦▾ 🗷 ✕	
Address	C:\Desktop\1_Six Weeks\August 6-10		
	Name ▲	Size	Type
File and Folder Tasks ☒	Field Trip Form.doc	26 KB	Microsoft Office Word 97 - 2003 Document
	Games and Worksheets.doc	26 KB	Microsoft Office Word 97 - 2003 Document
Other Places ☒	Lesson Plans.doc	26 KB	Microsoft Office Word 97 - 2003 Document
	Parent Newsletter.doc	26 KB	Microsoft Office Word 97 - 2003 Document
Details ☒	Presentation1.ppt	99 KB	Microsoft Office PowerPoint 97-2003 Presentat...
	Video.flv	4,500 KB	Flash video file
	Reading Assignment.doc	26 KB	Microsoft Office Word 97 - 2003 Document
	Spelling Test.doc	26 KB	Microsoft Office Word 97 - 2003 Document

Figure 3.1   Organizing Using the Computer

Lesson-Planning Steps

These are the steps we go through when developing our curriculum for the year. You want to be sure you are covering your state standards and that students will be prepared for any state assessment to be taken that year. At the same time, you want to plan motivating lessons that are engaging for both the student and yourself.

1. Determine what you are required to teach. Look at a scope and sequence or overview of state-required essential elements for your subject or grade level. (Use the state department of education Web pages for this information.)

2. Organize that material into units. Try to make these units meaningful to students. For example, a unit on nouns is not going to motivate any of your students, but a mystery unit that integrates the study of nouns might.

3. Write an overview for the first six weeks on a calendar. This does not need to be detailed, but it should provide an overall picture of what you will cover during that grading period. If you teach several subjects, make a calendar for each subject area. This will be helpful to refer to when you write daily lesson plans.

4. Write lesson plans for the first week. In the beginning, you may want to go one day at a time unless your principal requires you to turn in your weekly plans. Use the following format:

   Date

   Objectives or state standards (what you want the students to be able to do)

   Materials (what you need to accomplish this)

   Procedures (what you are going to do to accomplish your objectives)

   Assessment (how you know you met your objectives)

The following pages show examples and templates for planning. A sample calendar and daily lesson plan are included for elementary and secondary students to show this process in action.

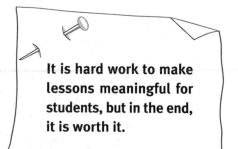

It is hard work to make lessons meaningful for students, but in the end, it is worth it.

Sample Elementary Calendar with a Six-Week Overview

A sample lesson plan is provided for the Tuesday plans outlined as follows. Blank templates ("Lesson Plan Template, Elementary Grades" and "Lesson Plan Template, Secondary Grades") are in the back of this chapter. Secondary teachers can do each course on one calendar or one calendar per course taught.

Monday	Tuesday	Wednesday	Thursday	Friday
Get to know	Get to know	G.T.K/T.B./Org.	Design team	Design team
Team building	Team building	Writing steps	Prewriting	Life map
Organization	Organization	Graphing	Graphing	Graphing
Space unit introduction	Galaxies	Stars	Constellations and myths	Constellations and myths
Round-robin stories	Mystery/horror	Science-fiction/ fantasy	Adventure/history Fiction	Rough draft
Place value	Thousands	Millions	Decimals	Math test
Gravity	Tour the solar system	Figure distances	Elliptic orbit	Solar system fact facts
Drafting/reading-writing workshop	Drafting/reading-writing workshop	Drafting/reading-writing workshop	Drafting/reading-writing workshop	Drafting/reading-writing workshop
Symbols	Area and Dimension	Multiplication quiz	Multiply by one digit	Multiply by one digit
		Timeline/*Apollo 13*	"The Planets" with Patrick Stewart (2000)	Field trip to planetarium
No School	No School	Global response	Global response	Revising
		Repeated addition	Addition practice	No math today
Introduction to space project	Teach note taking	Write paragraphs	Pop-up book visual	Oral presentations
Revising	Second draft	Second draft	Proof draft	Final copy
Multiply (two digits)	Two-digit practice	Subtraction (take away versus difference)	Subtraction with base 10	Visual word problems
Space exploration : Memorial to space shuttle crew	Moon: One Giant Leap	Lost on the Moon activity	Colonization simulation	Space test
Final copy due for book study	Book study	Book study	Book study	Final copy due; share written stories and book studies
Long division	Long division word problems	Unit math test (no long division)	Long division: two digits into two or three digits	Long division word problems

Sample Elementary Lesson Plan for Tuesday

Objectives:	To be able to understand place value using base 10
	To be able to transfer numbers from standard to numerical form
	To be able to write a story as a team
	To be able to discuss the place humans hold within the galaxy
	To be able to use a time line to record historical facts
Materials:	Base 10 pieces (yellow), long white paper, time line copies, universe video, black construction paper, small white paper
Homework:	Math – Place value
	Reading – Read for twenty minutes, write a response to reading in log
	English language arts – Write one sentence for each vocabulary word using it correctly
Journal:	If you had x-ray vision, what would you do?
Words of the day:	*galaxy* – a large group of stars, planets, gas, and dust
	Light year – the distance that light travels in one year – about six trillion miles
	Space – the expanse in which the solar system, stars, and galaxies exist
Daily oral language:	Read the following sentence and identify the helping verb: *All the stars in the sky are part of the Milky Way galaxy.* Is this the only helping verb that can be used for this sentence? Why or why not? [Answer: The word *are* is the helping verb. It is the only possible choice because the noun is plural.]
Daily geography:	(A) Which ocean is the largest in the world? [Pacific]
	(B) Which hemisphere is south of where you live? [Southern and Western]
Daily math:	Write the following numbers in numerical form:
	(A) Three thousand four hundred twenty-nine
	(B) Nine hundred forty
	(C) Ten thousand seven

Classrooms that Spark!

Procedures:

8:00–8:30	Announcements, homework calendar, word of the day, journal
8:30–8:45	Daily oral language
8:45–9:00	Daily geography
9:00–9:45	Daily math: Introduce/review basic place value using base 10 blocks:

(a) Create a place value chart—divide long white paper into thirds and make a ones column, tens column, and hundreds column.

(b) Students take out base 10 pieces—discuss pieces.

(c) Give random numbers to students, and have students place pieces in the correct column (assessment activity).

(d) Continue to practice with students—have students come up with their own numbers (extension activity).

(e) Write out numbers in standard form to get ready for homework.

(f) Closure—students write in math journal what they learned today.

9:45–9:55	Bathroom break/go to specials.
10:50–11:20	Reading workshop: Students read for twenty minutes. They may sit anywhere in the room—no talking! Teacher either reads with students on an individual basis, or monitors students reading. After the twenty-minute buzzer rings, students return to seats to write response in log.

Reading response: Where will the main character be twenty years from now?

11:25–12:00	Round robin writing: Give each table a different topic: "A Day at the Beach," "I Think My Mom Is an Alien," "Summer Picnic," "A Crazy Soccer Game," "The Day the Sky Turned Black," "The Hungry Spider." Each table gets one topic (on index cards to be drawn), each child has notebook paper, each person starts his or her own story, say go, wait three minutes and stop, pass the paper to right, read the story and continue it. Do this until you get your story back (approximately three or four times).
12:00–12:50	Lunch/recess
12:50–2:30	Set up mission log—white folder—title it Student Log.

Middle section: Cover page (mission log, name, teacher, and grade), time line pages, blank paper.

Students write in the dates on their time line.

Students write in the first time line event and discuss it.

Watch galaxy film to introduce galaxy unit.

Students make model of galaxy by punching holes in black paper and back it with white paper (use pencil to punch holes).

Assessment will be finished time line at end of unit.

2:30–2:50	Read aloud or journal and clean up room.

Closure Activity: Sample Lesson Plan for Ninth-Grade Creative Writing (Two Class Periods)

Objectives:	To be able to compose a narrative using real-life experiences
	To be able to design a life map of important events
Materials:	Real-life story (from my life), object to go with the story, large white paper, markers, crayons, color pencils, large sheets of paper for each student
Homework:	Write a draft of a story based on real-life experiences.
Focus activity:	Read the news article about the ozone layer on the overhead (or the handout), and relate the events in that story to your life. How is this affecting your life, or how might it affect your life in the future?

Procedures:

9:00–9:05 (1:20–1:25)	Students enter and work on focus assignment. Teacher checks attendance and visits with each student around the room, checking homework calendar.
9:05–9:10 (1:25–1:30)	Share a few journal entries as a class.
9:10–9:25 (1:30–1:45)	Lesson: real-life writing (a) Read own real-life story to the students: "My Golden Puppy." (b) Discuss: What made this story enjoyable? Did you think it was good? Why or why not? What about it was fun or interesting? Move into class discussion about how real-life experiences can make a better story because we are able to add more details. We are writing about what we know. (c) Show students the object related to the story and explain that the story was based on a real-life experience.
9:25–9:45 (1:45–2:05)	Pass out large sheets of paper. Explain to students that we will be writing and illustrating a life map, which will help us remember important events in our lives. Students create their own life map.
9:45–9:50 (2:05–2:10)	Closure. Students write on index cards: Why should we use experiences and knowledge from our own lives in our writing? Pass in cards. Clean up to leave.

Assessment and Evaluation: Homework

"Homework for tonight is . . . ," we say, and as we dole out their duties for the evening, our class often groans, whines, and whimpers. Why do we put ourselves through the aggravation of assigning homework only to hear loud protests? Often we only receive a halfhearted effort—if it gets completed at all. Is homework really necessary?

Over the past century, our society has gone from the belief that homework is essentially bad to the belief that homework is good and back again. In their book, *Who's Teaching Your Children?* Vivian Troen and Katherine Boles trace this transition from the 1900s to recent times. It seems we have come full circle.

Although ten years ago, the consensus was that homework was beneficial, Troen and Boles point out that "parental backlash against the ever-growing burden of homework is clearly spreading nationwide" (pp. 125–126). In addition, current research shows that while homework given in sixth grade and increased through high school is beneficial, it is a complete waste of time for students in kindergarten through fifth grade.

From our experiences in the classroom, we have seen that homework in the elementary grades is not necessary to enhance student learning. During this crucial learning period, it is vital to give students time to complete their work in class rather than at home, for these reasons:

- The teacher can supervise student work, and students get immediate feedback on their efforts.

- The teacher can correct misunderstandings and incorrect answers immediately. Students therefore do not repeat wrong information over and over that they must then unlearn during class.

- The teacher can assess student learning and acquisition of skills while monitoring students. Student practice of skills and knowledge during class time is a much more effective measure of assessment or an extension of learning than sending it home, where it may or may not be completed by the student.

Assigning homework in moderation can be useful to instill values of self-discipline and responsibility in older students. Homework is effective in helping to build a work ethic in our students. However, it must be done in moderation.

What is the goal of your homework assignments?

Teachers should remember that when homework is assigned, one student could easily spend hours on the same assignment that takes another student just fifteen minutes to complete. Why do we need to assign twenty-five two-digit multiplication problems when five problems will show us whether students can apply the concept?

Keep in mind the following factors that influence a child's ability to complete homework:

- A chaotic home environment with many children and in which the student may have adult responsibilities
- Students who are without parental supervision for most of the time after school
- Students living in poverty who may not have a place to complete homework or the supplies needed
- Older students who might work after school
- Busy family and extracurricular lives, including sports, church, clubs, community service activities, and family events

Parents often disagree with the methods used by the teacher and attempt to help their child do the homework either by doing it for the child (in which case the student learns nothing) or teaching their child a different way to complete the homework (often incorrectly). Now the student must unlearn the incorrect methods and relearn the correct ones in class. This does not help the student or the teacher in any way.

The homework issue is one that has many sides and will not easily go away. Assigning outside work has long been a part of school. No doubt all teachers have faced (and are facing) the challenge of getting students to turn in their work. When parents enter the fray with excuses for their child, it makes it that much more difficult to get the assignment. At the same time, we need to be understanding of the need for families to spend time away from school work and not assign so much that it becomes an unmanageable burden. Like everything else in the classroom, a delicate balance is needed. So we must ask ourselves: Is there too much homework, not enough time, or both?

Organization Skills

If you must assign homework due to parental or school demands, it is vital that you teach students how to keep themselves organized. It is difficult for students to keep up with homework assignments for several classes along with the materials needed to complete those assignments. Here are ways to make that easier:

- Keep an "unfinished" folder or "homework" pocket folder where students can place work to be done on one side and work completed on the other side. Label each side clearly. Secondary students who use binders should have tabs with pockets separating each subject or class period. The front pocket can be used for work to complete and the back pocket for work to turn in.

- Train students to keep materials, hand-outs, and work completed in a specific section of their three-ring binder for each subject area.
- Train students to use an academic calendar to copy homework for each class. Check that this information has been copied down correctly, and initial it each day.

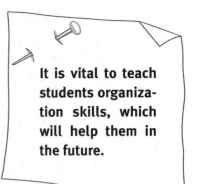

It is vital to teach students organization skills, which will help them in the future.

Homework Procedures

Procedures are important to help students and parents know what you expect in regard to homework assignments. Type out your homework procedures and expectations to give to students and parents. One copy should go in the student's binder, and the other should be posted at home. (An example can be found in the next chapter.) To stay green, post these procedures on your class Web site or wiki. Your procedures should address these issues:

- What homework stays the same each night or each week.
- Whether you expect parents to sign the academic calendar once a week.
- When and where you expect assignments to be turned in.
- What your policy is for absences and late work. How long do students have to turn in the assignment? How will their grade be affected?

The sample homework procedure that follows is for a fifth- or sixth-grade class. Younger students may not have homework as part of these procedures, and older students may have more. In addition, primary teachers may want to use a calendar format rather than listing out procedures and regular assignments. A list can be overwhelming and shouldn't be used with younger students.

Sample Homework Procedures

MONDAY

Homework:
- Read for twenty minutes, and write a response in log.
- Vocabulary sentences. Due Thursday.
- Other homework written in calendar.

TUESDAY

Tuesday envelopes go home with information from the school and grade
level. Look for parent newsletter from grade level each week and progress report every three weeks.

Homework:

- Testing skills practice.
- Read for twenty minutes, and write a response in log.
- Vocabulary sentences.
- Other homework written in calendar.

WEDNESDAY

Tuesday envelopes returned with parent signature.

Testing skills practice due from previous week.

Homework:

- Read for twenty minutes, and write a response in log.
- Vocabulary sentences.
- Other homework written in calendar.

THURSDAY

Vocabulary homework due.

Homework:

- Read for twenty minutes, and write a response in log.
- Study for vocabulary test.
- Other homework written in calendar.
- Parents check over and sign student binder and academic calendar.

FRIDAY

Spelling and vocabulary test.

Teacher checks binder for parent signature and reading response log.

Communicating Homework

Post homework assignments on the class Web site or class wiki for parents and
students to access. Be sure to tweet important due dates coming up, including
the end of the grading period, to remind students to get work turned in.

Post homework tips and strategies on a blog for parents. Many parents
want to help their student but don't know how. Educating parents about current vocabulary and strategies will help ensure consistency between home
and school when completing homework.

Grading Homework

Homework should be used only to instill the values of self-discipline and responsibility within students. It is not a valid assessment tool for student learning since so many variables can influence completion of the assignment. That being the case, homework assignments can be graded with a system of checks for the level of completion—for example, a check can mean that the homework was completed and a check with a minus sign for homework that was only partially completed. This system holds students accountable for the work, but no more.

These types of grades might count toward a participation grade but individually should not account for much of the student's overall average. In-class assignments and assessments should make up the majority of the student's grade in order to accurately reflect learning.

In Defense of No Homework

If you feel you will have a difficult time defending the decision to not assign homework, whether to your administrator, district administrators, or parents, we suggest that you read *The End of Homework: How Homework Disrupts Families, Overburdens Children, and Limits Learning*, by E. Kralovec and J. Buell, for supporting research. In addition, several articles available on the Internet that point out the deficiencies in assigning homework may help you defend this position. *The Homework Myth* by Alfie Kohn is another useful source.

When thinking about homework, keep the following in mind:

- Do more work during class time.
- Do not assign homework to younger students.
- When assigning homework to older students, lighten the load.
- If homework is necessary, make the assignments meaningful.
- Do not use homework to assess student learning.

Conclusion

Detailed lesson planning is one of the major keys to a successful classroom. Without it, teachers are unprepared and unorganized, which causes students to be unruly and disruptive. Lesson planning encompasses so much more than broad topics in a small box. It involves thinking through objectives carefully, developing engaging activities to motivate students and enhance the lesson, and creating meaningful assessments of knowledge learned. To use an analogy, lesson planning is the jar that contains our methods for teaching students. When used properly, everything flows out smoothly into each container. Without it, our ideas and strategies have no guidance and spill haphazardly around the room.

References

Hunter, Madeline. "Teaching Is Decision Making." *Educational Leadership,* 1979, *42*(50), 62–65.

Kohn, Alfie. *The Homework Myth.* Cambridge, Mass.: Da Capo Press, 2006.

Kralovec, E., and Buell, J. *The End of Homework: How Homework Disrupts Families, Overburdens Children, and Limits Learning.* Boston: Beacon Press, 2000.

Patrick Stewart Narrates the Planets Epoch 2000. BMG Special Product, DVD, February 2000.

Troen, Vivian, and Boles, Katherine C. *Who's Teaching Your Children?* New Haven, Conn.: Yale University Press, 2003.

Web Site Resources

Lesson Plans Page, http://www.lessonplanspage.com/
A to Z Teacher Stuff, http://atozteacherstuff.com/
Write a Lesson Plan Guide, http://www.eduref.org/Virtual/Lessons/Guide.shtml
Education World Lesson Planning Center, http://www.education-world.com/a_lesson/

Lesson Plan Template, Elementary Grades

Date: _____

Objectives:
  To be able to
  To be able to
  To be able to
Materials:
Homework:
  Reading:
  Language arts:
  Math:
  Science:
  Social studies:
Journal:
Words of the day:
Daily oral language:
Daily geography:
Daily math:
Procedures:

Note: These times are in half-hour blocks, but you may need to individ-
  ualize your schedule. See the sample lesson plans for examples.

8:00–8:30 _____
8:30–9:00 _____
9:00–9:30 _____
9:30–10:00 _____
10:00–10:30 _____
10:30–11:00 _____
11:00–11:30 _____
11:30–12:00 _____
12:00–12:30 _____
12:30–1:00 _____
1:00–1:30 _____
1:30–2:00 _____
2:00–2:30 _____
2:30–3:00 _____

Lesson Plan Template, Secondary Grades

Date: _____

Objectives:

 To be able to

 To be able to

Materials:

Homework:

Journal:

Word of the day:

Daily sponge activity:

Procedures:

1. _____

2. _____

3. _____

4. _____

5. _____

6. _____

7. _____

Rethinking Assessment

Part of planning includes knowing how you will evaluate the results of your efforts. In laying the foundation for a fire, you know you will see and feel the results of your work. You'll be able to see whether the fire is large enough, whether it provides enough light, and whether it generates enough heat. The purpose of the fire is determined during the planning stage. Having the ultimate purpose clear in mind, you are better able to evaluate the results. In turn, the results of your evaluation may cause further action on your part.

It is the same with learning. Assessment must be considered in the planning, implementation, and evaluation stages in order for it to be effective. First, you need to know what you will evaluate (your objectives). Then you need to conduct ongoing assessment to determine necessary changes. Finally, you need to appraise the final results.

Often teachers skip the first two parts of assessment and focus solely on the third: the final evaluation. This may come in the form of an end-of-chapter or end-of-unit test. It may include multiple choice, essay, fill-in-the-blank, or something in between. But what about those informal assessments that help determine whether students are on track? What about the prior planning for assessment within lesson plans?

Also, if you do decide to pull in assessment during the planning and implementation stages, how will you accomplish it? What strategies will you use? How effective will these strategies be in evaluating student knowledge and progress?

When thinking about assessment, remember:

- It is important to continually check your assessment philosophy and techniques. By doing this, you make sure your assessment presents a true picture of student achievement.
- Proper assessment can be a challenge.
- It is important to vary and adapt assessment tools to fit different learning styles and instructional needs.

Effective teachers continually reevaluate their assessment techniques.

Moment of Reflection

Is assessment something you actively consider when planning, or is it just tacked on to the end of your unit so you can enter a major grade in your book? Do you find yourself merely copying the chapter unit test out of the textbook and using it as a major assessment? What else could you be doing to ensure you adequately assess student knowledge and use those assessments to help increase student learning?

Philosophy of Assessment

Assessment is much more than assigning a letter grade. It should provide you with detailed information to share with parents. Moreover, assessment conducted throughout the school year will measure the progress students have made, show students' strengths and weaknesses, and allow you to check for how much students understand.

By varying the ways you measure student achievement, you can tap into different kinds of learners and accurately represent student progress and achievement. For example, if a student has difficulty with writing and every single method of assessment in a social studies class is an essay test, what kind of grades do you think this student will receive? If, however, you vary your assessment tools and give an oral interview or observe this student discussing concepts with other peers, then that student has a chance to show you what has been learned. This student may be able to tell you the entire history of the Civil War if you asked him, but when he has to write it down, he fails and receives a poor history grade. Is that a fair assessment of his historical knowledge? This is an important issue for teachers.

Your lesson should reflect the type of assessment tool you use. If you are going to have students create a time line of important dates during the American Revolution, you need to teach your lesson or give students notes in a time line format. Essay questions require a classroom discussion where students can express their thoughts and opinions.

If a student does not understand what your expectations are, it will be difficult to get a true picture of what that student has really learned. For example, if you expect your students to be able to compare and contrast fractions with decimals, make sure you tell them. Students cannot meet your expectations if you do not communicate them.

Directions for any evaluation should be clear and precise. When students are confused, they cannot show their knowledge of the skill or concept being assessed. Use simple language and sentences, for example. Too many compound or complex sentences will cause your students to bog themselves down in your instructions. Follow your own directions exactly as you have written them to double-check the clarity.

Kinds of Assessment

Formative assessments evaluate student comprehension of material both during and after lessons. It is a vital part of the instructional process because it provides a way for you to adjust your teaching methods as needed. When it is clear students are not getting it, you can reteach or refocus the lesson to capture a better understanding of the material by the majority of the class.

Summative assessments occur at specific points during the learning process: at the beginning of new units of study, at the end of a unit, as benchmarks throughout the school year, or to show student learning at the very end of the school year. These evaluations show a student's progress and mastery of goals set out by the district or state. These assessments include national and state standardized tests and tests at the end of a unit, a chapter, or a semester. Typically these exams are multiple-choice, fill-in-the-blank, matching, or standard essay questions. In addition, alternative assessment strategies can be used in place of these more traditional tests.

Authentic performance assessments allow students to demonstrate the knowledge and skills they have learned in a meaningful way. Often they are asked to apply their knowledge to real-world situations such as writing letters to government officials discussing community issues. Another example is a business class assessment requiring students to create a business plan and projection of start-up costs. After a unit on friendly letters and the persuasive mode of writing, younger students may write a letter to a parent or a friend persuading them to do something the student has chosen. After the skills and knowledge applied in this letter have been evaluated and perhaps revised in light of the evaluation, the student can mail it to the recipient, which then leads to an assessment of envelope addressing skills.

How Often?

Formative assessments should occur every day, after every lesson. It is not something that should come only at the end of a unit. You should be checking for understanding and student comprehension throughout the day. Here are some ideas:

- Sticky notes: Ask students to write three facts they've learned from the lesson on a sticky note. Bright and fun colors, such as hot pink or neon green, are motivating for students. You can also buy sticky notes and little memo pads at dollar stores that provide that spark of motivation at the end of a lesson. Once the students have written their three facts, you can walk around the room and scan their answers to check for understanding.
- "Ticket out": Students answer a question or give a quick fact as their ticket to get out of class at the end of the period or day.
- Tweets: Students individually or as a class sum up what they learned in 140 characters or fewer.

Alternative Assessment Tools

A common dilemma among teachers is how to find ways to conduct summative assessments other than paper-and-pencil examinations. Here we have provided alternative ways to evaluate your students' learning. You might not use every method and you may vary your assessment tools with each class or each student. Whatever methods of appraisal you choose, just be sure to use a variety.

Observations

Teachers observe students in various situations and keep records for grading purposes. Clipboard cruising is one way of keeping records on observations of each student. Attach several sheets of mailing labels to a clipboard. Keep it with you and jot down comments on each label—one per student. Depending on the size of the labels, multiple comments could be recorded on a single label for the student being observed.

One way to observe is to walk around the room. Students often freely share their knowledge when they are not intimidated by the pressure of getting graded. Another way is to observe students in cooperative group discussions. Are students participating? Are they showing knowledge of a concept or comprehension of a reading passage by the comments made in a discussion? Are students correctly using a skill taught in class?

Student Reflection

When students are asked to reflect on their own growth and knowledge of a concept or theme, they take responsibility for their own learning. Students create their own meaning instead of memorizing and regurgitating information, which provides a clear picture of what the student learned and internalized. You might use this assessment tool after students read a book or passage, have studied a unit, or finished with their projects. Be sure to give students examples of the kind of reflection you expect. Otherwise you may end up with broad statements that do not help in assessing what they actually learned.

Clear and Unclear Windows

In this variation of student reflection, students fold a piece of paper into two or more sections. They label half of the paper as clear windows and the other half as unclear windows. In the clear window boxes, students write what they have learned and understand about a topic, reading, or concept. In the unclear window boxes, they write about the concepts they do not understand or where they need clarification. This is a useful resource because you can shape future lessons to address unclear windows.

Semantic Web or Mind Map

This is a fabulous method of assessment and is also a super way to teach students how to organize information. Students need to learn how to make connections and find relationships among varying facts and concepts. For the web or mind map, they place a main topic in the middle of the paper and then branch off with related details. Each branch might have another branch off it connecting that fact or statement with another detail. This can be written or drawn. Using this as an assessment shows how a student organizes the knowledge or if a student doesn't understand a concept at all.

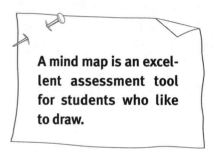

A mind map is an excellent assessment tool for students who like to draw.

As with all of the other types of assessment, it is important to model for students what you expect to see when they turn in their work. Model how to create a web or mind map around a specific concept or skill.

"I Learned . . ." Statement

This assessment can be used after a short activity, such as a lesson or film, to show whether your objectives were met. It could also be used as a culmination to a large thematic unit in place of the unit test.

In the "I learned . . ." statement, students express what they have learned orally or in writing. It is best to narrow this assignment to five or fewer statements so students are forced to prioritize the information instead of throwing out trivial facts. This is another assessment where Bloom's keywords can come in handy. (See Chapter Seven for more information on Bloom's.)

Summary Statement

A summary statement is longer and provides more depth than the "I learned" statements. Students are asked to summarize what they have learned in a paragraph. This may also be an oral or written assignment. A summary should require the students to make connections among the various facts they learned instead of simply stating isolated data. This type of activity requires higher-level thinking skills on the part of students.

Interview

Oral interviews can be held with individual students on any topic to see how much that student learned or to check for understanding. The interview should last no longer than five minutes. The questions should include a range from lower-level to higher-level thinking. The lower-level questions will provide opportunities for success and build student self-esteem. The higher-level questions will allow you to assess student reasoning ability. Take notes during the interviews for grading and record-keeping purposes.

> " My second year of teaching, I had one student in particular who was a concern. It seemed that he could not pass any test that I gave him. However, I knew he understood the content because of discussions we'd had in class. After a while, I gave him some oral examinations to see how well he would do. He passed every time. This student had a hard time getting the information from his head onto paper. Had I not thought of varying my assessment for him, he would not have passed my class. "

Visual or Pictorial Assignments

Visual learners can often express their knowledge beautifully through many types of artistic and creative assignments. Here are some great examples of visual assessment tools:

Illustrations to go with writing and to show comprehension of material	Pictures with captions
Cartoon drawings	Murals
Mobiles	Dioramas (shoe box scenes)
Maps	Charts
Graphs	Posters
Travel brochures	Mind maps

Chapter Ten provides activities of this nature that can be used to assess student learning.

Project-Based Assessments

Creating products is not only a motivating activity for students when they are learning new information or applying skills learned in the classroom; it also makes an excellent performance assessment. Students must discover answers to questions posted by the teacher over the spectrum of Bloom's taxonomy of cognitive skills. These answers are then used to complete several tasks to show comprehension and apply learning. Some projects may be research of information, while others may require students to simulate real-world or historical situations. In addition, students may be required to build objects, machines, or structures that meet specific requirements. (For examples of these types of products and projects, see Chapter Seven.)

Checklist of Objectives

When students have a lengthy assignment or project, a helpful tool for teachers to evaluate student progress is to have the students fill out a checklist. When students are given time to work on the project in class and you don't want to grade in depth until the final project, you can ask to see the student's checklist along with corresponding work. A brief glance shows you whether a student is on track. An easy grade can be given at this point for effort and progress or completeness of that particular section. Bloom's keywords can be used to create a checklist so students are required to use all levels of thinking. (We discuss this further in Chapter Seven.) This checklist can be put on your wiki or blog for parents and students to refer to at home. Two examples follow:

Example Checklist for a Native American Project

- ☐ Identify, locate, and illustrate on a map the area(s) where your tribe lived. (Knowledge)
- ☐ Explain the culture and daily life of your tribe. (Comprehension)
- ☐ Construct a visual teaching tool to demonstrate the lifestyle of your tribe—for example, a diorama, model, poster, video. (Application)
- ☐ Compare and contrast your tribe with another tribe when looking at food, dwellings, religious ceremonies, and geographical location. This will require you to communicate with one other group. (Analysis)
- ☐ Organize a presentation that incorporates all of the information you have gathered about your tribe in order to teach others. (Synthesis)
- ☐ Determine how well your tribe would be able to survive in America's modern environment. (Evaluation)

Example Checklist for Student Evaluations

Evaluate your group on the following elements using numbers 1–4, 1 = poor and 4 = excellent:

_____ Cooperation within the team
_____ Individual participation
_____ Information gathered
_____ Amount, correctness, elaboration

_____ Visual teaching aid
_____ Creativity, best quality, accuracy, use in presentation
_____ Presentation
_____ Individual participation, clearly spoken and loud enough, creativity

Moment of Reflection

What is your philosophy of assessment? Are your assessment techniques accurately representing student achievement and progress? What types of assessments are you using? Do you have a balance of formative, summative, and authentic performance assessments? What could you do differently?

Portfolio Assessment

Many teachers do not rely on portfolios when assessing students because they are confused about what a portfolio is and what it should be used for. Should you use only the best student pieces or put in a range of pieces to show improvement? Also, how do you grade the portfolio? If the work is already graded, do you grade it again? This section provides a brief primer on how to use portfolios.

Goals

Decide on an overall goal. What is the purpose of the portfolio? What is unique about you and your students? Your goal should reflect your classroom and your students. Some possible goals might include the following:

- Student improvement
- Mastery of certain skills
- Amount of learning that took place
- Collection of student work

Remember that your goal should reflect you, your classroom, and your students.

Assessment

Before beginning to use portfolios, decide how you will grade them. Once again, what is the purpose of this portfolio? Assessment of the portfolio is closely tied to your goal.

- Quality of work in the portfolio
- Amount of work in the portfolio

- Improvement
- Knowledge of skills

The easiest way to assess a portfolio is on a rating scale, and it too must reflect your goal. You must decide what you are looking for in each portfolio entry, or in the portfolio as a whole, and then create a rating scale to reflect that. For example, let's say your goal is to show the amount and quality of learning that has occurred over the semester. You might evaluate each entry as correct (mechanics), complete (information), and comprehensive (thought provoking), with the student receiving a score of 1 to 4 in each area:

1 = not at all   2 = somewhat   3 = mostly   4 = entirely

The scores are added up to give a grade for the entire portfolio.

Ask another teacher to help you assess the portfolios in order for the assessment to be reliable. The reason is that we sometimes grade according to the student, although not purposefully. If the work in the portfolio is not very good, but we know that this is the best the student can do, then we might be more lenient on our rating scale than another teacher who does not know the student. An impartial evaluator helps to make the portfolio a more reliable and accurate form of assessment. The grades from the two evaluators can be averaged and used as the grade for the portfolio.

Student Involvement

Student involvement is an important part of the portfolio process. After all, it is the students we are evaluating. There are three main components to student involvement.

Understanding

It is important that students understand what a portfolio is, your goals, your rating scale, the sorts of pieces you want included, and how the portfolio will be used. Explain this information at the beginning of the year. If you wait until the end of the semester, your students will not be as involved with the portfolio, and you will not get a true reflection of their thoughts and feelings about their work. If your students understand what is required of them, they will be much more likely to create what you want in a portfolio.

Choice

Choice is an extremely important aspect of the portfolio. There are some pieces you will want students to include so you can accomplish your goal, but there should be some entries that express and reflect the student's personality and preferences. You may be able to give students some choice even in the work you require, but it is vital that your students be allowed to choose work that reflects them or their progress.

Reflection

Students should write a reflection of their thoughts and ideas about each portfolio entry. You may want to ask them to write why they chose to include certain pieces or how they felt about an assignment. These reflections will give you an even clearer picture of the student's work, learning, and progress throughout the year.

Another important aspect of reflection is a discussion between teacher and student of each piece and reflection in the portfolio. A dialogue needs to occur between student and teacher so that a clear understanding of the portfolio occurs. The student and the teacher should be able to explain each entry. If you do not feel your students are mature enough to reflect and self-evaluate their own work, don't include this element in your portfolio requirements.

You could also use the portfolio as a way to collect and hold student work to show progress over the course of the year. This is an excellent way to show parents student improvement in knowledge and work product. You can also use the portfolio as a way to pass information about individual student abilities to their next year's teacher.

Teacher Tip

Student reflection on portfolio entries is an important part of the process. However, it is important to remember that student reflections must be done in a timely manner. If you wait until the end of the year for reflections, most students won't remember what the assignment was for in the first place.

Sample Portfolio Outline

An outline of details regarding how you plan to use the portfolio will make things much easier for you in the long run. It will also help you remember what you decided at the beginning of the year. Here is a sample portfolio outline for a language arts class. It is not absolutely necessary to produce an outline with the same detail, but it does help.

Portfolio Assessment

Goal:	To show the amount of learning that has occurred over the semester.
Focus:	The focus will be on the reflection statements for each entry since most of the work has already been graded.
Items to be evaluated:	Students must include one narrative, two expository (how to; compare/contrast, etc.), journal entries, and three poetry pieces. In addition, students must choose five other assignments from class to put in the portfolio.

Student involvement:	Student choice of five assignments should show what they have learned over the semester. These entries can be both good and poor work samples. Students must write a reflection on each entry. The reflection should express the purpose of the entry in the portfolio, the skills it shows accomplished (or working on), any thoughts or feelings about the entry, and why the student put it in the portfolio. Before the portfolio is evaluated, the student and teacher will have a conference to discuss the entries included and the portfolio as a whole.
Criterion:	Each reflection/entry will be evaluated on correctness (mechanics), completion (information), and comprehension (thought provoking), with the student receiving a score of 1 to 4 in each area, where 1 = not at all; 2 = somewhat; 3 = mostly; and 4 = entirely.
Reliability:	Two teachers will score the portfolio. One teacher will be myself, the main instructor, and the other teacher will be someone who is not as familiar with the students. These two scores will be averaged and used as a final grade for the semester.
Validity:	This portfolio will have content validity because it measures the student's awareness of what was taught in class. Students reflect on what they learned through each experience or project done in class.

Idea Share

Have students take home their portfolio at the end of each grading period or semester to present to their parents or other caregivers. Students can discuss the entries and reflections with their parents. You might provide a way for parents to then respond to their child's portfolio. These responses can be kept inside the portfolio for comparison later in the year.

Moment of Reflection

In what ways can a portfolio be used in your classroom? How might you use a portfolio as an assessment?

Grading with Rubrics

Subjective grading is one of the hardest parts of evaluating students. How do we judge the work? Are there specific criteria to use? Do we compare different student results? It is important to grade writing, projects, and other types of subjective assignments in a fair manner.

The rubric is one way to evaluate student performance in a manner that is equitable and judges each student on his or her own merits. It also provides an overall picture of the assignment and a set of criteria to use when grading. Here are a few strategies for using a rubric when grading:

- Decide what skills you want the student to show and objectives to meet.
- Write these down in a checklist format.
- Grade each skill or objective on a scale of 1 to 4 (0 to 4, where 0 = not at all, 1 = poor, 2 = fair, 3 = good, and 4 = excellent).
- Average the numbers to get a total score for the assignment.
- Final scores might look like this:

0–1 = 60   1 = 65   1–2 = 70   2 = 75
2–3 = 80   3 = 85   3–4 = 90   4 = 95   4+ = 100

Example Rubric for a Diorama of the American Revolution

Score	Category	Scale			
3	Scene from American Revolution	1	2	3	4
3	Correct information	1	2	3	4
4	Complete sentences used on index card	1	2	3	4
3	Colorful	1	2	3	4
2	Creative	1	2	3	4
3	Neat	1	2	3	4

18 total points: 18/6 = 3 = Grade 85
Comments:

Grading Writing Assignments

Writing assignments are difficult to grade because of the subjective nature of writing, and personal opinions enter into both the writing piece and the grading process. Here are a few strategies to help with this challenge:

- Use a rubric like the one discussed in the previous section. Grade only the skills you have covered in class.
- Use an overall rubric. With this, students receive one grade for their entire paper. A sample overall rubric is provided at the end of this chapter ("Writing Rubric Sample"). Also, your district, school, or perhaps the state may have developed a writing rubric that you are expected to use. Ask other teachers or the language arts department chair for this information.
- Give students two grades for their paper: one for content and one for mechanics.

When giving two separate grades on writing assignments, the content grade can be scored from 1 to 4 on the ideas expressed and how well they followed the writing mode. The mechanics grade can be on a scale of 1 to 100 with 1 point or 1/2 point taken off for each grammar error. You can then average the two grades, or you can keep them separate for your grade book. Be sure you are grading grammar learned previously. Correct the mistakes, but do not count off for rules not yet taught or learned in a previous grade. How do you know this information? Your school may use vertical planning and have a chart of skills taught for each grade. You can also check state or district standards and curriculum requirements to see what skills are taught at each grade.

> It really concerned me as I was grading student work that they were receiving a grade that reflected effort as well as the grammar skills demonstrated. During my student teaching, my cooperating teacher told me to grade one and then judge the others according to that first paper. They would be either better or worse. In my mind, that is not acceptable. It does not take into account the individual differences of my students. In the end, I decided to give students two grades: one for grammar and one for content. Through this method, students are able to see some success and get the constructive feedback needed to improve. With an overall grade, students do not receive the specific feedback in either grammar or content to become better writers.

Testing and Test Anxiety

Whether or not you agree with standardized tests as a valid assessment tool for student performance, they are here and it doesn't look as if they will be going anywhere for a while. In fact, it seems that the public is leaning more toward these types of tests than they ever have before. Basically this means more stress for us and our students.

We are stressed because, for many of us, our jobs are directly affected by how well our students perform on these tests. Some of us feel the need to "teach to the test" while others take a "back to the basics" approach with students.

One factor that is not often discussed, though, is student test anxiety. Low student scores are often a result of fear and frustration rather than lack of knowledge. This is especially true of borderline students and students who are on the verge of a passing score.

Just imagine yourself in their place. You know how to work multiplication word problems. You've done it a hundred times in class, and most of the time you pass with an average grade. Then a test is placed in front of you. You are told that this is a very important test and that how well you score will determine what you have and have not learned. You might even be told that this will affect whether you go up to the next grade level. Now you are getting nervous and your palms are sweating. You have butterflies in your stomach. You think that you can do this, but you aren't quite sure. The more you think about it, the more nervous you get. Suddenly all you can think about is how nervous and scared you are. The teacher announces that it is time to open the test booklet. You see the first question, and your mind goes blank.

Have you ever experienced that same sensation? Many people have both as a student and as an adult. This is test anxiety. It is a fear that causes your brain to downshift to a lower gear. When going through test anxiety, it is virtually impossible to concentrate on working through individual test questions.

Understand How the Brain Works

It doesn't take long to teach your students how their brain works. No matter how old or young, your students should be able to understand the basics. (We discuss this theory in Chapter Six.) Here are other ways you can use this research to help your students.

- Explain the basic theory to your class. Be sure to put it into terms they can understand.

- Discuss and brainstorm different events that can cause them to shift from their "thinking" brain to one of the smaller sections of their brain. These might include being hungry, having to use the bathroom, fighting with someone, being angry, being frustrated, being tired, being afraid.

- Work out with students ways to overcome these stumbling blocks during a test. Prepare, with your students, a classroom environment that will help them stay in thinking mode throughout the test.

Create Favorable Testing Conditions

Taking the time to create a calm and relaxed classroom environment can ease student anxiety before they are given the test. Creating a comfortable working atmosphere can help students feel more engaged on the task and less distracted by their atmosphere.

- Have healthy snacks, high in carbohydrates if possible, available for students in the classroom. Always approach this as both a necessity and a privilege for students. Be sure to explain your expectations regarding food in the classroom in detail. When students understand why food is available and your expectations, they will be less likely to take advantage of the situation. Small fish-shaped crackers, Triscuits or healthy crackers, apple slices, trail mix, and popcorn are good snacks for testing days. Be sure you have disposable bowls and napkins as well.

- If you teach younger students or have a morning testing class, provide a small breakfast—perhaps muffins and juice or a piece of fruit.

- Be sure the lighting in your classroom is adequate. If not, bring a few lamps from home to add soft light. Also, check the temperature of the room. If the conditions are too cold or hot, students will be more concerned about the temperature than the test. Finally, are students moderately comfortable? You don't want things too cozy, but if a large student is crammed into a small desk, his or her brain will not be on the test.

- Explain restroom procedures to students. Make sure everyone understands they are not required to wait until the end of the test, but they do need to give you a signal. Some teachers like to give each student a small piece of colored construction paper folded in half. The student places this card on his or her desk to signal the teacher when he or she is in need of assistance, a snack, or a restroom break. You might want to laminate these cards and use them regularly in the class.

- Encourage students to eat a good meal and get at least eight hours of sleep the night before a big test. This will help students arrive at school rested. Also, you want to encourage students to arrive a little bit early so they do not feel rushed before taking the test.

Teach Students Calming Exercises

What do you do with a student who has severe test anxiety or freezes up suddenly during a test? Here are the steps you can teach your students when they are feeling nervous or tired during a test:

1. Close your test booklet, and place your answer sheet in the middle of the booklet or turn the test over.

2. Close your eyes.

3. Imagine yourself in your favorite place—somewhere quiet where you feel calm and relaxed.

4. Slowly count to ten, or take several slow deep breaths.

5. Don't think about the test, but try to keep your mind empty or calm. In other words, don't start thinking about what you are going to do later in the day after the test.

6. When you feel ready, open your test booklet and begin again.

Moment of Reflection

Are you concerned with the issue of test anxiety? Is this something you have faced yourself? What issues do you think affect your students' ability to take a test? What can you do to help them?

Conclusion

In order to be effective, you must think about how you will assess students in the early stages of lesson planning. The fact that many classroom activities can be used as a way to assess student learning is a time saver. However, if you do not take this into consideration, you could find yourself trying to evaluate students in a manner that is neither valid nor reliable. Always be sure that your assessment matches what you have taught and that it addresses different learner needs. This can be done by varying the type of activities you use. Also, take into account your special needs students, and determine ahead of time how to modify assessments so they are valid. In short, student assessment should not be an afterthought to lessons, but rather a preplanned effort in order to effectively evaluate learning.

Web Site Resources

Kathy Schrock's Guide for Educators—Rubrics, http://school.discoveryeducation.com/schrockguide/assess.html

Teaching Today—Alternative Assessments, http://teachingtoday.glencoe.com/howtoarticles/alternative-assessment-primer

Emerging Technologies—Assessments, http://www.emtech.net/Alternative_Assessment.html

Portfolio Conference Sheet

Student Name: _____

Date: _____

Teacher Name: _____

Directions: Make comments about the discussion under each entry of the portfolio.

Title of entry:

1.

2.

3.

4.

5.

6.

Portfolio Grading Sheet

Teacher uses this form to assign a grade for each piece in the student portfolio.

Student Name: _____

Grade: _____

Class: _____

Teacher Name: _____

The grade is marked in the smaller box with comments in the larger box.

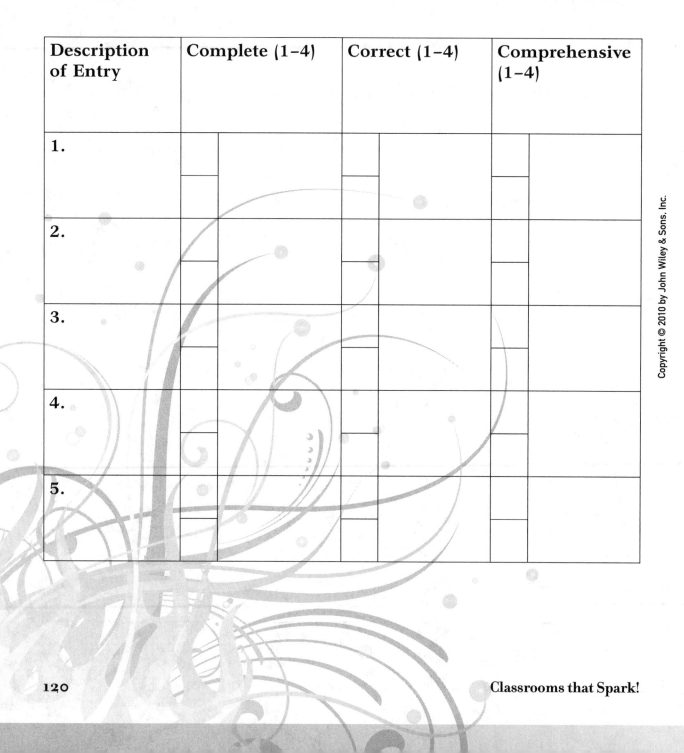

Description of Entry	Complete (1–4)		Correct (1–4)		Comprehensive (1–4)	
1.						
2.						
3.						
4.						
5.						

Classrooms that Spark!

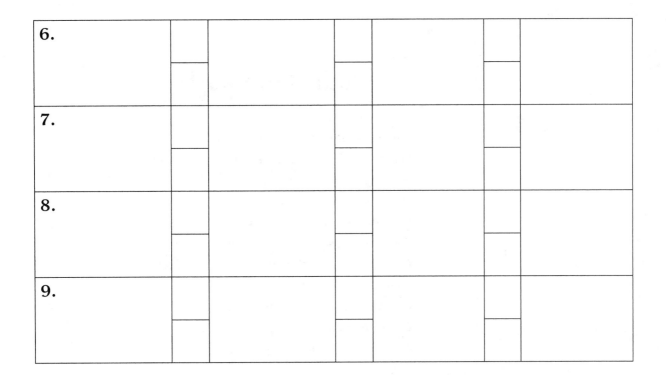

6.						
7.						
8.						
9.						

Each student should have a reflection of about five to ten sentences for each entry (upper elementary).

Writing Rubric Sample

Score	Characteristics
4	Correct purpose, mode, and audience
	Elaboration for each point and in each paragraph
	Consistent organization
	Clear sense of order/completeness
	Smooth flow; almost no grammatical errors
3	Correct purpose, mode, and audience
	Moderately well elaborated (a few points/paragraphs)
	Somewhat organized
	Clear language, few grammatical errors
2	Correct purpose, mode, and audience
	A little elaboration (one point/paragraph)
	A few specific details
	Lists items rather than describes them
	Gaps in organization
	Many grammar and spelling errors
1	Attempts to address the audience
	Brief, vague, no elaboration at all
	Off topic, thoughts wander, no organization
	Wrong purpose, mode
	Major grammatical errors

Classrooms that Spark!

Midterm Progress Report

Student's Name: _____

The grades below reflect your child's grade midway through the current grading period.

Reading_____   Language Arts_____   Art_____
Math_____   Science_____   P.E._____
Social Studies_____ Foreign Language_____   Behavior_____

CONCERNS

☐ Low grades on homework
☐ Does not complete assigned work
☐ Poor homework/study habits
☐ Does not pay attention in class
☐ Does not make up missed work
☐ COMMENTS:

- -

I have seen my child's midterm grades.

Student:_____ Date: _____

Parent:_____ Date: _____

Progress Report

Student Name: _____ Date: _____

WORK HABITS	E.E.	M.E.	N.I.	Comments
Completes assignments on time				
Follows directions readily				
Uses time wisely				
Contributes to activities, discussion				
Works neatly, carefully				
Works independently				
BEHAVIOR				
Follows school/class rules				
Respects authority				
Considerate of peers				
Cares for school property				
Is self-disciplined				
ACADEMICS				
Reading				
Writing				
Social studies				
Math				
Science				
Extracurricular				

E.E. = Exceeds expectations. M.E. = Meets expectations. N.I. = Needs improvement.

Parent Signature: _____ Date: _____

Source: Developed by Spring Branch ISD, Spring Branch, Texas.

Classrooms that Spark!

Missing Assignments

Name: _____

Assignments (put down the list of assignments that the student did not complete):

Parent Signature: _____

Part Two

Lighting the Fire

When you appeal to the highest level of thinking,
you get the highest level of performance.

Jack Stack

The mediocre teacher tells. The good teacher
explains. The superior teacher demonstrates. The
great teacher inspires.

William Arthur Ward

Great Beginnings

It's summer, and I'm sleeping. The house is quiet, and all is peaceful. Then the phone rings. I stretch and lazily reach over for the phone. "Where are you? Your classroom is empty, and school starts in ten minutes!" I hear the principal shout into the phone. I jump out of bed and start stressing. *I'm not ready!* I think to myself. *I don't have plans for the first day. I haven't set up my classroom.* My heart beats rapidly, and I start to sweat. Suddenly I sit up in bed. It is still summer, I remember, and school doesn't start for another three weeks. I breathe a huge sigh of relief and start to calm down.

Why do we have these kinds of dreams? Probably because we all realize that the first day of school is the most important one of the entire year. You make or break your classroom environment on this day. The first day and the first week are your best chances to build a classroom climate of mutual respect and understanding. You want students to go home with a feeling that learning will be fun as well as challenging and have a clear sense of your expectations.

This is just like lighting the fire. You need a good spark from the match to get the fire going. If you have a dud match, you'll never get it lit! What you do on the first day and during that first week of school is the match for the fire. If you want that fire of learning to become a blaze, you must have a great beginning. This chapter contains ideas and strategies to help that spark along.

While most ideas presented here may seem familiar, we think you'll find a new idea or two to help light the fire in your classroom.

Random Seating Ideas

Using random seating will give you a good idea of which students should and should not be sitting next to each other as you develop your class seating chart. There are a number of ways to do this:

• Cut up squares out of different colored paper, and laminate them. Each color represents a table or a row of desks. Have enough squares of each color for the seats at that table or in that row. Tape one colored square to each table or on the first seat of each row. When students enter the classroom, greet them and have them pull a square from a bag or basket. They then locate a seat for that color. This is an organized way of seating students, yet it is random and does allow some choice. It is also less time-consuming because this is accomplished as students enter the room.

• If you are working with tables or groups of four, another way to seat students randomly is to use the four suits of playing cards or numbers. This works the same as the colored squares.

• Label each row with a team name. Have laminated cards with the team name ready to pass out to students as they enter the room. You could also use subject area vocabulary, names of famous people, or objects that relate to your subject area.

• Instead of colors or playing cards, use pictures of famous mathematicians, scientists, historical persons or events, current events, novels that will be read during the year, chemical elements, laws of physics, artists—or whatever else goes with the subject you teach.

• To add a sense of fun to the start of class, let students sit wherever they want. Then after the bell rings, pass out a set of quick puzzles, poems, challenging math equations, or a series of clues. There should be enough for the number of rows or tables and seats in each (for example, six sets of puzzles with five copies each). When students solve the mystery and get their answer, they find the answer in the room on their row or table.

Will this be a little chaotic on the first day? Sure it will, but the first day is chaotic anyway. Will this be fun and get students thinking right away? Definitely!

For primary students, use these same ideas, but cut out shapes for each table or use the die-cut machine to punch out animals, stars, or something else.

Think about using shapes from your first unit of study to introduce and reinforce the concepts you will be teaching. Laminate the shapes so they can be used all year long or in future years, if possible.

For a fun "mystery," use rhyming words. Example: A student is asked a question: "What rhymes with bun?" Students then find a picture of a sun to locate their table. These should be written on a set of cards with enough questions to fill the seats at each table. These cards can be shuffled for the random affect. Once students are seated, give them a name tag to put on their desk. This encourages a little pride as students label their desk as their own.

Ideas to Welcome Students

Have a welcome packet ready on each desk. This packet might include a blank desk name tag, a note from you, a peppermint or pencil, and any information you want students to have. For younger students, you may want to hand out the prewritten name tags once they are seated. The packet may also include a welcome letter for students to take home to their parents (see the "Letter to Parents" at the end of the chapter).

Type up your general welcome note, and copy it on brightly colored paper. This is a nice way to say hello and welcome students entering your classroom. You might even think about having a student information sheet copied on bright yellow paper for students to start filling out as soon as they sit down (see the "Student Information Sheet" and "All About Me" at the end of the chapter).

Although name tags are used mostly at the elementary level, this concept may help secondary teachers get to know their students a little more efficiently during the first week. Use card stock paper (or a five- by seven-inch index card), and have students fold it in half lengthwise, then write their name on the card. You will find they will want to decorate it as well. This table-top card is a way to help you call on students by name during the first week or so of school until you know them better. Have students keep these folded in their binder or personal classroom in-box ready to use for the next class.

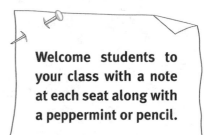

Welcome students to your class with a note at each seat along with a peppermint or pencil.

Type a welcome message and have it showing on your presentation station or whiteboard. To make it animated, use ready-to-use animated graphics in PowerPoint along with colorful backgrounds and text.

If you are tech savvy, use an animation program to create an animated welcome banner. Post this on your First Day wiki page, which then shows on your whiteboard. Search the Internet for freeware programs you can use. Many make it easy to create simple animations.

Add a bit of mystery and ask students to locate the hidden message or picture within the welcome banner or online welcome letter. This message or picture can relate to your subject area or first topic of study.

Planning Ideas for the First Day

Alternate your class time between formal procedures, expectations, and fun team-building or icebreaker activities. Also take some time to discuss your personal standards such as, "I believe in doing your personal best," "Character counts in this class," or "Honesty and integrity are traits I value highly." You may have students write down the character traits or life skills that are important to them. Older students may write a personal statement of their values. This could be a personal vision statement and can help you better understand each student.

> " I like to use the poem 'Pretty Good' by Charles Osgood to introduce the concept of personal best. We take some time to discuss the poem and how it relates to each of us in the classroom, myself included. It usually stirs up a great discussion, and I get across my point of how important it is for each student to do their own personal best. "

Here are some other ideas for the first day:

- Post the daily schedule on a poster, the overhead, presentation station, or interactive whiteboard and explain it. Students like to know what to expect for the day. Going over this information near the beginning of class will also deter them from asking repeatedly, "When is lunch?" or "What's next?" If you do get questions such as these, it takes less class time to say, "Look at the schedule."

- Secondary teachers can write the class agenda on the board for students to follow along and go over the semester syllabus. The syllabus should outline as many assignments and projects ahead of time with due dates. This will help prepare students for the eventuality of college or vocational school.

- Prior to the students' leaving your classroom for any reason, explain hallway rules and procedures.

- Prior to lunch or recess, go over any cafeteria and playground rules.

- Students feel appreciative when you display their work. Have them do activities on the first day that you can then hang up in the classroom or hallway immediately.

Displaying student work on the first day shows students they are valued. While this may not seem like much to you, our students want to know we value the work they do in the classroom. Younger students especially like to see their work posted on the walls for everyone to see.

- Have the students fill out a student information sheet with all necessary information.
- Go over your procedures and expectations. This will include homework expectations, daily assignments, quizzes and testing information. You can also provide an announcement sheet that gives the wiki page or classroom Web site where this information is posted all year long. It is helpful to provide students with a copy to take home.

Sample Lesson Plan for the First Day for Intermediate Elementary Grades

Objectives: To become familiar with rules, schedule, and procedures

                      To be able to work with others in a team situation

Materials: cut white paper, crayons, student information sheets, schedule, class procedures, rules, themes and units, regular-sized white paper and construction paper, progress report, welcome letter

Procedures:

8:00–9:35   Students come in and work on creating a name plate on a small piece of white paper. Explain to them, "Be creative using crayons and lots of colors. I want your name plate full of color with no white spaces. You can decorate it with pictures of your favorite things or use a theme to decorate it. Make sure that your first name is very large and clearly printed." While students are doing this activity you need to call roll, take up supplies, and check off student list.

            Teacher introductions (5–10 minutes)

            Introduce and practice the quiet signal (10 minutes).

            Name game: Students get in a circle. The first person says his or her name, the second person repeats the first student's name and then says his or her name. Go around the circle, building the list with each student. The teacher should be last and say everyone's name.

(Continued)

9:35–9:45	Quickly go over line and hallway expectations with students.
	Bathroom break/go to specials (art, PE, or music).
9:45–10:30	Specials: Art/PE/music rotation
10:35–10:50	Play the game Simon Says. After playing, discuss the objectives of the game: listening skills and following directions.
10:50–12:00	Review school rules, discipline policy, reward system, and consequences. Student groups create a written and oral presentation of one assigned rule telling what it looks like, sounds like, and feels like. Presentation can be a simple discussion or a skit.
12:00–1:05	Bathroom break/lunch/recess
1:05–2:30	Student presentation of expectations
	Introduce the year-long theme and six-weeks units and life skills.
	Object activity: Say to students, "Write down the first object that comes to your mind when you think of yourself. Draw that object. What does it reveal about you?"
2:30–2:55	Clean up.
	End-of-the-day journal on topic of first-day jitters
	Go home.

Sample Secondary Lesson Plan for a Fifty-Minute Course

Objectives:	To be able to learn names of classmates
	To be able to list and explain classroom policies and procedures
Homework:	Create a mind map or web of the expectations discussed in class. Be prepared to share.
Materials:	White paper, index cards, classroom policies and procedures handout

Procedures:

5 minutes	Housekeeping: Students complete information cards with name, address, phone number, parents' names and phone numbers (if different), birth date, class schedule.
	While students are working, you should call roll and do other opening-day procedures.
5 minutes	Teacher introductions
10 minutes	Name game: Students get in a circle. The first person says his or her name. The second person repeats the first student's name and then his or her own name. Go around the circle, building the list with each student. Teacher should be last and say everyone's name.

20 minutes	Classroom expectations, policies, and procedures
10 minutes	Closure: Emphasize the importance of working together to learn. "I am your guide. What you put into your learning is what you will get out of it." End-of-class journal: What are your goals for this course? What expectations do you have for me as the instructor?

If you have blocked scheduling and have ninety minutes with each class, alternate between going over classroom procedures and fun get-to-know activities.

For example, you might add the following before closure:

15 minutes	Student pairs develop a mind map of the expectations discussed.
10 minutes	Student pairs group together and share mind maps. Ask: "How are they similar? How are they different? Can you see the thought patterns of other students? What does this tell us about working together in groups as opposed to working individually?"
10 minutes	Share these results as a class. Why is it important to know the expectations of the leader or facilitator at the beginning of a venture?

Setting Goals

Setting goals is an important activity that should be done during the first week of school. Have students think for a few minutes and jot down their goal for the class or for themselves for the year. Then go around the room and have everyone individually share these goals with the rest of the class. Compile these into a list of class learning goals.

Use the student-set goals to help you get to know them better as well as to set goals for your teaching throughout the year. Post these goals immediately, or type them up so that each student has a copy.

Student Supplies

To avoid fielding constant questions from students about where they should put things, think about the following:

- Do you want each item stacked separately?
- Do you want certain items returned to you and have the students keep others?
- You can also ask everyone to hold on to their supplies until later in the day. Just make sure to decide this in advance so you are consistent.
- Create a poster and hang it over the supply location so that students (and parents) can easily see where the supplies should go.

- Supplies are not the only element you need to consider and plan for when getting ready for the first day of school. We have included a "First Day Checklist" at the end of the chapter to help you prepare for this important day.

First Day Opening Activity Ideas

It is a good idea to have an activity for students to begin working on when they enter the classroom on the first day. This sets the procedure for focus assignments, warm-ups, or sponge activities at the start of class each day. It also keeps students occupied while you talk with anxious parents, seat latecomers, and prepare yourself for first-day administrative tasks. Here are some short, fun, and easy assignments for students to complete as soon as they arrive at the classroom:

- *Name plates.* Give students half a sheet of white copy paper and instruct them to create a name plate. It must be colorful, creative, and fill the entire page. The students may use a theme such as favorite things or family. Write the instructions on the board or overhead. (Have crayons and paper ready.) This is an easy and colorful way to decorate the classroom that first day. Hang the name plates up as students finish or laminate them to hang up the next day.

- *Journal topic.* Write a fun and interesting journal topic on the board or overhead and have students write about and illustrate it.

- *Student fun facts.* Prepare a sheet that asks students different questions to learn fun facts about each one. For example: What is the craziest thing you've ever done? Where is the most exotic or different place you've ever visited? What is the weirdest name for a pet you've ever had or heard? What does your name mean?

- *Crossword or word search puzzle.* There are Web sites that allow you to plug in terms and definitions or clues to create a crossword or word search puzzle. Use terms about you, the school, the community, or even your first unit of study as a preassessment (e.g., www.puzzlemaker.discoveryeducation. com, www.puzzle-maker.com, and www.crosswordpuzzlegames.com are just a few Web sites you can use).

- *Student information packet.* Your welcome packet might include a student information sheet, a puzzle, a fun story to read, and a page to color. Secondary students may simply have a student information sheet to fill out.

- *Coloring pages.* These work well for younger students, as do wooden puzzles and books. Primary teachers may want to have several activities ready to be used on each table.

- *Brainteaser or challenge.* This is a fun way to start every class, not just on the first day. Most students enjoy the challenge of a puzzle and find them fun; these types of activities also stimulate the brain and encourage higher-level thinking skills. Books of logic puzzles and brain teasers can be found at most bookstores. Barnes & Noble has published a series of brainteaser books that are readily available. Also, the Critical Thinking Company publishes books that get children of all ages thinking through puzzles and other brainteasers.

- *Show me what you know.* Create an activity to help you determine student prior knowledge about your first unit of study. This may include a word search or crossword puzzle as well as journal prompts, a K-W-L (what I know, what I want to know, and what I learned) chart, and a web of information with only the middle circle completed. You'll want to make it a little more fun than a quiz because it is the first activity of class but your objective of preassessment is still met.

- *Create a cartoon.* Using a blank template with three or four squares, have students create a cartoon. This could show their favorite event over the summer, their feelings about having a new teacher, their favorite book, what they want to learn in your class, or whatever other topic you'd like them to think about on the first day.

- *Create an avatar.* Have students draw a picture to use as their classroom avatar. Students can color these to make them more interesting. Scan these into the computer so students can use them when they are posting to their Web site or blog.

Idea Share

Have students busy and engaged while you chat with parents and take care of house-keeping duties so they get off to a good start.

Get-to-Know Activities

Here are some activities you can do during the first few days and weeks of school:

- *Name game.* Students get in a circle. The first student says his or her name. The second student repeats the first name before saying his or her own. The third student repeats the first and second students' names and then adds his or her own name. This continues around the circle to the end. The teacher should be last and say everyone's name at the very end.

Idea Share

One way we show students we value them is by remembering their name. The name game is an excellent way to help you remember student names from the first day of school. As the students go around repeating the names, you do the same. Silently mouth along with each student during their turn. As you silently say each name, look clearly at the student for name-face recognition. By the time it is your turn, you will have said everyone's name several times in your head and should have no difficulty in remembering them the following day.

- *Ball throw or pillow throw.* Students form a circle, with one student in the center. The student in the center throws the ball (or a pillow) gently to another student and must call out the student's name before throwing it to him or her. The student who now has the ball throws it gently to another student, first calling out his or her name. If none of the students knows another person in the class, do basic introductions before playing this game. Students must throw the ball within five seconds, or they are out of the game. If a student says a wrong name, he or she replaces the person in the center. This is a fast-paced, fun, get-to-know game, especially for older students.

- *Scavenger hunt for signatures.* Students use the "People Scavenger Hunt" sheet at the end of this chapter and try to find other students to fit each description. When they have found someone, they get that person's signature in the box.

- *Picnic basket.* Tell students you are going on a picnic. Say your name aloud and one or two items you are taking with you on the picnic—for example, "My name is Julie Rogers, and I am taking jam." Then ask students, "Who wants to go on the picnic with me?" Students raise their hands and tell their name along with an item. The item must start with the same letter as their name, but do not tell your students this. They should discover it for themselves as part of the game. Tell the student they cannot go on the picnic if they bring the "wrong" item, but they can try again until they find the right item.

- *Seat scramble.* Use enough chairs or desks for everyone in the class. All other chairs or desks are off limits (you may need to mark these). As the teacher, you start the game. Call out a feature or fact about yourself—for example, blue eyes, red shirt on, birthday in September, traveled out of the country. All students who also have this feature or fact then stand up and look for a new chair. They cannot sit in an empty chair that is directly next to them. You, as the teacher, grab an available chair. This forces one student to be left standing. That student is now the caller and must choose a feature or fact about himself or herself to call out. These can be as specific or general as the caller wishes. The caller cannot repeat a feature or fact used previously. Every time this is played, one person will be left standing. Each caller should say his or her name as an introduction before choosing a feature or fact to call out. Play the game until every student has had a chance to be the caller or for a specific time period. Be sure to set a timer to keep track of the allotted time for this activity. You may find yourself so caught up in the game that you lose track of time!

- *Back-to-school bingo.* This activity is similar to the scavenger hunt except that it uses a bingo chart. See the "Back-to-School Bingo" sample and blank template at the end of this chapter.

- *M&M/Skittles game.* Pass around a large jar or can filled with M&Ms or Skittles. Instruct students to take some as it comes around. You may request that they not take more than a handful, and make sure they know not to eat the candy until you say so. After everyone has taken some M&Ms, each student must tell one fact about himself or herself for each M&M he or she is holding before eating any. This is a fun game and usually gets a lot of laughs as students try to come up with little details for each M&M in their hand.

• *Star activity.* Students use the "Star Activity" handout at the end of this chapter, and fill in each point with their own answer. Afterward they walk around the room to find another student with the same answers. If they find someone, that person needs to sign the back of that point.

• *Match-Up.* Develop a set of pairs for the number of students you have. For example, if you have thirty students, you need fifteen pairs of people or objects that go together. Using a mailing label, put one name or object on the back of each student. The student does not know who or what he or she is. Everyone travels around the room asking others yes or no questions to determine who or what they are. For example, "Am I a person?" "Am I dead?" "Am I fictional?" "Am I used in the house?" A student who guesses who he or she is then finds his or her pair. Here are some examples of matches:

Peanut butter/jelly	Einstein/$e = mc^2$	Newton/law of gravity
Hannah Montana/Miley Cyrus	Bunsen burner/graduated cylinder	Cloud/rain
Earthquake/tectonic plates	Emma/Jane Austen	Patton/World War II
Harry Potter/J. K. Rowling	Paul Revere/Revolutionary War	Circle/sphere

Once paired, students then proceed to the partner interviews activity, listed next. This is a fun random way for students to get a partner.

• *Partner interviews.* Students pair up or are paired up with someone they do not know. With the class as a whole, brainstorm five or six questions to ask. Students then interview each other using index cards. When everyone is finished, each person must stand up and introduce his or her partner to the rest of the class and share interesting facts about this person. This activity is used often in a middle school setting.

• *Groups activity.* Have each student brainstorm for two or three minutes and list the different groups they belong to. These groups include any and every way that students could categorize themselves—for example:

Daughter	African American	Texan
Son	Student	Football player
Pianist	Babysitter	Shopper
Christian	Sister	Friend

Be sure you give examples of the groups you belong to in order to help students begin brainstorming.

Once everyone has a list, go around the room and allow each person to introduce himself or herself and share the groups he or she belongs to. Ask students to listen for commonalities in the lists.

This is an excellent activity to lead into a discussion about tolerance, accepting differences, and focusing on similarities as ties to friendship. It is also a great way to help you identify different strengths and talents among your students.

Team-Building Activities

The activities listed below provide an opportunity for students to get to know each other in small group settings and encourage a sense of camaraderie among students. Team-building activities also set the stage for cooperative learning groups, an active learning strategy that requires students to work together in small groups.

If You Were . . .

In this activity, a great way to get to know each student's personality, all students answer the questions and then share them with the class—for example:

- If you were a car, what kind of car would you be?
- What kind of animal are you like when you are angry?
- If you were a bug, what kind of bug would you be?
- Name something that always makes you smile.
- If you could be like any other person, who would it be?

An adaptation of this idea is to use one of those "get to know your friends" e-mails that is often circulated with different questions or statements to complete—for example:

- What did you have for breakfast today?
- Do you prefer the beach or mountains?
- What is your favorite soda?
- What is your favorite color?
- Which movie star do you think you are most like?
- Who was the last person you talked to?

Older students might enjoy answering this type of questionnaire; just be sure to check the questions for appropriateness.

Assumption Game

Students work together as a class to figure out "what happened" or "why" by asking yes or no questions. For example: "A man, on his way home, saw the masked man coming toward him, so he turned and ran."

Students might ask, "Was the first man scared of the second?" You have to answer each question with a yes or no. No answers are just as helpful as yes answers. For example, if the answer is "No, the man is not scared," then students do not need to ask whether he is a burglar. There is no limit to the number of questions asked unless you want to set one. The goal is to get students to listen to each other's questions and use logic to think about how the answers change or affect their understanding of the scenario. This type of activity encourages higher-level thinking skills.

The answer to the example is a baseball game: the man is running to home plate and the catcher is coming toward him with the ball. These types of scenarios are often called story logic problems and minute mysteries. You can find them online and in books of logic games. Be careful about the types of questions you ask or modify the questions to make them appropriate for the age you teach and for school in general. The Critical Thinking Company publishes the Red Herring series with these types of puzzles specifically for school-aged children and adolescents.

Cooperative Learning Games

There are many books available with cooperative learning activities to help students learn how to work as a group. One is *Cooperative Group Problem Solving: Adventures in Applied Creativity,* by Douglass Campbell. These types of activities, similar to the "Desert Survival Activity" found later in this chapter, are fun to do at the beginning of the school year to help students see the importance of working together as a team.

In addition to books, there are courses also designed to help people learn how to work as a team. The Ropes Challenge Courses, also known as *Ropes* or *Ropes courses,* provide opportunities for people of all ages to meet physical and social goals through obstacles, both low and high. High ropes include activities that occur at heights including cable walking and mountain climbing. Low ropes include activities that utilize props low to the ground and require more group cooperation skills to complete. The following two cooperative learning games were developed as part of a low ropes course in Spring Branch, Texas.

Chicken Hawk Game (from Ropes)

In this game one person is the chicken hawk, and everyone else is a chicken. The chicken hawk tries to tag chickens. Everyone must stay in the boundaries, which will vary depending on the size of your students. Depending on the area available, you'll want the space to be at least as large as half of a soccer field so that there is enough room to run.

When a chicken is tagged, he or she must stand on one leg and flap wings and say, "Help me! Help me!" This chicken may be untagged when two or more chickens hold hands in a circle around him or her and sing "Happy Birthday." The chicken hawk may not tag any chickens who are in a circle, holding hands singing "Happy Birthday." If all the chickens are tagged, the chicken hawk wins. If the chicken hawk can't tag any chickens, the chickens win.

It is possible for the chickens to win if they all get in a huge circle holding hands and sing "Happy Birthday." It is important that the students work together to try to solve this. Do not give them the answer, but let them figure it out on their own. It will take a while before they get it, and you may have to stop the game periodically to repeat the instructions. If it goes on too long, you may want to start giving hints. This game has instructional value because the students learn that they have to listen to each other and work together to solve the problem.

Paper Plate Game (from Ropes)

Game Instructions

1. Place the nine paper plates in a row.

2. Each team of four students stands on the four plates located at each end of the line. One empty plate should be between the two teams.

3. One team is from Jupiter and the other is from Mars (or you could make it two cities, two cultures, or something else). Tell the teams that there is a bridge between the two planets and they have to cross the bridge to get to the other side. If they fall off the bridge, they are sucked into the vacuum of space.

4. The goal of each team is to change places with the other team. They may NOT step off the plates.

Rules

Stay on the plate. If your foot touches the floor, everyone starts over.

You may jump around one person at a time. You may only jump around people on the other team (not your own team).

You must go from your space to an empty plate. You may step forward onto an empty plate. When your team gets stuck (no one can move), you have to start over.

First team to finish wins and must show the other groups.

Answer to the Paper Plate Game
Read this carefully and work it out on paper prior to the game.

Label each team A1–4 and B1–4	B3 jumps A1
A1 steps forward	B4 steps forward
B1 jumps A1	A1 jumps B4
B2 steps forward	A2 jumps B3
A1 jumps B2	A3 jumps B2
A2 jumps B1	A4 jumps B1
A3 steps forward	B1 steps forward
B1 jumps A3	B2, 3, and 4 all jump one space
B2 jumps A2	A1, 2, 3, and 4 move into final place

Draw-an-Alien Activity

Break students into groups of four, and have each student select a different colored marker or overhead pen. Then give each team one transparency or a large sheet of white paper. Students are to draw a team alien without talking. Each student must only use the marker he or she has chosen and may not switch colors. Set a time limit for this activity. Two to five minutes is a good limit. Directions for students are in the back of this chapter on the "Team Draw Activity Instructions" page.

This activity is designed to show students the importance of working together and communicating with each other. You will notice that some colors are used more than others. Lead students to the idea of team roles. There are leaders and followers in every team. Who are your leaders? Which colors were not used at all or were used very little? These are students who need to be encouraged by the group to participate.

Desert Survival

Break students into small groups. Each group receives a sheet that explains they have been stranded in the desert. (See the "Desert Survival" sheet at the end of the chapter.) Each team has a list of materials available. They must choose a certain number of items to use for survival and prioritize their list. This is a great activity to get students working together as a group.

Design Team Activity

Break students into groups of four, and choose something for them to design according to your unit or theme. You can offer students a choice of two or three possibilities. You might also have students design the perfect classroom, cafeteria, gym, or playground. Students need to work together as a team on this project. Make sure you give them lots of time to brainstorm, sketch, and do a final copy.

Conclusion

The first day and first week of school are like a match that lights a fire. Although the first day is often hectic, it is vital that you strike it just right. If students see you flustered and unorganized, they will carry that picture of you in their heads for the rest of the year. Following expectations and staying organized will not be a priority to your students because of it. However, if students see before them an organized teacher who is prepared, cares enough to learn about each student, and sets clear expectations, they will be more likely to develop into a class that loves to learn.

Your tone of voice and posture also affect how students view you as a teacher. Be firm when going over expectations, but also let students see your unique personality. Take the time to get to know your students and train them in what you expect to happen within the classroom. In essence, the first day is a time for you to "strike the match" and light that fire of learning!

Reference

Campbell, Douglass. *Cooperative Group Problem Solving: Adventures in Applied Creativity.* New York: McGraw-Hill, 1994.

Web Site Resources

List of Activities for the First Day, http://www.ilovethatteachingidea.com/ideas/subj_first_day.htm

Back to School, http://www.proteacher.com/030005.shtml

Ice Breakers, http://www.educationworld.com/a_lesson/lesson/lesson317.shtml

Education World Back to School, http://www.educationworld.com/back_to_school/index.shtml

Welcome Letter to Parents

Dear Parents:

Hello! I am excited to have your child in my class this year. I feel confident we will have a terrific year full of learning and fun. I look forward to talking with you throughout this year.

Communication is very important to me, so please feel free to ask any questions and express any concerns or ideas you may have. Your child's education and well-being is my number one priority this year. I want to work together with parents and students to make this year a success for all of us!

Sincerely,

Cut at the dotted line and return filled in.

- -

Name of child: _____

Name of parent(s): _____

Daytime phone: _____

Evening phone: _____

Cell phone: _____

E-mail address: _____

Explain any special interests, sports activities, and hobbies your child has:

List any allergies your child has with foods or other products:

List any medications your child is currently taking that may affect his/her performance in class:

Are there any special notes or comments you would like to make to help me better interact with your child this year?

Student Information Sheet

Name:

Address: Phone:

Mother's Name: Phone:

E-mail:

Father's Name: Phone:

E-mail:

Guardian's Name: Phone:

E-mail:

Siblings and age of each:

Your birth date:

What is your favorite . . . :

Sport: Food:

Book: Movie:

TV Show: Subject:

In my spare time I like to:

I collect:

I enjoy playing:

I like to read:

Do you have any special talents and interests? If so, what are they?

All About _____

My Favorites

Sport: _____

Kind of book: _____

TV show: _____

Song: _____

Color: _____

Movie: _____

My Interests

Hobbies: _____

Places I've traveled: _____

Future occupation: _____

My Wishes

Where I'd like to travel: _____

My one wish for me: _____

My one wish for the world: _____

First Day Checklist

Use this checklist to make sure you are ready to start your first day!

☐ I know how I am going to seat my students when they arrive.

☐ I know how I am going to greet students and parents when they arrive.

☐ I have a short note welcoming my students, along with a pencil, peppermint, or other small token on each desk. (You don't have to write names on these notes.)

☐ My board is set up with the date, my name, an agenda for the class or day, and opening assignment instructions.

☐ My lesson plans are written out in detail and are where I can get to them easily.

☐ My class lists are with my lesson plans.

☐ My attendance sheets are with my lesson plans.

☐ I know what students are going to do with their supplies when they bring them to me.

☐ I need the follow materials for today:

☐ The materials are out and ready for students to use.

People Scavenger Hunt

Find someone in the classroom for each phrase below and have them sign on the line. You may use each person's name only twice.

New to this school this year _____

Has on something red _____

Has an older brother _____

Has a younger sister _____

Was born in September _____

Read a book this summer _____

Has a dog for a pet _____

Went swimming this summer _____

Has blue eyes _____

Can play a musical instrument _____

Walks to school _____

Went on a vacation trip this summer _____

Has visited a foreign country _____

Has visited at least five states _____

Has exactly seventeen letters in entire name _____

Is the youngest in the family _____

Knows how many centimeters are in a meter _____

Is an only child _____

Back-to-School Bingo

Find classmates to initial each square. Work to get five in a row. If you want a real challenge, try filling the whole box!

Read more than five books this summer.	Moved into a new house this summer.	Flew on an airplane this summer.	Has traveled to a foreign country.	Has visited five or more states.
Likes to play soccer.	Has a younger sister.	Has visited Washington, D.C.	Has a dog as a pet.	Plays more than one sport.
Is wearing a watch.	Has exactly 15 letters in their full name.	FREE	Has a four-digit house number.	Has blue eyes.
Has a bike.	Earned perfect attendance last year.	Will celebrate their birthday this month.	Has relatives in other states.	Can play a musical instrument.
All of his or her grandparents are still alive.	Has relatives in other countries.	Has an unusual pet.	Made honor roll last year.	Was born in June.

Classrooms that Spark!

Back-to-School Bingo

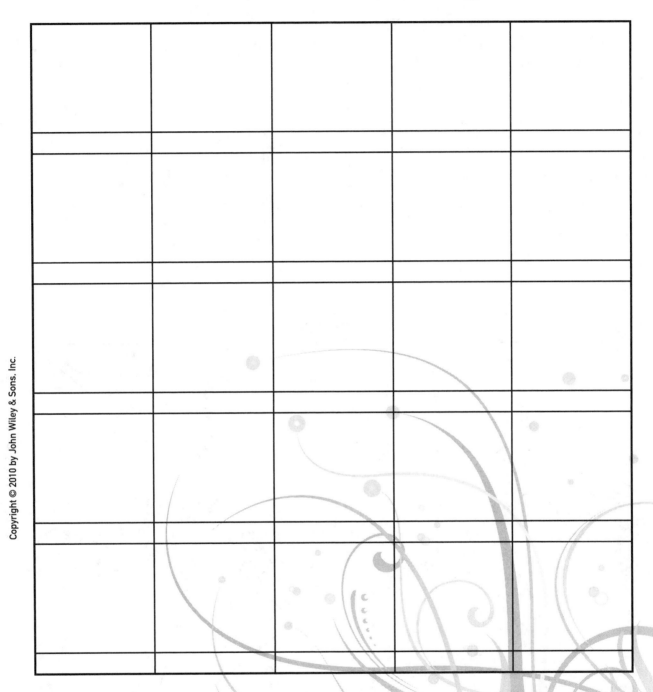

Find classmates to initial each square. Work to get five in a row. If you want a real challenge, try filling the whole box!

Star Activity

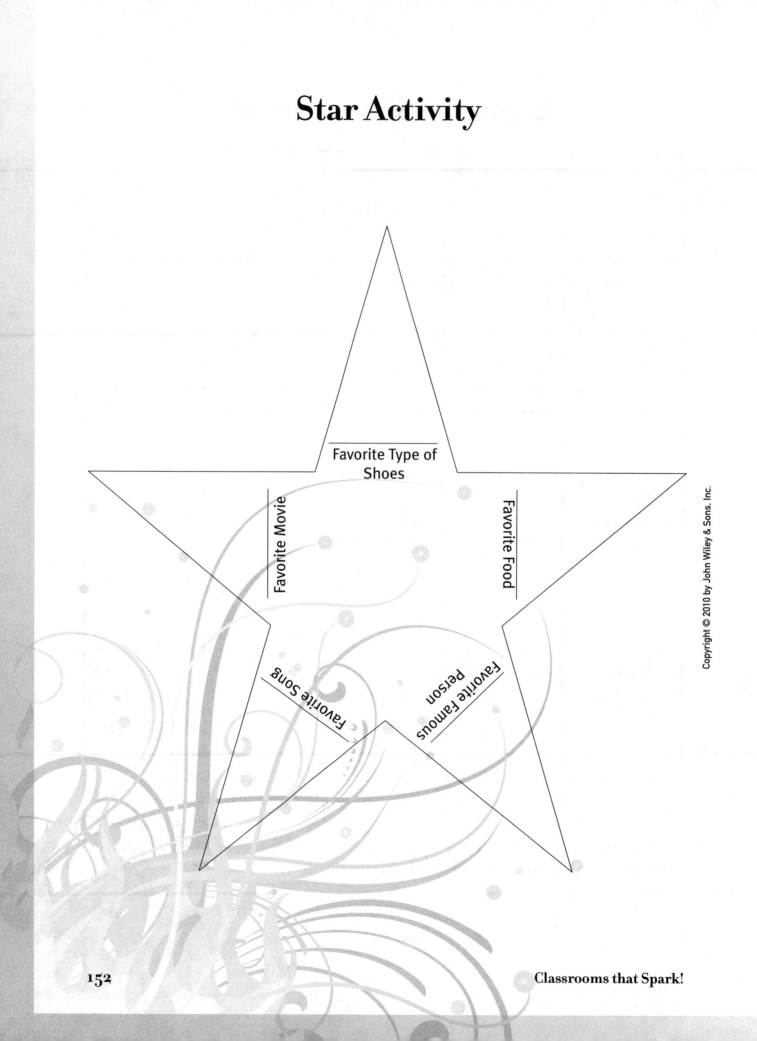

Favorite Type of Shoes

Favorite Movie

Favorite Food

Favorite Song

Favorite Famous Person

Classrooms that Spark!

Desert Survival

You are on a small airplane that is forced down in the Sahara Desert in North Africa. The plane is off course. It was traveling at two hundred miles per hour and lost radio contact five hours ago. All passengers are okay. There is no guarantee of a rescue or survival. It is a three-day walk north to the nearest settlement city.

As a group, you must choose the items from the following list to take with you. You can carry only seven of the twenty items to help your group survive the desert trek. Your group must be ready to defend the seven items chosen with supportive reasoning.

Desert Survival Box

A hand mirror   A long-sleeve jacket
A parachute   An umbrella
A pencil   A safety pin
A book of matches   *TV Guide*
2 cans of a soft drink   Nail clippers
Scissors   A compass
An electric fan   A portable radio
1 tube of toothpaste   A case of water bottles
A ten-dollar bill   A hunting bow and 1 arrow
A school math book   A box of saltine crackers

Team Draw Activity

In your teams, have each person select a marker. Using only your own color and with no oral communication, create a team picture on your blank paper.

Once your illustration is complete, discuss your handiwork and name your creation.

Learning-Centered Classrooms

Don't let the spark of a great beginning go to waste. Some fires have a great start, but then fizzle and die because necessary elements, such as oxygen, are missing. The ultimate goal is to build a roaring fire of learning in your classroom that will last all year long. You can do this by developing a student-centered classroom. This is a place where students feel comfortable to take risks and know they are safe from emotional, mental, and physical hurt. It is a place where relationships are built and develop into mutual trust and respect. This special environment takes thought, preparation, and work on your part to be successful. In this chapter, we discuss the three elements that are essential in creating a learning-centered classroom:

- An understanding of content
- An understanding of human nature
- An understanding of how the brain learns best

Understanding Content

The more knowledge you have about a particular event, concept, or skill, the better you are able to teach it. The wealth of information you have stored in your brain through study and experience makes it possible for you to expand on the basic information presented to students in textbooks.

Could you teach a subject straight from the textbook and cover the required objectives? Probably. Would it be considered effective teaching that will follow the students throughout their lives? Most likely not. Knowing your subject material brings with it the confidence that you know what you're talking about. You'll be able to share stories and fun facts that add depth to student learning. And you'll be better prepared to help students apply this learning to their lives and the world around them.

Consider an example of two classes that are reading a chapter in social studies about the early U.S. government and the first president. After students in the first class read the chapter, their teacher, whom we will call Teacher A, discusses the information from the text and assigns a worksheet with various questions to assess comprehension of material read.

In the other class, while students read the chapter, Teacher B stops at various points to check for understanding. When students read about the first president, Teacher B pulls out two white squares the size of teeth and passes them around the class. When students wonder about the squares, she asks, "How do you think George Washington may have used these?" Students brainstorm and discuss possible uses. The teacher then goes on to tell them that George Washington actually had false teeth. Students are then encouraged to look on the Internet for other interesting facts about the U.S. founding fathers or early presidents.

Which students will remember and retain the lesson: those with Teacher A or Teacher B? Consider Teacher A. She discussed the history of U.S. government and presented a required objective. Will her students remember the information presented once the formal assessment is completed? Probably not. Now consider Teacher B. Do you think that using the fun fact and concrete object of false teeth grabbed student attention? Definitely! In addition, the extension activity is motivating for students and encourages further thinking on their part. Students were not merely told that George Washington had false teeth; rather, they were led to this fact through a study and discussion of the two objects. They are likely to remember this lesson for years to come.

Taking information about a famous person and relating it to students' lives helps make that person real to them. Getting students actively engaged in a discussion about how life in the 1700s was different from today will stick in their mind and stay with them longer than a two-sentence or two-paragraph statement about George Washington from the textbook.

Staying Knowledgeable

There are many ways you can be sure you are able to extend and enrich student knowledge on topics and concepts you don't know much about or understand.

Idea Share

Kids Discover magazine is an outstanding source of interesting information, fun facts, and eye-catching photos on a variety of topics: science concepts, famous people, historical events, current events, and world cultures. Check the school or public library to see if you can gain access to this magazine.

Read and Keep Reading

Nonfiction books and magazines can be interesting and fun to read. Consider science journals such as *Discover* and, of course, newspapers. Remember: the more you read, the more you know.

Research

As you do lesson planning, write down keywords from the textbook or other resources from which you plan to teach. Then use those keywords to do an Internet search for information. Type in the words "fun facts," along with the keywords, to see what comes up in your search. And as you work, ask yourself how the particular skill or concept is applied in the real world.

Other professionals must stay well informed of content for their field as well as current practices, and so must teachers.

Dyan: Several years ago my husband and I were remodeling our bathroom when he found that he needed to enclose a vent at an angle. Neither of us knew how to figure out the measurements to cut the board. so I turned to the Internet, used the search engine "Ask Jeeves," and typed in, "How do I figure the measurements to cut an angle?" and "construction" as my keywords. The information was right there. We found we needed the Pythagorean theorem. This is a real-world application of geometry skills. You could also type in "real-world geometry" (or any other skills) to find plenty of information to use when planning lessons.

Practicing and Preparing

Before planning lessons, be sure to

- Practice the skill to be taught.
- Read the chapter or selection you plan to use in class.
- Practice the experiment.

By doing these things before you plan your lesson, you'll find you are better prepared for potential questions, glitches in procedures, problems, and misunderstandings that may occur during the lesson. It will also help you know what to expect when you actually present the lesson to students.

Understanding Human Nature

Why do teachers need to know about human psychology? The more you know about human behavior, the more you will be able to motivate students to want to behave and learn in your class. In addition, you'll better understand possible underlying causes for student actions and behaviors in the classroom. This understanding leads to better interactions with students. Take some time to review the concepts you learned in your psychology courses during undergraduate or graduate work. Then use this information to come up with ways you can adapt your own behavior to create positive relationships with your students.

Each student in your class is a unique individual who has specific needs. It is easy to forget that when dealing with a classroom full of faces. We can get caught up in curriculum, deadlines, grades, and accountability, and forget that we hold in our hands the fragile psyches of children who often need more than just good grades to help them bloom into successful adults.

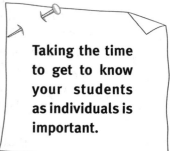

Taking the time to get to know your students as individuals is important.

Knowing Your Students

Get to know your students as individuals. Be flexible, and know that you cannot react exactly the same to every situation and every student.

Be understanding. Look further into what may be causing a problem rather than immediately assuming the child is a troublemaker and "out to get you."

Also take the time to talk with students. Don't make assumptions, but rather talk out any problems, assist with mediation between students, or just take time to talk with the student about life in general.

Erikson's Developmental Stages

Erik Erikson's research on psychosocial developmental stages of growth provides some insight into student behaviors. A person passes through these stages of growth with a certain level of success. Some are highly successful and some highly unsuccessful, and of course there is the range in between. The important thing is that the level of success at each stage affects how successful the person will be in accomplishing the following stages.

When you are dealing with student behavior and interaction issues in the classroom, an understanding of these stages and how they affect each individual may help you in developing strategies. For example, if you see an innate sense of mistrust in a student, you might focus on building a relationship of trust through consistency and flexibility depending on the circumstances. Students who constantly question themselves may need encouragement and affirmation from you on a daily basis to build their sense of autonomy and initiative. Understanding provides you with further tools to help those students.

A highly simplified explanation of each of Erikson's stages and the major psychological milestone passed during that stage follows. Several charts of Erikson's work can be found online, highlighting other equally important milestones of physical and social development as well. We strongly encourage you to learn more about these stages and how they affect student behavior and relationships.

Oral Sensory Stage: Birth to Eighteen Months

- The child develops a sense of trust or mistrust.
- The infant must form a loving trusting relationship with caregiver or develop a sense of mistrust.

In this stage the infant forms a sense of trust when his or her needs are met consistently. This includes feeding, burping, changing soiled diapers, sleeping, and love. If these needs are not met or are met inconsistently, the infant will develop a sense of mistrust. How the child emerges from this stage, with an innate sense of trust or mistrust, affects all future interactions he or she will have with others. We see the outcome of this in the classroom when interacting with students who tend to trust everything we say and do or, by contrast, question everything we say and do.

Muscular-Anal: Eighteen Months to Three Years

- The child develops a sense of autonomy or shame and doubt.
- The child must successfully develop physical skills including walking and toilet training, or a sense of shame and self-doubt may develop.

The child is attempting to master several physical skills, which will lead to more independence. A successful child feels pride in his or her abilities. A child who doesn't meet with success may develop a lack of confidence. You may recognize this in the classroom with students who need constant reassurance that they are doing their work correctly. These students may be less likely to take risks and participate in class discussions. Students who emerge from this stage successfully are more likely to take risks in terms of participation and will complete tasks without constant reassurance.

Locomotor: Three to Six Years

- The child develops a sense of initiative versus guilt.
- The child becomes more assertive during this time and takes more initiative, but if he or she is not supported or is too aggressive, the child may develop guilty feelings.

During this time the child is learning to be more independent. Goal setting occurs, with the child determining his or her own actions. It is important that the child is able to envision and pursue goals without guilt or the fear of punishment. However, if caregivers constantly question or hover without allowing the child to exhibit independence, a sense of guilt can develop. The child then feels that anything he or she might choose to do is always wrong, which leads to constant questioning of his or her decisions and abilities. In the classroom, students who do not successfully navigate this stage may seek constant direction and have difficulty in making choices.

Latency: Six to Twelve Years

- The child develops a sense of industry or inferiority.
- The child deals with demands to learn new skills or risk a sense of inferiority.

During this stage, the child enters school and must learn many new skills throughout the elementary grades. A child who feels unable to meet these new demands may develop a sense of inferiority, failure, and incompetence. This is also the time that a sense of self-worth is developed. A child who successfully navigates this period develops a sense of industry, allowing him or her to continue successful learning strategies. Depending on how successful the child is during this time, either a positive or negative attitude toward school and teachers will develop. Some students react to their feelings of inadequacy by shutting down and refusing to complete work, while others do the bare minimum to pass.

Adolescence: Twelve to Eighteen Years

- The teenager develops a sense of identity or role confusion.
- The teenager must achieve a sense of identity in occupation, sex roles, politics, and religion.

During this time, the teenager tries integrating many roles into a self-image under role model and peer pressure. He or she may look to parents, teachers, and other adults as role models to determine his or her own values and morals. The teen also looks to peers for this same information. The young person tries out new ideas in an effort to determine who he or she is. A teenager who is unable to make this determination may become confused, which could lead to making unhealthy decisions that will affect his or her future life. We see this identity search in the classroom when students imitate pop icons and peers, frequently change attire and attitudes, and constantly question the world around them.

Moment of Reflection

Why do you think it is important to get to know your students? How will this knowledge of each individual help you in managing behavior and providing effective learning for each student? What strategies do you have in place for building strong working relationships with students? How do they typically respond to you? Why do you think this is the case? What can you do to improve your relationships with students?

Home Life

Another element that affects student interactions and behaviors in the classroom is home life. Of the innumerable factors of life at home that affect students, we'll focus on three major categories. Although these are not ones that you can change, it is helpful to have a basic understanding of how family and home life affect student behavior.

Security of the Home

Students who have an insecure home life can exhibit behaviors ranging from withdrawal to aggression. A student who is constantly on the move from home to home, state to state, or country to country may be less likely to open up and create bonds with the teacher and other students. Why bother when you'll just be picking up and moving away shortly? Others may build a wall around their feelings for emotional protection and come across as uncaring or aloof. Students who come from an insecure home due to abuse or neglect may exhibit signs of shyness. Others may lash out in anger because school is the only safe place to do so.

Parenting Styles

Parenting styles fall into four major categories, with a range from extreme to moderate within each:

- *Authoritarian.* Parents are strict and expect unquestioning and immediate obedience from their children. Little flexibility is evident. Parents are demanding and do not take into account the child's wishes or desires at all.

- *Authoritative.* Parents have clear expectations and standards but are not necessarily restrictive. This parenting style is more supportive than punitive, and parents often listen to the child's wishes and desires when making a decision. This parenting style provides clear boundaries but is flexible.

- *Permissive.* Parents are lenient and undemanding. The child's wishes and desires usually win the day. Very few standards and expectations are in place for the children.
- *Uninvolved.* Parents do not set standards and don't care what their children do. This parenting style can include neglectful behaviors.

Parenting styles greatly influence student attitudes and behaviors in school. Children living under the authoritarian style tend to be either submissive to or overly antagonistic toward adults. Children with authoritative parents tend to be responsible and perform well in school. Children with permissive parents tend to take less responsibility for their actions and often feel that obedience is not necessary when interacting with adults. Children from uninvolved parents either shy away from relationships with other adults or cling to an adult offering caring attention.

Family Structure and Cultural Background

Whether students are living with a single parent, a guardian or grandparent, a newly combined stepfamily, in a foster home, or with an original mother and father, the family structure has an impact on the attitude of the student toward building other relationships. Culture is another element that colors a student's perspective and behaviors. In addition, your own culture has bearing on how you interact with your students, your expectations for them, and how they interact with you. It is important to learn more about the cultures represented in your classroom so you have better understanding of your students. If you get a chance, take a world cultures class at a local college to help you in this venture or read one of the many books on the topic.

Peers and Past Experiences

The older your students are, the more likely their attitude will be affected by their peers and previous school experiences. Decisions and behaviors of preteens and teens are often influenced by their friends. Pay attention to those the student is hanging out with to get a better understanding of this influence.

Past school experiences also affect student behavior. A student with negative experiences of teachers often starts a new school year with an attitude that says, "I'm going to get into trouble anyway, so why not start it on my own terms?" Because of past treatment, this student has already determined what you will do as the teacher and is acting accordingly.

As with most other misunderstandings, these assumptions on the part of both student and teacher can make a situation bad before it even has a chance. You are the one in charge, and this means you have to take the first step in moving away from the assumptions and toward better understanding. Once you've taken that first step, the student is better able to follow. With a little time and patience, you may find that your most challenging and troubled student becomes your greatest asset.

Boys in the Classroom

Most classroom teachers, being female, have difficulty understanding boys and how they operate. Perhaps you find yourself at a loss in trying to help boys find a way to be successful in the classroom.

For the longest time, girls have been a major focus in teacher training because they were often left out of class discussions when competing against more assertive boys. The goal of this training was to help girls become more assertive themselves in the classroom, allowing them to receive the attention they deserve. This has been an issue of concern in the past and is currently being addressed. The following information is not in any way intended to propose that we stop encouraging girls to be successful in the classroom, only that we also need to better understand boys.

Psychologists and social scientists are warning our society that we are in the middle of a major crisis among boys. We can see this ourselves when we look at the number of boys committing horrifying violence. As a teacher, the more you know about the types of behavior most likely exhibited by boys, the better prepared you will be to handle it.

> One of the boys in my room was very active and had difficulties with prior teachers in the school. He was brilliant but often caused disruptions because of his need for movement. I moved his desk to a place where he would not distract others and let him stand or wiggle while working. This gave him just the outlet he needed.
>
> The year before, he had been in and out of the principal's office all year long. The year I had him, he went to the principal's office maybe two times all year. His parents were pleased with the progress, and he was able to be a positive member of my class.

James Dobson (2001), in his book *Bringing up Boys*, states that understanding how boys are "hard-wired" is the first step. Let's take a look at the information he provides:

- Higher levels of testosterone in boys cause traits of high-risk behaviors including physical, criminal, and personal risks. The more testosterone in a person, the more risky behavior this person exhibits.

Taking away recess from boys will only increase your own frustration level.

- Boys have lower levels of serotonin, the hormone that calms the emotions and facilitates good judgment.

- Boys have a large amygdala, the fight-or-flight part of our brain. It does not think or reason, but puts out a chemical that causes a knee-jerk reaction that can lead to violence in some instances.

All of these elements are the backbone for why boys tend to engage in risky behaviors, including acting out in class, wrestling with other boys, and an apparent lack of common sense.

We must understand the needs of most boys to be physically active. We also need to have an understanding behind the cause of often irrational reactions by boys to events and people in the school. For example, boys are much quicker to shut down when in a controversial situation with a teacher.

We strongly recommend that you read Dobson's (2001) *Bringing Up Boys, The Wonder of Boys* by Michael Gurian (1996), or *Raising Cain* coauthored by Dan Kindlon and Michael Thompson (2000). These are excellent books on understanding and helping boys.

In addition, keep in mind the strategies for knowing your students discussed earlier. Provide opportunities for active boys to move around or wiggle, letting them stand, bounce up and down, or use squeezey balls while working. Perhaps seat them in the back of the room where they cannot distract others.

Finally, provide a place where students can calm down until they are ready to join the class—for example, the reading corner.

Difficult Students

There are a number of reasons for students to be angry or difficult. These students may

- Be picked on by others
- Assume they will always get in trouble (from past experiences)
- Have issues at home
- Feel that no one likes or appreciates them
- Feel the need to prove they are tough
- Feel stupid
- Not trust the teacher because of past experiences

Most of these are effects from the stages of development and other issues described earlier in the chapter.

To determine the root of the problem

- Identify the specific behaviors the student is exhibiting.
- Determine whether this is happening in just your class or other classes as well.
- Consider whether this behavior is recent or has been happening for several years.

If the behavior has changed recently—you've seen a change in behavior in attitude or the student was not behaving this way last year—then ask if something has happened recently to the student at school or home, such as:

Being bullied	Family issues	Changes in family life
A recent move	A friend moved	Death in the family

These types of events can affect a student's attitude and behavior possibly resulting in a shut down in the classroom. Once you've identified what appears to be the cause of the change in behavior, work toward a solution:

- Offer a place for students to go to calm down. They may rejoin class when they are ready.
- Talk with the student to determine the cause of the anger or problem. Talking out issues often helps build a relationship of trust.
- Allow the student to talk to the counselor.

> **Sometimes all it takes is a kind word or "I believe in you" to turn an angry or difficult student around.**

If the student's behavior is long term, begin to work with student, parents, and the counselor to resolve the problem:

- Don't make assumptions.
- Be flexible rather than rigid.
- Offer a place or way for the student to calm down when angry or frustrated.
- Offer encouragement.
- Encourage positive behavior.
- Use the student's leadership qualities in a constructive way: "I really could use your help as a leader in the classroom."
- Talk with the student instead of making assumptions.
- Slow down and take your time when working with the student. This shows you care.

> One year I had a fifth-grade student who was the angriest child I had ever seen. He was in complete shut-down mode. The mere hint of another kid touching him would result in a complete meltdown. I looked in his cumulative folder and saw that he had had problems with this since first grade. He was in special education, but only for speech. However, he kept telling me, 'I can't do that. I'm stupid.' After talking to the mom, who threw up her arms in exasperation, I decided that extra care was needed with this one. Whenever I saw him get angry, I would let him go to the quiet corner and calm down. When possible, I would go and talk with him about whatever had happened. After a while, he began going to the corner less and less. One day I saw him doing some of the more complicated math problems with ease. I said to him, 'Boy, you sure are smart. Look at what you can do!' He beamed. I gave him this kind of encouragement over and over. By the time winter holidays rolled around, it was as if I had a totally different child in my class. You know the best part? This year he graduated with a master's degree in accounting. I was so proud of him!

The more time spent builds trust, which leads to respect. Many angry or difficult children are ignored, yelled at, and demeaned at home. They need something better from you if you want their cooperation. Implementing a nonthreatening environment in your classroom will help.

Understanding the Brain

Researchers have shown that certain elements increase students' chances of learning. Here we will present a simplified explanation and application to the classroom, but in order to fully understand how the brain learns best, we strongly recommend you read work by Eric Jensen, Howard Gardner, Leslie Hart, and Susan Kovalik. We have listed several books in the Resources section that we recommend for review. In addition, the Institute of Heart Math (2006) has a collection of resources designed to help both students and adults understand how the brain works.

The first element of a brain-based classroom is a nonthreatening environment in which students feel comfortable sharing their thoughts, ideas, and dreams with the teacher and other students. You want to strive for an atmosphere in the classroom where no one is judged by anyone else. Every idea is welcomed, no one is ridiculed, no one is fearful of overly harsh punishments, and no one is put down. Your classroom should be a place where students can make mistakes and still be cherished.

You can create a nonthreatening environment in these ways:

- Insist on positive life skills: kindness, cooperation, teamwork, flexibility, friendship, integrity, honesty, dedication, and loyalty.

- Provide character education to create a positive classroom climate. Character education focuses on positive life skills and good manners. There are many resources for character education in the classroom available in bookstores and on the Internet. Some Web sites you might find helpful are www.charactercounts.org, www.character.org, and www.charactered.net.
- Do not allow bullying, teasing, gossiping, and other negative behaviors in your classroom.
- Implement the consequences you set out for negative behaviors, and defend students who are being hurt by others. Show that you will not tolerate this behavior.

Keep in mind that if your classroom is full of negative and hurtful behavior from either the teacher or the students, the amygdale (the part of the human brain that controls the fight-or-flight reflex) activates and student learning shuts down. We explain this phenomenon in more detail later.

The Triune Brain

Current research on the brain continues to change and improve our understanding, but it is also very complex. Here we provide an overview of the basics.

Simply put, the brain has three parts. We will use a term from author and researcher Leslie Hart (1985): the *triune brain.* There are technical terms for each part, but we use more simplified terms here:

- *Brain 1: The reflex brain:* This smallest part of our brain (the amygdale) resides just below the second brain and just above the spinal cord. It takes care of all our bodily needs, such as eye blinking, swallowing, digesting, heart beating, and eating. In addition, the fight-or-flight reflex is exhibited through this part of the brain. This is really the survival part of your brain.

- *Brain 2: The feeling brain:* This part of the brain is slightly larger than the first and resides between the first and third brains. This area controls our emotions and territoriality. We also gain hindsight from the second brain that allows us to learn from our mistakes.

- *Brain 3: The thinking brain:* This is the area where we learn, store, and retrieve knowledge. Solving problems, creating goals, reflecting over behavior and actions, and making choices all stem from the use of this brain. It is the largest of the three and provides us with foresight, allowing us to plan ahead and determine consequences for our behaviors and actions.

Explaining this concept to students helps them better understand how they learn and why sometimes it seems so hard to concentrate and learn. There are several things that can keep us from using our thinking brain. For example, if we are hungry because we haven't eaten anything all morning, our brain downshifts into the reflex part, and all we can think about is our hunger. No learning can take place because every thought revolves around food.

Another strong example is anger. If someone makes us angry, our brain downshifts to the feeling brain, so that it, rather than the thinking brain, is in control. All thoughts revolve around that anger. No learning can take place while we are emotional. This goes for all emotions, from joy to fear.

Think about a time someone made you really angry. Were you able to think straight? Often this is how people describe a haze of anger. How can students learn if their thoughts are consumed by hunger, bodily needs, anger, or other emotions? Also, how can we teach well if we are consumed by those same things?

Let's apply this theory to the classroom. What would happen if our students walked into a classroom where they were constantly picked on by other students, ridiculed or belittled by the teacher, and punished for every minor mistake they made? Can learning occur in the classroom? Definitely not! Students will enter that room and immediately downshift to their feeling brain so they are better able to protect themselves from possible harm—physical, emotional, or mental.

What about a classroom where chaos rules? Before long, the teacher is the one who becomes fearful. The entire class is spent with the teacher operating in survival mode. No quality teaching can take place when the teacher is spending every minute using his or her feeling brain.

Moment of Reflection

What are you doing, if anything, to encourage a nonthreatening environment in your classroom? What could you do differently to develop this type of classroom environment? What kind of classroom environment do you promote? How does it affect student learning?

Creating a Brain-Based Classroom

At the beginning of the year, explain to your students the concept of the triune brain. Give specific examples from your own life of times when you've downshifted. Here's an example. Emma: When I was taking the Graduate Record Exam, I arrived very early and brought a book to read while I waited. Although the test had not yet been passed out, a test monitor came by my seat, snatched the book out of my hands, and threw it on the floor near the opposite wall. "No outside materials allowed," she harshly told me. After that heated exchange I was so angry I couldn't think of anything else except for the way she treated me for a full fifteen minutes or more into the test. I couldn't concentrate at all until I had calmed down.

After sharing examples and discussing with students, this is a perfect time to explain the strategies discussed in this section and Chapter Two for making your classroom brain-friendly. Be sure to discuss at length your expectations for student use of these privileges and freedoms along with the consequences if they are abused.

To help students stay in their thinking brain, keep a huge jar of pretzels, goldfish crackers, or some other healthy type snack available for everyone. If a student comes to you hungry for whatever reason, offer a handful of crackers to help ease that hunger.

In addition, allow students some freedoms. When they need to use the restroom, allow them. Require students to let you know, sign out using your sign-out sheet (not during instruction, of course), and then sign themselves back in when they return. This allows you to keep track of where and when everyone has gone. It also shows students more respect than demanding they ask permission to leave when nature calls. We as adults would never stand for that kind of treatment and should similarly respect our students. However, if students abuse this freedom, there should be consequences. (See Chapter Two.) Remember that students need boundaries. Unlimited privileges without accountability can result in students' taking advantage of you.

Moment of Reflection

How does an understanding of the triune brain affect your teaching style and your classroom? What are some strategies you might implement in your classroom to help overcome some of these issues? How does this knowledge help you relate to students?

Conclusion

A brain-based classroom is one where collaboration between students and teacher occurs daily. It is a place where everyone feels comfortable working and sharing ideas with one another. Can it occur in the real world of teaching? You bet! We've experienced it ourselves. However, it is up to you to create this environment through your knowledge and actions. By being a lifelong learner, you foster a love for learning in your students. By reading and researching all you can about the concepts you teach, your students see your own desire to learn more. And when you take the time to get to know each of your students as individuals, they begin to trust and respect you as their guide. Finally, when you understand how the brain works, you can better meet student needs. When these needs are met, learning takes place every single day, which is your ultimate goal.

References

Dobson, James. *Bringing Up Boys.* Carol Stream, Ill.: Tyndale, 2001.

Gurian, Michael. *The Wonder of Boys.* New York: Putnam, 1996.

Hart, Leslie. *Human Brain and Human Learning.* Black Diamond, Wash.: Books for Educators, 1985.

Institute of Heart Math. *The Inside Story: Understanding the Power of Feelings: The Heart-Brain Connection.* 2006.

Kindlon, Dan, and Thompson, Michael. *Raising Cain: Protecting the Emotional Life of Boys.* New York: Random House, 2000.

Web Site Resources

Applying Brain Research to the Classroom, http://www.brains.org/

Institute of Heart Math, http://www.heartmath.org

How Can Research on the Brain Inform Education? http://www.sedl.org/scimath/compass/v03n02/brain.html

Engaging Students in Learning

Another necessary element to building a roaring fire of learning in your classroom is actively engaging students in the learning process.

Take a look at the learning pyramid to see the average retention rate for different styles of teaching. Which of these encourage passive learning through listening or watching and which encourage active learning through doing? (See Figure 7.1.)

Boredom is a sure-fire method of cultivating unruly students. Dry and dull lectures accompanied by repetitive worksheets are more than enough to have even the most well-behaved student feeling a little restless. What, then, is the effect on more active students who already have difficulty sitting still in class?

Students need to be actively manipulating information through a variety of activities in a learning-centered classroom. Being actively involved is motivating, and you'll find that students won't want to leave your class because they are having so much fun. In a learning-centered classroom, students are being challenged to think at higher levels, create products that demonstrate and apply their learning, and teach others what they have learned. Let's start by taking a look at higher-level thinking skills.

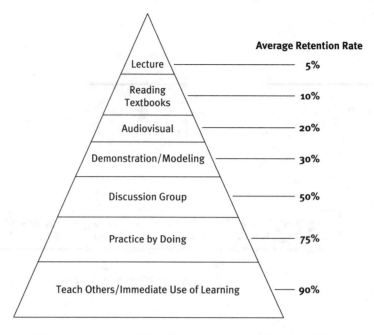

Figure 7.1   The Learning Pyramid

Source: Reprinted with permission from NTL Institute for Applied Behavioral Science, 300 N. Lee Street, Suite 300, Alexandria, VA 22314. 1-800-777-5527

Bloom's Taxonomy

In the late 1940s and early 1950s, education professor Benjamin Bloom (1913–1999) and a group of colleagues worked to develop a system to identify and organize the process of thinking and learning. Their goal was to take a process that seemed complex and simplify it, with the purpose of sharing it with teachers, who could then use this system to help them better plan lessons and teach students.

How do we think? How does that thinking turn into learning? What is the process, and how can we better understand it? These are just some of the questions that dominated Bloom's team during their six years of working together. In 1956, Bloom's group published the *Taxonomy of Educational objectives: Handbook 1,* which is now commonly known as Bloom's taxonomy. Since then, this chart of thinking skills has been used not only by classroom teachers but by trainers across the world in all areas of work and learning. Bloom's taxonomy is a standard that continues to prove its worth. A closer look at Bloom's taxonomy will help us better understand how to use it in our own classrooms.

Taxonomy: A System of Classification

A taxonomy is a system of classification. Bloom's taxonomy in particular is a structure for classifying learning principles. Bloom's group identified three domains in their taxonomy and devoted a handbook for each one. Handbook 1 looks at the cognitive domain: it focuses on thinking and learning objectives and answers the questions, What is thinking? and How does it develop? Bloom and his colleagues then developed a chart to help teachers better understand how thinking occurs and the different levels of thinking and learning.

Bloom's original and widely used chart of learning has six categories: Knowledge, Comprehension, Application, Analysis, Synthesis, and Evaluation. The first level of knowledge focuses on the recall of information. Comprehension is concerned with understanding meaning. The third level, Application, is the use of knowledge or theory into practice. Analysis requires the ability to interpret various elements to determine further information. At the Synthesis level, learners should be able to create or build something new (or new ideas) from existing information. Students then evaluate, assess, and critique the viability of the information they learned and created in the Evaluation level.

This chart is hierarchical. Before learners can determine meaning, they must have the basic facts and information. Before they can interpret various elements, an understanding of those elements must first be in place. Our job as teachers is to help students move from the level of basic knowledge and comprehension through the higher cognitive skills.

In fact, we need to do more than lead them from one level to the next. It is vital to teach them how to recognize the thinking process they are using. We must use the vocabulary of Bloom's taxonomy with our students so each can understand where he or she is in the learning process. However, the first step is for us to become familiar with the terminology ourselves as well as its use in the classroom. Only when we become confident in our understanding and use of this chart will we be able to teach it to students.

Now that we have the basic categories listed, let's take a look at a tool that will help you use this chart. The tool consists of a list of verbs underneath each category. With a list of verbs at your fingertips, you now have a way to plan learning objectives, develop questions, and assess student progress within a particular unit. Following are three sets of keywords or lists of verbs under each category: one for primary, intermediate, and upper-level students.

Bloom's Taxonomy of Cognitive Skills: Primary Students

Knowledge	Comprehension	Application	Analysis	Synthesis	Evaluation
List	Explain	Show	Compare	Build	Agree
Choose	Describe	Draw	Contrast	Design	Disagree
Circle	Retell	Practice	Examine	Model	Support
Find	Give example	Act out	Sort	Draw	Give opinion
Name	Calculate	Use	Ask	Create	Decide
Count	Write	Do	Group	Plan	Recommend
Tell		Write	Put in order	Put together	Rank

Remember when working with primary students that most of your work will be at the first three levels as your students learn new skills. They will move into the higher three levels throughout the year. However, you may have students entering your classroom who have already mastered certain skills and are ready to move forward in their learning. Be prepared with activities that will allow students to think about and use these skills in the higher three levels.

Example: A kindergarten student arrives in your class and is already reading. Further observation shows that this child can read both aloud and silently and comprehends the story. Rather than having this child practice identifying the letter "D/d" in a story with the rest of the class, you might have him or her put together words from the story (already written on large strips) to create original sentences.

Bloom's Taxonomy of Cognitive Skills: Intermediate

Knowledge	Comprehension	Application	Analysis	Synthesis	Evaluation
List	Explain	Show	Compare	Build	Defend
Label	Describe	Illustrate	Contrast	Design	Critique
Define	Retell	Practice	Examine	Develop	Support
Identify	Give example	Present	Infer	Rearrange	Justify
Name	Calculate	Develop	Classify	Create	Debate
State	Summarize	Solve	Sequence	Imagine	Recommend
Select	Estimate	Demonstrate	Categorize	Hypothesize	Rank

Bloom's Taxonomy of Cognitive Skills: Upper Grades

Knowledge	Comprehension	Application	Analysis	Synthesis	Evaluation
List	Explain	Demonstrate	Compare	Construct	Defend
Locate	Describe	Illustrate	Contrast	Design, create	Critique
Define	Paraphrase	Apply	Distinguish	Develop	Support
Identify	Give example	Present	Infer	Rearrange	Justify
Recite	Calculate	Develop	Deduct	Incorporate	Debate
Recognize	Summarize	Solve	Classify	Suppose	Recommend
Quote	Estimate	Manipulate	Categorize	Hypothesize	Prioritize
Memorize	Interpret		Dissect	Combine	Verify

Classrooms that Spark!

Some examples follow of using Bloom's keywords in the classroom:

Content	Knowledge	Comprehension	Application	Analysis	Synthesis	Evaluation
Letter "D"	Circle the letter "D"; underline words that start with the letter "D."	How does the letter "D" sound?	Write the letter "D." Write a word that starts with the letter "D."	Sort objects that start with the letter "D" from a group of objects.	Fill in the blanks of the sentence or story with words that start with the letter "D."	After listening to a sentence, decide whether it was easy to understand with the words used. What other "D" word [from a word bank] might have made more sense in this sentence?
States of matter	List the properties of a gas.	Explain how a gas is different from a solid.	Demonstrate how a liquid becomes a solid or gas.	Analyze different substances, and determine the state of matter for each.	Suppose we breathed liquid rather than a gas (oxygen mixture). How would our lives be different?	Which is better to breathe: solid, liquid, or gas? Support your opinion.
Landforms	Locate Hawaii in the atlas.	Explain how an island is born.	Demonstrate how a volcano can create an island in the ocean.	Compare and contrast an earthquake and volcano.	Design your own island using three different land features.	Using what you know about landforms and tectonic plates, criticize or support the notion that California will one day "fall into the ocean."

Why Use Bloom's?

Bloom's is a planning tool. Think of it as a visual chart showing the learning process from the simple to the complex. Bloom's taxonomy shows the order in which human beings, both children and adults, acquire and master new knowledge and skills. The verbs identified with each level will help you develop questions, activities, and assessments to use during your lessons. You can also use these keywords to help identify student levels of knowledge and abilities. This information can then help you plan lessons and enrichment activities designed so that your students move from one learning level to the next.

Recommendations for Using Bloom's

We recommend keeping handy reminders of Bloom's both at your fingertips and on the wall:

- Create a small strip of paper that lists each category across the top and the relevant verbs underneath. Set your page orientation to "landscape" so you can fit all six categories across the width of the page. You might be able to fit several of these strips on a single page. The list we provided previously is by no means fully complete. You might be able to think of other verbs that would fit in each category. Also, be sure to use verbs that are appropriate for the age group you teach.

- Separate the strips and laminate them.

- Keep one at your desk, one at your podium or overhead station, and one anywhere else in the classroom you feel you might need it. These strips will serve as a quick reference sheet for you. Because they are small and can easily be taped up or kept handy, you will be more likely to use them.

- After reading a story or textbook section, take out the Bloom's strip and use it to ask questions ranging from the knowledge level to the evaluation level.

- Create a poster to put up in your room (if possible). This poster will serve as a reminder and will begin to reinforce the vocabulary for both you and your students. Although you may not yet be ready to teach this chart to your students, the written terms and your use of them in class will serve as an introduction and will help students become familiar with the vocabulary.

Most of us get so caught up in our lesson and flow of the class (or staying on top of discipline issues) that we forget new concepts that have not yet become habit. However, when you look up and see the poster or other reminders, perhaps it will jog your memory to use some of the verbs found in the chart.

In addition, most of us have a tendency to ask only knowledge and comprehension questions. The constant reminder may nudge you to ask a few questions using terms from the three higher categories as well. Finally, it is nice to have something in your hand that is not bulky or hard to manipulate. This way you can easily look down and create an off-the-cuff question, reading response, or journaling prompt.

Learner Differentiation

Classrooms have anywhere from fifteen to forty unique individuals. Each student has a different set of abilities, a different level of intelligence, and different background experiences that make up his or her knowledge and skill base. To meet the needs of each student when everyone might need something different is where learner differentiation comes into play. *Differentiation* means giving each student what he or she needs to move forward in the learning process from the simple to the complex.

This is yet another way Bloom's taxonomy helps. By understanding that each person must move from the simple to the complex in thinking and learning, we can see that each of our students is on his or her own continuum. While teaching a particular topic, you will have students ranging from those who have never heard of or studied the topic to those who have a passion about it and may know more than you do. Your job is to plan lessons and a variety of activities that will help students master each level and move forward. Keep in mind that learning is spiral, and throughout their academic career, each student will revisit certain topics again and again in more depth. If you are teaching younger students, you cannot expect all of them to fully master each level for a particular topic. You can expect, however, that they will master the part you are teaching them.

Differentiation most dramatically comes into play with special education, English as a Second Language (ESL), and gifted learners: those who are most often in need of lessons that are modified or adapted for them. Special education students have an I.E.P. (Individualized Education Plan) that tells the teacher what modifications must be made for that student. (We discuss this in more detail in Chapter Ten.) ESL and English Language Learner (ELL) students who have recently entered the country generally received the bulk of their learning from a ESL/ELL teacher, but those who progress enough to enter the regular classroom also have special needs. (We discuss these in more detail in Chapter Ten.) Finally, we have gifted learners who generally are far more advanced than the rest of the class and can be quite a challenge for a regular classroom teacher.

Because most gifted students are functioning on a highly advanced level, they often perceive assignments as mundane and a waste of time, especially if the assignments are more practice of skills. Why, they wonder, should they complete thirty two-digit multiplication problems when they've been able to solve them for some time? These students have already mastered the skill and are ready to move on. By holding these students back to perform the same tasks as everyone else, you are setting yourself up for major attitude and behavior problems.

These students often refuse to complete the work, even though it could be done in half the time as the rest of the class, as a way of protesting. You'll see signs of boredom, which then often leads to off-task behavior, distractions for the whole class, and other misbehaviors. These students need more than simple knowledge, comprehension, and application questions and activities.

They are ready to move on to more complex thinking and the next skill. This is where Bloom's comes to the rescue. By using the keywords, you can create more challenging questions and activities for these students to complete.

Following are some strategies for learner differentiation:

- *Assess student level of knowledge and/or mastery prior to the start of a unit.* This can be done as a short pretest, a K-W-L chart (see Chapter Four), or answering a journal prompt. If you use the pretest method, keep it short. This is not a full-blown test that will be recorded in your grade book, but is rather an information-gathering tool. You want to see what each student does and does not know prior to planning the unit. Give this preassessment several weeks before you start the unit to help you plan. Doing a pretest the day you start the unit will not give you much help in planning your lessons and activities. If you suddenly find that everyone in your class is already functioning above the level you had planned to teach, you'll bore everyone and have a classroom full of misbehavior, or you'll have to come up with lessons off the cuff, which are not effective.

- *Plan activities that fall in each category of Bloom's.* Be prepared with a variety of questions and activities for each day's lesson that fall into each category. You'll have activities ready for each student no matter what level he or she is currently functioning at. This will allow you to challenge students to think at higher levels rather than always in the lower three levels. Although you may not use every activity you have planned, you will be prepared in case you have a student who quickly completes and shows mastery of a lower-level activity. When that student hands in the assignment, pull out the next one for him or her to complete.

- *Use learning and thinking centers.* Depending on what grade level you teach, you'll want to have either learning centers or thinking centers. (We discuss learning centers and thinking centers in more detail later in this chapter.) Create activities for these centers using Bloom's keywords. Label each activity as to the category in which it falls. Students should then complete a certain number of activities at each level. Some students will be assigned to work on three or four categories while others may be required to complete one or two activities in every category. Each student should complete the activities that will help him or her gain mastery, as well as challenge this student's thinking.

- *Require a different level of completion of basic skills.* For students who have already mastered a skill level and are ready to move forward, require them to do only a portion of the practice assignment. However, require that the portion be completed with 100 percent accuracy. Then provide those students with independent projects at higher levels to complete.

> Working with gifted students can be quite a challenge. It is so difficult working with a student who often knows more about different subjects than you do, and it can be easy to feel resentment toward that child. Rather than lowering myself to a childish level, I decided to do what I could to modify lessons and make them more motivating to my higher-level students. For example, I had five students in my fifth-grade math class performing on a seventh- or eighth-grade level. Rather than forcing them to do exactly the same as the rest of the class, I required these students to complete 20 percent of the math assignment given with 100 percent accuracy. Then I had them working on seventh- and eight-grade-level math for the rest of the class period. Because these students would be required to take the state achievement test, I needed to make sure they could complete the basic curriculum, but then they were able to work on their own independent studies throughout the year.

Moment of Reflection

Why is it important to keep students actively engaged in the classroom rather than passively listening? What are some ways you can keep them actively engaged? How might you implement discovery or experiential learning in your classroom?

Team and Group Activities

Another aspect of the brain-based classroom is cooperative learning. Working together as a team is an important skill used throughout life. Moreover, when students work together as a group, they learn from one another.

Although you may not see some of the benefits immediately, your students are learning important social skills and different ways to think and respond to situations by observing the others in their group. Properly managed group activities not only motivate students but also enhance student learning.

Expectations

Take some time to brainstorm your expectations for collaborative groups in your classroom. What would you like to see when students are working in groups? What behaviors are acceptable and not? What kinds of outcomes do you expect from group work? Write these expectations down to clarify them in your own mind, which will help you communicate them clearly to your students. You might even work up a procedures or expectations chart or poster for students to use as a reference while working in groups.

Example: I expect to see students taking turns to talk in a group. I expect to see each student participating. I expect to see each student doing his or her job within the group. I expect to see a completed project or assignment at the end. I expect for students to learn how to work through their differences. I expect for students to learn how to work with students who are not necessarily their buddies. Students talking quietly and working quietly is acceptable. Loud discussion or yelling is not acceptable. Students walking around the classroom with a purpose (to get supplies, resources, or something else) is acceptable. Students walking around the classroom to chat with friends is not acceptable.

Team Roles

It is important to discuss team roles with your students so that they know what is expected of them. In the beginning, model what you expect each role to look and sound like. Just telling students, "Okay, you are the leader," does not teach them how to be a leader. Instead model what the leader of a group might say and do. Even if your students have worked in a group situation before, they need a refresher course.

Example: Leader: "We are supposed to read this chapter and respond using the questions on this sheet. Why don't we break up the chapter and each read a section aloud. Who would like the first two pages?" When the group is getting off task, the leader might say, "I think maybe we are getting off topic. Who is supposed to read next?"

Primary teachers can give the students some simple guidelines for each role. You might even script out what they should say to help train them in this role. Your goal at this point is to begin training students for each role within the group.

Idea Share

Looking to get students actively engaged in a lesson? Try putting them together in a group to become "experts" of a section in the chapter or to create a product using the skill or concept you just taught.

A good book to read besides Roger and David Johnson's (1996) *Cooperative Learning* is Rabow, Charness, Kipperman, and Radcliffe-Vasile's (2000) *William Fawcett Hill's Learning Through Discussion*. It will give you additional ideas on how to model a good team for your students. *Choice Theory* by William Glasser (1998) also discusses the concept of teaming within the classroom.

We have seen that the best results from cooperative learning come by having students review the roles and rules of working as a team before starting the activity. This should happen each time you use cooperative learning groups. Here are a few roles you might use:

Leader: This person guides the group. He or she begins the discussion, leads the team in the activity, and redirects when the group gets off task.

Recorder: This person writes down the specifics of the activity and takes notes.

Reporter: This person presents information to the class.

Materials: This person gathers necessary materials.

Timekeeper: This person watches the clock and makes sure the group meets their deadline.

Idea Share

Use Bloom's keywords to help structure group discussions or group activities. We sometimes use a concept called "cube it" shared with us at a gifted and talented training. The idea is to take a box, cover it with colorful paper, and put the keywords for each level on each side of the box. Give one cube to each group of students, and have them create their own questions or activities based on one or more of the keywords listed on each side. You could tell students to "cube it," and have them do one question or activity for each level, or you could assign a level to the student groups depending on what you wanted them to do.

Strategies for Successful Teaming

Provide structure for the activity. Have a list of questions for reflection or discussion, an envelope of tasks, or a checklist of activities ready to give each group. This helps make sure that students have a clear understanding of what they are to do in the group. A specific starting point, rather than a vague command of "discuss this," will focus students.

As they work, constantly monitor students. We use the clipboard monitoring method discussed in Chapter Two. A simple spreadsheet on a clipboard will help you keep track of student behaviors and academic progress.

Using bonding activities at the beginning of the year, or any time you change groups, helps students work better as a team. Several activities listed in Chapter Five could be used for this purpose. In addition, you might look up information on Ropes activities, which are designed to build trust between groups of people and emphasizes problem-solving skills. Your community may have a local Ropes course, but if not, several low Ropes activities can be found on the Internet.

Remind students of expectations prior to the activity, and take some time to model what you want to see and hear—not just one time but throughout the year.

Example: "We had some problems during group work today. Let's remind ourselves of what group work looks like and sounds like."

You cannot say to your students, "Okay everybody. Get into groups of four, and discuss the implications of war on a new country," and expect a good result. In fact, you probably won't even be able to get them to do a simple activity such as illustrating a concept just taught.

Keep in mind that students will not work as a perfect group in the beginning. Regular use of group activities will help students become adept in this skill. You have to show them how to work together or how to guide and participate in a discussion. It is a lot of work on your part, but it is worth the effort in the long run. Just stick with it, and keep reminding your students what is expected of them. Before you know it, you'll have students actively engaged in their learning rather than bored to tears.

Grouping: Strategies and Ideas

Below are a few different ideas for using student groups for self-directed learning, discussion, and practice of skills:

• *Think-pair-share.* With this strategy, students take a minute to think about the topic or question you have posed. They then share what they think with a partner or neighbor. After a few minutes of sharing, the pairs choose another pair and share again as a larger group. This activity gives students a chance to think both independently and gain new ideas from others.

• *Jigsaw.* This strategy calls for small groups of two to four students. Each small group becomes an "expert" about a reading selection, research, or a particular skill or concept. Every group is responsible for a different passage or concept. Then one "expert" from each group gets together in new larger groups: they all share their information with each other. This activity helps make an otherwise boring assignment exciting and different. It also allows students to see how others work, and it keeps them moving.

• *Group to individual.* When you are presenting a new skill or concept for students to manipulate, work through an example as a whole class. Next, have students do the activity as a group. Then have students do a similar activity with the skill in pairs. Finally, have students show application of the skill or concept as individuals. This strategy allows students the opportunity to practice the skill or concept several times and gather input from other students before having to show comprehension and application on their own.

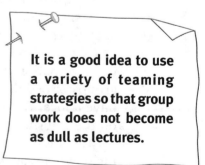

It is a good idea to use a variety of teaming strategies so that group work does not become as dull as lectures.

Group Activities to Enhance Learning

Just about any activity that engages students actively in their learning can be done as a group. Below are a few ideas to help you get started:

- *Games.* Playing board and other types of games such as Scattergories, Mastermind, and Monopoly encourages thinking skills and require students to take turns.

- *Scavenger hunt.* Students read through a chapter or part of a chapter and work together to create scavenger hunt questions for the class to answer.

- *Scripts.* Students work together to turn a historical event or a story into a play. Students can work together to explain a concept or skill through a skit or play. Require a written-out script to show the different reading parts.

Moment of Reflection

What kinds of cooperative learning do you use in your classroom? What issues keep you from using group work versus individual work during class time? How might you overcome those issues?

Puzzles

A Puzzling Classroom

See if you can figure this out:
George, Helen, and Steve are drinking coffee. Bert, Karen, and Dave are drinking soda. Is Elizabeth drinking soda or coffee?
The answer is at the end of the "Puzzles" section.

Most of us love good puzzles. Some people are more drawn to spatial puzzles, others enjoy a good logic puzzle, still others math or situation puzzles. In fact, you may even be distracted from reading right now because you are trying to figure out the puzzle shown in the box. Mazes, jigsaw puzzles, brainteasers, and short mysteries pose challenges that capture our imagination and our thoughts. Puzzles are also an excellent way to capture the attention of students and encourage them to think on higher levels. Below are some ideas for incorporating puzzles into your classroom, no matter what you teach:

- Pose a puzzle of the week every Monday. Students have all week to try to answer it. Have students place possible answers in a folder or large envelope to be opened on Friday. With younger students, you might let them try throughout the week and tell them whether they are "cold" or "hot." Students who are "cold" might go back and rethink their answer. Students who are "hot" know they have it. You could post this new weekly puzzle on your wiki or blog for the kids to try to solve and discuss online. See the Further Resources at the end of this chapter.

- Add an object to your room that has to do with the topic or skill you are teaching. Challenge students to find it.

- Have a jigsaw puzzle station in the back of your classroom that students can work on during free time or when they finish their work early. A jigsaw puzzle is fun, but it also requires students to think logically and use spatial relationships to determine where pieces fit. If you can find a puzzle that relates to something the class is studying, all the better. Use the Internet to find topic-related puzzles for students to solve. When working with preschool and kindergarten students, have a permanent puzzle station for students.

- Copy and paste logic puzzles and brainteasers on the inside of a manila folder, and laminate the folder for durability. This makes a portable "thinking center" that students can take to their seats and work on when they have finished a class assignment or test. (This concept is discussed later in this chapter.)

- Combine a read-aloud and puzzle solving together with *The Puzzling World of Winston Breen* and *The Potato Chip Puzzles* by Eric Berlin. These books offer a mystery to read, brainteasers as a part of the plot line, and extra puzzles the main character solves. The official Web site includes information about the books and author, more puzzles to solve, and a puzzle blog hosted by Winston, the main character of the books (www.winstonbreen.com).

- Have students create their own jigsaw puzzles. Students could draw the setting or character in a story, create a time line, draw a historical figure or event, or create a mind map or semantic web. If you have them do this on card stock, turn the page over and have students draw different shapes and figures that interlock on the back, then cut along the lines to separate the puzzle pieces. Craft stores also sell jigsaw puzzle paper that is already shaped and pierced. Students simply draw on the sheet and then punch out the pieces. Additionally, if you scan the pictures into the computer, students can create online jigsaw puzzles at www.jigsawplanet .com. These files can be saved and e-mailed to friends and family as well.

- Use a situation puzzle for a transition or time filler. A situation puzzle is a logic puzzle posed in story format that usually includes a misleading word, phrase, or statement. Pose the situation to students and give them twenty questions to solve it. The key to solving these types of puzzles is questioning assumptions. We typically make assumptions with regard to a scene described. Encourage your students to question these assumptions. Two sources of situation puzzles are Nathan Levy's book series, Stories with Holes (www.storieswithholes.com), and the Red Herring books put out by the Critical Thinking Company (www .criticalthinking.com). You can also use a search engine to find situation puzzles. Just keep in mind that many are minimysteries and can include a homicide or other crime. Always check the puzzles for appropriateness for your students.

- Bring a wrapped object that relates to your topic of study to class, and place it where everyone can see it. Don't mention it or talk about it. When students ask, wave them off as if it is nothing to remark about. This will drive them crazy with interest. You might then pose a challenging question, and tell students that the first to answer will get to open the wrapped object. Ask your students to discuss why they think this particular object was chosen. This is an intriguing way to introduce a new topic.

- A variation on the previous idea is to put objects in a box with an opening large enough for only a hand. Students feel the objects and try to guess what each is. What do these objects have in common? How are they different? How does each object relate to the topic currently studied?

- Have a sudoku challenge on Fridays. The older that the students are, the more complicated the puzzle should be.

- Use crosswords and word searches when practicing definitions and vocabulary words. Cryptograms also provide vocabulary and sentence practice. These are puzzles that substitute one letter for another. For example, a is really s, p is really a, and o is really t. The word might be "sat," but in the puzzle, it will show as *apo*. Once a word is deciphered, students use the key letters from that word to determine other words. Cryptograms are usually sentences and phrases. Students must use their knowledge of how sentences are formed to determine the key words that will help them decipher the puzzle. You can offer certain vocabulary words as clues to help determine the key.

Puzzles are fun and challenging, and they require thinking critically in order to solve them. We must use our knowledge of spatial relationships, numbers, number relationships, words, and experiences in the world to solve different puzzles. This makes them not only enjoyable but also effective learning tools. The next time you have a humdrum worksheet or activity, take some time to think about how you can turn it into a puzzle or mystery for students to solve. Look for different ways to incorporate puzzles into your lessons for students to solve as part of your class and outside class.

Still wondering about the puzzle at the start of the section? Thought we'd leave you hanging, did you? Here's the answer: *Elizabeth is drinking coffee. She has two e's in her name, just like everyone else in the puzzle drinking coffee (as well as coffee itself).*

Problem Solving

Problem solving is an important life skill for all students to learn. It cannot be memorized from a book; in fact, we each have our own unique process of solving problems.

Theorists have generally defined problem solving through six steps that everyone should use to reach results. The following, offered by Michael Hacker and Robert Barden (1992) in their book, *Living with Technology*, is an organized process that people practice in order to conserve time, materials, and money when problem solving. The point to get across to students is that if they use these steps, they will waste less time, fewer materials, and less money:

1. Define the problem clearly.
2. Set the goals (desired results).
3. Develop alternate solutions.
4. Select the best solution.
5. Implement the solution.
6. Evaluate the actual results and make necessary changes.

It is important to explain to your students that through experience, they will each develop their own technique for problem solving. Eventually they will become aware of the mental steps they use when they work on a project. When they become aware of this process, they will be able to refine that skill in order to be more efficient.

Moment of Reflection

How frequently do you use puzzles in your classroom? Why do you think adding a puzzling element to your class is both motivational and engaging for students? How do puzzles encourage students to think at higher levels? How might you incorporate more puzzles into your lessons?

Discovery and Experiential Learning

Another aspect of the brain-based classroom is discovery, or learning through experiences. Students learn best when they experience something and add that experience to their knowledge base, or schema. Science and social studies provide excellent opportunities for this type of learning. For example, most major cities and some rural areas have places of historical interest or reenact ways of life from various times in history. This type of experience brings history to life for students.

Allow your students to find and experience the knowledge for themselves. If that seems the easy way out to you, you are wrong. From an outsider's point of view, it may seem as though the teacher is doing nothing. However, students need guidance and encouragement to find the right answers.

Some students need an extra push to do more than just what is expected of them. Your job, contrary to popular belief, is not always the purveyor of knowledge. It is also to guide your students and teach them how to gain that knowledge for themselves. We look here at ideas to promote this kind of learning.

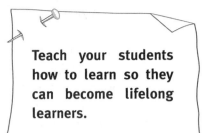

Teach your students how to learn so they can become lifelong learners.

Expert Advice

This is a slight twist on the jigsaw teaming activity. Break your students into groups of four or five, and assign each group a section of the unit or chapter from the textbook. Instruct them that they have a specified amount of time to become an expert on their section or concept. They need to read the section, discuss it, and be prepared to teach it to the rest of the class.

Encourage them to ask questions of each other and you. Also, their presentation should be creative. Then hold every student accountable for the information presented through a test or other assessment. You will be surprised at how motivated students are to read when they are the ones who have to teach everyone else.

Independent Study

Have each student choose one concept, person, or idea related to your unit to research. Create a checklist for them to follow in order to write a research paper, create something visual, and present the information to the class. Hold students accountable through an assessment over the information presented.

Discovery

Pose a question to your class, and discuss it. Help them to discover the information through questions and discussion. For example, you might say to your students, "I wonder why George Washington was elected the first president." Then guide them through a discussion to help them discover the answer. This will encourage questioning skills that will help in student research.

Use objects to lead to "I wonder" questions. Pass around an object and say, "I wonder what this is used for." Encourage students to come up with their own "I wonder" questions about the object.

> On a field trip to an old farmhouse in Texas, Heritage Farmstead, we had each child hold a tool or object that would have been commonly used on a farm in the 1800s. They made guesses about what that item may have been used for and wondered what it was. When we revealed to them the actual use, it was like uncovering a mystery. This really gave them a feel for life long ago and the modern conveniences we now take for granted. "

When students ask a question about a particular topic or ask a "why" question, help them use the Internet to discover the answer for themselves. Then they can share their information with the rest of the class.

Another discovery method is to take students on an exploration walk and pose "I wonder" questions about the world around them. These questions do not need to stay within the confines of nature and the environment. Is there construction going on nearby? As you pass by, ask, "I wonder why they are doing this work." This may spark some interest in students to research further in order to answer your question. With construction questions, students could learn more about math and science in their quest for knowledge.

Example: You might pose a question regarding the use of triangles and other shapes in building bridges and other structures.

Experiments

Don't just discuss a question or concept, try an experiment instead. Are you discussing Egypt and the Nile? Try an experiment showing how the Egyptians were able to use the floods to their advantage in farming. Discussing space exploration? Experiment with balloons to show how a rocket works. Discussing plant life? Have students design and plant a garden.

The AIMS Education Foundation has some wonderful experiments that are easy and can be connected to all subject areas. Additionally, the Delta Education Science division puts out a series of science big books, the K–6 Delta Science Readers, complete with teacher's guide, which includes classroom experiments. Scholastic and Teacher Created Materials also have some books available of experiments that can be done in any classroom. Get your students doing, not just reading!

Idea Share

The Internet is an excellent source for experiments you can do with your students. When doing a search, be sure to type in "student experiments" and the keywords of your topic. You might also try Yahooligans when searching (www.yahooligans.com)/.

Children's Stories

Have students read a chapter from the textbook and rewrite it as a children's story. It must be from one person's point of view (for example, Caesar's story about the fall of ancient Rome) and should include all of the important information from the chapter. Have students share their stories. You could even have them share their stories with younger grade levels.

Children's stories are also a way to introduce a unit and make connections between literature and the subject area. Everyone loves to be read to, no matter what age they are. And middle and high school students often enjoy "reliving their past" through fun activities. Though the activities may seem childish, we can capture student attention and revive otherwise dull lessons.

Getting ready to learn about the human body? Why not read the book *Dem Bones?* You could incorporate music into the learning. Primary students especially love the combination of stories and songs. Older students could work together to turn the book into a rap rather than trying to sing the actual song.

Getting ready to learn about onomatopoeia for a poetry unit? Why not read the book, *Mr. Brown Can Moo?* Although a simple Dr. Seuss book, *Mr. Brown Can Moo* is full of onomatopoeia and provides excellent examples. Your students will get a kick out of listening to a book from their childhood, and you've just used something different to introduce what could be a boring lesson.

Getting ready to study point of view? Start with *The True Story of the Three Little Pigs,* which is told by Mr. Wolf. There are many such stories that take well-known fairy tales and folk stories and rewrite them using a different point of view. The animated film *Hoodwinked* shows the story of Little Red Riding Hood from four different points of view. Watching this movie would be another way to introduce the concept of point of view. Students could then take their own favorite fairy tale and rewrite it from another character's point of view.

Getting ready to study Egypt? Start out with *The Egyptian Princess,* a Cinderella story that is told in Egypt. Have students point out the differences between the familiar story of Cinderella and this one. This discussion could lead into listing different aspects about Egyptian life and culture and be a good start to a new unit.

Getting ready to solve word problems? Introduce your unit with the book *Math Curse.* The main character spends an entire day encountering different math problems that he must solve. This is a stimulating way to introduce something that can be a struggle for students.

Uncounted children's books reach across subject areas. If you are not sure what you are looking for, do a search through an online bookstore with the concept as your keyword. Certain online bookstores allow you to browse specific sections or genres to help refine your search. For example, you can go to the children's book section and browse titles in just that section. Otherwise you may end up with a larger list of suggestions that are not useful for meeting your objective.

Research Projects

In this information age, research skills are some of the most important and useful tools we can impart to students. These skills should be taught and practiced from first grade all the way up through high school. In our opinion, students should be required to complete at least three research projects each year. In the upper grades, the requirements should become more stringent to prepare students for work in college or vocational school, where research is a common learning tool.

Research Paper Tips

Children are naturally curious about the world around them, and there is no better way to learn than to discover the answers to questions through research. You may say to yourself, "My kids aren't ready for research." In truth, perhaps you are the one who is not ready. For those of us who remember twenty-page writing assignments, the word *research* can have a negative connotation. But research can be as simple as looking up the answer to a question. Below are some tips to help you along.

Start Out Simple and Easy

In primary grades, have students use books, their parents, other teachers, and the computer to find the answer to a question. Have older students use primary and secondary sources to find the answer to a question relating to your topic of study. Require a paragraph and a creative product, such as a pop-up book or diorama. With secondary students, set a limit of three- to five double-spaced typed pages for each paper. Every ninth grader should be able to write a three-page paper and every twelfth grade should be able to write a five-page paper.

Be sure to teach note-taking skills before requiring any formal research. The note-taking strategy we outline later in this chapter is an excellent tool to help keep students from plagiarizing when taking notes from other sources.

Take It Step by Step

When you do your first research project, take the students through the process step by step. Model each step for them as a class and then allow them to complete that step for their own project.

One way to help students get comfortable with research projects is to do the first one as a group project, the second one as a partner project, and the next ones individually.

Allow Student Choice

Choose a timely and global topic, and then allow students to choose the specific area within that larger topic. For example, if animals is the topic, students choose the animal they want to learn more about.

Determine Ahead of Time What You Expect

What elements do you expect in the project? Do you want a written part, a visual part, and an oral presentation? Within each of these, what do you expect? Is this to be a group or individual project? Can the written part be creative, like a story or skit, or do you expect a formal essay of some sort?

Create a Checklist for Students to Follow

Make sure you include every aspect that will be assessed. Include directions for the project at the top of the page. You can make the checklist as specific and detailed as you feel your students need.

A checklist can show students the steps to follow when completing their project as well as tasks and products to be done for each section. Some students need a lot more structure than others. You might even consider including due dates for completion of each section.

Teach Students How to Write the Formal Paper

When it is time for students to write their essay, go through the process with them step by step, especially the first couple of times.

> Projects are a great tool to use in the classroom. Students are excited to learn and enjoy the collaboration.

> "I teach students how to write an introduction in class. Then, independently during class or for homework, they are required to write an introduction for their paper. The next day I read and help students revise their introductions. We follow the same process for the body and conclusion of the paper. It really helps students to go through the process one step at a time, especially if this is their first formal paper."

Monitor Students Constantly

This is not the time to sit behind your desk. Monitoring is not difficult as long as you are prepared. Use the Clipboard Monitoring form in Chapter Two to help keep track of who is on task and who is having trouble with the process.

Teaching Note-Taking Skills

In order to be successful at research projects, students need to be taught how to take notes from a source. Even the youngest ones can be taught through modeling. Although you may not ask a kindergartner or first grader to copy down notes, modeling the skill during a nonfiction reading begins building a schema for note taking. For example, when reading a science big book with younger students, you may use a chart pad to record the main idea and supporting details found on each page (as shown following).

The more this vital skill is taught in elementary and middle school, the better students will be at note taking as they progress through the grades.

Use Big Books to Introduce Note-Taking Skills

Using primary big books to introduce note taking is easier on the teacher and the student because small chunks of information are presented on each page.

The student is not overwhelmed by a large amount of text and the teacher has the advantage of simple paragraphs with a clear main idea and supporting details. Additionally, the large print of big books makes it easier for students to see when reading as a class. Big books are available on a variety of topics. These are very informative, can be easily used to connect to the current topic being taught, and have fantastic pictures.

Idea Share

You can model note-taking skills for the whole class on an overhead transparency, a large sheet of butcher paper, or on a chart pad. This activity will build the background knowledge and skills for independent note taking.

Introducing Nonfiction Books or Magazines

Choose a book or article that is easy to read (never use an encyclopedia to start because students become overwhelmed by the large amount of text) and either make transparencies or enough copies so that each student can easily read the information. Follow the steps below several times with your students as a class, then have them work in small groups, then as pairs, and finally individually. This process helps give students confidence to take good notes:

1. Write the title or general topic of the book as your main heading or topic.

2. Read each page, including the picture captions, carefully.

3. Write what the page was mostly about, which will identify the main idea.

4. Write the main idea as your subhead on a transparency or butcher paper.

5. Supply details from the page that support the main idea. Write these as one- or two-word details under the subheading.

6. Look at the pictures and each caption. Is this material necessary or extraneous? If it is relevant, include the supporting detail into the appropriate subheading.

For example, for information about the solar system, you might end up with this information:

The Solar System

The Sun
- A medium-sized star
- Eight planets orbit: Mercury, Venus, Earth, Mars, Jupiter, Saturn, Uranus, Neptune
- Provides light and heat

Inner Planets
- Mercury, Venus, Earth, Mars
- Solid—mostly rock
- Closest to the sun
- Short orbits

Have students apply this knowledge of note-taking skills when researching and taking notes from any source, including the Internet. Instruct them to take notes exactly as they have practiced in class. When they begin taking notes in this manner, using only one or two keywords for each detail, you'll find that they are not able to plagiarize from the source. You may even want to practice taking notes from an encyclopedia or other nonfiction book to help them make the transition from simple paragraphs to more complex source material. Make sure they don't forget to write down the title of each source at the top of their notes.

Here is a set of instructions you can give to older students to help them during the research and note-taking process. A reproducible copy of these instructions are also provided at the end of this chapter.

Instructions for Taking Notes

1. Read each paragraph, and determine whether it contains information you need. If it does, go to the next step. If not, read the next paragraph.

2. What was that paragraph mostly about? Write the main idea on your paper.

3. What are the details in this paragraph? Write the supporting details in no more than three words as bullets under the main idea.

4. Read the next paragraph, and follow the same instructions. Remember that you do not need to copy everything down. Taking notes is the art of pulling out only the information you need.

Using the Internet

It is important to spend some time talking with your students about ways to discern valid sources of information on the Internet. The wonderful thing about the Internet is that it encourages anyone to post their thoughts and ideas. The downside is that not everything posted is valid or true. Students need to find corroborating sources that show similar information to help them determine whether the facts they gain from the Internet are correct. Comparing their research from the Internet to research done from print resources or even primary resources is the best way to validate the information. Also, encourage students to access reputable Web sites, including those of the Smithsonian, Encyclopedia Britannica, American Museum of Natural History, U.S. government sites, or any other well-known agency. (See the list of Web sites at the end of the chapter.)

When doing research with younger students and encouraging them to obtain online sources as well as print, have a list of preapproved Web sites ready for them to access. Post these, along with your checklist and other pertinent information, on a wiki site specifically for the research project. Students can access the site immediately without possible issues retyping the address. For an example of how this might work for you, the following sample wiki page shows an example:

Revolutionary War Time Line

For the next two weeks, you will be creating a time line of events leading up to, during, and right after the Revolutionary War. I will provide poster board, and you will be responsible for researching the information. You must include:

- Three major events leading up to the war (15 points total)
- Five American Revolution battles (25 points total); must include Battles of Lexington and Concord and Battle of Yorktown
- Four other important events that happened during the Revolution (20 points total)
- Ending result of the Revolution (10 points total)
- Four pictures (20 points total)
- Two paragraphs on two people of importance (10 points total)

For each event or item you list, write three to five sentences describing their importance. End the time line with information on how the American Revolution ended and what the result of the war was. I will give you time to research in class, but you will need to work at home as well. Your social studies book has plenty of information, and you can get books from our library. This is a 100-point grade!

Battles (Some)	Important Men	Important Women	Important Events
Battle of Bunker Hill	George Washington Minutemen	Abigail Adams	"The Star-Spangled Banner"
Battle of Long Island	Samuel Adams Crispus Attucks	Mercy Otis Warren	Paul Revere's ride
Battle of White Plains	Francis Marion William Dawes	Patience Wright	Declaration of Independence
Battle of Princeton	Benjamin Franklin	Betsy Ross	First Continental Congress
Battle of Trenton	Paul Revere	Elizabeth Zane	Second Continental Congress
Capture of Fort Ticonderoga	John Hancock	Nancy Ward	Washington crosses the Delaware
Battle of Charleston	Patrick Henry	Molly Pitcher	Winter at Valley Forge
Battle of Camden	John Jay	Deborah Samson	First American flag
Battle of Eutaw Springs	Ethan Allen	Anne Bailey	"Common Sense" is published
Battle of Saratoga	Thomas Paine	Rachel and Grace Martin	French Alliance
Battle of Monmouth	Benedict Arnold	Angelica Vrooman	Articles of Confederation
Battle of Brandywine	Nathanael Greene, Francis Scott Key		

GOOD LUCK!
Here are some Web sites to use for your project:

Causes of the Revolution

http://americanhistory.about.com/od/revolutionarywar/a/boston_massacre.htm
http://americanhistory.about.com/od/revolutionarywar/a/amer_revolution.htm
http://www.usahistory.info/timeline/revolution.html

(Continued)

Women of the Revolution

http://library.thinkquest.org/10966/bios.shtml
http://www.americanrevolution.org/women.html
http://score.rims.k12.ca.us/score_lessons/women_american_revolution/

Men of the Revolution

http://library.thinkquest.org/10966/bios.shtmlhttp://www.theamericanrevolution.
org/ipeople.asp
http://en.wikipedia.org/wiki/Francis_Marion
http://www.francisscottkey.org/

Major Battles

http://library.thinkquest.org/10966/battles.shtmlhttp://www.usahistory.info/
timeline/revolution.html
http://www.theamericanrevolution.org/battles.asp

Important Events During the Revolution

http://www.ushistory.org/declaration/account/
http://library.thinkquest.org/10966/tour.shtml
http://www.usahistory.info/timeline/revolution.html
http://www.usahistory.info/American-Revolution/Lexington.html
http://www.usahistory.info/Revolution/foreign-aid.html
http://www.kidport.com/RefLib/UsaHistory/AmericanRevolution/AmerRevolution
.htm

Conclusion of the Revolution

http://www.usahistory.info/timeline/revolution.html

Photographs and Pictures

http://library.thinkquest.org/10966/flags.shtml

Source: Thanks to Holly Jaye, McAdory Elementary School in McCalla, Alabama, for sharing her wiki page with us and allowing us to share it with others.

Utilizing the Librarian

The librarian is a treasure trove of knowledge about resources available through the school and even the district. The librarian should be the first person you contact as soon as you know the topic you plan to teach because of the many ways in which the librarian can help you. Here are just a few of them:

- The librarian knows what nonfiction and fiction resources are available in the library that are related to your topic.

- The librarian knows what magazine resources, such as *Kids Discover, National Geographic,* and others, in the library are related to your topic.
- The librarian can help teach research skills to your students.
- The librarian often knows about online resources that will be useful for your topic. He or she can also help corroborate information students find online to make sure it is valid.
- The librarian has access to a network of other school librarians within the district and can often get resources you cannot.
- The librarian can help you locate audio and video resources, as well as book resources.
- The librarian is a valuable resource of ideas and strategies for approaching different topics in instruction. As someone who has contact with other teachers in the school, he or she can direct you to another teacher who might also be able to help.
- If there is a special book or video resource you feel would be helpful to many teachers, the librarian can order it for the library.

As you can see, the librarian is a very useful member of your school staff. Don't neglect this valuable resource! When preparing to plan your lessons for a particular unit or topic, visit the librarian first and get his or her input. You may find a plethora of ideas, strategies, and resources just waiting to be shared!

Presenting Information

Students can present information they learned during a research project in a number of ways. Below are a few ideas:

- Reenacting a historical event in a skit
- Dressing up as a historical figure or character from a novel
- Giving a simple speech presenting knowledge obtained
- Teaching the class a minilesson
- Creating a podcast (an online record of student audio presentation that can be uploaded to a class Web site, blog, or wiki page) presenting information learned
- Creating a poster board presentation or a concept board presentation
- Modeling an experiment
- Creating a PowerPoint presentation
- Creating a video presentation
- Using the digital camera to integrate pictures into a visual presentation (Animoto.com and PhotoStory3 allow students to create a short photo story with pictures and music)
- Reading a formal essay written

Moment of Reflection

Why should you consider using research projects throughout the year rather than just once a year? With what topics during the year might you incorporate a research project? How might you use smaller research activities in your units?

Making Connections Among Subject Areas

Another effective teaching strategy is integrated study. This section offers some of our thoughts on why you should integrate as well as some suggestions for your classroom. Most of these ideas come from Susan Kovalik's (2003) *Integrated Thematic Instruction*. Another excellent resource for integrating is a book entitled *The Way We Were, the Way We Want to Be* by Ann Ross (1995), written for middle school teachers. Both of these will make a fine addition to your professional library.

Reasoning

With everything we are supposed to teach each day, it often seems as though we can never fit it all in. However, by integrating subject matter, concepts, and skills, not only can you cover everything you need to, but you can also help students make important connections in their learning.

Integration is the connection of several subjects under a topic or theme. Brain research shows that students learn best when ideas are connected across subject areas. As adults, we know that science cannot be separated from math, and social studies concepts are closely linked to both language and science.

> An effective teacher helps students see connections across their learning.

How then can we ask our students to learn in isolated compartments for each subject? In doing so, we push students further back rather than leading them forward in their studies. One way we can work toward making connections is through thematic units. Kovalik states that themes should be motivating to students and relate to the real world.

> Making connections in learning encourages higher level thinking and is supported by brain-based research.

Getting Started

Start with a topic of study required for your grade level. Science and social studies are the easiest to use as a starting place because they include English language arts and math objectives within their own objectives.

Brainstorm skills and objectives usually taught for that topic, and brainstorm connections with other subject areas. Then find the common links in skills and concepts—for example, graphing is a skill used in math, science, and social studies.

Example: Let's say you have an upcoming unit on volcanoes. List the skills and concepts to be taught for the topic. Then brainstorm social studies, math, and language arts connections with volcanoes. (See Figure 7.2.) Some of your ideas might include these:

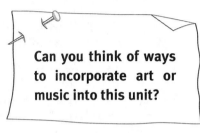

- Have students locate volcanoes along the ring of fire using latitude and longitude (social studies). This could even include a video about the ring of fire.
- Students read about or research famous historical events surrounding volcanoes such as Mount St. Helens or Mount Vesuvius (language arts and social studies).
- A study of landforms could arise since many mountains began as volcanoes. In addition, students can learn how new islands are created (which goes well with the Ring of Fire study). With the study of islands, students can learn mapping skills. Those skills can be applied by creating their own "island" and using graph paper to create a map of cities, rivers, and other features on this island (social studies).
- A volcano eruption follows a sequence as to what happens and how it creates an island over time. This works well for including the reading concept of sequencing (reading).
- Students can study the geometry of volcanoes by discussing cones and triangles and how seismic instruments work to measure pressure (math).

Use a graphic organizer when planning the unit of study, like the one shown here:

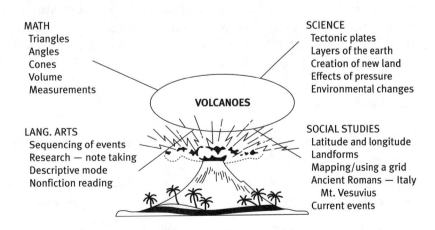

Figure 7.2   Graphic Organizer for Volcano Study

Start Small

If you jump in with both feet, you may meet with disappointment. Not only does it take a while to get used to a new idea, but it also takes some time to implement a new type of strategy in the classroom. Just like our students, we all have different ways of learning. Some of us need to go for the gusto, but others need more of a trial period before being ready to undertake a project like this. Integrating takes experience and logical thinking. It works best when two or more teachers are working together to brainstorm the connections and make them work in a lesson or unit.

Here are a few ways to start out with small steps:

- When reading a story or novel, incorporate history from the time period used in the setting.
- Provide students with a time line of interesting events that occurred during the time the author wrote the novel or during his or her life-time. One way to do this might be to create an "In the Year Of" poster that shows the prices of everyday items, popular music, famous people, and other categories for that period.
- Point out cities and countries on the map for authors, story settings, famous scientists, or mathematicians.
- Point out ways the environment—landforms, temperature or seasons, climates, animal and insect life—affects a story, historical event, or world culture.
- Use time lines to show other events happening at the time of a scientific discovery.
- Use research projects in science and social studies to study a topic in further detail.
- When teaching a concept or skill in math or science that has a practical application, show these or discuss them with students.

An example is a unit used with fifth graders on integrated science (specifically environmental science—biomes, environments, habitats) and social studies (U.S. geography and Native Americans). The theme, trekking across the United States, addressed these topics:

Topics of Study

- West Coast to East Coast—tracking the natural movement of early peoples across North America
- Eastern Pacific tribes: coastal environment, habitats weather
- Southwestern tribes: desert environment, habitats, weather
- Plains tribes: grasslands environment habitats, weather
- Eastern tribes: forested environment, habitats, weather

Skills

- Graphing—math
- Collecting current data on precipitation and temperature from each geographical area and graph—science and math
- Comparing and contrasting regions—language arts (essay)
- Discussing the effects of environment on Native American culture for each region—science and social studies
- Comparing and contrasting Native American cultures—social studies and language arts
- Native American mythology (comparing and contrasting stories)—language arts
- Environment of each region—science and social studies
- Habitats found in each region—science and social studies
- Food chain—science
- Energy cycle—science
- Settlement of early peoples—social studies
- Research on various Native American tribes—social studies and language arts
- Group presentations of research—social studies and language arts

> An effective teacher keeps a balance between basic skills instruction and integrated thematic units.

Notice that basic math and language arts skills are not included in this integrated unit. We believe that there must be a fine balance between basic skills and integration. We used our daily oral language, daily geography, and daily math to practice these basic skills. We also tied this practice into our integrated lessons. In addition, we added in a skills time into our day for math, reading, and writing.

Here is an example of a lesson plan that uses integration throughout the day:

Sample Integration Lesson Plan

Objectives:	To be able to average a group of numbers
	To be able to create a poetry book using original poems
	To be able to complete a book study for a novel
	To be able to explain how a habitat, ecosystem, and environment are different and how they are related
Materials:	Science book, notes on averaging, large white paper, colored pencils
Journal:	Imagine that you live in a forest. Describe everything you see: animals, plants, weather.

(Continued)

Homework:	Reading: Read for twenty minutes. Write a response from questions in your log.
	Language arts: Write one sentence for each vocabulary word.
	Math: Practice averaging and mean.
Words of the day:	*ecosystem*—a community and its nonliving environment
	community—all the populations in one ecosystem
	population—all the organisms of one species that live in a certain place
Daily language:	Locate the commas used in the following sentences. Explain the two different comma rules used:
	"Ecosystems can change constantly. They comes in all sizes, and they can exist in a puddle, log, ocean, or forest."
	Answer: Sentence 1: Commas are used to separate items in a list. Sentence 2: A comma is needed before the "and" in this sentence because it is a compound sentence.
Daily geography:	(a) What sea surrounds Jamaica?
	(b) What city is 23 degrees S latitude, 43 degrees W longitude?
	Answer: (a) Caribbean (b) Rio De Janeiro
Daily math:	Estimate the following to the nearest hundreds place:
	(a) $790 + 3,756 + 2,345$, (b) $490 + 5,645 + 8,205$, (c) $608 + 6,457 + 10,790$
	Answer: (a) 6,900, (b) 14,300, (c) 17,900

Procedures:

8:00–9:30	Announcements, copy homework into calendar, copy words of the day, write in journal
8:30–8:45	Daily oral language: Students complete and go over in class
8:45–9:00	Daily geography: Students complete and go over in class
9:00–9:45	Daily math: Students complete and go over in class
	Introduce averaging with word problem: "Mrs. Hershman went on a shopping spree last week. Monday she spent $20.00, Tuesday she spent $30.00, Wednesday she spent $40.00, and Saturday she spent $50.00. What is the average amount of money she spent last week?"
	Give notes in math spiral on average and mean.
	Do a few practice problems in the spiral.
	Practice with page 95 in the science book. Use the diagram of the average number of ants in a particular ecosystem to calculate the total ant population.
9:45–9:50	Bathroom break/go to specials.

9:55–10:45	Specials: Art
10:50–11:20	Reading workshop. Students complete predictions for main character for book study.
11:20–12:10	Writing workshop: Students continue working on poetry book.
12:10–1:00	Lunch/recess
1:00–2:30	Brainstorm with the students things they might find in a forest environment: pond, fish, bushes, trees, birds, small animals.
	Discuss and take notes using ecosystem diversity sheets on ecosystem and difference between habitat, ecosystem, and environment.
	Students create a visual as a group to show their understanding of the difference between a habitat, ecosystem, and environment, and how these three are related.
	Group presentations
2:30–2:55	Read aloud: "Flight of the Sparrow" (a poem).
	Review homework.
	Clean up.

Here are some samples from integrated units that we did for fifth and sixth grades to give you some idea of how to organize units of study. The first unit is more detailed to show you how we categorized the concepts taught.

Sample Integrated Units

Fifth Grade—Year-Long Theme: Exploring Our World

First 6 weeks: The Outer Limits	Topics—galaxy, solar system, moon, space exploration
	Math
	number line
	place value
	basic operations
	Science
	galaxies
	constellations
	solar system
	gravity
	moon
	spacecraft/ exploration
	probes

(Continued)

	Language arts
	news articles
	science fiction
	narrative (mode)
	Social studies
	Time line
	Space exploration (history of)
	Modern American history
	Reading
	Genres
	Attributes of a story: setting, characters, plot
	Main idea
Second 6 weeks: Our Island Earth	Topics—formation of earth, volcanoes, islands, rain forests
Third 6 weeks: A New World	Topics—Native American tribes, ecosystems
Fourth 6 weeks: Across the Ocean	Topics—ocean life, exploration of Americas
Fifth 6 weeks: Westward Bound	Topics—colonization, growth of America, government, westward expansion
Sixth 6 weeks: Exploring My Own World	Topics—family, self, 50 states

6th Grade—Year-Long Theme: On My Own

First 6 weeks: Knowing Myself	*Unit One: This Is the Real Me (2 weeks)*
	Knowing myself mentally: student information, learning styles inventory
	Knowing myself emotionally: individual values and morals, emotions and the way they affect different people
	"Last Summer with Maizon"
	Knowing myself physically: physical appearance, describing people, adjectives, physical skills
	"Cecilia Dowling"
	Prewriting skills: life map, freewriting, looping, brainstorming, mind mapping, jot list, hot topic list
	Reading skills:
	poetry: "Cecilia Dowling"
	details: "Last Summer with Maizon"
	Individual novels
	About the author

	Unit Two: My Heritage (2 weeks)
	The Great Ancestor Hunt—trade book (begin reading before unit)
	The World in the Classroom: Map skills, identifying cultures and countries
	Family: family tree, prefixes, suffixes and root words
	"Child of the Owl"
	Traditions: family customs, personal narrative, parts of a book
	Opera, Karate and Bandits
	"Fiddler on the Roof"
	Unit Three: My Goals (2 weeks)
	Personal: Resolutions, friendly letter, main idea, setting goals
	Brother to the Wind
	Professional: setting goals, actions have consequences
	Guest speaker on careers
Second 6 weeks: Finding My Place	Topics: continents, map skills, early humans, family, communication skills, early settlements, time lines, ancient civilizations, climates
Third 6 weeks: Applying Myself	Topics: Résumé, biographies, charts/graphs, population, government, economics, the "how-to" essay, interviewing
Fourth 6 weeks: Improving My World	Topics: Inventions, persuasion, cause and effect, nonfiction, exploration of world, ocean, Renaissance
Fifth 6 weeks: Dealing with Others	Topics: Relationships, cultural borrowing, trade routes, economics, conflict and resolution, war, the Holocaust, governments, advantages and disadvantages, heroes
Sixth 6 weeks: I'm All on My Own	Topics: Survival skills, critical thinking skills, freedoms and responsibilities, spread of democracy, world geography, environments

Interdisciplinary Study

Integration is not an impossibility in a departmentalized setting. If you are truly interested in integrating subject matter, there are several ways to go about it:

- You and your team members need to agree that integration is the best thing for your students.
- Share the skills and topics that will be taught throughout the year.
- Work together to determine a year-long theme and subsequent six-week themes.

- Planning together will make integration much easier for everyone.
- Each class will cover part of the lesson for the day.

For example, if you were doing a mini-unit on volcanoes, each class would build on the others:

- Science would discuss how volcanoes are formed and would experiment with volcanoes.
- Social studies might plot various known volcanoes on a map of the world and study latitude and longitude.
- Language arts might read about some historical volcanic eruptions such as Mount Vesuvius or Mount St. Helens and may write an essay on how to make a model volcano.
- The art teacher could be a part of this unit by having students make a volcano (or it could be done in another class).
- Math might be able to study cones, ratios, percentages, and probability.

Learning Centers

Another way of enhancing your instruction is through learning centers. Upper elementary and middle school teachers often do not use the learning center, saying they take up too much room, take too long to create and organize, take too much effort to monitor, and take too long to evaluate students.

In our classrooms, we found a way to use learning centers so that they were not a burden but a helpful tool.

Enrichment Centers

Students use the enrichment center when they are finished with a class assignment and have nothing else to do. We also use it as a reward. Here is how to set it up:

- Create a "thinking folder" for each student with a manila folder. This folder is used to hold any puzzles or other enrichment activities they have completed and are ready to be assessed.
- Place these folders in an easily accessible place, such as a student filing cabinet, standing file organizer, or plastic crate with hanging file folders.
- Copy logic puzzles, think-a-grams, and other word puzzles; glue them on colorful construction paper; and laminate them.
- Separate puzzles by type and place them in clearly labeled manila folders. You might want to paste one puzzle in each folder or keep similar puzzles in a single folder.

- Write the directions for the puzzle on the manila folder.
- Place vis a vis pens in a can on a table.
- Students choose a puzzle, complete it, and write the answer on their own sheet of paper.
- Have students wipe the original puzzle clean and put it away.
- Students can work these puzzles at their own seat, which means you don't have to keep a center area prepared. All you need is a spot to hold the puzzles.
- Every three weeks, check the folders, and grade the puzzles.
- Give students extra credit for correct answers and feedback for wrong answers.

Rotating Centers

Another idea for learning centers is to use rotating centers. Set up each center on a table or group of desks, and separate students into rotation groups. Each group works on a center and then at a predetermined time rotates to a new center. A disadvantage is that some students finish more quickly than others and may become behavior problems.

A variation is to create a checklist and allow students to work at their own pace. Each student visits each center when he or she has an opportunity. For management purposes, set limits as to how many students can be at each station.

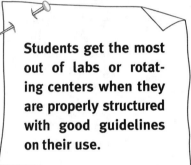

Students get the most out of labs or rotating centers when they are properly structured with good guidelines on their use.

In order for this to work, you must monitor carefully. Have your clipboard in hand, and be ready to help students, note hardworking students, and note behavior problems. Have an alternative activity ready for students who are not mature enough to handle this type of assignment.

Here is how to set up these centers:

- Type or copy directions for each center, paste them on colorful construction paper, and laminate.
- Set the directions and materials on each table or group of desks.
- Pass out checklists to students.
- Students record the answers on their own paper.
- Students place their checklist, answers, and any products they created in their manila folder to be evaluated.
- Evaluate the work done in the centers using the checklist. Give each activity a score of 1 to 4, and then average the scores to determine the overall grade. (See Chapter Four for more information about rubric scoring.)

Example: Each of these questions goes with a science experiment to perform to find the answer:

STUDENT CHECKLIST
☐ How does salt water help keep whales afloat?
☐ How big are whales?
☐ What keeps whales warm?
☐ What helps keep whales afloat?

Blogging

If blogs are a foreign language to you, please do not panic. Blogs are virtual communities where creativity, self-expression, and interactive discussion are encouraged. They are easy-to-use, journal-style entries that are published on the Internet. Through blogging, students can read each other's ideas and make comments on one another's work. They equalize the opportunity to share ideas. Your most bashful student, who lacks the ability to do well in classroom participation, may open up in a whole new way. Blogging is not difficult; moreover, students love it, and it can bring enormous success to their learning. With a little planning, you can set up a blog in about two hours.

Why should you consider choosing the use of blogs as a strategy? Blogs accommodate, encourage, and engage many learners. If you feel the need to get into the minds of your students and help them reflect on how their behaviors affect the lives of others, this is an excellent strategy. With high-stakes tests looming over daily lessons, learning to answer an open-ended response has become an essential skill. Using critical thinking skills and connecting literature to the real world are necessary competencies to score the highest point value on standardized tests. Allowing students to blog and talk online with their peers cuts to the heart of the adolescent world. You will be able to meet your curriculum objectives, prepare students for proficiency tests, and engage students in the process.

Blogs can be used in almost any discipline and in a number of different ways—for example:

- *Science:* An exchange of ideas learned after a scientific experiment.
- *Math:* A discussion of fundamental concepts to better understand the logic behind a mathematical formula; a beginning-of-the-school-year chat about how numbers are a part of many aspects of the world around us.
- *Current events:* Nonfiction can help students situate themselves in a real-life context, and blogging can promote an exchange of ideas.
- *Social studies:* Student discussion of research about politics or culture during an appropriate time of history.
- *Art:* Articulation of artistic impressions of famous works of art.

- *Creative writing/language arts:* Build-a-story; poetry interpretation; author study research; literary criticism.
- *Language arts:* Discussion of important or famous quotations: what they mean and how they relate to student lives.
- *Classroom management:* To inform students of classroom requirements; post handouts, notices, and homework assignments; or serve as a question-and-answer board between students.
- *Online mentoring:* A class of older students can assist a class of younger students to develop more confidence in their writing or critical thinking skills.
- *Cooperative learning:* Each student in a group can take a specific role and relay the research findings through a blog.
- *School-to-school:* Use blogs with another school in your own or another district as a way to communicate with each other and share ideas on common curriculum.
- *Clubs or extracurricular activities:* A great communication technique for groups that cannot meet as often as they like yet need to complete a task.
- *Discussion:* Any issue, any discipline, any grade level. You control the question, and let the students burst with their answers.

Well-managed blogging has the following results:

- Encourages reading and writing while increasing comfort with computers and the Internet and allows the infusion of technology with any discipline.
- Offers a personal space to read and write, alongside a communal one, where ideas are shared, questions are asked and answered, and social cohesion is developed.
- Is appropriate for different age groups and both genders.
- Prepares students for the future.
- Easily accessible inside and outside the classroom.
- Provides homework and class work assignments that students are excited to complete.
- Is a powerful and effective technology tool for students and teachers alike.

To get started, use these implementation steps:

1. Set your objective, and decide how the blog will work to achieve your goal.
2. Find a hosting site that fits your needs. Most important, you want to be sure to find a site that offers privacy settings so that the blog is not made public. Several sites that host education related blogs are listed at the end of this chapter.

3. If needed, prepare an explanation for parents and secure their permission.

4. Determine how you will assess the blog (if needed) and keep students accountable and, in so doing, decide on the student's posting requirement.

5. Decide your requirement for student language use (their own language or the English language).

6. Get student log-in (screen) names and passwords. This step is required only if you are going to take on the role of setting up student accounts. Most blogging sites also offer the choice of having students set up their own accounts.

7. Sign up at the hosting site. This process takes about ten minutes to complete. Once you register, the blog is created. The site will likely offer many options for you to personalize your site. You can add a picture, change the fonts, and so forth. The process of personalizing the page is optional, and probably the most time-consuming part of setting up a blog. Once you give your page a personality, the blog is set for discussion.

8. Create paperwork and logs for bookkeeping if needed for your assignment.

9. Post your assignment or discussion questions.

10. Give students a due date. The first round of blogs will bring about questions, but after the first time students participate, they know the routine and expectations.

Consider these important points:

- When creating the blog settings for students (on the site), always think about their safety first. Using a blogging site designed specifically for teachers and students provides the most safety.

- Consider that you might want to review each blog entry (scan) before it is published. This option is important during a blog discussion that includes a hot topic.

- Limit the visibility of your blog to members only. You do not want your blog to be seen by anyone you do not allow in the process.

- Opt for creating student accounts for them rather than having students create their own accounts and log-in information. It is more time-consuming (maybe an extra hour), but it give you total control. The age of the students and the topic of discussion can help you make this important decision.

- Start small with one class, one group, or just one small educational unit. Tweak the problems before you open it up to a larger forum.

- If students are using an anonymous blog, have them provide you with a new username before you begin the next unit which uses the blog.

- Do not overuse this strategy or, like anything else, students will get bored with the idea. If you use it for a second unit, change your requirements or how you use the blog (as part of a cooperative project, for example, rather than a question-and-answer discussion). For example provide a story starter, and when students log on, they need to add to the story from the point where the last person left off.*

Moment of Reflection

What is your opinion of integrating subject areas? Is this something you might implement in your classroom? Why or why not?

Field Trips

Field trips are important discovery learning tools. They provide hands-on learning for students and serve as a way for children to experience their community. Moreover, students love them. However, without planning and organization, field trips can be a nightmare for teachers. We have discovered over time that prior planning is the key to a positive field trip experience. This does not mean just planning out where, when, and how you're going on the field trip. It also includes providing structure and guidance for both chaperones and students and getting permission slips in for all students (see the "Field Trip Permission Form" at the end of the chapter).

Here are some strategies for having a successful and effective field trip:

- The more chaperones you have, the lower the student-to-adult ratio will be. Smaller groups give parents and others volunteers greater control over their charges.
- Whenever you go on an inside field trip, you want lots of structure and control to maintain a quiet and nondisruptive environment.
- Sign up parent volunteers well in advance of the trip.
- Notify other teachers in the school of the dates and times for your field trip.
- Notify the cafeteria if you will be out during lunch. This helps them better prepare for lunch that day. Also, you may have several students who need a sack lunch from school. A lunch count needs to be done at least two weeks before your trip.

---

*The entire section on blogging is reprinted with permission from Jeri Asaro, Pequannock Valley M.S. and Inspiring Teachers Publishing, Inc. Original article location: http://www .inspiringteachers.com/classroom_resources/monthly_columns/new_teachers/blogging_is_ beneficial.html.

- Put in a request for a field trip to your principal as soon as you begin planning.
- Have a clear educational objective for your field trip. Why are you going? If it is just for a free day or to give students a break, the trip probably won't be approved.
- When signing up parent volunteers, write down their names and phone numbers on your calendar so that you can call them with reminders.

> "As a kindergarten teacher, one activity I did after a field trip, as closure, was to have my students each make up one sentence about the trip. I typed out each sentence on half a page using the presentation station. Next, I printed off each sentence (two per page) and asked students to illustrate their own. Then we gathered each half-page together and created a class book about our field trip. It was a fun closing activity that incorporated technology and ended with a product my students were proud to show everyone."

Hold students accountable for their learning, and be ready with a scavenger hunt or focus questions for adult volunteers to use with their groups to help make the most out of this educational experience.

Organize and write down your expectations of both students and adult volunteers during the field trip. Give each adult leader a clipboard with the following information attached (also see the "Field Trip Instructions" form at the end of the chapter):

- Their assigned bus
- A list of students in their group
- Teaching tips for the trip
- Questions they should ask students during the trip
- Topics to discuss during the visit
- Special exhibits for students to focus their attention
- Backup procedures for supervising difficult students

Visit your destination ahead of time so that you can prepare this information for the field trip. Take a notebook and jot down questions and ideas for a field trip activity.

> ## Idea Share
>
> When going to a museum or other less interactive field trip, consider giving each student a clipboard or pocket folder to hold focus questions, a scavenger hunt, or some other type of activity that helps them get the most out of their trip. Some places have scavenger hunts or other activities available for students to use. Be sure to ask prior to creating your own.

Here are some tips for two other areas of the field trip:

Working with Chaperones

- Have name tags ready for everyone. This helps the volunteers identify the students in their group and the other chaperones.
- Thank the volunteers for joining you even before the field trip begins.
- Ask volunteers to arrive fifteen minutes before departure time to receive instructions.

Organizing

- Have signs made up for the buses (especially when taking a large group) so that students can easily identify their assigned bus.
- Get several large plastic tubs on wheels to hold lunches. I like to have one for each group, but some people simply have one for each class. If you or the school can't afford to get these types of tubs, gather several large empty boxes to use. They aren't as easy to get from the bus to the eating area, but they do work to keep lunches together.

Conclusion

A brain-based classroom is one in which students are actively engaged in the learning process. All of us naturally have a sense of curiosity about the unknown. Unfortunately, the isolated nature of traditional lectures and textbook reading has a tendency to squelch that curiosity. Students become bored and refuse to learn. We hope that this chapter has inspired you to use cooperative learning tools such as discovery learning, integrated content, and learning through experiences to foster life-long learning within your students.

References

Bloom, B. S. (ed.). *Taxonomy of Educational Objectives. Vol. 1: Cognitive Domain.* New York: McKay, 1956.

Glasser, William. *Choice Theory in the Classroom*. New York: HarperCollins, 1988.

Hacker, Michael, and Barden, Robert. *Living with Technology*. New York: Glencoe/McGraw-Hill, 1992.

Johnson, Roger, and Johnson, David. *Cooperative Learning*. Minneapolis: The Center for Cooperative Learning, 1996.

Kovalik, Susan. *Integrated Thematic Instruction: The Model*. (3rd ed.) Village of Oak Creek, Ariz.: Susan Kovalik and Associates, 2003.

Rabow, Jerome, Charness, Michelle, Kipperman, Johanna, and Radcliffe-Vasile, Susan. *William Fawcett Hill's Learning Through Discussion*. Thousand Oaks, Calif.: Waveland Press 2000.

Ross, Ann. *The Way We Were, the Way We Can Be*. Village of Oak Creek, Ariz.: Susan Kovalik & Associates, 1995.

Web Site Resources

National Geographic, http://www.nationalgeographic.com

This Day in History, http://www.historychannel.com/thisday/

The History Channel, http://www.historychannel.com

Yahoo! Countries http://www.kids.yahoo.com

U.S. Government, http://vvww.vote-smart.org/index.html

White House for Kids, http://www.whitehouse.gov/kids/

Time for Kids, http://www.timeforkids.com

Bill Nye—The Science Guy, http://billnye.com

The 8 Planets, http://www.nineplanets.org

The Exploratorium, http://www.exploratorium.edu/

National Park Service, http://www.nps.gov/parks.html

American Museum of Natural History, http://www.amnh.org

NASA, http://www.nasa.gov/

Magic School Bus, http://scholastic.com/MagicSchoolBus/

Weather Channel, http://www.weather.com/

Cells Alive, http://www.cellsalive.com

San Diego Zoo, http://www.sandiegozoo.org/

Science Hobbyist, http://www.eskimo.com/~billb/

How Stuff Works, http://howstuffworks.com

21 Classes, http://www.21classes.com

Wiki Spaces for Educators, http://www.wikispaces.com/site/for/teachers

Gaggle, http://www.gaggle.net

EduBlogs, http://www.edublogs.org

Blogmeister, http://classblogmeister.com/

Instructions for Taking Notes

1. Read each paragraph, and determine whether it contains information you need. If it does, go to the next step. If not, read the next paragraph.
2. What was that paragraph mostly about? Write the main idea on your paper.
3. What are the details in this paragraph? Write the supporting details in no more than three words as bullets under the main idea.
4. Read the next paragraph, and follow the same instructions. Remember that you do not need to copy everything down. Taking notes is the art of pulling out only the information you need.

Remember, you do not need to copy *everything* down. Taking notes is the art of pulling out only the information needed.

Field Trip Permission Form

Dear Parents,

We are taking a field trip to _____.
For the students' safety and well-being, it is important for you to know where we will be going and the purpose of this trip. Please note the following important information about our upcoming event.

Place: _____

Date: _____

Time: _____

Purpose: _____

_____

_____

Please fill out and sign the form below. Detach the bottom portion, and return it to me in the next couple of days. If you have any questions or concerns, please feel free to contact me at school during my planning period from _____to _____, or leave a message with the school secretary for me to return. School phone number: _____.

Sincerely,

- -

I, _____, give my permission for _____ to attend the field trip to _____
_____.

I will _____ send a lunch _____ purchase a school lunch.

My child has the following special needs to take into consideration
_____
_____.

Parent Signature: _____

Date:_____

Field Trip Instructions

Date: _____

Time: _____

Place: _____

Group: _____ Volunteer Name: _____

List of Students	Schedule for the Day (Including Rotation Schedule of Exhibits)

Please be sure to ask your group to think about or discuss the following:

Be sure to visit the following exhibits:

Making Connections

Reading and Writing Across the Curriculum

When striving to build a fire of learning in the classroom, we cannot forget about the foundational skills of reading and writing. These skills are vital in all aspects of learning and life. Without the ability to read and write, students cannot function efficiently and successfully in the classroom and in the rest of the world, not to mention on those "oh-so-important" standardized tests.

Many teachers believe that the teaching and practicing of reading and writing is the domain of the language arts teacher. This is absolutely not true. With the current crisis in student achievement, it is important for every teacher in the school to incorporate reading and writing skills in the classroom and across subject areas.

And yet none of us has the extra time to add another item to our overloaded curriculum. How can we reconcile this need with the reality we face? This chapter provides a variety of strategies that will help students practice vital reading and writing skills and enhance the teaching of your subject area. The question and challenge we put to you is this: How can you rekindle the spark in your own subject area by integrating reading and writing strategies into your lessons?

Poetry in Math

When you think of poetry, do you think of cafés where people drink coffee in a small dark room and listen to other people spout out unintelligible lines? Or do you associate poetry with those huge anthologies forced on you for Literature 101? For some people, poetry is an outlet to express their thoughts and feelings. For others, such as Shel Silverstein, it is an outlet for humor. We would like to challenge you with some different ways to use poetry in your classroom, whatever subject you teach.

There are many different types of poems, but we will point out just a few and show you how to use these in math, science, social studies, art, or even music and physical education class. The first is the haiku: a three-line poem with the first line of five syllables, the second line of seven syllables, and the third line of five syllables (5-7-5). It does not rhyme and is usually written about nature—for example:

> The sun shines brightly
> It warms all air and all life
> The flowers blossom

Have students write a haiku about a concept you just taught to assess their comprehension. Do you know how difficult it is to write a structured poem about a topic you do not understand? This really gets them thinking creatively about the topic!

Geometry
Shapes surround our lives
Squares, circles, triangles too
We use them to build

The Atom
Atoms are tiny
They have protons and neutrons
Electrons as well

Poems are a great way to assess learning and get students thinking at higher levels. Writing poetry forces them to think in a new way rather than just answering a question, filling in a blank, or choosing the correct answer. Structured poems also force students to learn how to write concisely. They have to figure out how to say what they want within a specific set of rules. Poetry also allows students to express themselves differently from their classmates. You can see student personalities and different levels of understanding through poetry. Poems can be used to

- Evaluate prior knowledge. What do students already know about this topic or concept?
- Assess comprehension of a specific concept discussed or read.

- Analyze, synthesize, or evaluate information from several concepts or topics (higher-level thinking skills).

Haiku is not the only type of poem to use. Another is the bio poem, which follows this format:

Line 1: Name
Line 2: Four words that describe your topic (name)
Line 3: (Relative—brother, daughter, father) of . . .
Line 4: Lover of . . . (three ideas or people)
Line 5: Who feels . . . (three ideas)
Line 6: Who needs . . . (three ideas)
Line 7: Who gives . . . (three ideas)
Line 8: Who fears . . . (three ideas)
Line 9: Who would like to see . . .
Line 10: Resident of . . .
Line 11: His or her last name

Example

Martin Luther
Husband of Coretta Scott King
Lover of human rights, freedom, and peace
Who feels passion, fear, and pride
Who needs respect, voting rights, and desegregation
Who gives a voice to the people, his own time selflessly, and hope
Who fears retaliation, violence, and failure
Who would like to see all races living together peacefully
Resident of Atlanta, Georgia, and Montgomery, Alabama
King, Jr.

A variation of the bio poem can be used for any topic or concept. It follows this format:

Line 1: Person or concept name
Line 2: Two adjectives to describe
Line 3: An action phrase with an -ing word
Line 4: An action phrase with an -ing word
Line 5: An action phrase with an -ing word
Line 6: Wrap-up word or phrase that is a synonym for line 1

Here is an example:

Volcanoes
Hot and fierce
Spitting out ash and rocks
Spilling out lava
Covering everything in sight
New land is formed

Another possibility is the acrostic poem, also called the name poem. Write one word or phrase starting with each letter that describes the person, concept, or topic. Together, the first letters in each line spell the name of the person, concept, or topic down the page vertically:

Built of bones, muscles, tissues
Only one per person
Digests food for energy
You

Consider other types of poems you could use to evaluate student learning or use as a different kind of assignment to encourage students to think about your concept in a different way.

Where do we get this valuable information to create poems of different topics and fields of study? One excellent resource that adds flair to your classroom is a quality classroom library that serves as an area for reference, research, and leisure time.

The Classroom Library

Every classroom, no matter what subject area, should have a classroom library with books and other materials to encourage students to read. Here are a few tips on creating and managing a classroom library:

- Choose one corner of your room to dedicate to reading. It doesn't have to be huge, just a space big enough for two or three students to sit comfortably.
- Partition it off a little from the rest of the room to make it a special quiet place.
- Have books and other types of reading material, nonfiction and fiction, available for a wide variety of reading levels.

Stock the reading corner with a variety of materials:

- How-to books
- Historical fiction and other genres of fiction
- Fun facts books
- Nonfiction books related to the subject area you teach

- Magazines
  - *Kids Discover*
  - *Discover*
  - *Ranger Rick*
  - *Scholastic DynaMath*
  - *Scholastic Math*
  - *Chem Matters*
  - *Science Weekly*
  - *3-2-1 Contact*
  - *Smithsonian*
  - *World Kid*
  - *TIME for Kids*
  - *Midlink Magazine*
  - *Sports Illustrated for Kids*
- Student publications
- Newspapers
- Poetry books
- Biographies and autobiographies

Idea Share

Magazines, how-to books, and other nonfiction books are sources of information for in-class research. Scholastic and other educational publishers in the areas of science, social studies, and other subject area topics publish a wide variety of books. Check out Scholastic's Web page, http://click.scholastic.com/teacherstore/, or go to an online book store to browse for nonfiction books to include in your reading area.

A reading area can be a place for students to sit quietly and read, a place for research, or a quiet area for students needing to take a break and calm down. Design your area so it can meet one or all of these purposes throughout the school year.

As a middle school teacher with language arts/social studies classes, I really wanted to set my reading corner apart from the rest of the room. I decided to pull in a comfy rocking chair, some beanbag chairs, colorful carpet squares, big pillows, and a floor lamp. There was not a window near my corner, so I created a window out of butcher paper and 'hung' curtains to make it seem homey. I also stuck a big palm tree way in the back of the corner. All of my kids enjoyed that corner, and I often used it for more than just reading.

Make the corner conducive to research by adding a long skinny table. Set out several trays or containers to hold supplies: paper, pencils, pens, highlighters, and sticky notes.

Managing the Reading Area

Now that you have everything set up and ready to go, here are a few strategies for managing this area:

1. Set up a check-out system.

   - Use library check-out cards and folders. These can be found at office supply stores and some teacher supply stores. Or check with your school librarian. Depending on your school, you might be able to ask her to order some for you and charge it to the language arts department or your grade-level budget.

   - For each book write the title, the author's name, and the cost to replace it on its book check-out card so a student who loses a book knows how much he or she must pay to replace it. This helps at the end of the year with any books that have been permanently lost.

   - Have a system in place for organizing and managing the reading area. To check out a book, students fill out the card from the back of the book and place it in an index card box behind the letter of their last name. Appoint a student librarian to replace books in the shelves or have students do it individually.

   - Use a checkout log in a three-ring binder. Students write their name and the date when they check out a book and again when they check it back in. Be aware that this method is one of the easiest ways to permanently lose books. You may want a backup accountability system where you initial when a student returns a book.

2. Organize the books for easy reference.

   - Use color-coded dots and write out a key where it can be clearly seen. For example, a red dot may mean science fiction and a blue dot a mystery book.

   - Set aside each shelf for a different genre. If you do this, make sure that students are familiar with genres.

   - Keep a separate section of nonfiction books.

   - Put books in alphabetical order by the author's last name. Be warned: this is difficult to maintain unless you have a student librarian to help you.

> "One way I use my reading corner is as a quiet place where angry or frustrated students can calm down. I start out the year by reading Judith Viorst's *Alexander and the Terrible, Horrible, No Good, Very Bad Day.* Then I explain to my students that when we are having a horrible day for whatever reason, it keeps us from learning properly. I encourage them to let me know when they need to cool down, and I send them to 'Australia' which is my reading corner with a palm tree in it."

Reasons for All Teachers to Have a Reading Corner

- Area for quiet time
- Student research
- Access to books
- Enrichment of content
- A place for students who are finished early to read

Monitoring Students

When students are in the reading corner, walk around and use the clipboard to help with observations. Keep notes on who is doing what during silent reading time. (For more on this technique, see Chapters Two and Four.)

A second way to monitor students is to have them keep a reading log with daily responses to their reading. They record the title of the book, author, and number of pages read each day before completing their response. A page of reading response questions is included later in this chapter.

Idea Share

Use Bloom's keywords to help you develop reading responses on a variety of levels.

Moment of Reflection

What purposes can a reading area serve in your classroom? What types of books and other materials would you include in your classroom library? Do you foresee e-books or the computer as part of your reading area in the future? Why or why not?

Literature Circles (Reading Groups)

The literature circle, or reading group, is a strategy that all teachers can use. While language arts/reading teachers may be using groups to read a novel, other subject area teachers may use this same strategy when reading a nonfiction source or textbook.

This strategy offers students a way to read and discuss in a cooperative group setting. It allows students to work together and is very motivating. Nevertheless, setting up literature groups can be confusing and sometimes hard to manage. Following are strategies for effectively setting up literature groups in the classroom.

Assigning the Books

These groups of four of five students are often heterogeneous, containing students at a variety of reading levels. You can have the students choose their own book to read as a group, they can choose a book from several you have picked out, or you can choose the book you expect them to read. As a subject area teacher, you may assign a section of the textbook or other nonfiction reading. The novel read in a literature group can relate to a topic studied in science or social studies or might be a genre that you are studying.

Each group either reads the book or text together aloud in class or assigns chapters or sections to be read each evening. During class time, students discuss the material in their groups.

It is important to provide students with guiding questions to use during discussion, and each person should record the answers to discussion questions. Keywords from Bloom's taxonomy of thinking skills can be used to help develop thought-provoking discussion questions.

Another option is to provide statements about characters or events within the story or text for students to prove or disprove. Have students go around the circle and either agree or disagree with the statement. Require students to state their reasons and provide specific quotes or events from the story to support their position. Here are some examples:

- *Charlotte is a nosy spider who should mind her own business.* Do you agree or disagree with this statement? (Using *Charlotte's Web*)

- *The count of Monte Cristo is the true villain.* Do you agree or disagree with this statement? (Using *The Count of Monte Cristo*)

- *The electoral college is an effective method for electing the president of the United States.* Do you agree or disagree with this statement? (Using the textbook or other resources)

- *The atom is the smallest particle in existence.* Do you agree or disagree with this statement? (Using textbook or other resources)

Groups can also create small products to show their comprehension of the story: a storyboard of events, an illustration of the setting, a time line, a pop-up book with information, a PowerPoint presentation, or a photo story.

It is vital to remind students of class procedures, your expectations, and how to work together as a group every time they meet. This should be done before students get together in groups. When you begin to see student discussions that do not meet your expectations, model exactly what you want to see.

Teacher-Led Literature Groups

Another option is to break students into smaller groups by ability level. Literature groups are a great way to practice decoding, comprehension, and other reading skills. Once again, each group should be assigned or allowed to choose a different book to read. Students are assigned chapters to read and gather during class time to practice reading and discuss the book with the teacher.

These ideas help with group management:

- Students keep books in a large plastic bag with a zipper lock that can hold the book and any related materials to the discussion.
- Use index cards as bookmarks. The students write down the assigned chapter to read for that evening, along with the date. This will keep a good log of reading assignments.
- Assign students either a guiding question for them to answer as they are reading a chapter or a reading response of some sort to have ready for discussion. Sample responses can be found later in this chapter.

Managing Teacher-Led Literature Groups

How do you manage working with one group of students while the rest are still there? What will the rest of the class be doing? All students should know exactly what to do each day during literature group time. Generally you expect the other students in the class to be working quietly on seat work while you are reading with each group. This will not happen without training. In the beginning, you will find you are interrupted frequently to quiet the class or get them focused on their assignment. You should get to a point where all you need is a look or to ring a small bell to remind students that they should be working quietly. This is not the time for group work activities for the rest of the class because you can't be walking around and monitoring. The students should be working quietly on self-directed activities.

Idea Share

Assign meaningful seat work for students who are not reading with you: practice work on a specific skill or concept taught earlier, finishing other assignments, individual work in thinking or learning centers, or individual research projects, for example.

Determine how much time you want to spend with each group. Do you plan to work with one group each day for twenty or thirty minutes or two groups each day for ten or fifteen minutes? This decision is the first step toward preparing for how you will spend your time. Next, break up the allotted time into five- or ten-minute segments:

- One segment of the allotted time is for students to read to you.
- One segment is for basic comprehension questions.
- One segment is for higher-level thinking and discussion about the book.

A number of activities can foster a good discussion or enrich student learning—for example:

- Students create a storyboard that shows the major events happening within that chapter.
- Students create a time line that shows the major events happening within that chapter.
- Students keep an index card for each character. As they read, they write down traits of each character. This could be extended to include relationships between that character and others, as well as any changes that occur to the character over the course of the story.
- Use agree or disagree statements to start discussion. Students must support their opinion with reasons and with quotes or events from the story.

Internet Application

When students come across a concept that they have no prior knowledge about, use the Internet to help extend their knowledge.

Help students make a list of keywords related to the concept for an Internet search. The group can then use the classroom computer to search for information, print out information, and share their new knowledge with the rest of the class.

Have a list of preapproved Web sites on a wiki page or classroom Web site for younger students to click and visit immediately without having to search and filter inappropriate sites.

Teach older students how to discern valid and reliable information when searching. To start, direct students to government and well-established national organization Web sites to gather information. (See the list of Web sites at the end of Chapter Seven.)

Whole Class Reading Strategies

There are several methods for reading a passage as a whole class, and they can be used in any subject area.

Choral Reading

Students all read together out loud. A variation is to assign each student a different sentence that each reads in turn. Or break the students into groups, and assign each group a different passage to read aloud. Or you could assign half the class to read every other paragraph.

Oral Reading

Students take turns reading aloud. The following techniques are fun to use:

- *Popcorn reading,* which requires a student to read anywhere from two to eight sentences aloud. When finished, this person calls on another student to pick up the text.
- *Pass the ball reading,* where a student has a squishy ball or wadded-up piece of paper. When the student is through reading the paragraph, he or she gently tosses the ball to another student, who continues the reading.

Reader's Theater

In this technique, students sit in the front of the room, and each is assigned a character. One student is the narrator. While reading a story, each student reads the dialogue spoken by his or her character and the narrator reads the rest of it. You could also assign several narrators. A variation is to break students into groups, and assign each group a section of the textbook or chapter in a novel. Student groups take the text and turn it into a script to read the following day. Make copies of the scripts, assign parts, and begin reading.

Reader's theater is just one way you can integrate the required curriculum element of theater into your classes. Creating a script from a textbook chapter to read aloud in class is another way this skill can be integrated. A third strategy is to have students act out the main events or main idea of the passage they are reading.

How can you integrate theater into other subjects? When teaching in social studies or history, students could act out scenes from battles, famous speeches, trials—the possibilities are endless if you have an open mind. Students will remember history they have had to plan, write a script for, and act out. This brings history to life.

When teaching science, students can be atoms, protons and electrons who act out their reactions with each other, chemicals, planets revolving around the sun, and so much more. Your imagination can bring a boring reading passage to life!

Individual Reading Time

This may be called silent reading time, D.E.A.R. (Drop Everything and Read), or another name. The idea is for students to find a place in the room to read on their own to encourage reading for pleasure. Students often enjoy this time, especially if you dim the lights and play some soft music. Allow your students to sit anywhere they want so they will be comfortable and motivated to read.

Writing Activities with Reading Passages

Use writing activities to enhance reading. Whether you teach language arts or another subject area, reading and writing go hand in hand. Here are some ways you can use writing activities to enhance student reading in your class.

Reading Logs

Have students keep a daily record of what they read in and out of class. You could also give students an easy-to-fill-out log sheet to help you keep track of what they are reading and how much they are reading.

Dialectic Journals

A professor at Emory University in Atlanta, Georgia, used to make her students keep dialectic journals to enforce active reading. Students fold a piece of paper in half and draw a line down the middle. On one side they write any words or quotes from their book that capture their attention. On the other side, they write what they were thinking while they read that word or passage. This helps them track their train of thought throughout the reading. See the following sample dialectic journal.

Example

Student Response	Quote from Book
I would be mad if my mom ignored me all the time. This woman sounds totally selfish! I guess as long as they could sew and talk, it didn't matter if they knew anything else. What a waste.	"To the education of her daughters, Lady Bertram paid not the smallest attention. She had no time for such cares." (*Mansfield Park*, p. 17)

She sounds like an eighteenth-century version of a couch potato. How boring to sit all day without TV. How did they do it? I don't think I could just sew all day long. I bet she gets fat because she sits all day. I totally can't imagine sitting around basically doing nothing. Did all women do this?	"She was a woman who spent her days in sitting nicely dressed on a sofa, doing some long piece of needlework." (*Mansfield Park*, p. 17)
No brain and no beauty? How did she ever get married in the first place?	"Of little use and no beauty" (*Mansfield Park*, p. 17)

You might use this with younger students using a combination of words and pictures. Perhaps the words they record from the story are their vocabulary words.

Genres
Teach students the different genres, and have them write their own stories using the critical attributes of mystery, horror, science fiction, fantasy, fairy tales, adventure, fables, historical fiction, or biography.

Idea for Primary Grades

You could model the dialectic journal concept to students by using the whiteboard or chart paper while reading a fiction or nonfiction story. This helps model active reading for younger students.

Moment of Reflection

What type of reading strategies do you use most in your classroom? How effective are these in helping students comprehend and retain information?

Reading Responses
Have a question ready for students to answer about their reading for the day. Students can record this in a journal. Collect these responses every week or every couple of weeks so you can record participation grades for individual reading time.

Idea Share

Use the reading skills listed in the next couple of pages to create your own responses. Also, using Bloom's keywords makes creating reading responses easy for the teacher to come up with both basic and higher-level questions!

The reading response journal or log is also an opportunity for students to practice various reading skills. Instead of always asking for a summary of the pages read, you could have students do one or more of the following:

- Create a storyboard showing at least four major events (events that are important to the outcome of the story or other characters) from the pages read.

- Create an illustrated time line showing at least four major events from the pages read.

- Explain what the pages were mostly about. What are some specific details that support this main idea? Support the main idea with words, phrases, and actions from the story. Write down the page numbers where you found these details.

- Describe two or three different cause-and-effect patterns within the pages you read.

- Write down two fact statements and two opinion statements from your reading.

- What do you think will happen next in the story or text? Why? Support your reasons with quotes from the book. Include page numbers.

- What events in the story or text caused your character or others to react in an unusual manner? What events in this part of your reading have caused an unusual reaction? If there were none, why do you think this is the case?

- What events are affecting your character, and in what way is the character affected?

- Compare and contrast the reactions of two characters to the same event, or compare and contrast two characters from your story or text.

- For subject area teachers: Have students respond to the text when reading about historical events, people, objects, places, or concepts.

- What made you like or dislike the main character?

Using these types of reading responses as assessments helps prepare students for state tests.

- What animal does the main character mostly resemble? Explain your answer.
- Choose one of the characters to invite to a party. Which one did you choose, and why?
- Would you be friends with the main character? Why or why not?
- Describe the tone of the story.
- Describe the mood of the story.
- Does the weather in the setting affect the story? If so, how?
- What would happen to the story if the setting were a thousand years into the future?
- What would happen to the story if the setting were 250 years in the past?
- How might the setting be different if this were a different genre?
- If you were the main character's brother or sister, what advice would you give him or her?
- How might you describe the main character to a friend in a letter?
- What problem did the main character face? How would you have solved it differently?
- Which planet is the main character most like (e.g., icy, hot, burning balls of gas, lots of hot air, colorful, rugged terrain, and so on)? Why?
- Which character would you like to be? Why?
- If you were one of the characters in this story, how would your life be different from the way it is now?
- Describe the relationship the main character has with the other characters in the book.
- Write about one funny thing that happens in the story.
- Would you end the book differently? If so, how?
- Did anything happen in the story that made you feel angry? What is it, and why did you have that reaction?
- Write about one sad thing that happens in the story.

Reading Skills to Be Taught and Practiced

This section looks at reading skills that should be taught in reading and practiced in every class. If you do not specifically teach reading, you should still find it relatively easy to integrate either a review or use of these skills in your class:

- Identify the main idea.
- Summarize a passage.
- Distinguish fact from nonfact.

- Sequence events.
- Identify supporting details in a passage.
- Determine word meaning (vocabulary).
- Determine cause-and-effect relationships.
- Compare and contrast ideas.
- Make observations and analyze issues within a passage.
- Locate specific information in a passage.
- Use graphic sources to help interpret reading.
- Make generalizations, and draw conclusions from a passage.
- Identify the purpose of a text.
- Make predictions.

The best way to help your students recognize that they use these skills daily is to use the vocabulary and point them out in your own lessons. For example, you could say, "What was the sequence of events that caused the Civil War?" or "We just identified a cause and effect. That is an important reading skill."

As you read the objectives, ask yourself, How many of these am I already doing without being aware of it? How many science and social studies teachers, for instance, require students to locate facts from the textbook? Sequencing is another commonly used skill in math, science, social studies, music, art, and physical education classes.

"Well," you may ask, "since I'm already reinforcing many of these skills in the classroom, what more is there?" Awareness is the first step. However, you must also make your students aware that these skills can be applied in all areas in academic and real life.

Example: A science teacher is planning a lesson on electricity. Before the textbook reading, he introduces important vocabulary terms. At this time, it would be easy to incorporate a short discussion on how the prefix or suffix of a word gives a clue as to its meaning. This little bit of reading instruction doesn't take long, but now two reading skills have been emphasized in the class. To take it a step further, the teacher could point out how prefixes and suffixes help determine word meaning in everything they read, from VCR manuals to advertisements. In the course of a few minutes within a lesson, the science teacher has reinforced reading skills, applied it to the curriculum, and applied it to the real world.

Moment of Reflection

How might you incorporate various reading objectives into an assignment to read a textbook chapter?

Spelling Skills

Students who are not taught spelling face obstacles in both reading and writing. Poor spelling habits that are not corrected can lead to difficulty in writing and even lower literacy skills. A child who becomes frustrated and discouraged may end up falling behind. Many young readers are puzzled by the rules and exceptions of spelling. Research has shown, however, that learning to spell and learning to read rely on much of the same underlying knowledge. Students need to learn the relationships between letters and sounds. An understanding of spelling mechanics can lead to improved reading.

A new way of looking at spelling in today's fast-paced classrooms is word study, an alternative to traditional spelling instruction. It is based on learning word patterns rather than memorizing unconnected words and using spelling words that relate to the current classroom topic of study. Word study is a more integrated approach to spelling instruction that addresses word recognition, vocabulary, and phonics as well as spelling. It provides students with opportunities to investigate and understand the patterns and meanings in words.

One example we could study in understanding patterns of spelling is how to know when the /j/ sound as in *age* is spelled with "dge" as in *ledge*. In most cases when a word has the short vowel sound as in *ledge, bridge,* and *judge,* it is spelled with "dge." When the word has the long vowel sound, it is spelled with the "ge," as in *age, stage,* and *rage.* Knowledge of patterns gives students confidence for future spelling in reading and writing. Of course, for every rule, there are exceptions. Students learn, though, that spelling patterns exist and these patterns help to explain how to spell, read, and write words.

Word study is designed to build word knowledge that can be applied to both reading and spelling. Because it is closely tied to reading instruction, it also develops students' abilities in phonics, word recognition, and vocabulary. Using vocabulary words that fit with the science or social studies curriculum being studied is an added way to give meaning to words and put them in real-world contexts.

A good idea is for students to hunt for words in their reading and writing that fit the pattern being studied. Teachers and students may construct a word wall illustrating examples of the different patterns studied. Students may keep a word study notebook to record the patterns they learn and their new understandings about words. A fun way to study spelling words and patterns is to play games and activities to apply their word knowledge.

Whether you are doing traditional spelling instruction or word study, here are some activities you can use to spark interest in spelling:

• *Go to Spellingcity.com.* Students can enter their spelling words for the week and play games, pretest, and do other fun activities.

• *Crossword puzzles with spelling words.* Students complete crossword puzzles that have spelling words as the words in the boxes and definitions or synonyms as the clues for the across and down categories. There is language arts software for teachers that have the crossword format already created. The teacher just plugs in the words and clues and the software creates the puzzle, so the teacher just prints it out for the class.

• *Word searches.* Students find their spelling words in a jumble of letters on a page. Software for teachers exists that has the format already created. The teacher just plugs in the words and the computer creates the word search ready to print.

• *Spelling Scrabble.* Students use Scrabble tiles to make their spelling words. After they make a word, they must record how many points the word was worth. They can determine which words were worth the most and least. This activity is an easy way to check that students are really making their words.

• *Spelling code breaking.* Teachers choose a font on the computer that prints out symbols instead of letters. Type the entire alphabet at the top of the page. Type out each spelling word in this new and different font, in other words, the teacher is substituting a symbol for each letter in the alphabet. At the top of the page, list the letter of the alphabet and its symbol below it. Teachers then render the spelling words in the code and students decode their spelling words. Students love to "break the code" in figuring out what each disguised spelling word is.

• *Spelling journals and word walls.* Teachers are regularly bombarded with questions from their students about how to spell words. It seems like it is often the same words being asked about time and time again. To discourage this, give each student a spelling journal. At the top of each page, they write a letter of the alphabet. So page 1 is "A," page 2 is "B," and so forth. A child who asks how to spell a word must write it correctly in his or her journal or add it to the classroom word wall. Before asking the teacher again in the future, the student must look in the spelling journal or on the word wall to see if the word is already there. By the end of the year, their spelling journals will be a great resource.

• *Spelling games.* Divide students into groups, and give each group a store-bought board game, such as checkers or bingo. (Each group needs a different board game.) Next, have the students design a new set of rules for that game, where they incorporate spelling words into it. For example, a group may decide in the game of checkers that a player must spell the word given to him or her correctly before gaining permission to move a game piece. You'll be amazed at how creative your students will be! After the new set of directions is written for each game, groups can get up in front of the class to explain the new rules. They can rotate the games so that each student can play the new version, or games can be placed in a reading center for free time.

• *Sparkle.* Have the children line up against a wall so they are shoulder to shoulder. Start at either end of the line, and give the group a spelling word. The first person says the first letter, the next child says the next letter, and so on until they reach the end of the word. The next child says "sparkle," and the next one has to sit down. If a child gives the incorrect letter on his or her turn, he or she must sit down. Continue the game until you are down to one child. Children love this game, which is a great review.

Strategies for Incorporating Reading into Any Subject

This section offers practical ways to incorporate reading strategies into your curriculum, no matter what subject you teach.

Vocabulary

Introduce vocabulary terms before beginning a unit or lesson. Discuss how the root word, prefix, or suffix offers a clue to the meaning of the word. Here are some activities:

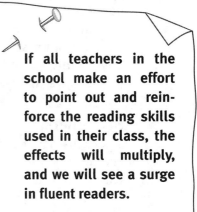

- *Have students guess the meaning of a list of words on a sheet of paper.* Next to their guess, ask them to write down the clue that helped them determine the meaning. Next, pass around a handout that gives students the correct definition of each word along with the clue or clues. Allow students to share their meaning and clue for each word and then the actual definitions. To add an element of fun to the activity, offer incentives for students who get the definition correct. You could also offer a prize to the student with the most creative definition, local reasoning, or creative clues for each word. This will encourage students to take risks in guessing the meaning and show them that you reward effort as much as correctness.

If all teachers in the school make an effort to point out and reinforce the reading skills used in their class, the effects will multiply, and we will see a surge in fluent readers.

- *Create a word wall for important terms.* You can keep the word wall up all year or change it for each unit of study. Another option is to create portable word walls for each unit using trifold display boards that can be moved around the room easily or folded up and put away when not needed. Upper-level teachers may have one board for each class they teach. A permanent word wall might include terms that are needed all year, and portable word walls would show the important terms for a specific unit. A word wall is easy to create. Simply divide a section of a classroom wall or the display board into rows and columns to show each letter of the alphabet. You might need several rows to accommodate all letters. Then, using Velcro or sticky tape, place a laminated card with each letter in the appropriate column or row. As new terms are introduced, write them on laminated construction paper or card stock and stick them under the appropriate letter. Older students could keep a vocabulary notebook with a "word wall" of their own inside.

• *Clap the syllables of each new word to help students remember it.* Another way to help students remember a word is to rap it or sing a song with it. Jazzles (http://phonics.jazzles.com) has information about singing to remember words.

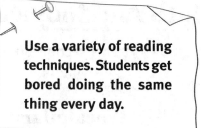

Use a variety of reading techniques. Students get bored doing the same thing every day.

Reading a Textbook

Use reading objectives to help focus the purpose of student reading.

Locating Information from a Nonfiction Reading

Create a scavenger hunt of questions for students to answer when reading through a chapter or section of a textbook. Students can work in groups or pairs, reading aloud (quietly) and helping each other locate the answers, or they can work individually. A scavenger hunt is also a fun homework assignment.

An alternative for older students is to have students read through a section of the chapter as a group, in pairs, or individually. They create their own scavenger hunt questions, and you compile the questions for the entire class to complete. The scavenger hunt activity also works well for a take-home assessment.

Sequencing

There are several good sequencing activities you can use in the classroom. For example, students who are learning a scientific procedure or math equation can write out the steps to completing the procedure or solving the problem. Another idea is to then write a "how-to" essay explaining the specific steps.

Students reading about a historical era or events can create an illustrated time line to show the correct sequencing of events or present a sequence through a storyboard.

After students read a chapter about a scientific procedure, math equation, or historical time period, give them an envelope with the events and steps typed on slips of paper. Have students close their books and put the events or steps in the correct order. The class as a whole can then paste or tape their strips on colorful construction paper or butcher paper.

Another possibility is to use Photo Story or Animoto.com to create a sequence of photos with music to represent a visual retelling of events or a story.

Idea Share

When presenting a new activity, have students do the work as a class the first time to model and answer any questions they may have. Then allow them to work in groups, then in pairs, and then individually. This sequence gives students the opportunity to help each other and learn from one another before applying what they have learned on their own.

Fact Versus Nonfact

After students read a chapter or section in their textbook, have them create two to four statements: two of them true and two false (but not outrageously so)—for example: (1) Whales are mammals. True or false? and (2) Whales are related to fish. True or false? Students will have to have pay attention to write the statements and answer them correctly. Encourage students to try to trip up the rest of the class with their statements. This will motivate them to read and listen carefully.

Graphic Organizers

After reading a passage, novel, or nonfiction book or textbook in class, have students fill in a graphic organizer. Graphic organizers reinforce main ideas, sequencing, compare and contrast, fact or nonfact, and many other skills.

If you decide to extend the reading into an essay or other written product, a graphic organizer is a useful prewriting activity. Several types of graphic organizers are available at the end of this chapter to help you get started.

Webbing

Students draw a circle in the middle of their paper and write the title of the book in it. Then they draw other circles off the main one for each chapter and write the main idea for one chapter in each of the smaller circles. A web can also be used to break down a textbook chapter by putting the chapter title in the middle and then having main ideas sprouting off the circle in the middle. For example, if the text chapter is on the solar system, the circle in the middle could be shaped like the sun and the main ideas could all be shooting off from the center sun.

Venn Diagram

The Venn diagram is a good way to organize compare-and-contrast information (see Figure 8.1). Students draw two circles with a small portion overlapping. In one circle, they write traits of one object and in the other circle traits of the second object. In the overlapping section (middle), they write traits that the two objects have in common.

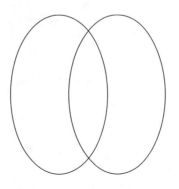

Figure 8.1 Venn Diagram

Listing
Students can draw boxes down their paper or number a column down the left side of their paper from 1 to 10. They then put events from the book in order.

Table
Students make a chart by drawing a line across the top of a piece of paper and one down the middle of it to form a T-chart. They can use this for comparing and contrasting and listing advantages and disadvantages, pros and cons, or fact and nonfact.

Mind Mapping
This is the same as webbing, except that students use pictures or illustrations instead of words.

Bloom's Taxonomy Keywords
To encourage higher-level thinking skills in all areas of our classroom, we recommend using Bloom's keywords to help develop reading discussion questions, reading responses, and writing activities. Use these keywords to create responses on a variety of reading responses:

Knowledge	Comprehension	Application
Define	Explain	Demonstrate
List	Summarize	Show
Identify	Interpret	Operate
Describe	Rewrite	Construct
Match	Convert	Apply
Located	Give examples	Illustrate
Analysis	**Synthesis**	**Evaluation**
Compare	Create	Judge
Contrast	Suppose	Appraise
Distinguish	Design	Debate
Deduce	Compose	Criticize
Infer	Combine	Support

Example: The following questions could be used with *Charlotte's Web:*

- Identify the main characters.
- Describe the setting of the story.
- Explain why Charlotte is helping Wilbur.
- Give examples of how the other animals felt about Wilbur.
- Compare Charlotte with Templeton.
- Predict what you think will happen to Wilbur in the future.
- Compose your own message that Charlotte could use to help Wilbur.
- Design a web with a message for the farmer.
- Is Templeton a helpful character? In a paragraph, criticize his actions.
- Should Wilbur have taken Charlotte's egg sack back to the farm? Why or why not? Support your reasons.

> **Increase critical thinking skills by using higher levels of Bloom's taxonomy when creating reading responses.**

Example: Here are some sample questions for *The Count of Monte Cristo:*

- Describe the mood of the story.
- Explain why the count is helping Morrel.
- Give examples of how Danglars betrayed Edmond Dantès.
- Predict what you think will happen to the count now that his revenge has ended.
- Suppose Dantès escaped from prison without knowing the events that led to his arrest. Create an outline of events that might have happened were this true.
- In a paragraph, criticize the actions of Faria in regards to Edmond Dantès.

Responding to Reading

After students have read the assigned fiction or nonfiction selection, give them the following discussion and question starters. Be sure to use at least one starter from each level listed below to ensure students are using higher-level thinking skills. These starters can be written on a transparency, posted on a wiki page, shown using a document camera, or shown on a presentation station for students to respond to their reading or for a group discussion.

Example: Knowledge

- Define words from the reading that were unfamiliar to you.
- Identify three major events, concepts, or characters presented in the reading.
- Describe the setting of the story or event, OR describe the concept from the reading selection. Locate three facts or details from the passage read. Locate a place from the reading on a map.

Example: Comprehension

- Retell the event [or story or concept] from the reading.
- Summarize what you just read with the main idea and some supporting details. Give examples of . . .
- Explain how . . .

Example: Application

- Predict what will happen . . .
- Demonstrate how . . .
- Construct a model of . . . character traits of . . .
- Apply this reading to your own life.

Example: Analysis

- Compare and contrast . . .
- Make a T chart, and categorize elements from the reading.
- What can we infer from this reading about this character? Distinguish one aspect of the character, event, or concept from another.

Example: Synthesis

- Compose a letter to . . .
- Design your own . . .
- Create a new product that solves a problem from the reading.
- Suppose you were in the situation we just read about. How would you react?

Example: Evaluation

- Debate two sides of the issue or event in your reading.
- Appraise the usefulness of a concept, issue, or event from your reading.
- Criticize a decision made by a historical figure or character from the reading.
- What is your opinion? Support it with details from the reading.

Reading Novels in Class

It is very hard for students to sit still during an entire fifty- or ninety-minute class either reading or listening to someone else read. To keep students engaged during the entire class, alternate reading, discussion, and written activities.

You may be tempted to read the assigned novel every day or play a CD of the novel being read aloud for the entire class period. Not only is this incredibly boring, but it is not engaging students actively. It is important to stop at various times throughout the reading to check for understanding, discuss unfamiliar vocabulary, and relate the story to the students' lives.

Whenever teaching a novel, be sure to read it ahead of time, and think about ways you can relate it to the students:

- Look up information on the Internet about the time period when the novel is set to look for fun or interesting facts.

- Compare and contrast the life and times of the characters with those of the students.
- Bring in maps to integrate geography skills and help students determine location in relation to where they live.
- Look up information on the author to help students understand why he or she may have written the book.

Idea Share

How can you integrate information learned in other subject areas? For example, Charles Dickens lived during the Industrial Revolution and wrote about the deplorable living conditions of the time in his stories. What kind of story plot might your students use for a story about today's society? Another example: *My Brother Sam Is Dead* is set during the American Revolution—a perfect opportunity for integrating history into the lesson. Reading the novel before planning helps effective teachers integrate personal experiences and knowledge into the discussion.

Strategies During Reading

Activities done throughout the reading are more effective as teaching tools than when they are given after students finish reading the novel.

> Lesson planning for studying novels is more effective when the teacher has done some prior reading and research.

Activity: Paper Bags

Use plain brown lunch bags for this activity. Have students draw an image on a bag from the chapter or pages they read that stood out for them. The image could also be a scene from the book, the setting, or a character from the novel or story. If you are reading a textbook, the image might be a famous person or event described in the passage or a rendering of the concept being described in a textbook or nonfiction reading.

Students put other information inside the bag. Activities might include:

Main idea of the chapter/novel	Vocabulary words
Outline of the problem and solution	Drawing of plot events
Time line or storyboard of events	Character cards with basic information
Explanation of a skill or concept	Description of the procedure or events
Real-world application of skill or concept	

You can create additional activities using the Bloom's keywords mentioned previously in this chapter.

Activity: Venn Diagram

Use this graphic organizer to compare and contrast characters, events, or something else within the story. Require students to support this information from the text by citing page numbers.

Idea Share

Looking for more ideas? Go to Chapter Ten. Many of those ideas can be adapted to use during your reading lessons.

Activity: Letter Writing

Integrate two skills with the letter writing activity. Have students write an informal or formal letter to a character from the novel (or a person from the textbook) explaining his or her predictions about upcoming events or the outcome of the story. Students could also use the letter to draw conclusions about the novel or characters within the novel. A letter is a good way to apply any of the reading skills mentioned earlier in this chapter.

Students can also e-mail each other or students in another class rather than writing letters by hand. However, they should still follow proper letter writing skills. Just because the delivery method is different does not mean it is acceptable to disregard the appropriate format. Too many people forget to use these important skills when writing e-mails.

Letters and e-mails can be written to authors of books, current government officials, CEOs of corporations, and newspaper editors. In addition, letters can be written to famous historical figures, even if not living, as a way to express student knowledge of a subject in history, to draw conclusions, to ask pertinent questions, and to offer opinions. This assignment might include a return letter from the historical figure that is written by the student or another student in the class.

Activity: News Articles

Apply student comprehension of the novel or textbook reading through a news article. Have students use the reporter's method of the five W's (who, what, where, when, why) and one H (how) in analyzing the novel. Turn these into a news story complete with a headline. This activity can be used for both novels and in-class textbook reading.

Use Adobe Pagemaker or PowerPoint for students to type their articles into a newspaper or newsletter format. When completed, the final document can be posted in the room and sent home for parents to read. This strategy also provides parent communication about what students are learning in their own words.

Students can also use a digital camera to take pictures that relate to the news articles being written. For fun, have students dress up as historical figures and pose for photos when writing articles about history.

Moment of Reflection

What are some ways you might integrate writing activities that encourage higher-level thinking skills into your lessons?

Using Journals in All Classes

The journal is one of the best ways to assess student learning after a lesson as well as provide one-on-one feedback for each student. Here are a few tips to help you implement journals in your classroom.

Provide Structure

Students need structure to feel comfortable with any assignment, including journals. Simply directing students to "write down what you've learned today" won't work. An unstructured journal topic such as this leaves students feeling flustered and abandoned. They will spend the entire five minutes asking themselves, and you, "What are you looking for? What should I write? How much is too much or too little? Where do I begin?"

When planning lessons, use your objectives or key elements to form your journal topic. The topic question or statement should directly relate to your lesson and should be easy to answer in five minutes.

Examples

- Explain briefly how you would figure the sales price of a $20 pair of jeans with a 15% discount. (used after a lesson on percentages)
- What effect did the environment have on where early people settled and the type of home they built?
- What are the three branches of government, and which is your favorite? Explain your choice.

Have Expectations

Students need to know what you expect of them. Have your expectations written out in detail for the journals. Think about the following questions as you decide.

- What is your goal for the journal each day? What is the purpose?
- How much do you expect students to write?
- What kind of grade will they receive for their journal?
- What do you expect in terms of spelling, grammar, and other parts of the response?

Example: I expect my students to write at least three sentences each day. The journal entry must stay on topic and answer the question posed. I expect complete sentences and correct spelling. The journal is a way for me to check student learning each day and is also a way for me to talk with each student individually. A student who has something to say to me that he or she does not want to voice out loud may write it in the journal AFTER answering the question OR before class the next day. Students will be given a participation grade for the journal once a week.

Have a Procedure

It is important that you have a journaling procedure for your class. Students need to know exactly what to do for this type of assignment. The example here is a procedure when journals are used at the end of the class:

Example

- You must get your journal from the table before class starts each day. When it is time to write in your journal, put away all materials except your journal, and clean the area around your desk.
- Take out journal.
- Write your journal entry silently until the bell rings.

Grading

If you graded every journal on a subjective scale of 1 to 100, you'd be old and gray before getting through one year's worth of journals. Instead, it is important to hold students accountable for participating in this important activity. You can use the check system to give a quick grade that is easy to record. It shows students that you are reading their journal and that they are being held accountable.

Provide Feedback

Students want to hear what you have to say and look for your feedback every day. Be sure you have one or two things to say to each student in his or her journal. It doesn't need to be much, but be sure that you offer detailed comments in each student's journal at least once a week.

Your attitude affects whether journals will be a valuable teaching tool in your classroom.

Be sure to correct student mistakes in the writing. The more students are held accountable for their writing skills, the more they will improve. An employer in the real world will judge every piece of writing received from an employee, even informal notes.

Use this as one-on-one time. Have you noticed something particular about one student? Take some time to write this person a note and ask about the situation, or just let him or her know you are available to talk. The journal can serve more than just one purpose, and students respond to teachers who take time to learn more about them as a person.

Idea Share

I use spiral notebooks for my student journals and keep those for each class in a plastic crate. At the beginning of each class period, I pull out the journals for students to pick up as they enter the room. This is one way I check for student absences. I look to see which journals are still up front, check to see whether the students are actually in class, and mark the rest as absent. It works well and takes less time than calling the roll.

Evaluating Student Reading

Now that you have your students reading and practicing vital reading skills, how are you going to evaluate what they know or don't know about what they read? Whether your students read individually or as a class, you must determine three things:

- Did they read? How much are they reading?
- Did they comprehend what they read?
- Can they think critically about the reading?

The following assessments will help you answer those three questions.

Book Study

Create a book study with several assignments designed to test various reading skills. For example, you might ask students to write a one-page summary, create a diorama of the setting, make character trading cards, or write a poem about the main character. It is important to give students choice, so out of five activities, require students to complete three or four. It is also important to give students the requirements up front so they are able to think about these activities as they read. Two sample book study activities, "Beginning Book Study" and "Book Bonanza" are found at the end of the chapter. You can also use Bloom's keywords to create your own book study activities. The book study is a way to get students to actively think about their book and is more engaging than a straight book report.

Dialectic Journals

Collect student dialectic journals for a grade. This is an excellent assessment tool as students must record their own thoughts and feelings about the story as they read. The dialectic journal will give you a good indication of whether students are comprehending the reading.

Reading Responses

Collect reading responses every two or three weeks for grading. If the responses range from Knowledge to Evaluation over the two- or three-week span, you should get a good assessment of student comprehension and critical thinking with regard to their reading.

Formal Exam

You can give a formal exam to see which reading skills students have mastered. Set up these tests so they are similar to the state's standardized test. This will provide your students with practice in that format. The more familiar students are with the format of a standardized test, the better they will perform.

Moment of Reflection

Is it important to use to use and recognize the use of reading and writing skills in your class? Why or why not? Why do you think it is, or is not, important for specific reading and writing skills to be integrated in all curriculum areas?

Writing in the Classroom

This section discusses different writing modes and gives you some ideas on how to use these. For more detailed instruction on the writing workshop method, read Nancie Atwell's (1993) book *In the Middle*. It gives a structured program for teaching writing. Our goal is not to teach you how to be a writing instructor, but to give you some ideas for writing in your class.

The Writing Process

The writing process is the series of steps used when writing. Teaching children these steps can help them to think about their writing. It also teaches that writing is a process that takes time.

Writing Process Steps

1. Prewriting: Put thoughts on paper informally. Students can use jot lists, brainstorming, webbing, journals, and freewriting. (See the "Prewriting Notes" sheet at the end of the chapter.)

2. First draft: Students put their prewriting thoughts into paragraph form. This is also known as the rough draft.

3. Peer response: Students read their papers aloud to a partner, who makes notes on the following questions: What did you like about the paper? What questions do you have? (See the "Global Response" worksheet at the end of the chapter.)

4. Revision: Students add details, remove extraneous words and phrases, move words and phrases around, and hone their word choice. The teacher presents this as using colorful language and substituting blah words for more exciting ones. See the "Revising a Story" guidelines at the end of the chapter.)

5. Second draft: Students write a neat copy of their paper.

6. Proofread: Students look for and correct grammar and spelling mistakes.

7. Final copy: Students write or type a neat draft to turn in.

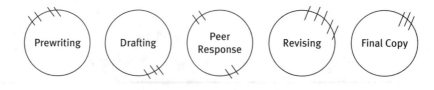

Figure 8.2 The Writing Process

Writing Modes

There are four major writing modes that students are held accountable for in most state exams. Teaching these writing modes in other subject areas, not just English class, will help students be comfortable responding to any topic or writing prompt they are given. In addition, when students are in older grades and college classes, knowing how to format these basic writing modes will help them create more effective term papers and essays.

- Compare-and-contrast essay (also referred to as the informative/ classificatory essay)
- Persuasive essay (also referred to as the persuasive/descriptive essay)
- Descriptive essay (also referred to as the informative/descriptive essay)
- How-to essay (also referred to as the informative/narrative essay)

Compare-and-Contrast Essay

In this essay, students discuss likenesses and differences between two objects, persons, or ideas:

Examples

- Tell how your shirt is different from your partner's.
- Tell how you and your mom or dad think alike and how you think differently.
- Compare styles of music.
- Compare and contrast kinds of movies.
- Tell how subtraction and division are alike and different.
- Tell how one problem-solving technique is different from another.
- Tell how SimCity and SimAnt are alike and different.
- Tell how flowers and trees are alike and different.
- Compare and contrast the respiratory and circulatory systems.
- Compare and contrast sailboats with ocean cruisers.
- Compare and contrast the British soldiers and the colonial soldiers.
- Tell how the villain and hero in your story are alike and different.

Idea Share

When doing a compare-and-contrast essay with a novel or when using sources of information, be sure your students support their statements with a citation of the source used and the page number. We need to teach students early on how to support their opinions with information from the story or source. (see Figure 8.3 on the next page.)

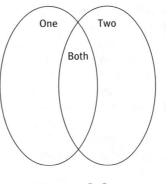

Figure 8.3

A fun way to organize a compare-and-contrast essay is to use yellow, green, and blue cards. Write information about one object on yellow cards. Write information about the other object on blue cards. Write their shared characteristics on the green cards (because yellow and blue make green). This provides excellent visual organization.

As students prepare to write the essay, advise them to have an equal number of entries for each side so the essay will not be lopsided. In addition, have them write in the page numbers from the text or story where they found words or events to support these characteristics.

The "Graphic Organizer for a Compare-and-Contrast Essay" at the end of the chapter is useful to students as they prepare to write this essay.

What do I look for in a compare-and-contrast paper?

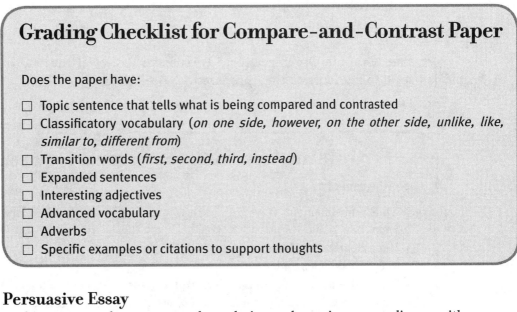

Grading Checklist for Compare-and-Contrast Paper

Does the paper have:

☐ Topic sentence that tells what is being compared and contrasted
☐ Classificatory vocabulary (*on one side, however, on the other side, unlike, like, similar to, different from*)
☐ Transition words (*first, second, third, instead*)
☐ Expanded sentences
☐ Interesting adjectives
☐ Advanced vocabulary
☐ Adverbs
☐ Specific examples or citations to support thoughts

Persuasive Essay

In this essay, students must make a choice and convince an audience with reasons.

Examples

- Should girls be allowed to play on the football team?
- Should students wear uniforms to school?

- Should students be allowed to use a calculator on math tests?
- Should students provide their own art supplies?
- Any concerns in the local or global community such as recycling, garbage dumps, nuclear war, war on terrorism.
- Any concerns in the school.
- Mini-persuasive writings: why I should be allowed to go to the library, to the bathroom, to see another teacher, or why I shouldn't have to do homework. This is the hardest purpose for students and the one often not given enough in class for practice. Mini-persuasive writings may help students learn how to offer solid reasons with support for choices.

Give a checklist to students that shows what elements you expect to see in their persuasive essay. You can also use the checklist to help you with the grading process:

- Position statement
- Introduction
- Three clearly stated reasons
- Specific examples and support for each reason
- Elaboration phrases (*as well as, one example, for instance, in addition*)
- Persuasive vocabulary (*obviously, clearly, noticeably, stands to reason, unmistakably, evidently, glaringly, plainly*)
- Transition words (*therefore, in conclusion, for example, nevertheless, another*)
- Interesting adjectives
- Specific verbs

The "Graphic Organizer for a Persuasive Essay" at the end of the chapter is useful to students as they prepare to write this essay.

Grading Checklist for Persuasive Essay

Does the paper have:

☐ A position statement
☐ An introduction
☐ Three clearly stated reasons
☐ Specific examples under each reason
☐ Elaborative phrases (*as well as, one example, for instance, additionally*)
☐ Persuasive vocabulary (*obviously, plead, visible, distinct, confidence, sincerely*)
☐ Transition words (*therefore, in conclusion, for example, nevertheless, another*)
☐ Interesting adjectives
☐ Specific verbs

Descriptive Essay

In a descriptive essay, students describe an object, picture, or event for an audience.

Examples

- Objects from a particular period in history
- Characters from a book
- Objects from a particular area in science
- A day in your life or in someone else's life
- Geometric figures
- An embarrassing event
- Historical or famous people
- An alternative setting for a book

Give a checklist to students that shows what elements you expect to see in their essay (also see the "Graphic Organizer for a Descriptive Essay" at the end of the chapter). Students need to know what is expected of them. Also, you can use the checklist to help you with the grading process:

- A topic sentence that tells the reader what is being described
- Location words (*up, down, below, above, next to, left, right, behind, in front of, beside, around*)
- Time words (*first, second, then, next, after that, finally*)
- Interesting adjectives (*radiant, sparkling, streaming, graceful, tinkling, delicate, gentle, ridged, cuddly, glistening*)
- Vivid verbs
- Specific examples for elaboration
- Use of the five senses (touch, taste, smell, sight, sound)
- Comparisons to other objects (*closer to, farther from, bigger than, smaller than, brighter than*)
- Use of adverbs (*slowly, quickly, intently, softly*)
- Metaphors and similes

Fun descriptive activities can also be used to prompt ideas for this essay:

- Give each student a peanut or apple, and have them describe it in an essay so that another person can identify it. Collect the essays and pass them back randomly. Which students can identify the correct peanut or apple from the description?
- Put an object in a bag, and have students describe it by touch only. What description came the closest to being complete?
- Have students sit together in pairs, with their backs to each other. One partner reads a description of an object and the other partner draws the picture of the object using the description as a guide.

Grading Checklist for a Descriptive Essay

Does the paper have:

- ☐ A topic sentence that tells what is being described
- ☐ Location words (*up, down, below, above, next to, left, right, behind, in front of, beside, around*)
- ☐ Interesting adjectives (*radiant, sparkling, streaming, graceful, tinkling, delicate, gentle, ridged, cuddly, glistening*)
- ☐ Interesting verbs
- ☐ Specific examples through elaboration
- ☐ Use of the five senses (how it smells, looks, feels, tastes, sounds)
- ☐ Comparisons to other objects (larger or smaller, thinner or fatter)
- ☐ Use of adverbs

How-To Essay

In a how-to essay, students write a sequence of steps on how to do something for an audience. See the "Graphic Organizer for a How-To Essay" at the end of the chapter.

Ideas for Practice Essays

Everyday activities:

- How to make a peanut butter and jelly sandwich
- How to bake a chocolate cake
- How to make a juice smoothie
- How to clean up the kitchen after dinner
- How to make a bed using military standards
- How to clean up your room

Teaching manuals and self-help essays:

- How to become a successful . . . (student, parent, teacher, friend)
- How to lose weight
- How to build muscle mass
- How to eat healthy

Humorous essays:

- How to be a failure at anything
- Five steps to losing your boyfriend
- Becoming a social outcast in ten easy steps
- How to befriend an alien
- How to teach a lion to dance

Subject area–related:

- How to locate a city using latitude and longitude
- How to solve a math problem
- How to create an explosion by mixing chemical elements
- How to perform a science experiment
- How to stay safe in a science lab

What Do I Look for in a How-To Essay?

- A topic sentence that tells the reader what is being done or made. What is the goal for this essay?
- Creative adverbs (*usually, slowly, lavishly, astonishingly, loudly*)
- Specific examples (materials, techniques, time frames)
- Interesting adjectives (describe persons, places, things using colorful, vivid language)
- Interesting verbs (not *run,* but *sprint!*)
- Phrases and clauses (begin with *which, that, who*)
- Other interesting vocabulary (uses content-specific vocabulary)
- Time-order words (*first, next, then, last*)

Grading Checklist for a How-To Essay

Does the paper have:

- ☐ A topic sentence that tells what is being done or made
- ☐ Creative adverbs (usually end in *-ly*)
- ☐ Specific examples (materials, techniques)
- ☐ Interesting adjectives (describing persons, places, or things)
- ☐ Interesting verbs (for example, *sprint* instead of *run*)
- ☐ Phrases and clauses (Begin with *which, that, who*)
- ☐ Other interesting vocabulary (content specific)
- ☐ Time-order words (*first, second, next, then, last*)

The following is a sample lesson written by a PE teacher to integrate reading and writing skills into his class. Although it is not a common occurrence for students to read and write when they go to the school gym, it is important for all school teachers to show they value reading and writing as important aspects of life. Even football players need to be capable of reading coaches' plays and plans! All areas of life require reading and writing skills!

Sample Lesson to Integrate Reading and Writing Skills into a Physical Education Class

Objectives:	Students will be able to use note-taking skills to read and research about Olympic athletes.
	Students will be able to use reading strategies of selecting main idea, sequencing, and finding supporting details throughout note taking.
	Students will be able to identify steps to becoming an Olympic athlete.
	Students will be able to write a formal business letter.
Material:	Video clips of Olympic athletes, TV and VCR, books and other print resources such as magazines on Olympic athletes and the Olympic Games, Computers with Internet and CD-ROM access, encyclopedias, paragraph on transparency to use to teach note-taking skills, clear transparencies to practice note-taking format, index cards, transparency of proper business letter format for letter writing, paper and pencils
Anticipatory set/attention getter:	1. Show the students video clip highlights of Olympic athletes. Most of the footage is of athletes participating in Olympic Games. Some are performing their sport during the games, some are in training, some are receiving medals, and others are in commercials.
	2. Discuss and brainstorm with students the following: "What does it take to become an Olympic athlete?" Begin a K-W-L chart to record "what we know" about becoming an Olympic athlete. Examples are hard work, dedication, ability, money.
	3. Review the K-W-L chart. Have students brainstorm questions to put in the "want to know" section. Examples: How do competitors get to the game? How do they get the money to train?
	4. Explain objectives to students: to research information and take notes on how they might become an Olympic athlete, then to write a formal business letter requesting help in their steps to obtaining their goal: gold medal!
	5. Mini-lesson on note taking.
	6. Students begin researching information individually and in groups on how a person becomes an Olympic athlete. Students should be recording the source information and taking notes on index cards.

Closure for day:	Have students explain different steps for taking notes from a source. Ask students to tell one new thing they learned about the Olympics today.
Homework:	"Tonight think about which Olympic sport you would like to participate in. Pretend you have mastered the sport and are ready to go to the Olympics. We will use this in tomorrow's lesson."

Continue lesson on day 2

Anticipatory Set:	Read a silly (though appropriate) letter from *Letters from a Nut* or a silly letter asking for donations. Ask students: How do you think a business would respond to this letter? If you were in charge of donating money, would you give this person any?
Procedures:	1. Put transparency of proper letter on overhead. Discuss with students. Identify the parts of the letter (heading, body, closing), and go over expectations for the activity (what you expect their letter to look like).

2. Students write first draft of their letter asking for a sponsor to help them get to the Olympics. |
| **Check for understanding:** | Monitor students work as they research and observe. Help as needed.

Ask students to share their information periodically while monitoring them.

Monitor students while writing letters. Help as needed.

Have students read letters aloud before writing final draft. Student correct errors as heard. |
| **Closure:** | Have students go to the chart and fill in one item they learned about becoming an Olympic athlete. Read them and discuss. |
| **Assessment of learning:** | Collect notes taken during research. Did students follow the correct format? Evaluate student understanding of main idea and supporting details (Texas Assessment of Knowledge and Skills) through notes.

Use rubric to grade the final draft of student letters. Grade content, correct knowledge, creativity, and neatness. |

Source: Thanks to Juddson Smith, physical education coach, Plano ISD, Plano, Texas, for sharing this lesson plan with us.

Conclusion

Reading and writing are skills that have importance in all courses. They are important in student lives daily and must be practiced in all subject areas. The more students practice reading and writing, the more proficient they will become. This is especially true of those learning the English language. The more we encourage the use of reading and writing skills in all classes, the more students will begin to see the importance of the written language in their lives. Many students feel that reading and formal writing are important only for their language arts classes. It is up to us to show them that architects, scientists, mathematicians, and others must be able to write formal papers and understand what their colleagues have written in journal articles and other types of reading text. The best way we can do this is by pointing out how we use reading and writing in our course requirements. Just think what can be accomplished when students are actively reading and writing in every class.

Reference

Atwell, Nancie. *In the Middle: Writing, Reading, and Learning with Adolescents*. Portsmouth, N.H.: Heinemann, 1993.

Web Site Resources

The Grammar Lady, http://www.aacton.gladbrook.iowapages.org/id3.html
Spelling City, http://www.spellingcity.comå
Creative Writing for Teens, http://fictionwriting.about.com
Research Paper Assistance, http://www.researchpaper.com
Journaling Life, http://www.journalinglife.com/
The Classics Archive, http://classics.mit.edu

Beginning Book Study

Each six weeks you will be required to complete a book study. During this book study you will read a novel of at least 100 pages and complete the activities below. This project is due _____
_____. If you read more than one novel of 100 pages or more, you may choose one of the books to use when completing the activities below:

1. Illustrate a scene from your book on the front of a paper bag with the title and author's name.

2. Write a summary of your book. Make sure you include the title, author's name, and the number of pages you read. The summary should be at least one page. Remember that a summary includes the main idea with some details from the book.

3. If you could give this book a different title, what would it be? Write your title for the book and why you think it should be named that on a slip of paper, and put it in your bag.

Book Bonanza

During this unit, you are to read a novel. After you have finished the novel, you will be responsible for completing the following activities.

This book study is due _____.

1. Write a summary of your book. Make sure you include the title, the author's name, and the number of pages read. Remember that a summary is the main idea and some details. Focus on major events that affect the characters or story.

2. Create a small vocabulary book. Choose five new words from your book. Write each word in bold letters (using a marker) on its own page, along with the definition and your own sentence using the word correctly. Then draw a picture of the word in a way that helps you visualize what it means. Try to think of creative ways to make your book!

3. Create a map of the important locations in your novel. Use a key with symbols to explain your map.

4. Project: Choose one of the following, or have your own idea approved by me:

   • Create a game based on your novel.
   • Write a play script based on a scene in your novel.
   • Make a mobile depicting the characters and setting.
   • Act out a scene from your novel.
   • Write a song based on your novel.
   • _____.

Prewriting Notes

Prewriting is the process of gathering ideas. There are five types:

- Freewriting. Write without stopping. Don't worry about spelling or punctuation. Just get your thoughts down.

- Jot list. List everything that comes to your mind about a topic.

- Webbing. Insert your topic in the center, and organize your ideas using a web as shown here.

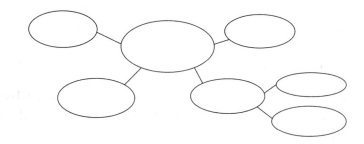

- Mind mapping. This is just like a web except you draw pictures instead of writing out the ideas.

- Looping. After freewriting, pick one important idea, circle it, and use it to start the next freewriting exercise.

Global Response

Writer/Reader

- Read your own story out loud to one or two partners. Be sure to speak clearly.
- You may correct mistakes you see as you read your story.
- While you read your story, your partners should be taking notes by filling out the following form:

  I think this story is about _____.

  What I especially like _____.

  I was wondering _____.

- Write down all comments made by the listeners on the margins of your story.
- Underline things the listener especially liked.
- Write down all questions in the margins.

Listeners

- Listen to the story carefully
- While you are listening, jot down specific words, phrases, or other things that you liked or were confused about. Write down questions about the story.
- After the writer has finished reading the story, tell him or her your comments out loud. Do not simply give the writer your sheet; say what you thought about the story.

When the first person is finished reading and all comments have been made and written down, it is the next person's turn.

Classrooms that Spark!

Revising a Story

A—Add details to your story. Use a caret ^ to add words.

R—Remove words, phrases, or sentences that are not needed, and strike out words you don't need.

M—Move words, phrases, sentences, or paragraphs around. Circle the words or phrases you want to move.

S—Substitute exciting words for boring words. Cross out the word and write the change over it.

In addition:

- Try to answer questions from other students or the teacher.

- You may need to revise your story more than once.

- A revised paper should look messy with arrows, carets, circles.

Graphic Organizer for a
Compare-and-Contrast Essay

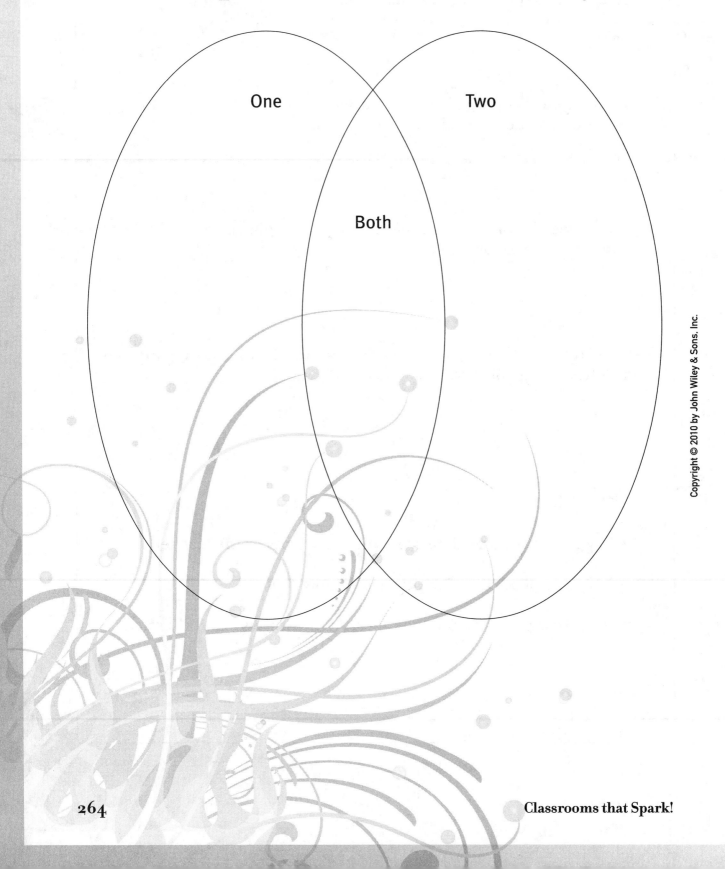

One

Two

Both

Classrooms that Spark!

Graphic Organizer for a Persuasive Essay

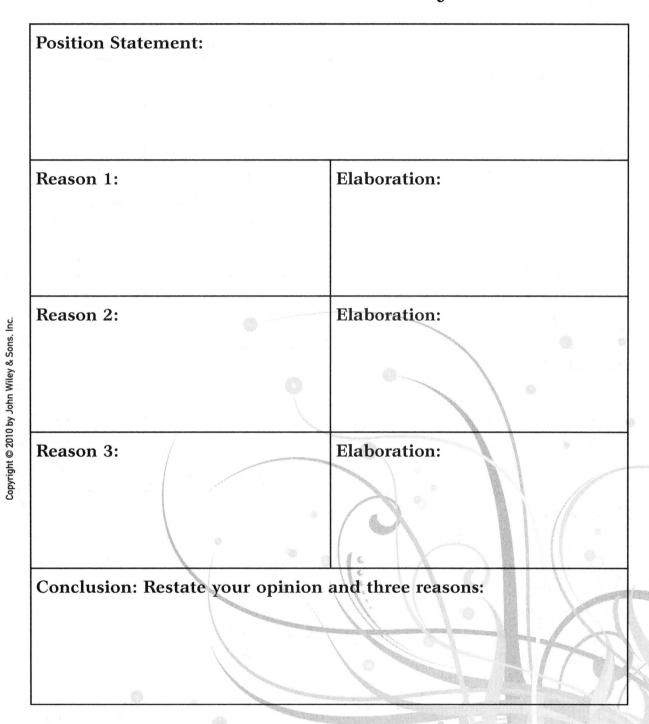

Position Statement:	
Reason 1:	Elaboration:
Reason 2:	Elaboration:
Reason 3:	Elaboration:
Conclusion: Restate your opinion and three reasons:	

Elaboration: Each point should be elaborated with a story illustrating a specific example, a quote, or statistics and data.

Graphic Organizer for a Descriptive Essay

	Object 1	Object 2	Object 3
Adjectives			
Vivid verbs			
Location and movement			
Looks like			
Sounds like			
Feels like			
Smells like			
Tastes like			
Metaphor			
Simile			

Graphic Organizer for a How-To Essay

Introduction
Step 1
Step 2
Step 3
Step 4
Step 5
Step 6
Step 7
Conclusion

Recharging Your Math Lessons

How do you light a fire in students to want to learn math? How can you make math interesting and fun and integrate it with other subject areas? These are questions we all struggle with each year as we strive to light that fire of learning in our students.

When trying to rekindle math lessons, think about your main math objectives for the year. How can you integrate some of these skills into other subject areas? For example, averaging and graphing skills can be used in science and social studies lessons. You could teach these skills during math and then apply them in an appropriate science or social studies unit.

Next, tackle the math textbook, released standardized tests, and other subject themes to develop a plan for teaching math concepts. Remember that you do not have to follow the textbook page by page. Teach math how it makes sense to you.

In this chapter, we offer tips to try throughout the year to make teaching math a little more fun. We also outline a step-by-step strategy for teaching math concepts, as well as different ideas for integrating math with other subject areas. Two key points guide us here:

- Integrating math with other subject areas
- Using practical and real-world applications with the math skills being taught

Integrating Math Concepts

Integrate math concepts into other subject areas through maps, tables, graphs, measurement, cooking, banking, logical thinking, and so on. Many math concepts can be taught during history, economics, science, language arts, music, and geography as well.

Other Academic Areas

Here are some ways to work with math in other academic areas:

- Have students calculate distances on a map using a scale and a ruler. This is an exercise in fractions, as well as multiplication, division, addition, and subtraction.
- Have students work with music notes, rhythms, and scales to practice counting and patterns.
- Create bar graphs, pie charts, and line graphs to connect math skills to social studies and science.
- Have students use a line graph to chart the growth of plants in a science experiment.
- Have students use a pie chart to represent any number of historical trends, such as the percentages of national origins of the people living in the first thirteen colonies.
- Organize information for research projects in tables.
- Teach coordinate graphing while studying latitude and longitude on maps.
- Study and compare health statistics. Teachers can write to any number of organizations to get statistics: government offices, the American Heart Association, and the National Cancer Society, for example.
- Have students calculate their weights on different planets while studying space.
- While studying different countries, have students calculate how to exchange currency. This is a way to practice multiplication, decimals, and working with money.
- Students can design, build, and test computer-controlled motorized vehicles and robots through the LEGO Mindstorms sets. This leads students to seek out and use knowledge from a variety of domains: programming, physics, engineering design, and, most unexpectedly for students, mathematics. In this type of a project, students are acquiring knowledge for use—such as learning a language by growing up in its country—an experience quite unlike

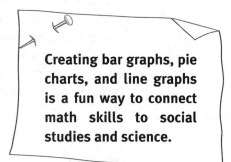

Creating bar graphs, pie charts, and line graphs is a fun way to connect math skills to social studies and science.

learning a language in order to pass a test. High-tech computerized model cars and other kinds of robotics are so rich in principles of mathematics that it is fun to apply the math. All children would be more enthusiastic to learn math if they met it in a context that is more alive than the ordinary paper-and-pencil curriculum.

Using Children's Literature

Use children's literature as a springboard to teach math. Bob Krech, author of *Meeting the Math Standards with Favorite Picture Books* (2002), offers ideas for teaching math in motivating ways. Among the titles he suggests are *How Much Is a Million?* by Ed Wiseman, *Counting on Frank* by Rod Clement, and *Sir Cumference and the First Round Table* by Cindy Neuschwander.

Idea Share

Books that incorporate real life and math are fun to share with students and contain examples of everyday math. Two books we've used are *The I Hate Mathematics Book* by Linda Allison and *Math Curse* by Jon Scieszka.

Games to Teach Math Skills

Teach math through activities and games. Don't be afraid to let the students play and have fun with these. Learning is still occurring.

- Cooking teaches measurement and fractions. Asking the students to double or halve a recipe teaches equivalent fractions.
- When teaching measurement, have a scavenger hunt for objects of different sizes around the classroom. You could do this in metric or standard units of measurement, or both if you were comparing the two.
- Have students practice coordinate graphing with art projects that require grids, such as cross stitching. You could also play "location race" by using maps with grids or using latitude and longitude.
- Have students go to their favorite store and list items they would like to purchase. They write down the cost of the item, any percentage discounts for items on sale, and the sales tax, if any. They can bring this information back to class, and you can use it to teach percentages, adding and subtracting decimals, estimating, and other calculations.
- Have students plan a fun trip to a place they'd like to visit. They need to develop a budget, determine distances on a map, figure out the time it takes to travel certain distances, and understand how to exchange money, for example.

- Many games require math skills including card games, dice games, Dominoes, Monopoly, and Life. Also, games such as MasterMind teach logical thinking skills, which help with math concepts.
- You can also find books of math games to play as a class. One example is *Mega-Fun Math Games* by Michael Schiro (1995).

Math with Holidays and Special Events

Create math problems and projects that relate to holidays and special events throughout the year. Word problems are a great way to do this.

Examples

- During Halloween, pumpkins are usually marked up in price at least 50% due to the demand for them. If in August a pumpkin that weighed 15 pounds costs $8.00, how much does that pumpkin cost on October 30?
- Last month Julie attended 4 professional football games. The tickets cost $44.75 each. She even got to see the Green Bay Packers play the Dallas Cowboys! How much did she spend on game tickets?
- At the grocery store in which Bobby shops, turkeys for Thanksgiving cost $1.89 a pound. If Bobby buys a 10-pound turkey, what will it cost?
- Kelly loves to make new friends. She has made 4 new friends each year for 5 years in a row. If Kelly received 2 flowers on Valentine's Day for every new friend, how many flowers did she receive?

Some of these word problems have extraneous information. This is an important lesson to teach students because problems on standardized tests often have extraneous information.

Day-long math projects centered around a holiday theme can also spark interest.

Example: Spend the day studying the mathematics of a pumpkin. Make sure to plan in advance with the cafeteria staff and your principal before you embark on this adventure.

- Measure the circumference and diameter of the pumpkin.
- Estimate how many seeds will be inside. Cut open the pumpkin and pull out the insides, including the seeds. This will be very messy, so ask students to bring large t-shirts or use art smocks to keep clothes clean. Give each student group a cookie sheet and a portion of the pumpkin innards. Students pull out seeds and place them on the cookie sheet. Have the groups count their seeds and share with the class. Who made the closest estimation? Next, spray a little olive oil on the seeds and lightly salt them. Take them to the cafeteria to bake. This makes a tasty snack in the afternoon or you can send the baked seeds home in baggies.
- Bake pumpkin pies for the whole class. The important part of this lesson is following the recipe for making the pumpkin pies. Let each group of students make their own pie. Take these to the cafeteria to bake.
- In making the pies, the measuring cups are a great way to explore fractions, and then the pies themselves can be used for a fractions lesson.

Relating Math to Students

When you are writing word problems, you can spark interest in them in several ways. One is to use your students' names. You can also make up funny stories and situations and include objects, famous people, and ideas that appeal to students.

Idea Share

Many students love hearing their name or, better yet, your name, in math word problems. This simple act can make word problems fun and motivating for students. Do you have a favorite hobby that would work well in a math word problem? Use real-life events to make word problems more meaningful to students.

Other Ideas for Relating Word Problems to Students
- Sports and sports celebrities
- Popular toys
- Trendy clothes and trends
- Popular celebrities
- TV shows and cartoons
- Cars
- Candy
- Music

Another way to appeal to students is to use pop culture in math lessons:

- *Sports. Sports Illustrated for Kids* often includes statistics and other data that can be used to introduce, apply, or enhance a lesson. Students can also compare and contrast different scoring methods. How are these methods implemented? What different kinds of math are needed to compute the scores or statistics?
- *Olympics.* Have students graph the number of medals won by different countries.
- *Racing.* This is the perfect sport for learning about time, distance, velocity, speed, and other math skills.
- *Celebrity magazines.* What is the net worth of different celebrities? Introducing place value when looking at celebrity income would be fun. How would you plot the place value for Oprah's yearly income? Compare and contrast salaries to show range, mean, median.
- *Television ratings.* Average and compare and contrast ratings for TV shows. Movies can be compared using their gross opening earnings. This information can be graphed or shown in other types of data charts.

- *Fashion.* Measurement skills, circumference, and other geometry skills can be studied through fashion. How do designers design their clothes? What are some common shapes used for different types of outfits? How do tailors take three-dimensional measurements, two dimensional-fabric, and create clothes for us to wear?

Moment of Reflection

What math strategies have worked for you in the past? Why were these successful? What are some different ways you can incorporate math skills into other academic areas for your grade level? What were your favorite board games when you were growing up? How can you use these activities in your math class?

Math Teaching Strategy

We have taught math concepts that combine various theories on the best ways to teach math. This strategy has three stages:

1. Visual and tactile concrete modeling
2. Math notebook
3. Real-world applications

Stage 1: Visual and Tactile Concrete Modeling

This stage encompasses the hands-on approach to teaching math. Introduce a new concept using manipulative pieces, models, diagrams, patterns, games, or student movement and involvement. Concrete models help children understand abstract ideas. You need to teach them to understand how numbers and relationships work, not just give them the rules of mathematics. Models allow students to have a visual picture, which can aid their comprehension. It is important in this stage to guide students in their learning through questions and prompts.

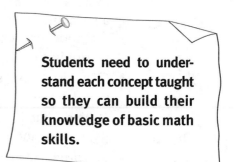

Students need to understand each concept taught so they can build their knowledge of basic math skills.

Examples of Guiding Questions
- What observations can you make?
- Compare and contrast these models.

- That is a good way to show this problem. But there is more than one way to solve a problem, so try to think of other possibilities.

- Can you explain how you solved that problem?

- Explain your reasoning.

- What were your thought processes while you were working on that?

- What will you do next?

Tips for the Hands-On Phase

This is a thought-provoking stage. Asking probing questions and having students make observations is the key to this stage. It will not feel comfortable for some students at first (some prefer paper-and-pencil activities), but all students benefit from concrete models.

Don't rush to correct students if they are not solving or demonstrating something correctly. Wait to see if they can figure it out on their own. If they are not anywhere near the correct answer, help them get back on track.

Encourage curiosity, logical thinking and reasoning, and expression of ideas. Allow students to verbalize their ideas and discover with each other.

Manipulative pieces and concrete modeling do not have to be expensive or fancy. Use common household items and things found in school—for example:

egg cartons	fruit	small candies
dried beans	straws	coffee stirrers
round oat cereal	popcorn	plastic interlocking bricks
blocks	plastic animals	marbles

Be sure to allow time for reflection of the student learning experiences before leaving this stage of teaching a math concept. If you are using rotating centers with math manipulative pieces, give students two or three minutes before switching to write their findings and describe what they did in their math journal.

Here are some examples of how you can use concrete modeling in your classroom:

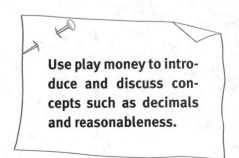

Use play money to introduce and discuss concepts such as decimals and reasonableness.

- If you are introducing decimals, let children work with play money. Ask them probing questions about the value of a dollar in comparison to twenty cents, seven cents, one dollar, and thirty cents. For example, you can have students demonstrate equal values, using different money pieces, for example: three dimes = thirty pennies = six nickels.

- When teaching the signs for "greater than" and "less than," have students participate in the lesson. Have several students stand at the front of the room. More students should be standing on one side than on the other. Either the teacher or another student is a "hungry alligator" in the middle. Which side would the alligator want to eat? The most people, of course! So the big open alligator mouth always faces the bigger number.

- If you are teaching multiplication principles to younger students, use colored tiles, rainbow cubes, dried kidney beans, or anything else that can be used to count in large numbers. Lead the students to discover that $3 \times 5 =$ three groups of five. Count (or add) them all up, and they equal 15. Practice this concept many times before moving on to the mathematical symbols. Students can actually see how multiplication works to support the facts they must learn.

- If you are introducing equivalent fractions, bring in egg cartons and cotton balls. Using the cotton balls, have the students show you what 6 out of 12 looks like, and then have them tell you how much of the egg carton is full. They should say half. This will prompt a discussion of how $1/2 = 6/12$. You can then ask the students to divide the carton up into three equal parts using yarn or markers, which allows you to discuss thirds.

As a kindergarten teacher, I used the alligator idea to help my little ones understand the concepts of greater than and less than. Each one loved to be the alligator and wanted to 'gobble up' as many people as possible. I would stand back and count each side of the room. Then I would ask the 'alligator,' 'Which side do you want to eat?' They, of course, would always pick the bigger side. 'Yes,' I would say, 'when we have two groups of numbers, the alligator always wants to eat the larger number.' Then we would practice on paper what we did as a class. I think the parents were really impressed that their little ones learned this concept so easily!

- Think about using oranges when teaching fractions. Peel the orange, and talk about how the whole orange is broken into sections. As you separate the segments, have students count them aloud and record the total number. Give students different segments and talk about how the students have two-tenths, four-tenths, and five-tenths. Which student has more of the orange?

- Another way to help introduce or conceptualize fractions is by cutting up drinking straws into equal parts. Oranges, egg cartons, straws, and

Classrooms that Spark!

any type of candy can be used to teach division as well. What other types of food can you use to teach math concepts?

Don't refrain from using manipulative pieces with older students. You can still introduce math concepts with models or manipulative pieces. If you are teaching geometry, you can use pattern blocks (different colored and sized blocks that form varying geometric shapes). Have students explore the many different sides and angles, teach perimeter with them, find equivalent shapes, and so on.

Using Manipulative Pieces in the Classroom

Let students explore with the manipulative pieces prior to starting your lesson. If you do not let them play before you expect them to listen, you will find that they are still playing and not listening. Actually, allowing students to explore is a learning experience in itself.

When the class is using manipulative pieces, monitor student behavior by walking around the room and asking probing questions to check for understanding. Listen to students and how they discuss and interact with one another regarding their observations. This can be a great springboard for your discussions.

Finally, provide time for students to record their thoughts in a math journal.

Idea Share

Set clear directions and expectations for students when working with manipulative pieces — or any other time students work in groups. Always review these expectations before you start the lesson or activity.

Ideas for the Primary Grades

These tips are geared to younger students:

- When looking at attributes of shapes, colors, and so on, use plastic hoops or baskets to sort items with similar attributes.

- For each shape, ask students to find as many of that shape in the classroom as possible. For example, with rectangles, students can identify windows, the whiteboard, or your desk. Have a treasure hunt to find different shapes in the room or a scavenger hunt that asks for one of each type of shape.

- Place mystery bags in a learning center, and put objects of different shapes in them. Students must feel the object without looking at it, guess the shape, and draw a picture of what they felt. This is a tactile activity for kids who learn kinesthetically.

- Play games such as Snap to match shapes or fruit salad with shapes instead of pieces of fruit.

- Use cookie cutters to cut out shapes from bread. You could also do this with cookie dough, and let the students decorate them before baking. You could also do this with play dough (but please don't let them eat it).

- Surround students with literature about shapes. Make a book about shapes with them using their own photos, drawings, and writing.

- Go for a walk around the school to find objects of different shapes and colors. The real world provides countless things to count and observe.

- Use beads and blocks to help students understand the concepts of units, tens, and hundreds.

Stage 2: The Math Notebook

In stage 2, students move from concrete models to the more abstract method of solving math equations using symbols. This can be used from second or third grade and up.

This is the more traditional way of teaching math by giving notes on how to solve a problem and allowing the students to practice in abundance. This method has been used for decades, and the children will continue to be exposed to this type of teaching for the rest of their school career.

Yes, we believe that giving notes and practice through paper-and-pencil activities is still important. As long as this method is used in conjunction with visual tools and real-life applications of math, the notes and practice part of teaching is vital.

The math notebook or math spiral is the center focus of this stage. Each student has a math notebook, which is separate from their student binder. You may choose to have students use a thick spiral notebook or a three-hole pocket folder with notebook paper inside. Set this up at the beginning of the year, and be consistent in using it all year. This notebook is for math notes and practice only.

Encourage your students to take their math notebook home every night to use as a guide in solving homework problems. Often your notes will be more helpful to them than the textbook.

This notebook is also an excellent reference for parents. By seeing how you have taught the skills, they will be better able to help their child with homework.

Once you have introduced a math concept with concrete models and exploration, the students are ready to move into solving problems using symbols. For some students, this will come as a relief: they are more accustomed to being given the steps for how to solve a problem and working out math problems on paper. Other students find this method boring and not as easily understandable.

Students need to understand that both of these stages in teaching math are equally important.

Using the Math Notebook

- Give step-by-step instructions on how to solve each math problem on the overhead, whiteboard, or document camera. Students should copy these notes into their math notebook. (See example page of notes following.) Use abundant examples of problems solved correctly.

- Provide opportunities for independent practice problems in their notebook after you have given notes and done several sample problems as a class. Always correct practice problems in their notebook as a class before moving on. This way, the students do not use incorrect information when doing homework.

- The students should have a contents page at the beginning of their notebook and make a new entry every time a new concept is taught.

- Monitor the students, and insist that they copy everything down in their math spiral or notebook. This is not a selective exercise where the students copy down what they want to. They copy everything, so you know that they have all the steps and notes.

- The math notebook is much more successful in teaching a concept than using just the textbook even if you get your notes from the text. You can add information and steps to help your students learn, because you know what they need more than anyone.

- When giving math notes, using an overhead projector is easier than writing them on a chalkboard. You can prepare the notes ahead of time and then reveal the transparency to the students a bit at a time.

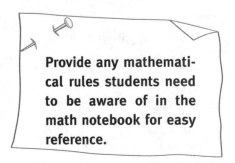

Provide any mathematical rules students need to be aware of in the math notebook for easy reference.

Adding Whole Numbers

Step 1	**Step 1**
Add the ones/units. If total equals ten or more, write the "tens" unit at the top of the Tens block (*Regroup*).	Th H T o ① 1 3 4 **2** + 7 8 **9** — — — — — **1**
Step 2	**Step 2**
Add the tens. If total equals ten or more, write the "tens" unit at the top of the hundreds block (*Regroup*).	Th H T o ①**1** 1 3 **4** 2 + 7 **8** 9 — — — — — **3** 1
Step 3	**Step 3**
Add the hundreds. If total equals ten or more, write the "tens" unit at the top of the thousands block (*Regroup*).	Th H T o ①1 1 1 **3** 4 2 + **7** 8 9 — — — — — **1** 3 1
Step 4	**Step 4**
Add the thousands. Write the total number under the thousands, and if necessary the ten-thousands block.	Th H T o **1** 1 1 **1** 3 4 2 + 7 8 9 — — — — — **2,** 1 3 1
Step 5	**Step 5**
Rewrite the total.	Answer is 2,131

Stage 3: Practical Applications

Once you have taught the students the concept and skills necessary to solve a particular type of math problem, you must make that skill meaningful for them. They need to be capable of applying that skill in real life. The key to this section is word problems and scenarios. They offer real-life situations, and the students must be able to solve the problem using the skills and concepts you taught them. This keeps your math instruction from dealing with rote memory and forces the students to use reasoning and their newly acquired skills.

Use real-world scenarios such as grocery shopping, cooking, figuring the tip for a restaurant meal, and sales tax, for example, to apply math skills and motivate students.

Tips for Real-World Math

- Bring ads and catalogues to class. Make up questions or word problems so that the students have to use these items to solve your problem.

  Examples

  - *To apply multiplication with decimals and practice working with percentages:* Find something that you would like to buy, and pretend that the store is having a 25% off sale. Calculate the new sales price of your item. Now add the 8.25% sales tax. What is the total price? How much money, in whole dollars, will you have to take to the store in order to buy this item?
  - *Apply addition and subtraction:* If you buy 5 apples for your teacher, on sale for 25 cents each in the grocer's ad, how much will the total cost be? How much change will you have if you pay with a $10.00 bill?

- Have students plan a trip to a destination of their choice and figure the costs and mileage. Older students can plan a trip to Europe to visit World War II battlefields or monuments or for a summer trip, an exercise that includes exchanging money as well.

- Let older students plan a class party given a certain budget.

- Have students design and build an invention or object using a variety of materials. They will need to use correct measurements in their design and apply those measurements when building their object.

- Explore careers in which math plays a prominent role: architecture, construction, engineering, catering, or owning a large or small business, for example. Explore the math associated with them.

- Use computer-aided design to design a home, office, or other building.

Solving Math Word Problems

Standardized tests are moving more and more toward real-life types of word problems. Many students can solve math equations, but have difficulty in reading and decoding what they are supposed to do in a word problem. Here is a refresher on teaching students how to solve word problems.

When solving a word problem, it is important to follow the steps needed to find the correct answer:

1. Read the whole question from beginning to end. Don't assume you know how to solve the problem without reading the entire question.

2. Reread the question and box key words. Some key words are:

total	product	sum
difference	more or less	each
how much	how many	altogether

3. Underline the question part of the problem. Think: What is this question asking for?

4. Determine the operation needed to solve the problem, and write it next to the question.

5. Cross out extraneous information—information that is not needed! Don't let anyone fool you!

6. Circle the numbers needed to solve the problem.

7. Write a number sentence next to the problem.
   Example: 58 − 9

8. Solve the problem showing all your work.

9. Write the solution sentence.
   Example
   - 58 − 9 = 49
   - There are 49 white doves left in the sky.

10. Check your answer. Is it reasonable? Does it make sense?

For a multiple-choice test:

- Locate the answer in the answer choices.
- Determine why the other answer choices are not correct.
- Circle the correct answer bubble on the answer sheet.

Idea Share

Integrate a common language arts strategy, the word wall, into your math classroom. Post the math vocabulary commonly used in word problems and on a portable word wall (something as simple as a poster) as a reminder for students.

Sample Problems

1. Josie went to a bird-watching festival on Sunday. There were 200 people at the festival. The music started, and 58 white doves flew into the sky. Nine of the doves flew into a nest in the tree. How many doves were left flying in the sky?

   258 people   67 doves altogether   49 doves were left   209 doves were in the sky

2. The teacher received flowers for her birthday. She had 64 yellow flowers, 21 white flowers, and 17 red flowers. How many more yellow flowers did she have than white flowers?

   102   85   60   43

3. The zoo had 2 beautiful peacocks and 6 zebras. Each peacock weighs 21 pounds. What is the total weight of both peacocks?

   8 pounds   11 pounds   42 pounds   19 pounds

4. It took Chad and his mom 4 weeks and 2 days to sew some shirts. How many total days is this?

   28 days   30 days   8 days   22 days

5. A teacher had 22 students in her class. Five students made the honor roll. The teacher wanted to give each honor roll student the same number of bonus points. She had 55 bonus points to share equally among the honor students. How many will each student get?

110   275   11   5

6. Sea World opened in Houston, Texas, in 1989. Today Sea World has 45 dolphins, 18 sea lions, and 2 killer whales. How many sea mammals does Sea World have altogether?

63   65   47   20

7. It takes Jill and her mom 1 hour to water the plants in their garden. Each day of the week for 7 days, they water the garden. How many minutes does Jill water the garden in 1 week?

420 minutes   60 minutes   49 minutes   7 minutes

Following is a short example of how to teach a math concept using all three stages of our math strategy.

Sample Math Lesson: Graphing

This lesson should be taught over several days. You cannot cram the whole lesson into one hour! Do not tell the students what you are doing before you begin your lesson.

Begin by explaining that graphs represent data that have been collected and give this definition: A graph is a visual tool that makes it easier for us to see information. Then explain the four kinds of graphs:

- Pictograph: Uses pictures instead of numbers and uses a key. *Example:* 1 pair of shoes = 1 person
- Bar graph: Shows information by the height or length of the bars. Show a sample, and draw a bar graph with the students for their notes.

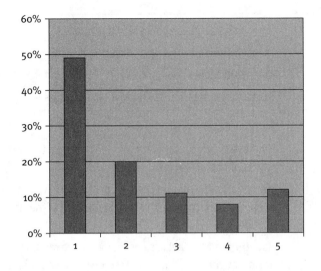

- Pie graph, also known as a circle graph: Shows how information is divided into parts of a whole.

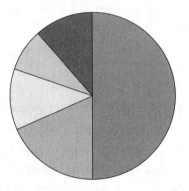

- Line graph: Uses dots and lines to show how things change and compare. Show a sample and draw a line graph with the students for their notes.

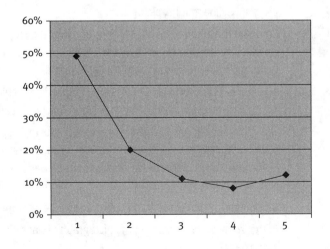

Objectives	To teach students the concept of a graph
	To teach students the four main types of graphs
	To teach students how to read and interpret different kinds of graphs
	To teach students how to create their own graphs
Stage 1: The Concrete Model	Birthday Graph
	Have every month of the year written neatly on twelve separate, rather large, sheets of paper. Prepare this before the lesson.
	Lay out all of the months of the year in order with some space between them, about 6 to 12 inches, on the floor in the front of the classroom, in the hallway, or outside.
	Have the students get in a line in front of the month their birthday falls. When they are in straight lines, have them remove their shoes and leave them in their place. Have all students stand back behind the pictograph and observe.
	Ask them if they know what they are looking at? (A pictograph)
	Have students draw the pictograph neatly on a piece of paper. They will need to sit on the floor where they can see it and they will not be able to put their shoes on yet.
	Have the students put on their shoes, clean up the papers, and return to their seats.
	Once all students are in their seats and have their drawn pictographs in front of them, have all students look at their graphs to discuss:
	What does each pair of shoes represent?
	What observations can we make by looking at this pictograph? Make them give specifics! Which month has the most birthdays in our class? Which month has the fewest? How many months have no class birthdays? How can you tell?
Stage 2: Math Notebook	Teach the concept of graphing.
	Give general information about graphs (Notes).
	Discuss, show samples, and give notes on different kinds of graphs: Bar graphs, pie graphs, line graphs, pictographs.
	Compare the different kinds of graphs and how they represent information differently. Are some graphs easier to read? Why? Would some types of graphs be better for representing certain types of data? Talk about specific examples.
	An excellent book on maps, charts, and graphs for teaching this graphing unit is *Maps, Charts, Graphs, and Diagrams* (1990 Teacher Created Materials, Inc.).
	You can make sample graphs on the computer using a spreadsheet program (like Microsoft Excel), or you can find graphs in newspapers, magazines, social studies and science texts. Show these graphs to the students and discuss them during your note giving.
	Demonstrate how to use graph paper, and make a sample graph as a class.
	Assign homework: To transfer the pictograph of class birthdays into a bar graph on graph paper.

Classrooms that Spark!

Stage 3: Practical Application

Study graphs and their use in real life.

Collect graphs from newspapers, magazines, and books. Copy them, and give samples to students to examine and discuss.

Ask the students to interpret and compare the information shown in the graph.

Have the students gather information of some sort and create their own graphs. Give a choice of graphs to create, but explain to the students that the kind of graph they choose must be useful for the type of information they are trying to represent.

Make sure the students consult their notes and samples for help in creating their own graphs.

Have students compare the birthday results in different graphs. Which graph best represents the information so we can understand it?

Moment of Reflection

What strategies from this chapter might you use to refresh your math lessons?

Conclusion

Teaching math is much more than skill and drill. Students must know the "whys" behind different concepts to understand and be able to apply these skills. Using manipulative pieces helps students begin with concrete visual examples that they can apply to abstract number equations. A math notebook will help keep students organized and offer a reference manual throughout the year. Finally, we need to help students understand how they will apply these skills to their lives in the real world. Real-world activities are not only motivating but also vital to completing the learning process.

References

Krech, Bob. *Meeting the Math Standards with Favorite Picture Books*. New York: Scholastic, 2002.
Schiro, Michael. *Mega-Fun Math Games*. New York: Scholastic, 1995.

Web Site Resources

Ask Dr. Math, http://mathforum.org/dr.math/dr-math.html
Math Forum, http://mathforum.org
Mrs. Glosser's Math Goodies, http://vvww.mathgoodies.com/
Eisenhower National Clearinghouse for Mathematics, http://www.goenc.com

Part Three

Fanning the Flames

*To waken interest and kindle enthusiasm is the
sure way to teach easily and successfully.*

—Tyron Edwards

*If what you're doing isn't working,
try something else!*

—NLP adage

Snap, Crackle, Pop

Ideas for Motivating Students

What do you do when the flames of your fire are burning low? This can happen quite frequently throughout the school year. The answer is to add some life to your fire: fan the flames! This can be tricky in the classroom. One of the most difficult aspects of teaching is motivating students. In fact, in his book *Choice Theory in the Classroom,* William Glasser (1998) states that trying to teach students who do not want to learn is impossible because they actively resist the teacher. The key, then, is motivating students to *want* to learn.

When you think about motivating students, it is important to first consider what is motivating to you. Most people are excited to learn new information about a topic that is meaningful or important to them personally. For a car enthusiast, everything that has to do with cars is meaningful and motivating. What topics are personally motivating to your students? That's your job to find out.

What else motivates people to learn new things? Survival is a motivation. Think about international students who are thrown into an English-speaking classroom or even an English Language Learners classroom where the teacher speaks only English. The survival instinct kicks in, and the student learns a new language in order to understand the new environment.

On the opposite end, what is not very motivating? Think about the times in your life when you were waiting in line, waiting to hear about that new job you want or to be accepted into a school, or perhaps waiting for an answer to a question. To sit and do nothing is not very motivating. We get restless, bored, stifled.

Now apply those thoughts to your classroom. Are your students given a purpose each day? Is there a meaningful purpose in each lesson? Or are your students merely warming a chair and desk day after day?

Listening to others, unless we are motivated to do so, is boring, boring, boring. Think about conversations you've had with people who were uninteresting or were talking way over your head. You may have felt like Charlie Brown listening to the adults in the cartoon. Do your students feel that way about you? Are you talking over their head? Are you going on and on about concepts your students would rather be experiencing?

Take a look at your lessons. How much talking on your part is involved? How much are students actively engaged in an activity that applies the concept? Reconsider your lecture and ask yourself, "Could I pull some of this information out and let the students learn it for themselves?" "Could I replace this part of the lecture with an activity that demonstrates the topic or concept instead?"

Ask whether your activities relate to the real world. For example, are your students just practicing their understanding of percentages, or are they applying it? A worksheet is easier for teachers, but using store flyers to figure sales prices (or original prices) of favorite items is more practical and motivational. Based on a student's allowance, how long would it take him or her to save for a coveted item? These activities require students to apply their knowledge (and can be used as an assessment), relate the concept to them personally, and are motivating.

The more engaged your students are, the more they will be motivated to learn. Engaging activities are ones where students must manipulate the information, skill, or concept in a variety of ways. This can include working in teams, discussion, projects, research, or creating a product. We've already discussed many of these ideas in more detail.

Now think about classes you've attended throughout your lifetime. Which ones do you remember as positive and motivating experiences? Which ones were so boring that you spent every minute counting the seconds until it was time to leave? Generally classes where the teacher or professor lectures or requires students to do meaningless work, busywork, or repetitive tasks are the most boring. Classes that get students actively involved in discovering their own learning and interacting with each other and that encourage respect between the teacher and students are the most motivating.

So what can you do? Come to class prepared with a variety of activities that will engage students in their own learning. If a lesson seems to be faltering or you notice a glazed-over look in their eyes, smile a big smile do a little dance, and pull out something different to capture their attention. Have you been doing all of the talking and action for the lesson? Think how you can get students involved instead.

The section below provides a list of the ideas and strategies described in detail throughout this book. It also offers additional ideas to help you engage and motivate students. Refer to them when you are planning lessons or pull them out as needed. The more actively involved your students are in the lesson, the more excited they will be about your classroom. In addition, students who are engaged and excited about their learning cause fewer discipline problems. So take a look at the following strategies and think about different ways you can make your students motivated and engaged each and every day!

Ideas and Strategies

About the Author
Have students add an About the Author section to their writing projects and assignments throughout the year. Begin by taking pictures of them using a digital camera. Then read aloud several different About the Author pages from a variety of books to give students an idea of what kind of information should be included in their paragraph. Next, have each student type a short paragraph in the third person about himself or herself and save it. Combine the picture with the paragraph, and include the title, "About the Author," centered at the top. Print these out, and students can add them to various projects and assignments.

Acting Out Main Events or Main Ideas
Get students up and moving by having them act out the main idea or main events of a reading passage. Get everyone participating by breaking up the chapter into sections and have each group act out their own section. These skits are fun for students to create and act out.

You can video the skits and show them to parents at open house.

Aliens in the Classroom
After teaching students a concept, check for understanding by having them write an explanation to an alien from outer space. You might even use a picture on the computer presentation station or interactive whiteboard to give students a picture of their alien.

Even better, let students draw their own alien, and then explain the concept on the back of their drawing. Encourage students to draw a different alien each time you do this activity. Think about awarding certificates for the aliens and explanations: for the ugliest alien, the cutest, the grossest, the clearest explanation, the most creative explanation, the simplest explanation, the wildest explanation, and so on.

This is also a way to review a previous skill and can be used across the curriculum.

Examples:

- Explain to your alien how to multiply two-digit numbers.
- Explain the scientific method to your alien.
- Explain how flowers grow to your alien.
- Explain how to get around town to your alien.

If you have a classroom set of computers, let students draw their alien using a paint program. The alien drawing can then be inserted into a Word document and the explanation typed below the picture. These can then be posted on your classroom Web site or wiki space so parents can view their child's drawing and explanation.

All About Me

As a bonding activity, pull some fun questions from the "Getting to Know Your Friends" e-mails that are passed around frequently. Be sure you choose appropriate questions for your students' age level. Students can answer these in small groups or pairs. Encourage them to elaborate their responses.

If you are studying graphing, use these questions as something different to graph than red T-shirts or blue shoes Some of these also make excellent journal prompts. Be sure to ask students to elaborate their answer.

Which Would You Choose and Why?

- Coke or Pepsi?
- Juice or milk?
- Mountains or beach?
- Shorts or jeans?
- Poetry or books?
- What was the last thing you ate?
- Who was the last person you talked to?
- What nickname does your family call you?
- What is your middle initial?
- What's your favorite kind of car? Color?
- What's your favorite food for dinner?
- Dog or cat?
- Hot or cold?
- Fast or slow?
- Wii or PlayStation?
- Handwritten letters and notes or e-mail?
- What kind of pet do you dream of having?

Atlas Activities

When studying cultures or geography, pick out a different latitude and longitude for each student to locate. Have them look up information about that city, town, or country: average temperature, precipitation, foods, dwellings, customs, and other data pertinent to your curriculum. This is a good way to begin research on various cultures. It also makes a fine prereading activity to do as a class before learning about historical events in a particular region or country.

If you are using an interactive whiteboard, consider an online atlas for this activity. The following resources can be used to research information using an online atlas:

- www.atlapedia.com
- www.onlineatlas.us (an atlas of the United States)
- www.worldatlas.com

Here are some other atlas activities:

- *Atlas race.* Have students race against one another to locate various places in the world using an atlas. If you want to make this a competition, you can start with the entire class. Play five different games to get five different semifinalists. These students play two rounds to determine the two finalists. The last two players play one round to determine the champion.
- *Activities with novels.* When reading a story or novel, have students find the city, town, or country of the setting on a map. Discuss where it is located in relation to where the school is located. Older students can determine latitude and longitude to practice geography skills. Discuss the culture, environment, and weather of the area. How does this affect the story, if at all? Is the setting a true representation of this actual city/town/country?

    If the story has a make-believe setting, where is the author from? Does the story reflect the culture and weather of the author's home town?
- *Activities with other subject areas.* Identify historical events on the map. Where did this occur in relation to where you live? Identify the place of birth or residence of different scientists, mathematicians, artists, musicians, sports figures, and other famous people. How did the culture, history, geography, or weather of where these famous people live affect them?

Big and Bold

Students love anything different from regular paper-and-pencil activities, so give them a large piece of butcher paper and markers. Let them make life-sized time lines in history, graphs in science and math, solve problems, create storyboards, or brainstorm ideas. When they are studying health, trace their body. Hang these creations around the room to create stimulation for your visual learners.

Blogging

Assign a blog entry for homework instead of a paper-and-pencil task. Get students discussing a hot topic or criticize a statement that relates to the lesson taught that day, or have them post their answer to a particularly challenging math problem, a scientific dilemma, or a brainteaser. If you have a full set of computers in your classroom, ask a question and have students blog or tweet their response in class.

Brainstorming

Brainstorming provides students opportunity for input in class decisions and class discussions. It also offers a way for students to voice out loud what they already know (or think they know) and generate ideas for everyone to think about. Brainstorming is an excellent prewriting strategy, as well as a way to stimulate thinking when beginning a new concept. Jot lists can be done independently and then shared with the group. Be sure that every idea is valued and none ridiculed. It does not matter how impossible an idea might be; during brainstorming, everything is to be included. We want to encourage students to think creatively rather than conform to one way of thinking. You can use brainstorming to

- Generate writing topics
- Generate questions for interviews or research projects
- Generate questions to ask guest speakers
- Generate a list of items to look for when on a field trip
- Generate a list of questions to answer before reading the textbook
- Generate discussion topics

Brochure

A brochure is a great way for students to show their creativity. They can use it to market a time-travel vacation to convince people to travel back to a specific time period in history. Who will they see? Where will they go? What will they experience?

Have students plan a trip to anywhere in the world. What will they see? What route will they take? How many miles away is it? Will they need to fly? What is the cost? Where will they stay? Math concepts are integrated by figuring the cost of gas and other travel and setting a budget for food, lodging, and attractions. How much will the total trip cost? For older students, how long will each leg of the trip take when traveling X miles an hour? Also, if they were able to save X dollars each month, how long would it take them to save up for the trip?

Here are other possibilities:

- When students are studying a new math concept, have them make a travel brochure to "Problem-Solving Land" with tips on how to solve this type of math problem.
- When studying world cultures, have students make travel brochures to convince people to travel to different countries or promote their country of choice.
- When studying any concept, have students create a travel brochure to visit the "Land of . . ." (atoms, volcanoes, baseball, etc.) in which they explain information about that concept.
- Let students create their brochures on the computer using programs that allow students to import pictures into the final product.

Character Cards

Give each student card stock paper to divide into six rectangles and cut out. On each card, draw the character (or historical figure) on the front. On the back, write the name, important features or characteristics, contribution to history (or to the novel), and other important facts about the person. These cards can then be used to study for an upcoming assessment.

Charades

Give students an object, person, or concept being studied. The student must then get the other students to guess the object, person, or concept through charades. The first student to guess correctly goes next.

Children's Books

Children's books are an excellent way to introduce units and lessons. Everyone loves to be read to, even if older students won't admit it! If you're not sure how to introduce a particular concept or skill, see if you can find a children's book that can be used as a jumping-off point for your lesson. Here are a few ideas:

Dem Bones by Bob Barner—skeleton/body unit

Me and My Amazing Body by Joan Sweeny and Annette Cable—body unit

The True Story of the 3 Little Pigs by Jon Scieszka and Lane Smith—point of view

It was a Dark and Stormy Night by Janet and Allan Ahlberg—how to write a narrative

Sidewalk Math—real-life math

Brown Bear, Brown Bear by Bill Martin Jr. and Eric Carle—patterns

The Pain and the Great One by Judy Blume—point of view

UFO Diary by Satoshi Kitamura—point of view

Hand, Hand, Fingers, Thumb by Al Perkins and Eric Gurney—rhyming

Mr. Brown Can Moo by Dr. Seuss—onomatopoeia

Math Curse by Jon Scieszka and Lane Smith—real-life math

Stellaluna by Janell Cannon—bats

Magic School Bus by Joanna Cole and Bruce Degen—science

Powerful Picture Books: 180 Ideas for Promoting Content Learning by Cathy Puett Miller is an e-book that lists over 180 picture books and lesson ideas for using these in elementary, middle, and high school classes.

Comic Strips

Give students a comic strip template with predrawn squares for a three-, four-, or six-scene comic. Have students create their own comic with characters to

- Explain a concept they recently learned (this can be done in the middle of the unit or near the end and used as part of the assessment)
- Describe or promote a book they read
- Demonstrate a cause-and-effect sequence for an event they are studying
- Show sequencing for an event they are studying
- Describe or show the characteristics of a famous person
- Compare and contrast two topics, people, events, or concepts
- Summarize a story they have read
- Support or criticize a decision made in history or from current events
- Create a story starter (have students switch and use the comic to start a narrative piece)
- Summarize a plot or describe a theme, mood, or climax of a novel
- Interpret the results of an experiment or lab activity
- Show how to solve a problem or prove an equation

Primary students could use a very short one- to three-frame comic to explore writing.

You can also have students create these through interactive cartoon creation Web sites. These two Web sites offer predrawn graphics and a variety of other elements:

www.makebeliefscomix.com, created by Bill Zimmerman, which includes printables as well. This program is easy to use, which makes it perfect for younger students.

www.readwritethink.org/MATERIALS/COMIC, created by ReadWriteThink; offers a few more features and options than www.makebeliefscomix .com, which makes it perfect for older students.

Computer-Aided Design

Use a computer-aided design program to design a home, office, or other building. This is a great activity when studying geometry and physics.

Concept Boards

A way for students to share and display their work is a trifold concept board. These are great when working on experiments in science or doing book reports. They also come in handy when reviewing previous skills, and you can display them for parents at curriculum fairs and parent nights.

Concept boards do not have to be large. Students can create small trifold boards out of a half-sheet of poster board or even a third of a sheet. Once they've cut the poster board into segments, they fold the remaining portion into three sections.

Concept boards can also be used to create larger-than-life brochures depicting information and illustrations of a topic recently studied. Students can use these to present information gathered during a research project. Concept boards also work for showing off graphic organizers with information, objects that have been sorted into different categories, or different elements of a concept or skill.

Create mini-centers using the same concept. Write the title of the center across the top. In each section, write the directions for one activity. You can have up to six activities or one section of information to read and five activities for each center. Attach materials needed (if any) to the board using plastic bags with zipper locks stapled to the board. The center activities do not need to be complicated.

Use Bloom's taxonomy keywords to develop activities for each center: matching, labeling, puzzles, seek and find, writing activities, reading and responding activities, and small experiments, for example. These portable centers can be easily sorted and taken to a student's desk or placed on a table when used by a group. Use a plastic crate and hanging folders to organize the centers by category for easy student access.

Create a Commercial

Divide students into groups, and challenge them to create a commercial promoting an object, skill, or concept taught during your unit of study. Students must use props and can create "backgrounds" using butcher paper. Record the commercials using a video camera. Students love to watch themselves on TV.

Creating a World

Have students create their own city, town, or country. They exhibit geography skills by drawing a map. Be sure they include important elements such as the legend or key, landforms, or a grid system. Give students crazy shapes as the boundary lines for their country.

Get students up and moving by having them "survey" a boundary line across the playground or a school field. Have one student start at one end of the field and the other start at the other end of the field and walk toward one another. Using silly string, duct tape, or spray paint (if allowed), have the students work toward each other marking the "boundary." Do they meet up? What will they do to make the two lines meet together? How will they placate each side to make sure no one is getting more land than the other? If equipment or trees are included (natural resources) within the boundary lines, you could engage in a hearty discussion about land rights.

This actually happened when two surveyors began marking South Dakota's boundaries. One started from the north and the other from the south, supposedly each following the same meridian. They missed each other by about a mile.

> One fun activity our students enjoy is the volcano island unit. First we study about volcanoes and how they often form islands. Then we make volcanoes in class and do the fun 'explosion' with vinegar and baking soda. Then students create a 'foot island' by tracing their foot on white paper. Students turn their footprint into their very own island country complete with cities, a capital, different landforms, roads and railroads, and any other element they've studied in geography and mapping. We have our students create their own legend and grid system for their map.

Debrief

Offer students two to five minutes to debrief during a particularly long direct instruction. After presenting a section of the topic, stop and allow students a few minutes to talk about it. When students are not familiar with this strategy, you will need to provide some structure in the form of a question to be answered or a statement to be discussed. This is a good time to incorporate blogging if your classroom has the necessary equipment.

Depending on the maturity of your students, you may allow options for the debriefing period, with some students talking about the lesson, others writing or asking questions they have about the lesson, and still others catching up on note taking or sitting quietly for a few minutes. This strategy provides an outlet for students to talk without interrupting direct instruction and also provides the brain with a few minutes to process the information presented.

Designing

Give students the opportunity to create or design something new using the skills learned in class. You could also offer a challenge in requiring them to design a product that combines certain concepts or skills. Students can then use their design to create the object, allowing an opportunity to evaluate whether the product met the criteria and produced the desired results.

Digital Camera

Digital cameras have a variety of uses in the classroom—for example:

- Take pictures to include in a class newspaper.
- Take pictures to include in a class newsletter to parents.
- Take pictures to include in brochures created on the computer.
- Take pictures of students working on projects in the classroom or simulation activities.
- Take pictures to use in student-created Web sites.

Dioramas

After reading or learning about a new concept, have students show what they've learned by making a diorama, or shoe box scene. Using a shoe box, they create a three-dimensional scene using construction paper and other materials, such as grass, twigs, plastic figures, or fishing wire. On the outside of the shoebox (on the top, sides, or back), students write a paragraph telling about the scene or explaining the concept. Display these in the school for everyone to enjoy.

Drawing

Have students draw something about a topic before reading or writing about it. This helps focus them on what they are about to learn and is a way to encourage students who do not feel successful when reading or writing.

Use mind mapping, which is very similar to webbing except that students draw pictures instead of using only words. Each thought or idea branches off the main topic. This can be used in all subject areas to show relationships between ideas, events, people, and so forth. Students can create mind maps on the computer using clip art or draw their own pictures. This allows those students who are more visual by nature to strut their stuff.

Use the storyboard strategy. Have students fold a piece of paper into four to six squares, depending on their age level. They then illustrate the sequence of events on the storyboard. This could be used to show the sequence of a story, historical events, steps to solve an equation, or steps in a particular skill. The storyboard is also a way to prewrite for a how-to essay.

Dress as a Character or Historical Figure

Students choose a historical figure to learn more about through research. As a culminating activity, each student dresses up as his or her historical figure and gives a speech. This speech should teach the rest of the class about the historical figure and should be written in first-person narrative. The class can then ask questions of the historical figure. If the student has done enough research, he or she should be able to answer these questions.

Experiments

Don't just have students read about a topic. Get them experimenting. Studying about whales? Use blubber gloves to feel how a whale is protected in cold water. A blubber glove is created using one small and one large sealable bag and shortening. Fill the small bag with shortening and seal shut. Mold the bag around the hand so that the bag of shortening completely covers the student's hand. Next, place the large bag over the student's hand and secure around the wrist. The student then places both hands in a large bucket of ice water. This activity leads to an excellent discussion about how the lining of blubber protects the whale in cold water.

When studying land forms, let students create models of mountains, plains, deltas, and plateaus. Get them messy with sand, water, and air as they see how rivers and wind help form land features. Experiments are fun, can be easy, and are incredibly motivating. When planning your unit, look for simple classroom experiments that relate to the topic of study. Experiments are a fun way to introduce a topic, apply a skill, or enhance comprehension of a concept, and they are not just for science.

Expert Advice

Students learn all they can about a particular topic within the unit of study and then teach the rest of the class. Allowing students to learn information for themselves is incredibly motivating, especially when they are allowed to create a product along with the research. PowerPoint is an excellent program to create visual presentations of information. Students might also use an interactive whiteboard if one is available. Older students should be encouraged to teach the class in a lesson format.

Freedom of Expression

Provide your students with lots of options. Every child, just like every adult, is better at one medium than another. Let them try their hand at writing music lyrics, poems, raps, and plays. Give students a chance to show what they've learned using their own personal style. Set up an area with odds and ends, paint, posters, and other materials so that they can create puppets, collages, and other artistic products. They will love the chance to explore their creative side.

Game Time

Many new and old games involve skills we teach in school. Monopoly and backgammon draw on the problem-solving skills we like to encourage, and Scrabble promotes vocabulary and spelling. There are junior versions of games for primary and elementary students. Many board games designed for young children are available and help teach skills such as taking turns and being good sports when winning and losing, as well as academic skills. Other games that also stimulate the brain are Scattergories and Mastermind. Games can also teach teamwork.

You can become a game creator as well. Students love to review for tests by playing bingo, overhead football, and jeopardy.

FunBrain.com is a way to introduce online games that challenge students' thinking. It has a great resource for teachers as well.

Students also love to create their own game. This type of activity forces them to use higher-level thinking. Have students make up a game using information they've learned. How will they teach others the skill or knowledge they've learned through their game? Is this a review-type game or a teaching-type game? Stress the importance of clear and precise instructions.

Teaching physics? Have students create a carnival game using the principles of physics studied so far. How might students use ramps, pulleys, wheels, gravity, and laws of motion in their game?

Review for spelling and vocabulary using spelling games. For spelling bee basketball, place strips of paper with spelling words in a cup or basket. Break the class into two teams. One student picks a word out of the basket and reads it to the next student, who must spell it. If the student spells the word correctly, he or she gets to try and make a "basket" with the basketball and a trash can. If the student "makes" the basket, the team continues to play. If the student misses the word or the basket, the other team gets a chance. The team with the most points at the end wins.

For the spelling bee race, group students into four or five lines. Call out the word, and have the first student in each line race to the board to spell it. Whoever spells the word correctly first wins that round. A variation is a spelling relay where each student writes one letter of the word for their team. The first team to correctly spell the word wins that round.

Spellingcity.com offers a variety of online games to help students practice their spelling skills.

Getting to Know Your Students

The more you know your students as individuals, the better you will be able to relate to them. Each child in your class is a unique individual with his or her own personality, wants, needs, likes, and dislikes. Do you really know each as a person, or do you see just another face? Students are often motivated to work harder for teachers who take time to get to know them on a personal level and show they care. This is often done in primary grades, but it happens less frequently as students get older. Nevertheless, it is equally as important, if not more so, for these kinds of relationships to occur in middle and high school.

Happy Sack

Whenever a student practices a random act of kindness, the recipient of the kindness writes the deed down on paper and puts it in the happy sack. Every week on a designated day, the teacher reads all of the kind acts collected in the sack. This encourages consideration and friendship among the students. A variation of this for older students is to use a Warm Fuzzy box or a Kool Kids box.

Having Fun

Don't be afraid to have fun and laugh with your students. Fun is an important need. Once you have established work time versus play time, enjoy humor in your classroom. Share a joke or funny story with your students, and encourage them to share some with you.

Helping Others

Helping others can be motivating to students. It provides them a chance to show what they know and to be appreciated. Students can help one another when they partner in class for activities and projects. Have students create study groups within the class to develop the skill of working with others.

Highlighting

Give students colored pens, pencils, or highlighters when they have to highlight or underline a reading passage. Another fun way to use highlighting is in teaching the parts of speech. Have students use a different colored marker to highlight each part of speech in a sentence. This is a great group activity where each team member has a different colored marker. The group must work together to identify the parts of speech in a sentence.

If You Were ...

Students learn more about each other when they answer offbeat questions:

- If you were a car, what kind of car would you be?
- What kind of animal are you like when you're angry?
- If you were a bug, what kind of bug would you be?
- Name something that always makes you smile.
- If you could be like any other person, who would it be?

Illustrated Time Lines

Students create time lines showing events in history. Encourage them to illustrate these and make them as colorful as possible. Use rolls of cash register tape for longer time lines or large sheets of butcher paper. Again, varying the size of paper offers something different for students than always using lined paper.

Is/Is Not

Get students thinking about what a concept "is" and "is not." Make a statement or state a word. Have students move to different corners of the room depending on whether they feel the statement or word is or is not related to the concept. For example, you might say 7 × 2 and 14 when discussing the concept of equal. Students would then walk to the "is" corner if they think 7 × 2 and 14 are equal OR to the "is not" corner if they don't think these two statements are equal. This activity can be used with students of all ages. Get older students thinking and moving faster by using a timer with this activity.

I Wonder

Pose a question to students that begins, "I wonder . . . " and challenge them to discuss and find the answer using whatever resources are available in the classroom. Encourage students to check out your classroom library and their textbook, and have a list of appropriate Internet Web sites ready for them to view. This is far more motivating than simply reading the textbook and answering the questions at the end of the chapter.

Examples

- I wonder why atoms have both positive and negative particles in them.
- I wonder why the U.S. Constitution did not abolish the practice of slavery.
- I wonder why bats use echolocation.
- I wonder why grass is green.
- I wonder why it is important to use active voice in writing.

Jobs

Have older students apply and interview for any class jobs you might have available. This will help students practice for the real world and will motivate them to do a fine job when they know they might get "fired." Change class jobs each semester so that other students have a chance to apply and interview. Having class jobs is extremely motivating because students love to be valued as a helper.

Do you have a particularly challenging student? Often the worst troublemakers are actually the best leaders. Capitalize on those leadership qualities and put them to work for you. You can say to them, "I noticed that many of the students in this class look up to you. That shows good leadership qualities. I could use a leader like you to help me." These students may simply need someone to believe they are more than what *they* believe themselves to be.

Being asked to help with an important and meaningful job can often turn these students into your biggest allies.

Journals

Writing out information often helps students conceptualize it and place it in their long-term memory. For example, think about how you would write out an explanation of "3 × 5." Writing out this concept requires students to really think about what "3 × 5" means.

Journals can be of use in all classrooms. In fact, the Olympic gold medal gymnast Kurt Thomas has his gymnastic students keep a journal of their work-out to solidify in their minds what has been done and what needs to be done. Journals can also be in fun shapes that relate to a particular unit. We discuss additional ideas for using journals in all subject areas in Chapter Eight.

Journal Starter Ideas

- Pictures: real world, real life, cartoons, political cartoons, from calendars
- Mystery statements: "It's nighttime, but I can see perfectly without the need for light. Why?"
- Hot topics
- Opinion statement for students to defend or oppose according to their own opinion
- Quotation: "Mathematics is the life of the gods."
- Creative thinking story starters
- Questions

Learning Vine

Make a vine of butcher paper or construction paper, and string it across the room or down a wall. Have students add "flowers" or "leaves" to the vine with facts from your unit. At the beginning of a new unit, take down the old leaves and flowers to make room for new ones. You could also use the vine as your word wall or to teach the parts of speech.

Letter Writing and E-Mailing

Writing letters to the president, governor, local congressman or senator, or other important figures is extremely motivating to students. Many addresses for government officials and businesses can be found in the almanac and on the Internet. This is an excellent way for reviewing both friendly and business letter formats with students. Not only do they have a real audience, but they also have a variety of topics to write about. This can also be used as a tool for assessment since students have to understand the subject in order to write a coherent letter. Everyone will be excited when they receive a reply in the mail.

For older students, *Letters from a Nut* by Ted Nancy and Jerry Seinfeld uses letters written in a serious format to poke fun at the world. The authors have written letters to actual businesses with either a compliment or a complaint and have published the return letter. This book is a fun way to introduce writing letters to businesses to either compliment or complain about a particular product or service. Note that you will have to edit some of the material in this book for appropriateness.

Letter writing can also be fun way to present information learned during a research project. Have students create a time warp in which they can exchange letters with a person, famous or not, from history. In the letters, the student asks questions about the time period, what the person does, how he or she is reacting to an event, and other information. (You establish the type of information expected for the project.) The "historical figure" then answers these questions in return through letters.

Students can get very creative using tea stains to make paper look old, using special fonts on the computer, and including black and white or old photographs (or drawings made to look like photographs) from the time period. Students with writing learning disabilities can use postcards to minimize the amount of writing. The letters are then displayed in a scrapbook in chronological order showing a clear picture of the conversation between the student and historical figure and knowledge gained.

Mini-Research

Have students research more often and less formally to establish a love of searching out answers. Research does not have to be massive, but can be an easy quest for knowledge. Assign mini-research topics using a variety of resources. Let students research information to answer questions they may have on a particular topic. Make it as nonthreatening as possible so that students will enjoy seeking information and reveling in the success of finding it.

Remember that research can be as simple as finding the answer to a question. When a student asks, "Ms. McDevitt, why does a hummingbird move so fast?" encourage that student to discover the answer through books, pictures, videos, and the Internet. A great answer to the question would be, "I don't know. Why don't we find out?" Then help the child learn how to find answers. If possible, don't make the child wait. Immediately satisfy that need for information and you'll be teaching a lifelong learning skill!

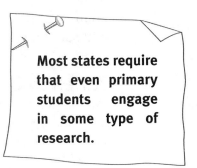

Most states require that even primary students engage in some type of research.

Mmm. M&Ms

The M&M game can be used not only as an icebreaker but also to review or test knowledge in various areas. Pass around a jar of M&Ms, and instruct students to take some. After everyone has taken some, have students tell you a fact or give a math problem for each M&M they take. This is also a way to review for a test or as a unit culmination. The AIMS Education Foundation has many hands-on resources for math teachers, including a math activity using M&Ms as part of a graphing lesson.

Mobiles

Mobiles can be used to display information. Students can make mobiles of atoms, story settings, and time lines and give written explanations of them. This is a great activity for visual learners and can be used as an assessment tool as well. We've used everything from coat hangers to dowel rods to make mobiles. Students can be creative in what they decide to hang when representing a concept.

Murals

On long sheets of butcher paper, students create large illustrations or scenes depicting objects, concepts, people, and events they've studied. Brainstorm the overall idea of the mural as a class, including what items should be included. Together as a class, create a rough outline on the whiteboard or on paper and show using the document camera. Students then choose the section of the mural they'd like to create. Alternatively, you can have groups of students design a portion of the mural and then put it all together. These butcher paper murals can hang in the hallway as a vivid representation of what students are learning in your class.

News Articles and a Newsletter

Get students writing about their learning in the form of news articles. These articles can be informative or descriptive and should show what students have learned during the unit. Compile all the news articles into a newsletter or newspaper format on the computer. Each student can type his or her own and include a picture as well if possible. Print the newspaper or newsletter, and share it with the rest of the school and parents.

Notes in Class

We are forever picking up notes in class, so adapt this tradition by encouraging students to write informal letters for information, send birthday notes to a classmate, or even write notes to their parents about their day.

With computers and specialty paper, it is easy to create personalized note cards to give to students. At the beginning of the year, you could use a card maker program to create a variety of cards with different messages on them. Then, throughout the year, pick a card and personalize it for the student.

Everyone likes to get a card that shows someone is thinking of them. If a student seems glum all day, give him or her a "Cheer Up" or "Hang In There" card. Use cards for more than showing appreciation for hard work and improvement; think of other situations where a personal card would make a difference to a student. If you make up a wide variety of cards with different messages, then you can just write in, "Dear _____," jot a quick note, and sign your name. If you have a few minutes, write more.

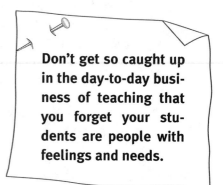

Don't get so caught up in the day-to-day business of teaching that you forget your students are people with feelings and needs.

Outside

Take students out and about on beautiful days. Walk around and pick up different kinds of leaves, look at trees and roots, pick up rocks to identify, or notice cloud shapes. There is so much to learn from our world that we should take advantage of it and spend some time outdoors. Who says that all learning must occur inside buildings?

You can also go outside to play team-building games or use chalk to do sidewalk math. Have students make butter, bricks, or other objects that reinforce your topic of discussion. Messy projects are best completed outdoors. Another activity you can do outside is to measure the distance from the sun to each planet with chalk, or have student groups use their bodies to create "live" mini solar systems with "planets" rotating around the "sun."

Doing a unit on birds? Have students go outside and pick things up like grass and leaves with a clothespin to imitate a bird.

Go outside to write poetry or stories, and let the great outdoors inspire your young writers and artists.

There are many different ways that you and your students can enjoy the outside world and learn at the same time.

Paper Bags

Students can use paper bags as an alternative to routine paper-and-pencil tasks. Fill the bags with flash cards, sequence strips, or character traits. Decorate the outside of the bag and put in exciting events from history, a script for a skit, events of a novel, or something else. Students can complete the activity found within the bag.

As a start to an activity with student groups, have them predict what the activity will be based on by looking at the outside of the bag.

Encourage student cooperation with paper bags. If each group has one or more items another group needs to complete their task, they will need to cooperate with one another in sharing and exchanging needed information.

Students can also put their work inside a paper bag and illustrate the outside. When using paper bags as part of a project, use a checklist so that students know exactly what is expected of them.

Book in a Bag is a creative way to have students do a book report. The outside can be decorated in any way (using glitter, stickers, construction paper cut-outs, crayons, markers, paint, felt, or other materials), and the design can be the student's choice or a scene from the book, for example.

You can have students complete different activities to place inside the bag: write a summary on an index card, provide the main characters on squares of paper, provide the setting on a colored index card, write questions about the book and provide the answers, or find new vocabulary words and write out the definitions, along with the page number where it was found. Once or twice a year, this is a way to spice up the traditional book report.

Young students can turn the paper bag into a puppet. For children who are shy, a puppet is a way to get them talking and participating in class.

Dyan: Once on a long airplane ride, I had my triplets use the white barf bags in the seat pocket to color and play with as puppets. It provided hours of entertainment!

Patterns

The Important Book by Margaret Wise Brown follows a specific pattern that students can use to explore any concept or problem. It is a circle book where the ending is the same as the beginning. The pattern looks like this:

_____ is important because . . .

It is . . .

It is true that . . .

It is true that . . .

It is true that . . .

It is also true that . . .

_____ is important because . . .

Begin by reading Brown's book aloud to the students, and have them use the pattern to write about colors, shapes, or some other simple concept. You can also use this pattern to write about any concept learned in class such as atoms or algebra. How could you use this pattern to explore a concept or assess student knowledge in your class?

Other pattern books are the Brown Bear Brown Bear series of books by Bill Martin Jr., *The Little Red Hen* by Paul Galdone, and *Who Took the Farmer's Hat?* by Joan Nodset. How might you use different patterns to get students writing about the topic at hand?

Pizza of Knowledge

When studying a concept, check to see if students are getting the main idea and supporting details by serving up a slice of knowledge pizza. Each student is given a large slice of pizza drawn on construction paper or cardboard, or they can draw their own on copy paper (for older students). Then give each student construction paper toppings (red circles = pepperoni, green squiggles = green peppers, brown triangles or cloud shapes = sausage, and so on). The teacher can create the key and say, "For each pepperoni, write a main fact; for each green pepper, write a supporting detail; for each sausage piece, write a fun fact," and so on. The students should have a few toppings of each kind. The teacher can easily see if the students understand the main topics versus the supporting ideas versus the interesting facts. This could work for language arts, science, or social studies units.

Poetry

Poems can be written about seasons, historical events, and even math. The more students write, the better writers they become. More information about using poetry in all classes can be found in Chapter Eight. A bio poem is one way to show knowledge about a historical figure or concept. It follows this pattern:

Line 1:	Person's name/Concept name
Line 2:	Two adjectives that describe
Line 3:	An action phrase with an –ing word
Line 4:	An action phrase with an –ing word
Line 5:	An action phrase with an –ing word
Line 6:	Wrap up word or phrase that is a synonym for line one

Here is an example:

Abraham Lincoln
Honest and just,
Fighting a bitter war,
Leading a broken nation,
Living on through time,
A Man for the Ages.

A name poem, or acrostic poem, is another type of poem that works well in describing concepts or famous figures. The letters of the person's name or the concept are written vertically down the page. Students write a word or phrase that describes the person or concept for each letter listed.

Let students type their poems on the computer and compile them into their own poetry book to take home at the end of the year. This is a perfect opportunity for that About the Author page as well! Bringing pop culture into the classroom is highly motivating to students. Bring in song lyrics when studying poetry. Begin by analyzing the lyrics for meaning, mood, and themes, then listen to the song. Discuss how the music reinforces these elements or not. For example, some song lyrics are particularly mournful, but are set to very upbeat music. You might discuss with students how the music affects individual reactions to the lyrics.

Pop-Up Books

When students are writing one or two paragraphs to answer a research question, have them publish their information in an illustrated pop-up book. They fold a piece of construction paper in half for their book, with the title written on the front and About the Author on the back, along with illustrations. Inside, students write their paragraphs on the bottom half of each side and illustrate the top. A pop-up image can be created by folding a small piece of card stock or construction paper in an L shape and pasting it on the page. You might also ask your art teacher to help you with other ideas for creating pop-up images.

PowerPoint

Students can use PowerPoint to create lesson presentations, visual and audio reports, and even put together a visual story with music. Allow students to create a report using PowerPoint instead of writing out an essay or using a poster.

Praising Students

Praising students is an excellent way to motivate them. When they share an answer with the class, thank them. Say, "Excellent answer!" or "Excellent effort!" You will be surprised at how many more hands will begin to go up when you do this.

Presents

Students describe a famous person, place, or concept on a sheet of paper. Encourage creativity with illustrations or objects that help represent the information. Have students put their information in a box, wrap it up, and exchange their "gift" of knowledge with another student. This can also be used for sensory activities where the student unwraps the "gift" blindfolded and tries to predict what it is by using their five senses.

When beginning a unit, find an object that relates to your topic of study. Place it in a box and wrap it up. If you teach several classes, you might want to use a gift bag instead so that it can easily be rewrapped and ready for the next class period. Place the wrapped box in a place where it will catch the eyes of students as they enter class. Begin class as you normally would and do not mention anything about the wrapped object. Students will be very curious to know what's in the box.

Use your creativity to think of a way to choose a student to open the present. For example, you could play a game that reviews prior learning that will then connect to the new unit. When the student opens the gift, have students work together in groups to try to figure out the new topic of study. You could also get students discussing how the object relates to what you'll be studying over the next several weeks. The wackier the object, the better.

Problem-Based Learning

Post a problem scenario, and challenge students to solve it. Provide resources in the form of books and a list of Web sites for students to research as they work in teams to resolve the issue. You might require students to create a product that meets certain specifications or develop a set of rules for a newly formed committee or even plan for the development of a new city or self-sustaining neighborhood. Your project should require students to learn concepts and skills outlined in your curriculum and show mastery of these concepts and skills through a final proposal or product.

Your job is to facilitate and help students find resources to solve the problem. Let student creativity run free, and you'll be amazed at the solutions developed.

Puzzles

Most students love a mystery and love to solve puzzles. Take a reading selection, and create a puzzle for students to solve. You can make it a logic puzzle (determine which explorer took which boat to which new land). Another option is to create a crossword puzzle with definitions of vocabulary words. You can also use cryptograms or missing letter puzzles.

If you don't feel up to creating puzzles, search the Internet, which has good resources for subject area puzzles. Use your favorite search engine, and type in the subject area and the keyword "puzzles" to locate ones that will work for your classrooms. One resource listing different puzzle Web sites is Education World—http://www.educationworld.com/a_lesson/lesson/lesson118. shtml. Also, check out our other ideas on using puzzles in the classroom in Chapter Seven.

Quotes

As students make profound or humorous statements, have them write these down on special paper, and then display them on a bulletin board or the walls of your classroom. What a great way to let students know what they say is important!

A variation to this activity is to have a quote of the day or a quote of the week from different famous figures. Use the quote as a springboard for your discussion that day or week. For example, a music teacher might use Shakespeare's, "We are the music makers and we are the dreamers of the dream."

Another variation is to have students finish the quote. Provide students with the beginning of a famous quote or saying and have them finish it in their own words. You'll enjoy reading the results, as will parents! Afterward discuss each quote and its meaning with students.

The Internet is an excellent source for books of quotes or Web sites full of quotes. A few of our favorite quote sites are

- www.brainyquote.com
- www.quotationspage.com
- www.quotegarden.com

Reader's Theater

Take a section of a novel or short story, and have students read as though it were scripted as a play. Students readers sit up front in a line facing the class. When a character appears and speaks, the student "playing" that character reads the dialogue. Assign one or more narrators to read the rest.

If student groups have scripted out a section in the textbook, you can have the group read the script with assigned parts using the reader's theater idea instead of having each group act it out.

Reading Toss

Reading aloud from a textbook can be fun when you use a soft ball. Have students choose who is next to read by lightly tossing the ball to another student. It is vital that you go over your expectations and consequences for off-task behavior before you begin this activity.

A variation is to have students stop in the middle of a sentence or paragraph. The next student must start at the exact place the last student left off. This should be approached as a game, not a punishment-based issue.

Red Herring Stories

Red herring stories are also referred to as situation puzzles or assumption games. Students are given a scenario in which they must determine the truth behind what happened. Typically the puzzle gives clues that are not needed, misleading information, or plays on our assumptions about the way the world works. Students must ask yes or no questions to determine what really happened in the scenario. Questions that receive no as the answer are just as helpful in solving the puzzle as questions that receive a yes answer. The key is for students to question their assumptions about the words and descriptions used in the puzzle. These are highly motivating for students to solve, especially older students. The Critical Thinking Company publishes the Red Herring series with puzzles appropriate for school-aged children and adolescents.

Remembering

Students are motivated to work for people who care about them. Remembering their name after the first day of school is one way to show that you care.

Birthdays are another area where students want to be remembered. Celebrating another year is important in our students' lives, and for some of them, it may be the only time that they get any personalized attention. Celebrate birthdays as often as you can. A birthday card, a cupcake with a candle, or any other simple act goes a long way with students.

Another way to celebrate is with a birthday bag. During the first week of school, have each student decorate a paper bag but not write their names on it. Throughout the rest of the year, pull out a bag at random and have the other students write short birthday messages to the birthday boy or girl. Place the messages, some candy, a bookmark, or a sticker page into the bag. At lunch, everyone can sing "Happy Birthday," and you can present the birthday bag to the student. This can be extremely gratifying since many students may not get a formal birthday party, and in some instances their birthdays go completely unnoticed by everyone else. Be aware, however, that some cultures do not believe in celebrating birthdays.

Round Robin

Get everybody involved by using pass-along stories, or round-robin stories. Each student writes one beginning sentence on their paper. They pass their paper to the next student, who adds another sentence or two continuing the same thought. The paper is passed around the table or down the row until everyone has had a turn adding to each story. This is an excellent way to teach the importance of staying on a topic and learning about fluent story lines.

The round-robin concept can also be used when solving equations. Have each student solve step 1 of an equation and pass it along to the next student. The paper continues to rotate until each problem is solved.

A third use for the round-robin concept is in writing out a sequence of events.

Scavenger Hunt

A scavenger hunt can be used in a variety of ways and is discussed extensively in Chapters Seven and Eight. Get students hunting for specific objects related to the unit of study that are hidden around the room. Students must be able to explain how the object is related to the unit. A variation is to get students hunting for answers to riddles or questions by reading through the textbook.

See the WebQuest listing below for an online scavenger hunt.

Script Writing

Divide students into groups. Then divide the textbook chapter into enough sections for each group of students. After reading an assigned section in the textbook, students work in pairs or groups to rewrite the section as a script. Student groups then act out their section in order.

Alternatively, you can have students work together to rewrite a section of the textbook as a children's story. Encourage them to illustrate their story as well. Then compile the sections in order to make a book. This book can be copied and shared with younger students to help introduce them to the concept or historical event. Let your students go to the younger classrooms and read the story aloud to the class.

Sentence Strips

Sentence strips have a variety of uses. Write different sentence parts on various strips, and cut them to size. Use nouns, verbs, connecting words, prepositions, and/or prepositional phrases. Mix them all up in each category. Have students choose at least one strip from each category to create their own sentences using the different parts.

For younger students you might want to color code each part of the sentence so that they can self-check to see if they have a correct sentence.

You can use this concept in just about any class. Use strips of paper to organize or categorize information into a T-chart, time line, Venn diagram, or any other graphic organizer. Type out statements, words, ideas, and themes, and cut them into strips. Have an envelope or bag with the strips ready for each student group. Students work together to put information in the correct order or correct category. They can paste their final product on construction paper or a large sheet of colored butcher paper. This activity helps students manipulate information in a variety of ways.

Shapes

Use octagons, squares, stars, and other shapes to help students see similarities and differences, categorize items, or order concepts. For example, a triangle is an excellent way for students to visualize hierarchies. A variation on this activity is to make these objects three-dimensional and place instructions or questions on each surface.

Have students make books cut into shapes that fit the current theme or topic of study. Shape books are lots of fun to make and easy too: punch holes in the tops or sides and thread with brightly colored yarn or O-rings. Shape books can be used as journals, to hold illustrations or time lines, or even to complete daily assignments.

Idea Share

In one of our Gifted and Talented training seminars, the presenter gave us all four-inch-square boxes and asked us to decorate each side with different colors of construction paper. Then we placed one Bloom's taxonomy level along with keywords on each side. When working with students, we can toss the box on each table and ask them to "cube it": students complete one task using each level found on the cube. All of our kids, not just the gifted ones, really enjoy this activity.

Sharing

Allowing students to share in class helps create a positive learning environment and makes students feel important. Have them share what they have written or learned. Encourage students to relate their learning to their life. Have they ever been in a particular situation described in the story or event? Have them share relevant experiences. Younger children especially love to share their own stories as a way of making learning meaningful for themselves.

Simulations

Get students up and moving and experiencing (as close as they can) historical events. Recreate Ellis Island and the immigration experience of that era (Ellis Island opened in 1892). Assign students roles from that time period, and have them move in the room to different stations: medical, language, education, and work experience. Some students can be immigration clerks, checking other students out to see if they will be permitted to enter America. Some students will be given a profile to use when getting off their ship—for example, "from Ireland, female, eighteen years old, work experience as a nanny, good health history" or "from Poland, forty-five years old, has tuberculosis, worked on a farm." Based on the criteria, the immigration clerks have a checklist with point values. After the immigrants stand in line and go to all the stations, they are given a green slip to enter or they are sent back home. This is a popular activity with the students to simulate the Ellis Island experience in American history.

Another simulation is to have students make their own adobe bricks and build a small hut with them. It takes only straw, mud, water, cardboard boxes, and sunlight. It is amazing to watch the pride in the students' eyes as they create homes in the way some Native American nations did. Get your principal's approval before doing this activity, because it take about three days to complete the process and everyone, teacher included, will need to dress in grubby clothes.

Get students to experience an international bazaar with booths set up for different cultures. Have students put together their own carnival with games they've created. Let students write with feather pens and ink, make their own quilt pieces, make candles, and play games popular in colonial America.

Online simulations are also available, starting with SimCity. Students create their own city and must provide water, electricity, and other needed elements to create the perfect city where people want to live and work. This is a great game to play when studying about civilizations.

Sticky Notes and Brightly Colored Paper

Have students do their assignments on extra large or extra small pieces of paper like sticky notes. You can find sticky notes in different shapes and in bright neon colors. Using them is a good way to check for understanding. Have students write their name and answer a question about the lesson on a sticky note and then pass it forward. Attach the notes together at the top with the sticky on the back and you can easily flip through the stack to see whether students are ready to move on or need more help. Another way to spruce up their work is by providing them with brightly colored paper or index cards. Doing work on neon yellow or green is more fun than writing on regular notebook paper.

Teaming and Talking

When students work in teams, they are motivated to learn. Student talking becomes more meaningful as they discuss what must be accomplished. In addition, working in teams gives students some time in class to socialize, which means they will be less likely to disrupt the lesson. If they know there will be time later when they can talk, they will be quiet and pay attention when necessary.

Traveling Checkpoints

When you face a worksheet full of questions that must be completed for your required curriculum, mix it up a bit. Post questions at checkpoints around the room. Have students travel together as a pair and visit each checkpoint on their journey, answering the questions posted there. Add a bit of spice and include a clue at the bottom of each checkpoint. Students must unravel the clue to figure out which checkpoint to visit next.

This strategy can also be used with activities. Students travel to each checkpoint, completing the activity outlined. Require students to complete a certain number of checkpoints for their journey to be complete. This allows student choice to play a part in the process.

True or False

Reviewing facts in class can be fun using the game True or False. Have student groups work together to create three to five statements regarding a recent lesson that are either true or false. Have the groups go to the front of the room to share their statements. The other students in the room then decide whether each statement is true or false. Students really enjoy this game because they have a chance to trick other students with their statements. It works well as a review too: you can stop after each statement and discuss why it was or was not true.

Video Game Creation

Have students create their own educational video game that relates to your unit of study. This would definitely be a project for the end of a unit, but once the game is created, it can be used in future years to learn and practice the skills and concepts. You can find game creation software to download or install on the computer to help students create their video game. These resources can help you get started:

- www.clickteam.com
- www.thegamecreators.com
- www.gamesalad.com (for Mac users)

Use the keywords "Online Game Creation" when searching for resources.

Video Interviews

When students dress as a historical figure or character from a book, spice it up even more by hosting interviews. Pair up students and have each brainstorm a list of questions to ask the other historical figure/character. Set up two tall chairs (if available) in front of the whiteboard or a background of some sort (the class can create this together). Students then interview each other as their historical character. For example, "Abraham Lincoln" interviews "Amelia Earhart," and then "Amelia Earhart" interviews "Abraham Lincoln." This is a fun twist on the historical figure activity. Students really love seeing themselves on TV, so be sure to record the interviews with a video camera.

Visual Stories

Students can use online software to create a story using pictures and music. This can be a retelling of a story read aloud in class or a representation of concepts learned during the lesson or unit. For example, after reading about the everyday life on plantations versus the city in the colonial South, students can choose to represent one or the other through clip art pictures. Next, they choose music to support the ideas expressed by the pictures. This idea can also be used for students to create original visual stories as an expression of creativity. One site that offers free photo creation of visual stories is http://www.animoto.com.

Walkabout Project

The walkabout is a type of research adapted from a traditional practice of Aboriginal Australian tribes in which adolescents are sent alone into the outback for several months to prove their readiness for adulthood. Maurice Gibbons, in his 1974 article, "Walkabout: Searching for the Rite of Passage from Childhood and School," adapted this practice to a form of real-life teaching to help students want to learn.

The Walkabout is a year-long project in which students explore one topic of interest to them. Students must go on an adventure, create something unique, research one aspect of the topic, do community service, or develop and showcase professional skills they attained. Pictures, journals, and information gathered for each section are organized into a three-ring binder and presented to a panel of teachers, peers, and parents at the end of the year.

While this project does require a good amount of time and effort on the part of the student, it is mostly completed outside class. It provides an excellent opportunity for students to learn in depth about a topic or career that interests them. You may want to provide due dates as well as some class time for students to report progress, ask for help, and share their project with other students throughout the year. Sharing allows students to learn from each other while completing the project.

> I've done the walkabout project with my sixth-, seventh-, and eighth-grade students, and it has been a huge success. One student decided to do her walkabout on veterinarians. She volunteered in a veterinarian clinic, interviewed the veterinarians, researched information about stray animals, worked in a pet shop, and learned how to properly bathe and dip animals. She used a journal and pictures to present her efforts and during the presentation demonstrated how to wash and dip a cat. All of my students were excited to show the new skills they had learned through this project!

Web Pages

Students can use Microsoft Publisher or even Microsoft Word to create their own Web pages. Microsoft Publisher provides more options and abilities for beginners and those who are already familiar with creating Web pages.

Instead of making a poster or writing a report, have students create a Web page or Web site that includes facts, pictures, and additional links for further information. Students can show their creativity and present information learned in a way that other students can access and use. Through a Web page, students can post surveys or quizzes, links, a way for other people to comment about the information presented, and other interactive features. This is much more motivating than simply drawing on a poster and showing it to the class.

Wiki Spaces are another way to get student work online. This is an easy way for students to post information about a topic they've recently studied.

WebQuests

A WebQuest is an inquiry-based learning method that occurs online. It can include an introduction, a description of tasks to be performed, and then each task along with a list of Web site links for students to follow in order to complete the task. Each task can be straightforward, or it can be set up similar to a scavenger hunt where students search the approved Web sites for answers to questions or specific information. At the end, students should have completed the tasks culminating in either a product or the answers to the questions. The WebQuest can be as simple or complicated, straightforward or creative as you wish it to be.

Alternatively, you can have students create WebQuest for younger students to follow. You would want your older students to include information they've learned about the topic being studied as well as tasks for the younger students to complete (or a scavenger hunt to follow). Students can use Microsoft Publisher or Word to create their WebQuest, or use one of the resources listed below:

- www.questgarden.com
- http://webquest.org

You can also use wiki pages to create a WebQuest very easily.

Whiteboard Discussion

Involve everyone in a class discussion by writing a question or thought-provoking statement on the board. Have each student write their example, thought, answer, or idea on the board under and around what you have written. Have different colors of marker available for students. This is a great way to start a discussion. This idea also works well with graphic organizers. Have students write their answer inside a graphic organizer posted on the board or large butcher paper.

Yarn and String

Younger students can use yarn to practice letters and match objects. Older students can match terms and definitions. Yarn is also a handy way to measure circumference and compare fractions. A pie chart can be created with yarn by tying several pieces of yarn, each the same length, together at one end. Then four or more students stand in a circle holding the other ends of the yarn, to demonstrate different fractions on a pie.

Zest

Add zest to your classroom by participating in the activities you require of your students. They will love to see your product and will be more motivated to put time and effort into it when they see how much effort you put into yours. This is an excellent way to model your expectations as well as a way to enjoy being with your students.

Be passionate about what you teach. This also adds zest to your classroom and motivates students. Enthusiasm is catching, even to those who don't want it. Students can't help but smile and get excited when they see you brimming with energy.

Zooming In

Have students take a broad topic and zoom in on one detail to explore fully. For example, when studying a culture, a student might focus on hair styles or fashions. It is also easy to zoom in with science by using microscopes and magnifying glasses to write about what students see.

A fun writing activity is to take students outside armed with a magnifying glass. Have each choose an object to view through the magnifying glass and then write a descriptive paragraph about it. Later, switch papers and have students try to guess the object from the written description.

Moment of Reflection

If you could use one word to sum up how to motivate students to want to learn, what word would you use? Why? Why is it helpful to have quick and easy ways to make learning fun? Is this something you strive to do for your students? Why or why not? What are some strategies you've learned so far that you might like to try with your classes?

Students Who "Won't"

What can be done when you have a student who refuses to complete the work assigned in class? This is very frustrating, and often our response is one of irritation. We may throw our hands up in despair or, worse yet, give up on that student and allow him or her to coast through class. All of these actions are a disservice to the student. Instead, we need to take some time, dig deeper into the situation, and try to determine the problem. What is causing this inaction on the part of the student?

There can be many causes to a "won't" attitude on the part of a student—for example:

- *Protection of reputation.* The student does not want his buddies to know he is smart and wants to learn because it would lower his status among the group.
- *Not motivated.* The student feels that the work is too easy or she has already completed similar assignments a million times and is tired of the same old thing.
- *Feels inadequate.* The student over the years has been unconsciously or consciously told he is not performing well and has decided that rather than continue to feel like a failure, he'd rather just not try at all.
- *Bored.* The student is bored with the lessons and assignments and gets in the habit of daydreaming or writing notes to her friends instead of doing class work.

Here is what you can do when faced with a student who has decided not to participate, turn in homework, or complete class assignments:

- *Start by getting at the root of the problem.* What exactly is going on with the student? Take some time and talk with the student one-on-one (away from friends). Talk with the parents to see if this has always been a problem or a steady decline. Talk with the counselor (or the counselor of the previous or lower school) to see what patterns he or she has noticed about this student.
- *Offer more student choice when possible.* Rather than assigning the same writing prompt, set of questions, project topic, or class activity to all students, offer several options. Allow students to choose the one that is most appealing.
- *Take time to talk with your student daily.* Ask about his or her day. Find out what is going on in his or her life. This is a way to discover hidden interests and abilities. It also shows the student that you care about him or her as a person. When students feel that you care, they try harder.
- *Make learning relevant to your students.* This is hard to do when you don't know your students very well. However, we are all motivated by topics and events that interest us. We are much more likely to spend time and effort on something that is important to us as opposed to something we are told we must do.

Andrea Peterson, National Teacher of the Year in 2007, often speaks about the three Rs of Rigor, Relevance, and Relationship and asserts that we need to change the emphasis to Relationship, Relevance, and Rigor. Her point is that building relationships with students helps teachers know how to make learning relevant to them. When learning is relevant to students, they apply themselves rigorously. In other words, when we get to know our students as people (build relationships), we discover what is relevant to each person. With that information, we are able to make lessons and projects meaningful for students. When students have work that is meaningful to them, they are motivated and tend to work rigorously to complete it.

This does not mean there is a one-size-fits-all solution. Each student is different. Some students respond quickly to efforts. Others take a long time to respond, and still others may not even seem to respond at all. Yet your efforts are not in vain. Those students will remember the teacher who cared. They will remember the teacher who held high expectations for each person in the class with no exception. You may not see the results of your work, but they will make a difference. Don't give up on students who have given up on school. Keep trying to reach them, and maybe one day, when you need it most, you'll get a phone call from that challenging student saying, "Thank you."

Moment of Reflection

Do you currently have students who "won't" do their work? What issues may be causing this attitude problem? How can you discover the underlying issues? What are some possible strategies to help you overcome this problem?

Students Who "Can't"

You've just handed out a class assignment. Most of the students get started on it, and as you walk around the room, you notice that everyone is getting into gear—almost everyone, that is. There sits student X with a blank piece of paper and a blank or sullen expression.

"What's going on?" you ask. "Do you need some help getting started?"

"I can't do this," replies the student.

At this point you might be wondering to yourself: Can't or won't? How can you tell the difference between a student who can't do the work assigned or who won't do the work? In addition, when we consistently see a particular student not meeting his or her potential, it makes us wonder whether the issue is one of "I can't" or "I won't."

The first thing to do is to check the student's records for an IEP (Individualized Education Plan). This plan will give you information on modifications that the student needs to be successful in the regular classroom. You might also speak with the special education teacher or department to see what strategies are recommended for using with this student if he or she has already been identified as having special needs. If the student is not already so identified, look for a huge gap between the student's ability/potential and performance. This is a definite sign that the student may need additional help to complete assignments.

Emma: One year I had a student named Marcus (name changed), a young man who confused me for the longest time because his participation in class discussions and his work product did not match. When engaged in a classroom discussion, he was able to fully explain the concepts discussed in class, and he showed a competent grasp of the material taught. However, when asked to write his responses to any question or to complete any kind of writing assignment, Marcus became a different person. He pouted. He sulked. He shouted. He obstinately refused to write anything.

When I finally coaxed him to write just one sentence, it became obvious why he put up such a fight. Writing was a true challenge for him. Although a middle school student, his sentences were incomplete, with most words misspelled and the letters a mixture of lowercase and capitals. It was like pulling teeth to get one sentence out of this boy. I can only imagine his frustration in not being able to get all of his thoughts on the paper. In essence, there was a huge gap between his mental ability/potential and his paper-and-pencil performance. Marcus needed additional help for a learning disability.

When faced with a student who truly can't perform to their full potential, it is our responsibility to make sure that he or she receives help.

- Talk with your special education coordinator or department chair. Ask if someone would be willing to observe the student and confirm your concerns.

- Speak with other teachers on the grade level or team to determine whether anyone else is also seeing a problem.

- Once you have confirmation of your observations, begin the special education referral process. There will be a lot of paperwork to fill out in your effort to help a child meet his or her potential.

- The referral process can be lengthy, so you might want to get suggestions from the special education department of ways to help the student in class. What alternative activities and assessments can you use to measure mastery of content? With Marcus, we tape-recorded his answers to essay questions for tests and he dictated writing assignments.

- Keep a record of all strategies used. Note what works and what doesn't. This will help later when trying to determine modifications for the student's IEP.

Moment of Reflection

How can you tell the difference between a student who "can't" and a student who "won't"?

Working with Special Needs Students

Special needs students are often the hardest students to motivate. Mainstreamed students include special education and ESL (English as a Second Language) students. As teachers, we know that our job is to teach all students regardless of their inherent ability. However, we also know that there are some students who are hard to reach for whatever reason. This section contains tips and reminders to help you cope with the varying abilities of your students.

Special Education Students
Remember . . .

- Do not treat these students any differently from the others.
- Pair them with someone in your class who is patient and willing to help.
- Read each IEP. If the IEP is confusing, ask the special education teacher to explain what that student needs. It never hurts to ask for help.
- You are required by law to follow each IEP exactly when modifying for the student.
- Get textbooks that you can highlight. Some IEPs request this. Your special education teacher will know where to get them or may have some you can use.
- Modify tests for these students before you hand them out. It takes only a few minutes to cross out or highlight sections for the student to complete. Don't embarrass the student by making him or her wait while you modify the test or assignment standing next to his or her desk.
- Do not tolerate jibes or funny remarks about special education students by anyone.
- Read to and with these students every day, even if it is only for a few minutes. That extra time reinforces that they are worth your attention.
- Do not make a big deal about special education students' leaving your class if they go to a resource classroom.
- Try not to lose your temper. But if you do, apologize. Kids understand that everyone has bad days.
- Be patient!
- Find out what that student is interested in, and use it.
- Be prepared to explain the concept or lesson in a different way for these students.
- Some students need to move to learn. Allow an active student to sit in the back and move around a little, as long as he or she doesn't disturb anybody else.

- Find out how that student works, and be flexible. If a student needs to draw to listen, then let him or her draw.

- If you don't feel comfortable with modifying tests and assignments, you also have the option of modifying grades for special education students. Modifying grades is a way of allowing the student's grade to reflect actual performance at his or her ability level. (See "Modified Grading System Grading Scales" form at the end of the chapter.)

- Trust your instinct.

- Don't get discouraged. It is hard when you know a student needs help but does not qualify according to the state requirements. Do what you can.

- Keep your eyes open for students who need help and are not getting it. Not everyone needs special education resources. Check it out first to make sure that the student is not just goofing off.

- Ask about other programs, such as tutoring and Big Brother/Big Sister, that might help your student.

- Have documentation of any behavior or academic problems the student has exhibited in your classroom.

- If your student does not qualify for special education services but you still feel he or she needs extra help, discuss a 504 plan or speech referral with your special education teacher.

- Remember that parents are not always happy about their child being referred for special education services. Many times parents feel that the teacher is simply trying to label their child as "dumb." Reassure them that you are trying to find a way for their child to be successful in the classroom.

Moment of Reflection

What is your attitude toward your special education students? Is this helpful or hurtful for them? How do you address the needs of these students? What might you change to create a positive learning experience for these students in your class?

Students with Attention-Deficit Disorder or Attention Deficit Hyperactivity Disorder

You may have in your classroom several students for whom it is difficult to pay attention and stay focused in class. This can be caused by attention-deficit disorder or attention deficit hyperactivity disorder (ADD/ADHD). You may be under the impression that only children and adolescents who misbehave in class have ADD or ADHD. This is not true. There are many very well-behaved students who suffer from this medical condition. As with most other mental issues, there are ranges and degrees of severity. Some students may be able to cope adequately with their condition, never needing medication. Others need medication to help them stay calm enough to focus and work during school hours. Some students sit quietly all day and seem to be the perfect student until the test arrives, and they fail. These are the daydreamers who mask themselves as teacher pleasers and don't upset the rhythm of the class with behavior disruptions, but still need help to learn. Still others need medication every day in order to function normally.

You may feel frustrated by your ADD/ADHD students, but they are in just as much need of your patience and understanding as special education and ESL students. You may be under the impression that these students are not trying hard enough, that they are simply dreaming away their days, and are unwilling to pay attention. This is an incorrect assessment.

An article written by Thomas E. Brown (2007), associate director of the Yale Clinic for Attention and Related Disorders, discusses a new understanding of attention deficit disorder. He notes that students suffering from ADD/ADHD are often ones who literally can't get their work done but often are treated as though they won't do the work. Brown explains the ranges of the disorder and how different people are affected by it. He also explains the chemicals the brain needs to operate properly and those that are missing in people diagnosed with ADD/ADHD.

Moment of Reflection

What is your attitude toward students in your classroom with ADD/ADHD? Is this helpful or hurtful for them? How do you address the needs of these students? What might you change to create a positive learning experience for these students?

Gifted and Talented Students

Students identified as gifted and talented may also pose a challenge. These children and adolescents are in as much need of modification as those with learning disabilities. The difference is that they need more opportunities to advance at a faster pace and participate in higher-level enrichment activities. Because of their advanced vocabulary, many teachers erroneously assume these students will be better behaved and are more mature than other students. However, the sensitive maturity of these students is often overwhelming for them resulting at times in tears or angry tantrums. Of course, there are ranges, and each individual must be assessed through observation to determine specific behaviors and needs.

When working with these students

- Don't get defensive when they correct you or subject you to additional information on a particular topic.

- Do encourage students with praise for what they know, and encourage them to share with the class.
- Don't just give extra questions or problems as enrichment. More is not necessarily better.
- Do give students opportunities to apply knowledge and skills in problem-based scenarios or real-world situations.
- Do offer opportunities to learn the topic in more depth and share this information with the class.
- Don't force students to sit bored while others are trying to understand the skill or concept.
- Do ask students to show their mastery of the skill or concept.
- Don't expect students to sit patiently and quietly while they wait for the rest of the class to learn the material presented.
- Do have work and activities available for students to complete quietly while you are working with the rest of the class. This work should either challenge the student or allow the student to move forward in the curriculum.
- Do hold students accountable for time spent and work completed.

Moment of Reflection

What is your attitude toward your gifted and talented students? Is this helpful or hurtful for them? How do you address the needs of these students? What might you change to create a positive learning experience for these students in your class?

ESL Students

It is frustrating to have someone in class who can't understand anything we're saying. How do we know that they are learning anything or that they are being successful? This is often the case with ESL students. Many times students arrive in our class having just entered the country. Others have been here for some time, but do not have a good grasp on the English language. Whatever the case, we need to be prepared to offer these students a good education. Here are a few tips from effective ESL teachers that you can use with ESL students in your classroom.

Respect an ESL student's need for silence when faced with a new language.

Students with No English Language Skills

- Provide ample listening opportunities.
- Use mixed-ability groups.

- Create high context for shared reading.
- Use physical movement.
- Use art, mime, and music.
- Put yourself in their shoes to gain perspective and understanding.
- Demonstrate.
- Restate and paraphrase.
- Use gestures.
- Explain or define all terms used in class.
- Use illustrations and photographs, and label items in the room.
- Remember that these students are scared and confused and do not understand anything that is going on in the classroom.
- Do not force them to talk until they are ready. Respect their silence.
- Pair them with a student who can fluently speak their language and can help translate.

Students with Extremely Limited Language Skills

- Continue to provide listening opportunities.
- Ask yes/no and who? what? where? questions.
- Have students label pictures and objects.
- Have students complete sentences with one- or two-word phrases.
- Use pattern books and picture dictionaries.
- Try to help them understand what is going on in your classroom.
- Pair them with a student who is fluent in English as well as in their home language if you can.
- Build vocabulary in the content areas using visuals and meaningful experiences.

Students with Less Limited Language Skills

- Ask open-ended questions.
- Model, expand, restate, and enrich student language.
- Have students describe personal experiences.
- Use predictable and patterned books for shared and guided reading.
- Use role play and retelling of content-area text.
- Have students create books.
- Do not assume that the students have the appropriate academic skills.
- Teach students academic language—what is a noun, subtraction, and so forth.
- Help students by modeling thinking aloud. Encourage students to use only English at school.

Students with Fluent Language Skills

- Pair them with another student who needs help.
- Use group discussions to help them continue practicing their language skills.
- Guide them in the use of reference materials such as dictionaries, almanacs, atlases, and encyclopedias
- Provide higher-level reading materials.
- Have students write their own stories.
- Provide realistic writing opportunities.
- Provide visuals to help with comprehension.
- Publish student writings.
- Encourage them to use both of their languages as a translator.

All ESL Students

- Do not let them use their lack of language skills as a crutch.
- Be understanding and flexible with ESL teachers. Ask for strategies and ideas to help you in the classroom.
- If you see that a student needs help and you do not feel that you do an adequate job, send the student to the ESL teacher for extra help.
- Begin with shortened assignments, and gradually increase them as they gain fluency.
- Do not make a big deal of students leaving your classroom for their ESL classes.
- Keep them as involved as you can in your classroom. They need to do everything the other students are doing.
- Have students do the regular assignment and then modify their grade if necessary.

Idea Share

Have students create "understanding" thermometers to help them show you their level of comfort and understanding. Use heavy card stock paper for the thermometer. Cut the page into three sections approximately four by seven inches. Label the top "Understanding Thermometer," and draw a line down the middle. On the right side of the line write "No Clue," then "Confused," then "Questions," then "I get it." On the left side of the line draw faces to represent these statements. Cut a hole at the top and bottom of the line. Thread a piece of yarn with a bead. Next, thread the yarn through the holes so the bead is on the front of the card. Tie the yarn in back. Students can move the bead up and down the thermometer to show you how they are doing. (See the example on the next page.)

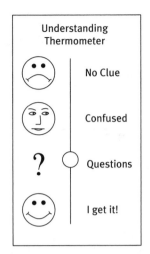

Understanding
Thermometer

No Clue

Confused

? Questions

I get it!

Moment of Reflection

What are some ways you currently help ESL students at different levels in your class-room? What are some other strategies you might implement?

Conclusion

The more motivated your students are, the more learning will take place. When students are energized and engaged, their minds are like sponges absorbing new information and storing it. This happens easily when they have a fun activity to connect with concepts learned. In addition, many of these activities help special needs students feel success and enjoy the learning process. Planning motivating lessons is not such a difficult task when you use simple activities like the ones in this chapter to add zest.

References

Brown, Thomas E. "A New Approach to ADD." *Educational Leadership*, Feb. 2007, pp. 22–27.
Gibbons, Maurice. "Walkabout: Searching for the Rite of Passage from Childhood and School." *Phi Delta Kappan*, May 1974, pp. 596–602.
Glasser, William. *Choice Theory in the Classroom*. New York: HarperCollins, 1998.

Web Site Resources

Motivating Students, http://www.vanderbilt.edu/cft/resources/teaching_resources/interactions/motivating.htm
National Society for the Gifted and Talented—What Is Giftedness? http://www.nsgt.org/articles/index.asp
Teaching Tips for ESL, http://www.everythingesl.net/inservices/
ADD/ADHD in the Classroom: Tips for Teachers, http://helpguide.org/mental/adhd_add_teaching_strategies.htm

Modified Grading System
Grading Scales

50%–75%	55%–75%	60%–75%	65%–75%	70%–75%
A 75 = 100	A 80 = 100	A 85 = 100	A 90 = 100	A 95 = 100
74 = 99	79 = 99	84 = 99	89 = 99	94 = 99
73 = 98	78 = 98	83 = 98	88 = 98	93 = 98
72 = 97	77 = 97	82 = 97	87 = 97	92 = 97
71 = 96	76 = 96	81 = 96	86 = 96	91 = 96
70 = 95	75 = 95	80 = 95	85 = 95	90 = 95
69 = 94	74 = 94	79 = 94	84 = 94	89 = 94
68 = 93	73 = 93	78 = 93	83 = 93	88 = 93
67 = 92	72 = 92	77 = 92	82 = 92	87 = 92
66 = 91	71 = 91	76 = 91	81 = 91	86 = 91
65 = 90	70 = 90	75 = 90	80 = 90	85 = 90
B 64 = 89	B 69 = 89	B 74 = 89	B 79 = 89	B 84 = 89
63 = 88	68 = 88	73 = 88	78 = 88	83 = 88
62 = 87	67 = 87	72 = 87	77 = 87	82 = 87
61 = 86	66 = 86	71 = 86	76 = 86	81 = 86
60 = 85	65 = 85	70 = 85	75 = 85	80 = 85
59 = 84	64 = 84	69 = 84	74 = 84	79 = 84
58 = 83	63 = 83	68 = 83	73 = 83	78 = 83
57 = 82	62 = 82	67 = 82	72 = 82	77 = 82
56 = 81	61 = 81	66 = 81	71 = 81	76 = 81
55 = 80	60 = 80	65 = 80	70 = 80	75 = 80

Classrooms that Spark !

C 54 = 79	C 59 = 79	C 64 = 79	C 69 = 79	C 74 = 79
53 = 78	58 = 78	63 = 78	68 = 78	73 = 78
52 = 77	57 = 77	62 = 77	67 = 77	72 = 77
51 = 76	56 = 76	61 = 76	66 = 76	71 = 76
50 = 75	55 = 75	60 = 75	65 = 75	70 = 75
D 49 = 74	D 54 = 74	D 59 = 74	D 64 = 74	D 69 = 74
48 = 73	53 = 73	58 = 73	63 = 73	68 = 73
47 = 72	52 = 72	57 = 72	62 = 72	67 = 72
46 = 71	51 = 71	56 = 71	61 = 71	66 = 71
45 = 70	50 = 70	55 = 70	60 = 70	65 = 70
F 44 = 69	F 49 = 69	F 54 = 69	F 59 = 69	F 64 = 69

Snap, Crackle, Pop

Parents as Partners

Developing a relationship with parents is one way we can help fan the flames of learning in our classroom. Parents have the greatest impact on their child's life, whether positive or negative, and we truly need them to be actively involved in their child's school life. We need to develop a partnership with them that ultimately becomes a support system for the student.

It is difficult to know when and how a positive partnership can begin with parents. Many of us may feel insecure or awkward when communicating with parents and try to get away with as little interaction as possible. However, this attitude of minimal contact is one that will ultimately hurt the student.

We must remember that the parents are their child's first teacher. As the child reaches school age, the parent passes the bulk of teaching and learning responsibilities to professional teachers. So in essence, we are "in locos parentis," and are taking the place of the parent for the time that the child is in our classroom. Therefore, it is vital that we become partners with the parents because of the dramatic roles we both hold in each child's life.

The Partnership

Webster's Dictionary defines *partner* as *two or more people working together toward the same goal.* This requires participation from both the teacher and the parent. Neither party can do all that is needed, so we must work together to accomplish the goal of educating our children.

The student should be included in this partnership as well. We can think of this partnership as a three-legged stool. Each leg must be of equal length in order for the stool to work properly. If one leg is unequal, the stool will be unbalanced. It is the same with the student-teacher-parent partnership. Each part must work together in unison with equal knowledge, involvement, and accountability in order for students to be successful.

When parents are not involved enough or even too involved, making decisions for both the student and the teacher, the partnership can become unbalanced and ultimately cause problems for their child. When teachers do not strive to involve parents, but rather make decisions without knowing the whole picture of the student's circumstances, such decisions may not be appropriate and may even be detrimental to the student's well-being. When a student makes no effort in taking on the responsibility of learning and continually points his or her finger at the parents or teachers, there is a pattern of dependence and lack of personal responsibility that can seriously affect the student's future.

Why Involve Parents

Not only do parents know more about their child than any other person, but they are the ones who are ultimately responsible for that child's well-being. Just because they are required by law to send their children to school doesn't mean they have relinquished their responsibility. It is vital that we involve parents in all aspects of their child's life, including school life.

As educators, we have a responsibility to involve parents because of their fundamental rights. However, it is also to our great advantage, as well as the student's advantage, to involve parents. Recent research documented by Fuller and Olsen in *Home-School Relations: Working Successfully with Parents and Families* (2007) shows that family involvement has a profound effect on student success in both academic achievement and behavior. Students who

have highly involved parents are more likely to be well adjusted and successful than those whose parents are not involved in their school life.

These studies began with the Head Start program created in the 1960s to help disadvantaged preschoolers. After extensive evaluations, it was determined that the most effective programs were the ones where both the parent and child participated and were regularly contacted by the teacher. In programs where parents and teachers were not involved with one another, R. McConkey (1985) noted in *Working with Parents,* the students lost any gains made after a few years.

Urie Bronfenbrenner (1976), in his study of the Head Start program, showed that children in these programs who were supported by active family involvement had fewer instances of failing a grade level, fewer referrals to special education classes, and higher levels of elementary and high school completion.

Informing and involving parents in your classroom has these benefits according to S. Swap (1987):

- Students strive for a higher level of academics such as
  - Earning better grades
  - Completing enriched course work
  - Enrolling in honors classes
  - Setting long-term goals for themselves
  - Participating in extracurricular activities that enhance learning
- Students tend to avoid negative behavior trends such as
  - Taking drugs
  - Running with a gang
  - Bullying other students
  - Giving in to peer pressure
  - Committing criminal activity
  - Leading classroom disruptions
- Students have a higher level of participation in school and community activities such as
  - Clubs
  - Athletics
  - Music
  - Religious activities
  - Community service
- Teachers experience more support and appreciation from parents. Parents feel a new appreciation for the commitment and skill of teachers.
- Schools are able to access a variety of resources from parents.

Barriers to a Positive Parent Partnership

Although the effects of parent involvement are obvious, teachers and parents often run into obstacles and attitudes that keep them from being true partners—for example:

- *Lack of family resources to complete required school activities and projects.* Some families lack the monetary and time resources necessary to participate fully in school and classroom functions.

- *Lack of information from the teacher to the parent.* If teachers do not inform parents about classroom and school events, a lack of involvement will result. Most parents do not have the time to initiate requests for information; therefore, teachers must make the effort. When teachers do not make the effort, parents assume that no news is good news, which is not always the case.

- *Fear on the part of the teacher.* Many times new teachers find it difficult to initiate parent contact. This fear can stunt the growth of a positive partnership between the parent and teacher and leave both feeling frustrated.

- *Fear on the part of the parent.* Sometimes parents come to the classroom with prior anxieties about school. These may be due to previous negative encounters with teachers or from their own unpleasant school experiences.

- *Lack of a supportive school environment.* If teachers and parents do not feel welcomed or supported within the school building, they will refrain from communicating with one another. It is vital for administrators to encourage both teachers and the parents to interact freely.

- *Teacher assumptions about family life.* If a teacher assumes that each student has access to everyday items such as a television or newspaper, then some families and students will feel alienated. Some families will not be vocal in communicating their situation due to embarrassment, which may come across to the teacher as hostility or indifference.

Moment of Reflection

What is your philosophy of parent communication and parent partnerships? Why?

Variables Affecting Parent Communication and Involvement

In order to have an equal working partnership between two individuals, there must be some level of understanding. This comes from finding out more about the person's background, attitudes, and relationships with others. By better understanding parents, we can work with them to ensure a successful learning experience for their child. Similarly, when parents understand us as people as well as our teaching philosophy and strategies, their level of trust will increase. When this happens, parents are more likely to work with us as equal partners rather than as silent partners.

As teachers we must deal with a wide diversity of family characteristics that influence the attitude of the parent and, in many cases, our attitudes as well. In addition, each family consists of both observable and unobservable traits, including traditions and a heritage unique to them, which can make communicating with parents difficult at times. It is important to take into consideration the general variables that affect families and the characteristics of human behavior when meeting with parents.

These are the variables that most affect parents and families:

- Availability of resources
- Parenting styles
- Parental beliefs about school
- Family structures
- Cultural background

Availability of Resources

Every family we encounter has a different level of financial security and available time that affects how much they are able to support their student and be involved in the classroom. This can range from profound poverty, where survival issues dominate family life, to working parents who are financially secure but do not have the time to volunteer in the classroom. Learning about the financial and time issues facing your students' families will help you better understand the attitudes of the parents you encounter.

Parenting Styles

Each family has its own set of values and beliefs that determine how parents discipline and interact with their children. D. Baumrind (1967), in an article in *Genetic Psychology Monographs,* identifies three parenting styles: authoritarian, authoritative, and permissive:

- *Authoritarian.* Parents are in absolute control and use mainly punishment strategies to improve behavior.
- *Authoritative.* Parents create a balance between setting limits and offering personal freedoms. Children are held accountable for their actions, but the focus is more on encouraging positive behaviors.
- *Permissive.* Parents have little or no control over the child. Limits are not set, and children are often not held accountable for their actions.

Our classroom leadership styles are also based on these behaviors. If our leadership style and a parent's parenting style clash, we may have some issues in communication.

Nevertheless, we must acknowledge parents' right to raise their children according to their own values and beliefs even if we do not agree with them. It is not our place to judge. We can offer suggestions and model positive strategies for parents, and we can encourage. If the situation is harmful to the child, we can take steps to protect that child, but we must remember that we are not that child's parent. It is a tough dilemma at times, but having a better understanding of each style will help us to better understand each parent.

Parental Beliefs About School

Each parent you face has had experiences with school that may have had a positive or negative impact on his or her life. This previous experience colors parents' perception of school and will affect your relationship with them. You may encounter parents who are fearful or insecure, angry, or positive and encouraging. The best advice is to remember that no matter what the parent's attitude may be toward you and the school, your attitude should always be positive and helpful. When we consistently serve others in a positive manner, we can overcome even the greatest obstacles. Parents who are fearful or angry may come to trust you and the school. Parents who are positive will have their beliefs confirmed and will go on to be advocates for the schools as well as for their children.

Family Structures

Although society generally labels a family as consisting of a mom, a dad, two children, and a pet or two, this is frequently not the case. There are many different types of families, and these differing structures may affect individual students. Since you are dealing with a variety of family structures in your classroom, it is important to gather information about each student's family, which will help you interact with both the child and parents in a positive manner. Consider the different family structures that may be represented in your classroom.

Traditional Families

Most teachers assume their students come from this type of a family, which includes a mother, father, and children. Be careful about making assumptions when you see what looks like a traditional family when in actuality it may not be one.

Single Mother

This family consists of the mother and the child or children. The burden of providing basic needs plus other parenting responsibilities lies with one person rather than two. This means that the single mom's time and energy are extremely limited.

Divorced or Single Parent

This family consists of one parent (mother or father) and a child or children. While similar to the single mother, this family has all of the time and energy struggles faced by the single mom plus the emotional devastation that occurs when parents break up or a spouse dies. These students may be operating in crisis mode, which will affect how they act in your classroom.

Stepfamilies

This family consists of two single-parent families joined together. Although this family looks like the traditional one, there are extra concerns. The children from the different families of origin may be jealous of each other and the attention their parent gives to the stepsiblings. Everyone may feel awkward in relation to the children that are not theirs by birth, and there may be other complications.

Guardian Parents

This family consists of a child or children being reared by someone other than a parent: grandparents, aunts or uncles, guardians, or foster parents. The variables with this type of family are so wide that it is important for you to get a general understanding of how each particular family operates so that you can better meet their needs.

Cultural Backgrounds

Our students and their families come from a wide range of cultures. It is important to learn as much as you can from the parents themselves or books about the basic customs and values from each culture. Within each cultural group, individual families are affected differently by the traditions and values passed down from their ancestors. These customs vary from country to country or state to state.

Tips for Working with Different Family Variables

- Before failing a student for not turning in homework, first consider whether you are punishing the student for his or her economic situation. Do not assume that basic supplies such as scissors, markers, paper, or glue are in the home. Parents in poverty are limited in the amount of support they can offer. The more you acknowledge their efforts, the more they will do for you and their child.

- Don't assume that parents don't care. Some parents may not show up for teacher conferences because they have no way to get to the school.

- Make an effort to welcome parents into your classroom whenever they can drop by. This shows you are willing to work with their schedule.

- Offer flexible conference times for parents who work long hours or several jobs. They may arrive at conferences feeling exhausted and overburdened. Offer to be a listener before you begin the official conference.

- A positive attitude and willingness to work with angry parents to help the child will help deflate them. Always keep the focus of your conversations on the welfare of the student.

- Put defensive parents at ease by starting with positive comments about the student.

- Be careful about the way you phrase concerns to authoritarian parents. Punishment at home can take many different forms, some of them abusive.

- Authoritarian parents may transfer their feelings of anger caused by frustration or embarrassment to the teacher. Let the parent vent. Then express a genuine interest in working together to solve the problem.

- Before making any major decisions regarding a student, solicit information from the parent regarding the child. It could be that they have already dealt with the problem at home. Be sure to take their advice seriously.

- If you have a student who is exhibiting disruptive behaviors or is not making any effort in school, call the parents. You may find that the student or family has gone through a serious life change that is affecting his or her behavior and schoolwork.

- Try to use a translator as often as possible when working with parents who speak a different language. Your school may have a faculty or staff member who speaks the language and would be willing to help translate. Another option is an online translation service that may provide help with translating letters and forms. Language can often be a barrier to both communication and involvement on the part of the parent.

Moment of Reflection

What family variables most affect your communication and relationships with your students' parents? What are some strategies you can use to overcome any barriers of positive communication and relations between you and the parents?

Making First Contact

There are several ways you can get off to a great start with students and their families. As we stated earlier, the first contact home is always the most important. It begins the relationship between you and the parents. Do you want the relationship to be one-sided or two-sided? Are you interested in a true partnership with the parent, or are you only giving lip-service to parent communication and involvement? Your tone of voice and the way you handle the conversation will communicate your attitudes and expectations to the parents.

The initial contact can set the tone for the remainder of the year, whether good or bad, and should occur before school starts.

Generally schools give out class lists along with other demographic information, including phone numbers and addresses, anywhere from two weeks to two days before school begins. Once you have your class list for the year, you can begin the communication process. This initial contact can be accomplished in a variety of ways even before school starts:

- Introductory postcard or letter
- Welcome package
- Phone calls
- E-mail

> **Always be aware of cultural differences when meeting with families.**

Introductory Postcard or Letter

Many teachers send a postcard or brief letter to students' homes before school starts. This is one of the easiest ways to get the year off to a fine start. Your welcome message should include

- An introduction of who you are
- A bit about your educational and training background
- A bit about your previous teaching experience
- The class you teach and your room number
- A statement expressing your excitement and interest in meeting the student
- A statement about the upcoming year
- You can use preprinted postcards, fold-over notecards, or colorful stationary to send your letter home.

Idea Share

Type up your welcome letter, save it, and print it out on colorful paper. This is especially helpful to secondary teachers who may have up to 150 students.

Phone Calls

A phone call is another way to welcome students and parents to the new school year and doesn't have to take a lot of time.

When making a welcome phone call, you might want to talk to the student first. Introduce yourself, and tell the grade or subject area you teach. Let the student know when to report to school and your room number. Then ask to talk to his or her parent or guardian.

Introduce yourself to the parent. Briefly explain your teaching style and background and your teaching philosophy. Ask if they have any questions for you, and answer them. Encourage parents to be active in the school to help with their children's school work when appropriate.

You may not always be able to make a call to the home before school starts. In this case, then a phone call needs to be made within the first few weeks of school. The parents need to hear your voice and know that there is a competent professional teacher in charge of their child's education.

Since this call is being made after school has started, you have already had a chance to get to know the students a little bit. This is a great opportunity to offer the parents specific comments about their child and even begin working on issues before they have a chance to develop into real problems. You might find the following "Sample Phone Conversation" useful.

Sample Phone Conversation

Hello, Mr./Mrs. _____

I am glad to have [student name] in my class this year. He/she seems to be very [positive comment]

witty	bright	attentive	vivacious	personable
talented	cheerful	friendly	cooperative	punctual
a class leader	spontaneous	hard worker	helpful	energetic

This is going to be a busy year for us. We will be studying [insert areas of study here]. I am really looking forward to a great year, and I hope you are too! Are there any areas of concern you'd like to discuss with me at this time? Is there anything I need to know about?

[If the student is already exhibiting negative behavior, this is the prime place to mention it.

[I want to share with you that I have noticed _____'s tendency to

talk too much	interrupt others	disturb the class
disrupt instruction	use time ineffectively	have difficulty working with others

[Have you had experience with this in previous years, or do you have anything to add about this type of behavior from your child? What strategies have you used in the past? I know that together we will be able to solve this problem and make this a successful year for _____.

[I wanted to let you know that I am hoping for open lines of communication between us, so if you have any questions or concerns, please do not hesitate to call me right away. My planning/team time is from _____ to_____ every day.]

It was great talking with you and I look forward to working with you and [student's name] this year.

Other Tips for Communicating with Students and Parents

- Create a Web site complete with a picture of you that explains more about who you are, your educational training background, and your previous teaching experience.
- Put your Web site address on your postcard or welcome letter so that students and parents with computers can get to know you better.
- There are easy ways for teachers to create and manage class web Sites (even for those not so tech savvy). Many school districts offer and support a Web site and course management system for teachers. If your district has this, take advantage of the resources and support. It really is easy and important to have a presence on the Web. Following are a few Web sites for teachers to create their own online presence:
  - Classnotesonline.com
  - Schoolnotes.com
  - Moodle.com
  - Blackboard.com

E-mailing the parent gives them your e-mail address to put into their contacts list so they can communicate with you more easily throughout the year.

Welcome Packet

Take some time before school starts to create a packet of information for parents. You can use colored pocket folders for this.

Create a label on the computer with the school name, class name, your name, and the grade level (if appropriate). We suggest that you use a shipping label so that it will look professional. Most office supply stores carry premade sticky labels that can be used with either a desk jet or laser printer.

Put forms that need to be returned on one side and information pages on the other. Be sure to label each side as "Keep" or "Return."

The packet should include

- A note of welcome
- Parent response sheet and survey form
- Classroom procedures
- Rules
- Discipline system
- Homework and grading policies
- Supply list
- Recommended book list for your grade level
- A general outline of your classroom curriculum
- School forms that need to be completed and returned
- Map of school with a star next to your room
- Names of the school administrators and office staff

For a middle school, create one packet for the team. On back-to-school night, each teacher can focus on one part of the packet as well as his or her own curriculum page. Parents take home the team packet so that it is all together. Send a packet home to parents who didn't attend so everyone has the information.

Idea Share

Make extras of these packets and keep them handy for when a new student enters your class during the school year. Parents will be impressed at how efficient you are! If you work in a school with a high mobility rate, be sure to have plenty of extras ready.

Parent Survey and Response Sheet

It is a good idea to send home a survey or parent response sheet to gather information about individual students within your class. Some teachers like to include this response sheet with their welcome letter. Other options include placing it in the welcome package or sending it home the first day of school. (See the "Sample Survey Questions to Include in a Parent Response" form at the end of the chapter.)

Idea Share

If you work in an area with a high population of non-English-speaking families, it is vital that they receive this information in their own language. Ask around the school, public library, churches, or other community services to find a translator for each language spoken. You may want to consider sending a copy of the letter in both English and their native language.

Grade-Level Meetings

Your school may want you to have a grade-level or team meeting with all of the parents. This is a great time to inform your parents about the policies, procedures, and expectations of the teachers in the grade level or department. This is for parents only and is more formal than the open house.

Have an agenda prepared. This can be a simple outline of the topics you will be discussing. An agenda will help keep you organized in your thoughts and will keep parents from changing the subject. A good way to keep from making unnecessary copies is to make a transparency of the agenda so that everyone can see it.

Example: Grade-Level Meeting Agenda

    I. Welcome and Introductions
    II. Discipline Program
        a. Rewards
        b. Absence policy
    III. Field Trips
        a. Planetarium
        b. Symphony
    IV. Schedule
        a. Daily activities
        b. Math
        c. English/language arts
        d. Science
        e. History
    V. Organization
        a. Procedures—homework, academic calendar
        b. Student binders
    VI. Grading
        a. Types of grades
        b. Progress reports
        c. Missing assignments
    VII. Volunteers
        a. Field trips
        b. Room parents
        c. Supplies needed

It is important for parents to understand exactly what you expect from their child. For example, you might say, "I expect all of my students to do their personal best on all assignments. If I see that a student has turned in a poorly done assignment, it will be returned ungraded. This means that the assignment when turned in correctly will be counted as late."

This type of meeting is the perfect place to garner parent volunteers for guest speakers, chaperones, tutoring, or other classroom events. Create a notebook of parent data that you can draw from when you need a helping hand. Use the "Parent Information Sheet" at the end of the chapter, and make enough copies for each family. Have the parents fill out this form during your meetings and leave it with you before they go. Take a three-ring notebook, and place the forms inside sorted alphabetically or by your class schedule. Tabbed dividers help keep this information organized when you have several different courses.

Moment of Reflection

What strategies do you use for initiating parent contact? How do you introduce yourself to students and parents? How do you set the tone for communicating with parents? What is one element of your parent communication you could improve this year?

Keeping Parents Informed

In order to help their child, parents need to have the whole picture of what is going on in school. Their only reliable link to this information is you. Here are a few ideas for relating this information to parents:

- Warm fuzzies
- Progress reports
- Academic calendars
- Newsletters
- Blog, Web site, wiki space

Warm Fuzzies

These are short notes of praise or "job well done" sent home with the student. This takes only a few seconds on the part of the teacher but can make a world of difference for the student and parent. Students feel appreciated and rewarded. Parents feel proud, happy, and thankful that the teacher is dedicated and paying attention to their child.

Even older students benefit from this type of attention. Many businesses have started using this type of praise and motivation with their employees to raise morale and satisfaction with their job. It is well-known that people like to be appreciated. Our students are no different.

Teacher Tip

Work up a half-sheet form with a graphic of a "thumbs up" or smiley face you can use for your Warm Fuzzies. Put a general statement of "Job Well Done" or "Good Going" at the top. Copy this form on brightly colored card stock paper. Put a stack of forms in several places around the room where they are easily accessible. Now all you have to do is pull one out and write on it. (See Chapter One for sample positive statements.)

Progress Reports

Progress reports help keep parents on top of what is happening with their students. These days, many of us have electronic grade books that make reporting easy. Take a look at the program you use to see if you can generate reports of missing work and average grades. (See the "Midterm Progress Report.") These types of reports are easy to print and send home with the students. Of course, if you think they aren't making it home, mail it with a return receipt. This will ensure that someone signs for the letter.

What if you don't have an electronic grade program? Parents still need to be kept on top of what is happening with their child in class. Make up a generic form with each student's name at the top. Make enough copies for the year and keep them in the student's folder. A checklist form takes a few minutes to complete, but still keeps parents up to date. (See the "Weekly Progress Report" and "Missing Assignment" forms at the end of the chapter.)

Some schools are starting to provide "home access" to parents. This is an online resource parents can use to view student progress/grades anytime during the semester. This online resource allows parents to keep up-to-date weekly as long as the teacher is consistent about entering information. This can cause a real issue for teachers if they fail to keep on top of entering student information daily. Some parents get very frustrated if they don't see grades entered on a timely basis.

If you have a program like this, don't assume that print progress reports are obsolete. Many parents do not access these online resources, even if they have the equipment necessary. Others may not have access to a computer or the Internet in order to view student grades online. It is still important for you to send out a progress report at the middle of each grading period to keep parents informed.

Academic Calendar

An academic homework calendar can work as a wonderful two-way communication between you and the parents. Having the students fill out their own calendar each day is also an excellent way for them to be held accountable for their class and homework assignments. This is a life skill you are teaching, so be systematic about it. This calendar should be kept in the front of each student's binder.

Plan class time each day to write in homework assignments, upcoming events, and other dates into the calendar. Be consistent in your use of the calendar. This will be helpful during parent conferences. For example, if a parent is upset because he or she wasn't aware of the assignments due, simply say, "Did you check the academic calendar? All of our assignments are written there and initialed by me each day for accuracy." Remind parents that the academic calendar is a tool to help them monitor their student's homework and other assignments such as projects and tests. There is no excuse for either parents or students to say they were not aware of an assignment or test when the calendar is used properly.

Here are some tips on how to use the calendar:

- Leave five minutes at the start of class or before the end of class for students to copy assignments.
- Require parents to read and sign the calendar at least once a week. Check that they have signed it.
- Encourage parents to make their own comments in the calendar as a way to communicate with you.
- Check calendars at the start of each class. Be sure you read the comments so that you can respond appropriately and in a timely manner.
- Assist special needs students with filling in the calendar. You might assign a buddy to help them copy the information as needed.

Newsletters

In our classrooms, we send home a weekly newsletter. If you are extremely busy with other duties, maybe a bimonthly or monthly newsletter would be more manageable for you. A newsletter is an excellent way of keeping your parents informed of

- Classroom activities
- Units and themes of study
- Upcoming events and field trips
- Important due dates for projects and tests
- The learning strategies you are using
- Ways to create a good learning and study environment at home

A newsletter does not need to be in print. Your wiki space or Web site can include a page with updates for parents about what is happening in the classroom. You can also send e-mail updates to parents with tidbits or reminders. If you have a classroom Twitter account, you can send short updates to parents who follow your account. These are all ways to keep your classroom green.

Using a digital camera, you can also integrate pictures into your newsletters. Parents love to see pictures of their children in print.

Some families come from backgrounds where they did not learn good study skills and don't know how to help their children establish them. As educators, we can help parents by giving tips, advice, and strategies in small increments that are not too overwhelming for parents to absorb and enact into their daily lives.

Here are some tips you can include in your newsletters to help parents create good study habits for their child. Be sure to put only one or two tips in each newsletter.

Tips for Parents

- Stress to your student that you are a team player in his or her school life. Your role is to help your child be a better student. It is important for your child that you create an environment where he or she can study and do homework with few interruptions and distractions.

- Schedule a time to complete homework when it is appropriate for both your student and the rest of the family. Routines are important: young people feel more balanced and comfortable when they know what to do each day. Don't expect your child to sit and work quietly on homework during a chaotic time in the house.

- Plan a "calm," "settle down," or "quiet time" for the family every day. Parents can spend this time reading, folding laundry, working on the computer, or doing something else quiet, but the TV and phone should be off limits during this time. This will send the message that we all need time in a quiet environment.

- Help your student set up a study area. This does not necessarily have to be the bedroom. Most kids do better when their parents are nearby and work well at the kitchen table. If younger siblings offer too much distraction, send them to their room or another room for quiet time. Decide on one location, and consistently use it as a place to work and study.

- Don't complain about homework in front of the student. If you have a comment or concern about homework or academic requirements, please call the teacher later. You have a huge impact on how your child views school and the teacher; don't let it be a negative one. You may be undermining the ability of the teacher to do his or her job.

- Keep in mind the goal of homework. It is an opportunity for older students to have additional practice in skills learned throughout the day, as well as a discipline-building activity. Homework gives your teenagers the opportunity to work independently and develop responsibility and self-discipline.

- Don't do your child's homework for him or her. Some parents may get carried away and want to do the project so that it is "done right." Doing the work may hamper your child's comprehension of the material and interfere in the teacher's reasoning behind the assignment. Instead, offer your help as a guide and advisor. Ask questions that will help the student come to his or her own conclusions about the assignment. If your student is having difficulties, call the teacher and ask for extra help before or after school.

- Make sure that your family is eating well. Just as cars cannot run without fuel, the human brain cannot run without food. Even a single missed meal can affect a student's behavior and learning. Please make sure that your child comes to school well fed and fueled up for the day and that snacks are readily available to help keep the brain going during homework time.

- Every day, check that your student has completed the homework listed in the calendar and has put this work in the appropriate section of binder or "finished" side of folder. Then check off the completed assignment in the calendar.

Parent Newsletter for Elementary Grades, September 1–5

This Week

In math this week we are practicing word problems using division and learning the steps in long division by two digits. In social studies/science, we are studying the layers of the earth as well as history of the earth as a planet. Students will be illustrating a time line of the earth's history and will choose one event to write a story about. In language arts we are exploring figurative language through poetry. Near the end of the week, students will create their own poetry anthology of favorites.

Birthdays This Week

John B. Student, September 3; Julie R. Student, September 4

Thank Yous

Thank you to all the parents who volunteered to go on our field trip to the planetarium. We appreciate your support. Thank you to Mrs. Jones for reading with several of our students.

Major Due Dates

September 22: Poetry theater presentations
September 29: Long division math test

Learning/Testing Strategies

Sequencing is an important skill. We are focusing on sequencing over the next three weeks. To help your child practice sequencing skills, read with him or her each night. Have your child tell you what happened first, second, third, and so on in the story. Another way to practice sequencing is to follow the directions in a recipe.

Classrooms that Spark!

Parent Newsletter for Secondary School, September 1–5

This Month

We begin our economics unit this month and will be studying different money systems, the exchange rate, the stock exchange, and real-life finances, including balancing a checkbook and keeping a budget.

Thank Yous

Thank you to all the parents who volunteered to go on our field trip to the Museum of Natural History and Science. We appreciate your support.

Major Due Dates

September 22: Life finance project due
September 29: Economics test

Wish List

If anyone has experience with the stock market, budgeting, accounting, or economics itself, we are in need of several guest speakers and materials during this unit. Please contact me at 555–456–7890 as soon as possible to discuss ways you can help us learn about world economics! Thanks!

Learning/Testing Strategies

Recent research shows that real-world experiences help students retain information and skills better than lectures and rote drill do. Take time this month to share how you handle your budget and checking account with your teen. This might also be a great time to open a bank account in the student's name so that he or she can begin to learn the skills of balancing an account and setting a budget for his or her own extra expenses. Another real-world experience that will enrich your teen's learning this month is to check stock reports in the newspaper. Pick one or two favorite stocks, and follow them each day.

Blogging for Parents

Unlike a newsletter, a blog is informal and can easily be done at home or school without the need for a copier. You can give your students and parents the blog address and encourage them to read it. While not every family will choose to use this resource, it will continue to be available for everyone. The other wonderful thing about blogs is that they are archived and topics can be easily categorized. You can provide links to other resources including district curriculum information and state information. Once a topic is addressed, you don't have to readdress it every year. Parents could be pointed to the relevant archived blog entries as concerns or questions arise. In addition, they can post comments and questions for communication between home and school.

Here are some ways you might use a blog to keep parents informed:

- Create blog entries to address specific questions from parents. Be sure to post both the question and the answer.

- Create a blog that defines terms and acronyms commonly used in your school and classroom that parents may be unfamiliar with. For example, ELA: English Language Arts; IC: Integrated Curriculum; ARD: Admissions, Review, and Dismissal; IEP: Individualized Education Plan; and ESL: English as a Second Language are just a few acronyms parents are unfamiliar with. Yet these are commonly used in communications to parents. Also, many districts have their own verbiage to describe different types of learners and learning situations. For example, one district refers to their Gifted and Talented students as PACE students.

- Create blog entries that explain the vocabulary used during specific content units for language arts, math, science, social studies, art, music, and so on (for example, *grouping* and *regrouping* are now used in math as opposed to *borrow* and *carry*, which are more familiar to parents). It is especially helpful for parents to use the same terms at home when helping their child with homework or studying for a test.

- Create blog entries offering basic practical ideas parents can use at home to reinforce concepts and skills learned in school. What is something you would like parents to do with their kids when you teach decimals, temperature, world cultures, or something else? Break these down into basic and easily understood directions that are free from educational jargon.

- Create blog entries that offer questioning techniques. How can parents start and continue a dialogue with their student that will stretch the mind? What kinds of questions could a parent ask his or her child in the grocery store, when viewing interesting events in nature, at construction sites, and so on that would encourage the student to think critically?

- Create blog entries that explain commonly used teaching strategies in plain language. This will help parents better understand what is happening in your classroom and why. You may find it reduces the number of times parents question your methods.

- Keep your blogs short and to the point. This will make it easier for you to write consistently and easier for the parents to read.

Another option is to use a classroom Web site or wiki pages to provide updates to parents. One thing to consider is that when using a classroom Web site or wiki page, certain information can be posted on a page and will not need to be changed or updated frequently. Examples are contact numbers and e-mail addresses, explanations of commonly used teaching strategies, and acronyms commonly used in the school and district. Other pages may then be updated daily, weekly, or each grading period depending on the information presented.

Building the Relationship

Building relationships take time and effort, and are the lifeblood of the school. Although many times we might prefer parents to remain distant and let us do our job, that is not the way to foster a partnership. We need the cooperation and the help of parents to help make our job easier and more effective in teaching students.

Keeping parents informed of what is happening in school is one way to begin the relationship, but it cannot grow without personal interaction. We need that two-way communication where we can each hear the other person's voice or see the other person's face. This means phone calls and parent conferences. The problem is that most of us wait until there is a major problem before we ever pick up the phone or meet face to face. By that time it is too late. More often than not, we end up facing frustrated and defensive parents who would rather blame us for their child's problems than work with us to solve them. So rather than waiting until the last minute, pick up the phone.

Tips for Calling Parents

- Decide in advance what is to be discussed.

- Rehearse in your mind what you plan to say. Jot down a few notes or a short outline to help you remember your points and stay on topic. If you are approaching a sensitive topic, rehearse out loud to see how it will sound to parents. You don't want to start the conversation by inadvertently offending them.

- Pick a time and place that will allow you to be calm and relaxed in your conversation. Calling a parent in the office two minutes before the bell rings will add an element of stress and can cause tension between you.

- Gather information and documentation to support your purpose for calling: grades, behavior records, health records, notes from the parents, student work, and so on. All of this information can be helpful to your discussion and having a folder for each student with this information included in it will be useful.

- Begin the conversation with a positive comment before stating anything else. Always tell the parent that you and the family need to work together as a team for the best interests of their child. Tell the parent that he or she is the most important person in that child's life, and it is in the child's best interest if you and they work together as partners.

- State your reason for calling in specific terms: "I need your help to . . ." or "Let's work together to solve this issue I am seeing, which is . . ."

- When appropriate, offer the parent assistance in disciplining or helping the child—for example: "You might want to start checking the homework calendar every night to monitor your child's homework assignments and check for completed assignments." Offer a consequence when possible for the behavior if it does not improve: "If your child does not _____, he/she will have _____ as a consequence. Please let's see if we can't try to solve this problem as soon as possible so we can move on with a terrific year."
- Before hanging up, summarize the conversation and reiterate any agreement that you came to. End the conversation on a positive note by trying to mention something the student did well that week.

Always follow up a parent phone call with a note acknowledging your conversation, reiterating any solution strategies, and thanking the parents for their time and support. Keep complete records of every parent phone call. You may want to keep a copy of the phone record in your student information folder (see the "Parent Phone Record" at the end of the chapter), or you can keep index cards on each student with the student's name, address, birth date, parents' names, and phone numbers. Under this information, keep a record of parent contacts with dates and comments. Whenever you are ready to make a phone call, simply pull the index card and take it with you.

Don't forget the importance of calling home for students who are doing well in your class. These phone calls are generally quick yet go a long way to building a relationship with parents.

Teacher Tip

Schedule some time every week to make positive phone calls home. Jot down the name of several students to call for each appointment.

Simmons, Paul		5th period
2211 St. Andrews Place		11/07/86
Wonderful, CA 34598		
Martha Simmons	(H) 456–9089(W)	329–0897
Peter Simmons	(H) 456–9089(W)	289–7658

2/1/97 called re: no homework—spoke with Mom, she will begin checking academic calendar and will sign every night. I will check in the morning that it was signed.

Communicating with Parents

There are times when you will have to speak with parents and assert yourself in asking for help. You need to phrase your concerns and requests in a way that is polite but firmly lets the parents know you need their cooperation.

Examples

- "I am very concerned for your child's well-being, and I thought that you should be aware of what I am noticing."
- "I understand your point [or feelings]. How can we work together to solve this problem?"
- "It is in your child's best interest that we work together to solve this problem."
- "Your child needs your help."
- "I need your support."
- "You are an important influence on your child. Your involvement is crucial for his or her success."
- "When students do not follow the rules and expectations, it is their responsibility to be held accountable for their actions."
- "If this problem isn't solved now, it could lead to greater problems later."
- "I need you to take stronger disciplinary action at home."
- "I want to help your child improve, but we need to work together!"
- "We need to talk together face to face in order to determine the best way to help your child. When can we meet?"

Idea Share

When talking with angry or frustrated parents, the best course of action is to let them vent their emotions at the beginning of the conversation. Take notes so that you can verify their concerns after they are finished. Next, explain that you want what is best for their student and that your job is to help him or her do well in school, not fail. Ask the parent if that is his or her goal as well. If the answer is yes, then say, "We want the same thing for [the student], so how can we work together here?" You do not want to get in a battle with the parent, anger them, or sound superior to them. You want them to realize that you need their help and support.

Some words and phrases will never elicit a good response from parents. Try using statements that are less threatening instead:

Negative Phrases	More Appropriate Phrases
Poor study habits	Not meeting her potential
Dirty/smelly	Is not using proper hygiene
Irresponsible	Can learn to make better choices

Negative Phrases	More Appropriate Phrases
Wastes time	Needs to use time wisely
Rude or mean	Inconsiderate of others
Lazy	Capable of more when he tries; not meeting his potential
Troublemaker	Disturbs the class
Cheats	Depends on others to do his work
Sloppy	Should try to be neater
Selfish	Does not like to share
Steals	Takes objects without permission
Stubborn	Insists on having her own way
Uncooperative	Difficulty in working with others
Obnoxious	Tries to get constant attention

Before using a strong or harsh word, rethink that expression and state your case in a more pleasant way. Remember that you are not only trying to help the student; you are also a representative of your school and district. It is imperative that you be professional in all communications with parents and other community members.

Each student you have in your class is the special pride and joy of his or her parents. Using diplomacy at all times goes a long way toward building a positive relationship with parents.

> ## Moment of Reflection
>
> How would you rate your interactions with parents? How do you think parents would rate your interactions with them? What can you do to improve your two-way communication and interactions with parents and families?

Homework: Too Much, Not Enough Time, or Both?

Have you ever faced a parent's complaint that too much homework was assigned for his or her child to complete due to family commitments? This is a two-part issue: too much homework and commitments outside school. Before addressing this issue, we need to think about both aspects.

First, young people spend seven to eight hours a day at school learning and completing work. When we then give them an undue amount of homework, it takes away the little time they have to play, socialize with peers, and spend time with their family. Children need time to play and relax just like everyone else. If all their time is spent completing outside school work, they might as well spend ten hours a day in school. Homework and outside projects certainly have their place, but too much can be more harmful than helpful. There are several excellent books on the subject of homework that offer solid research to back up the idea of either no or limited homework assignments. One excellent book on this topic is *The Homework Myth* by Alfie Kohn (2006).

However, we also have the issue of families' overcommitting their children in extracurricular activities such as sports, clubs, and outside lessons. Running directly from school to two or more activities every day also takes a toll on students. Even if students are given a smaller amount of work, when will a child who is constantly on the go complete it? Overscheduling is just as much a problem as large amounts of homework assignments. Where is the free time to play and socialize with friends when being shuttled from class to class by a parent?

It is important for us to reflect on the homework and outside project assignment load. Are you giving your students an abundance of work to do outside school? Also, reflect on how much time you give for students to complete outside projects. Do students have enough time to complete the work? Have you taken into account the fact they might be involved in extracurricular activities throughout the week? Make adjustments accordingly. This should help calm parents who are concerned that their child has too much outside school work.

If you determine that your homework load is reasonable and you are giving students plenty of time to complete outside projects, then you need to sit down with the concerned parents in a conference. First, ask the parents to express their concerns about the outside workload. Listen without interrupting, and take notes of all the commitments they list. Next, explain the amount of time you estimate it should take students to complete their homework assignments or the outside project (on a daily basis).

Example: Ms. Jones, if Eva spends half an hour each day working on this project over the two weeks she is given to complete it, there should be no problems in getting the project finished and turned in on time.

You also need to explain why you have the students working on this project at home versus in class so that the parent understands your reasoning. The parent may not agree, but that is not the point. The point is that you are not assigning this project on a whim. You have a reason—a purpose for the outside work. At that point, you need to gently talk to the parents about the fact that their child (and family) may be overcommitted. This is not an easy discussion because most parents do not want to have their decisions questioned.

However, if the child is spending three hours each day on additional commitments, there is no way the homework can be done as well. Use the notes you took earlier to help explain your reasoning. This issue needs to be addressed for everyone's sake.

Next, work with the parents to determine a compromise between the two of you that will help the child finish the outside work assigned. Perhaps you can assign a little less homework and the parents can have their child drop one or two of the outside activities. You can also provide a timetable and a structured outline of when each piece of the project should be completed.

An additional option is to discuss time management strategies with the parents. For example, take a look at the family's calendar and the free time available each day. Does the mother or father spend an hour or so preparing dinner? What is the child doing during that time? This would be a perfect time to complete homework assignments at the kitchen table. Ask the parents to describe how and when their child gets outside work done at home. Are there distractions? Does the child have a quiet place to get the work done? They should need to find only a half-hour to an hour in order to get the work done. If it takes longer than that, too much work is being assigned.

It is easier for parents to blame you if their child does not get a project done on time. A confrontation is hard but may be necessary. This situation is not one-sided, especially if the parents are using extensive family commitments as their reasoning. However, your tone needs to be one of working together on a solution. Stand your ground as far as the amount of work assigned (as long as it is reasonable) and do not apologize for outside work that has a solid purpose behind it.

You should also speak with your principal when this type of issue arises. Explain the complaints of the parent and your reasoning behind the assignments. Then, if the principal is approached by the parents, he or she is already apprised of the situation and will have a response prepared. The one thing an administrator hates more than anything else is being caught unprepared by a parent.

The Parent-Teacher Conference

Many teachers and parents worry about conferences. This shows in the fact that so many parents never show up for a scheduled conference.

For their part, teachers may feel nervous or fearful. This is normal, no matter how effective a teacher you are. Parents often feel uncertain and have mixed emotions about meeting with their child's teacher. They may want to please the teacher and make a good impression, but they also want to express their concerns or frustrations. Many parents have a hard time saying what they really think

Always start a parent meeting with an open smile and welcoming attitude.

and are timid, but some parents are extremely defensive and overbearing. Whatever the type of parent you may be dealing with, always remember that the objective of every conference is to develop a working partnership with the parents so that the student's best interests and learning is everyone's focus. You want to put the parents at ease by letting them know that your only goal for the conference is to build a positive relationship with them in order to benefit their child. Keep in mind the variables that cause each family to be unique and come to the conference with a positive attitude and willingness to compromise.

If you anticipate an explosive situation with a parent, let them know that a principal, counselor, team leader, or another staff member will be present. It is always better to have a support system in the room when working in this type of situation.

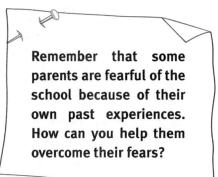

Remember that some parents are fearful of the school because of their own past experiences. How can you help them overcome their fears?

Preparing for the Conference

Decide in advance the purpose of the conference. Make notes to yourself of what is to be discussed. Learn about the home environment as much as possible to avoid uncomfortable topics or saying the wrong thing. You don't want to ask, "Where is Suzy's dad today?" only to find out that he recently passed away.

Collect information and documentation on the student: grades, your grade book, student work, behavior records, tardy slips, absent notes, and health records. You should have a student folder with all of this information together, but you may not want to bring everything you have compiled on this student over the year. Be selective: bring only what is necessary and could be helpful during the conference. Be organized with these materials before the parents arrive. And be sure to let the parents know where to meet you: in your classroom, the library, the principal's office, the school conference room, or somewhere else.

Prepare a plan or agenda for the parents to follow along. Knowing what to expect takes pressure off the parents. Both you and they can make notations on the agenda and write down any plans decided on. See the sample agenda at the end of the chapter: "Parent-Teacher Conference Plan."

Parents have busy lives too, Send home a reminder with the date, time, and location of the conference. You may want to have a tear-off portion of the note where parents can jot down questions and concerns they'd like to

Teachers look professional and organized when they are ready with student records and an agenda for the conference.

discuss with you, and send it back to school with their child, so that you can be even more prepared.

Hints for a Successful Conference

Here are some suggestions for a successful conference:

1. Stand when the parents enter the room and greet them with a smile. Thank the parents for making the effort to come, and show a pleasant, relaxed attitude. Try to put them at ease, and make them feel welcome.

2. Ask how the family is doing, and give them a few minutes to tell you about their day. It will give them a chance to vent a few feelings and give you insight into their life.

3. Begin your comments with a positive statement about their child—for example: "Bobby always keeps our class in stitches! He is a born comedian."

4. Share observations about the student. Ask for the parents' observations and compare them with yours.

5. Ask how the parents are feeling about their child's behavior, progress, and grades. Understanding the parents' attitudes will help you better understand the student's behavior.

6. Listen to what the parents say, and respond to their comments. You do not necessarily have to control the discussion.

7. Do not interrupt the parents while they are speaking. This often makes them feel defensive. Wait until they are finished speaking before you begin.

8. Discuss ways both you and the parents can help the student improve.

9. Make sure to have documentation in order to demonstrate your concerns. If the child has been having problems with grades, show the parent some of the student's work (or lack thereof), or maybe show them a negative pattern that is forming in your grade book. Do not make generalized statements; instead just state the facts.

10. If conferencing through an interpreter, discuss with the translator that you want a literal translation. Some interpreters take liberties, and you need to know exactly what is being said.

Teacher Agenda for Meeting with Parents

Here is a suggested agenda for conducting a student-parent conference:

1. Greeting. Smile and welcome the parents. Introduce yourself if this is your first meeting. Thank the parents for coming.

2. Start with a positive or encouraging comment about their child.

3. Explain the objective and purposes of the conference and why you feel it is necessary to meet in person—for example, you can better share work samples or can meet with student and parents together. Provide the parents with their own copy of the conference agenda.

4. Ask the parent for their observations or feelings about their child.

5. Provide your observations and concerns. Be specific on how you feel the student could make improvements.

6. Review the documentation that you have gathered for the conference.
   - Student work samples
   - Grade book
   - Discipline and other behavioral reports
   - Any special education forms or referrals
   - Scores and reports from standardized testing
   - Any input provided by other teachers who work with this student

7. Ask for parental comments, questions, and concerns.

8. Discuss ideas and develop a strategy for student improvement. Write down any plans on the agenda. Also, be sure to include a way to monitor student behavior and goals.

9. Plan a timetable for expectations of improvements made, and plan for a follow-up.

10. Summarize the conversation and reiterate any agreement that you came to. Thank the parents again for their cooperation, and try to end on a positive note.

Middle School Teachers and Student Conferences

Often middle schools work in teams that will use team planning time to conduct student or parent-student conferences. These steps for conferencing will work well for students as well as parents. Also, the agenda for the parent-teacher will be suitable for student conferences. It is helpful to have the counselor or another team member write notes on positives, concerns, and any plan that the group develops. Copy these notes and give to the parents before leaving the conference. This gives the parents a hard copy of what was discussed, giving everyone accountability, and provides a record for everyone of what was discussed during the meeting.

It is important when working with older students to give them input in a parent-teacher conference. This builds their self-esteem and will motivate them to change their behavior. Simple threats of conferencing with parents do not always motivate older students. Before bringing a student into a parent-teacher conference, notify the parents and make sure they agree to discuss these issues with their child present.

Devising a Behavior Plan

It may be helpful to bring a behavior plan with you to a student or parent conference. It may be completed when deciding on a course of action with the student. You and the student or parent can brainstorm both the goals and rewards to be used with the plan. (See "Behavior Plan" form at the end of this chapter.)

Another strategy is to gather the student's perspective on his or her progress and behavior. Have the student share a written evaluation of his or her experiences during the course in the previous grading period. You want her to include how she feels she has done academically and how she would rate her behavior.

Remember that behavior plans are a means to correcting student behavior, not punishment. Also, students and parents will be motivated to follow this plan if they participate in creating it.

Be sure to use rewards that are motivational to that particular student. Also, encourage the parents to use the plan at home as well. If the student realizes that he or she will be held accountable for behavior at school and home, you may begin to see a marked improvement in behavior.

Communicate Good News Too

Some students will never have an urgent need for a parent conference. They behave perfectly and do well in your class. Does this mean that you can simply dismiss ever contacting their parents? Absolutely not! Building a relationship with the parents of these students works to your advantage. It keeps your students motivated and builds a parent support base for you. Here is a sample letter you might send home:

Example

Dear Mr. and Mrs. Parent,

I am pleased to inform you that Joy continues to be a well-behaved and dedicated student. It certainly is a pleasure to work with her on a daily basis. Joy demonstrates a high level of effort in her class work and shows a positive attitude toward learning.

I sincerely appreciate all of your hard work in helping Joy to become a responsible student. If you have any questions or feel the need to communicate further regarding Joy, please do not hesitate to call or schedule a conference.

Encouraging Parent Involvement

Involving parents routinely in the classroom sends a positive message to students. First, they realize that their parents are aware of what is happening in the classroom. Second, the student sees that school is important to their parent. Many students, especially younger ones, also feel a sense of pride that their mom or dad is highly involved in their school.

Invite Parents to the Classroom for Special Events

Invite parents into your classroom for special events such as poetry theater, reader's theater, oral reports, and science project displays. Parents love to see these kinds of student presentations. You may need to arrange to hold class in the library, cafeteria, or auditorium to accommodate extra people. Plan ahead for special arrangements so that there are no mix-ups or misunderstandings.

Making a Special Phone Call

For upper grades, a special phone call may make more of an impression than a handmade invitation. Take some time to call the parents personally and invite them to your class presentation, open house, or other special event. While your students may get embarrassed that you called, the parents will appreciate the fact that you took time out of your day to include them. Leave a message on their answering machine or voice mail if no one is home.

If you know that you will be calling parents who speak another language, ask for the help of a translator. Perhaps someone in your school speaks that language and can help. A personal invitation means much more when the teacher or school makes an effort to use the parent's native language.

Bulletin Board

Post upcoming events on a bulletin board in your classroom and on a school bulletin board (if possible). Some schools have voice mail bulletin boards where parents can phone in to find out the latest assignments and news. Use whatever resources your school has available to post events.

Web Site

If you have a Web site for your classroom, give parents the URL at the beginning of the year so they can check for new assignments and upcoming events. You'll still need to remind them, but many computer-savvy students and parents appreciate the ease a classroom Web site offers.

When posting events, make it easy for parents to find what they are looking for. Keep your site simple and easy to navigate. Most parents aren't interested in cute graphics and sound bytes.

Our Web site, http://www.inspiringteachers.com, has free Web sites available to teachers to post their classroom information. We encourage all teachers to use this free resource.

Parental Help

When parents volunteer their help, determine where help is most needed. Every school and every classroom has different needs. You also need to consider the resources available to your parents. Does your school have parents with an abundance of time and money, no time or money, or something in between? When asking for help from parents, be sure not to ask more than they can give.

Supplies

Depending on the resources available to you through the school, you may need to ask parents to provide supplemental materials for the classroom. Generally the supplies needed for classroom projects are easily obtainable, such as household items. If you let parents know what you need near the beginning of the school year, they can begin collecting items such as paper towel rolls, paper bags, plastic baggies, baby food jars, mayonnaise jars, yarn, scraps of material, and anything else you might need.

Spend some time thinking about what projects you may want to do with your students throughout the year. New teachers should ask other grade-level or department members for suggestions since they may or may not know the curriculum right away. Develop a list of what you'll need so that parents can be informed in advance.

> One year we did a special project with our fifth-grade class that required a bale of hay, which was hard to find in April. Trying to locate the hay at the last minute was stressful, and we were afraid we might have to cancel the event. The next year, we created a list of special supplies and had a parent sign up to get us that bale of hay. Since the parent signed up at the beginning of the year, she had plenty of time to locate our hay and have it in time for the project.

Parent Volunteers

One of the biggest ways a parent can help in the classroom is by volunteering. There are many wonderful things all teachers would like to do in classrooms but are unable to because of lack of help. By encouraging parents to sign up as volunteers, you can plan to do a variety of activities for both older and younger students. Parents can volunteer to

- Help out with class projects and events
- Be a guest speaker
- Tutor students
- Chaperone field trips

Parents who volunteer are doing so because they know their help is important. However, their time is just as valuable as ours and they don't want it wasted. Have a list of duties or items you want completed ready for parents who come ready to volunteer in the classroom. (See the "Parent Volunteer Form" at the end of the chapter.)

Also, remember that no matter how often you see a parent, it is vital to refrain from chatting and sharing information about other students in the classroom. Not only is it bad form; it can backfire and cause an extremely difficult situation for everyone.

Offering a Helping Hand

One of the ways you can ask for parents to help is with classroom projects and events. Most parents will be happy to come to your classroom as long as they are doing something meaningful. Ask for help in monitoring lab activities, science fair projects, historical and cultural bazaars, and learning centers.

When parent come to help, be prepared. Explain the project and what you'd like for them to do with the students. Create a checklist of skills or activities you'd like the parent to monitor, for example.

Think of it as a job description. Parents are arriving with no prior knowledge and need to be instructed as to their duties while in the classroom. If parents arrive and find themselves simply hanging around because you aren't sure what you want them to do, the odds are that those parents will probably never volunteer in your classroom again.

Guest Speaker

Parents can be an excellent source of expertise that you can use to teach your students. Consider asking for volunteers to be guest speakers or demonstrators in your classroom. Among the parents may be writers, artists, musicians, practical mathematicians (an architect or someone in construction, for example), or scientists. Ask if they would be willing to share their expertise with the class.

Be sure to offer a warm and welcoming environment when you are hosting guest speakers:

- With a student, greet the parent at the door of the school.
- Have a name tag ready for the parent with his or her name and occupation.
- Offer a drink and simple snacks in the lounge area before heading to the classroom.
- Prepare students with appropriate questions to ask the speaker.
- Have a thank-you card ready to give the parent before he or she leaves.
- Write a second thank-you note, and mail it to the speaker the following day.
- Have students write a thank-you note to them.

Administrative Assistant

Many parents are willing to help out the teacher in any way they can. This may include stuffing weekly envelopes to go home with elementary students or copying handouts for the upcoming week. The parents who volunteer their time to help with these necessary but time-consuming tasks are important: they are helping you create and maintain the learning environment through their efforts. Here are some other ways you might use an administrative assistant:

- Laminating and cutting out materials
- Setting up bulletin boards
- Rearranging, straightening, or organizing the classroom library
- Preparing the class newsletter
- Copying administrative and management forms to use in the classroom
- Organizing classroom materials

Tutoring

Encourage parents to volunteer once a week or even once a month as a tutor in your classroom. You may even be able to get working parents involved with tutoring if they work for a business that encourages community service. Some parents will not want to volunteer as a tutor because they are unsure of their own skills. You can encourage parents to become tutors in the following ways:

- Ask for help in specific areas—for example, "I need someone to read to a student one on one."
- Give a specific amount of time, but be flexible as to when the parent can come: "I need someone to help for thirty minutes on Mondays."

- Give the parent tutor answers to the questions.
- Arrange for the parent and student to use a quiet corner in the library, PTA room, or conference room.
- When you see a need, make a general announcement through the class newsletter or bulletin board, or by calling parents you think might be able to help.

Some teachers feel threatened and frustrated when a parent expresses interest in taking their children to a private tutor after school. However, try not to take this as a personal critique or attack on your teaching methods. In the public school classroom, it is not possible to remediate for every child who struggles with reading, math, or study skills. Eventually we must move on to more advanced concepts, and some students get left behind. Often parents notice their children struggling at home in homework when they are working with them one-on-one.

It is a great thing when parents are involved in their children's school and homework activities, as parents catch things teachers cannot see in a classroom of twenty or more students. Welcome parental input rather than pushing it away. As teachers, we need to realize how crucial parental involvement is in the success of our students and let them help us! When parents offer to get their child extra help, we should really be saying, "Terrific! Let me know how I can work cooperatively with the tutor!" We all want the best for our students.

Conclusion

Parent involvement is vital to student success. Research shows that students who have actively involved parents are higher achievers in school. They cause fewer behavior problems and are more engaged in school activities. It is vital to develop a working partnership with parents throughout the school year. This cannot occur without some time and effort on your part.

Be sure to call parents regularly from the first week of school and throughout the year. Ask parents to offer their perspective. After all, they know the child much better at this point than you do. Keep parents informed of what is happening in the classroom. Regularly ask for volunteers to read and work with student groups, or invite parents as guest speakers. Whatever tools you use, be sure to keep up constant communication with parents to help ensure student success.

References

Baumrind, D. "Child Care Practices Anteceding Three Patterns of Preschool Behavior." *Genetic Psychology Monographs*, 1967, pp. 43–88.

Bronfenbrenner, U. "Is Early Intervention Effective? Facts and Principles of Early Intervention: A Summary." In Ann M. Clarke (ed.), *Early Experience: Myth and Evidence*. New York: Free Press, 1976.

Fuller, M. L., and Olsen, G. *Home-School Relations: Working Successfully with Parents and Families*. (3rd ed.) Needham Heights, Mass.: Allyn & Bacon, 2007.

Kohn, A. *The Homework Myth: Why Our Kids Get Too Much of a Bad Thing*. Philadelphia: Da Capo Press, 2006.

McConkey, R. *Working with Parents: A Practical Guide for Teachers and Therapists*. Cambridge, Mass.: Brookline Books, 1985.

Swap, S. *Enhancing Parent Involvement in Schools*. New York: Teachers College Press, 1987.

Web Site Resources

Education World Teacher Tools and Templates, http://www.education-world.com/tools_templates/index.shtml#parent

Scholastic – Parent Communication Strategies, http://www2.scholastic.com/browse/collection.jsp?id=107

SchoolNotes, http://www.schoolnotes.com

Sample Survey Questions to Include in a Parent Response Form

Name of child: _____

Parent or guardian names in full: _____

Parent address(s): _____

Parent e-mail: _____

Parent fax number: _____

Is it okay to fax you notices and letters at this number? _____

Student e-mail: _____

Daytime and evening phone numbers for both parents: _____

Special interests (sports, hobbies) of student: _____

List any allergies student has: _____

List any medication student is currently taking: _____

List special needs of student (both academic and medical): _____

Special notes or comments? _____

What are your goals and expectations for your child this year? _____

What motivates your student? _____

Any special family circumstances? _____

Do you have any areas of expertise that you feel would be helpful for the school or this particular class? _____

Circle three things you would be willing to do as a volunteer:

library   field trips   guest speaker   class parties/event

booster clubs   carnival   student clubs   lunchroom

reading to students   tutoring   monitoring the
                                  school grounds

Would you be willing to help translate? If so, what language(s)? Do you need a translator yourself? _____

Parent Information Sheet

Student name: _____

Mother's name (first, last): _____

Occupation: _____

Work phone: _____

Home phone: _____

E-mail:_____

Special abilities/interests: _____

How would you like to help our class this year?

tutoring   field trips   guest speaker

reading   classroom events   other

Father's name (first, last) _____

Occupation: _____

Work phone: _____

Home phone: _____

E-mail: _____

Special abilities/interests: _____

How would you like to help our class this year?

tutoring   field trips   guest speaker

reading   classroom events   other

Classrooms that Spark!

Midterm Progress Report

Student's name: _____

The grades below reflect your child's grade midway through the current grading period.

Reading _____   Language Arts _____   Art _____

Math _____   Science _____   P.E. _____

Social Studies _____   Foreign Language _____   Behavior _____

Concerns

☐ Low grades on homework
☐ Does not complete assigned work
☐ Poor homework/study habits
☐ Does not pay attention in class
☐ Does not make up missed work

Comments:

_____

I have seen my child's midterm grades.

Student: _____   Date: _____

Parent: _____   Date: _____

Missing Assignments

Name: _____

Assignments: _____

_____

_____

_____

_____

_____

_____

_____

Parent Signature: _____

Weekly Progress Report

Student Name: Date:

Work Habits	E.E.	M.E.	N.I.	Comments
Completes assignments on time				
Follows directions readily				
Uses time wisely				
Contributes to activities/ discussion				
Works neatly carefully				
Works independently				
Behavior				
Follows school/class rules				
Respects authority				
Considerate of peers				
Cares for school property				
Is self-disciplined				

(*Continued*)

Academics				
Reading				
Writing				
Social studies				
Math				
Science				
Extracurricular				

EE = Exceeds expectations. ME = Meets expectations. NI = Needs improvement.

MISSING ASSIGNMENTS: _____

Parent Signature: _____   Date: _____

If you have any questions, feel free to call me at: _____

Source: Developed by Spring Branch ISD Summer Program, Spring Branch, Texas.

Classrooms that Spark!

Parent Phone Record

Student's name: _____

Date call completed: _____

Subject(s): _____

Parent's name: _____

Telephone numbers (Home): _____ (Work): _____

Purpose of call:

Matters discussed:

Plan of action:

Parent Communication

Date:

Subject:

Today, _____

☐ was tardy to class.

☐ was unprepared for class.

☐ no pen/pencil

☐ no notebook

☐ no textbook

☐ did not have his/her assignment or homework.

☐ Other

This is the second occurrence of this problem. If the problem persists, I will call you.

Please sign this note and return it to school tomorrow. Thanks for your cooperation.

Sincerely,

Parent Signature: _____

Conference Request Form

Date:

Student's Name:

Teacher(s) Name:

Dear Parent(s):   It is important that we have a conference regarding your child's:

☐ Attendance

☐ Work habits

☐ Behavior

☐ Other

This conference has been scheduled for:

Date: Time:

Location:

If you have any questions, or need to schedule for a different time, please call me at: _____

☐ I will be at the conference. My questions and/ or concerns are:

☐ I cannot make this scheduled conference. A better time would be:

Parent Signature: _____

Parent Notification of Student Conference

Date: _____

Dear _____,

This note is to let you know that my teacher and I have had a conference, and we have decided that I need to improve in the areas checked below. If I improve my behavior, it will not be necessary to schedule a parent conference at this time.

☐ Poor attitude

☐ Showing respect for other students

☐ Showing respect for adults

☐ Knowing when to talk and when to listen

☐ Staying in my seat

☐ Behavior in the halls

☐ Behavior in the restroom

☐ Courtesy when teacher is talking with a visitor

☐ Good manners in the cafeteria

☐ Following guidelines of lunchroom behavior

☐ Getting assignments in on time

☐ Using time wisely

☐ Good sportsmanship: ☐ Playground P.E.   ☐ Classroom

Please sign to show that we have discussed this note. This will be in your classroom file.

Student: _____

Teacher: _____

Parent: _____

Classrooms that Spark!

Parent-Teacher Conference Plan

Please feel free to make any notations on the agenda.

1. Objective and/or purposes of conference.

2. Parents share any observations of the student they feel are important and that relate to student work and behavior at school.

3. Teachers provide observations, review documentation, and share any concerns.

4. Parents and teachers discuss possible strategies for improvement.

5. Parents and teachers decide on a plan of action.

6. Closure.

Parent Volunteer Form

Dear Parents,

It is our firm belief that when schools and parents work together, our students are more successful. We want to establish a partnership with you this year in order to better serve your child. Part of this partnership is parent involvement in the school. Research shows that when parents are actively involved in the school, students attain higher levels of success. We would like to invite you to be a part of our school in whatever way you feel you can. Please complete the following form and return it to your child's homeroom teacher so that we can better know how you would like to be involved. Thank you!

☐ Class parties
☐ Field trips
☐ Tutor in: ☐ reading   ☐ math   ☐ science
☐ Library
☐ Main office
☐ Special classroom events
☐ Monitor stations/learning centers
☐ School fair/bazaar
☐ Guest speaker
☐ Teacher assistant (copying, cutting, laminating, etc.)

Other: _____

We appreciate all you do to help your child have a successful school career and look forward to working with you this year!

Sincerely,

Behavior Modification Plan

Instructions: Work with the student and parent to determine five behaviors you expect the student to perform. Some examples include: stay in seat, use a respectful tone of voice, keep hands to self, take turns when speaking. Each day that a student exhibits one of these behaviors, place a sticker on or initial the box for that day. Reward the student on a weekly basis—for example:

  5 stickers   = a special job to do (erase board, line leader, run an errand)

10 stickers = a homework pass

15 stickers = special lunch with the teacher

20 stickers = computer time or library time

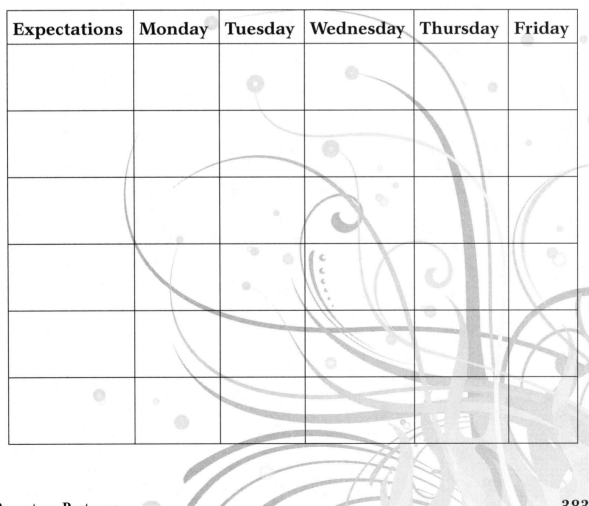

Expectations	Monday	Tuesday	Wednesday	Thursday	Friday

The Professional Teacher

Being part of the teaching profession is a noble act. As teachers we have a profound impact on society as a whole. In shaping young minds, we influence many lives and guide the learning of future leaders. Therefore, it is important for us to be positive role models in our school and the community. The way we are perceived by those around us influences whether we are considered part of a profession or glorified babysitters.

As Vivian Troen and Katherine Boles so eloquently wrote in their book, *Who's Teaching Your Children?* (2003), "Teaching is a complex skill that requires specialized training. Once we understand that teaching is much more than simply conveying information from one person to another, certain truths begin to emerge, and persistent myths disappear" (p. 148).

We can have an impact on how teachers are perceived by society if we all make a concerted effort to demonstrate our professionalism. Being a professional teacher requires

- Dedication through extra effort and time
- A professional appearance and demeanor
- Positive interpersonal skills
- Working collaboratively with other educators
- Mentoring others

- Practicing reflection
- Continuing professional education
- Resourcefulness and flexibility

This chapter is designed to be a guide or a "refresher" course on maintaining professionalism every day. Most of these tips and ideas are common knowledge. However, there are those times when we are so deep in the trenches that we forget many of these basics.

Dedication

Although we can get tired and stressed by the end of the school day, we must remember that our job is not finished when students leave for the day. As we all know, it takes time outside school hours to organize and manage the classroom, plan lessons, develop positive relationships with parents, work collaboratively with school staff, and attend professional development sessions. We have a heavy load: our mission is educating future leaders. Just remember that other business professionals also must work late hours and attend continuing education courses. This extra effort simply maintains our goal to be viewed as professionals.

Dedication means

- Participating in meetings
- Attending school events
- Tutoring after school
- Staying after school to plan
- Joining committees
- Calling parents

Maintaining a Professional Appearance and Demeanor

Being a professional includes maintaining a certain type of appearance and demeanor. Think about other professionals in the world. Generally they are sharply dressed and use language appropriate for their field. When you consult a doctor or lawyer, you expect a certain level of speech and attire. When that does not occur, do you still feel confident in that person's abilities? Now apply that to how others in the community view you as a professional educator.

Attire

Primary and special area teachers, who are on the floor half the time, must wear practical clothes, not a three-piece business suit. But what kind of image does wearing baggy shirts and stretch pants present to students, parents, and other members of the local community? This is something we all must consider when trying to show our professionalism.

> Remember that everything you say and do reflects on your professionalism.

Demeanor

The language we use with students, parents, and other educators helps to define us as professionals. Use care when talking. Be aware that others are responding to your level of dialogue. Before you get ready to say something, think through what you plan to say before you say it. This will help keep you from making serious communication mistakes.

Demeanor is also the way in which you carry yourself. Good posture and personal grooming all play a part in whether you appear professional. Below are some tips for maintaining a professional demeanor.

- Refrain from using slang.
- Be aware of your body language and facial expressions.
- Be diplomatic in your relations with other colleagues, students, and parents.

Interpersonal Skills

Our interactions with others can be positive or negative depending on our interpersonal skills. Look at the tips that follow to help you have positive relationships with your colleagues:

- Be respectful to all school staff, including office staff, maintenance staff, and paraprofessionals.
- Acknowledge the enthusiasm of newer teachers, and be willing to try something new, even if you don't agree with them.
- When implementing innovative strategies, be prepared to support your ideas with appropriate background reading and research.
- Be considerate of others:
  - Inform other school staff when using school resources, going on field trips, or holding an assembly.
  - Always ask before taking supplies or using resources.
  - Don't make assumptions.

- When working with others, be diplomatic in making suggestions or sharing ideas. For example, if another teacher leads the planning of a lesson and you want to offer your ideas, you could say, "What do you think about . . . ?"

Moment of Reflection

Do you feel you come across as a professional to others? Why or why not? What are some ways you could help others see you as a professional?

Are you a student of human nature? If you are a teacher or are planning to become one, then your answer to this question should be a resounding *yes!* Teaching is not just a matter of passing along information and knowledge from one generation to the next; it is also about understanding and interacting with others. When you are caught up in the rush of lesson planning, grading papers, school paperwork, meetings, and staff development, it can be hard to remember that you are dealing with a group of human beings on a daily basis. Whether you teach young children, youths, adolescents, young adults, or adults, they are all human beings at the core and will react and respond to you as a human being.

So what can you do to better understand and interact with the group of human beings you currently teach? Become a student of human nature. This means that you distance yourself from the actions and start asking, "Why?" Why is this student so angry when she comes into my class every day? What is causing this anger? Is it me? Is it school? Is it her parents or friends? Is it something happening outside school? Until you know the answers to these questions, your interactions will be based on half-truths and conjecture.

Why is this parent constantly in my face? Is it something I've done or not done with his child? Is it based on past interactions with teachers and false assumptions about me as a teacher? Is it based on past treatment from the school or other schools? Does it come from a true desire to be an advocate for the child, or is it a control issue?

When we take the words and actions of students, parents, and colleagues personally, we react as though what is being said or done is a personal attack on us. When we distance ourselves, ask the questions, and engage in communication with that person, we have better understanding. With clearer understanding, it is easier work toward a solution to whatever the issue may be.

Another part of this understanding comes from looking at both sides of the issue fairly. As human beings, we tend to want to look at only our side of a

Classrooms that Spark!

situation and not the perspective of the other side. This is human nature. Take some time to put yourself in the shoes of the other person and ask how you would feel and react in the same situation. This includes your students sitting in your class and the parents with whom you communicate. The more we can understand other people, the better we can interact in a positive manner.

As a student of human nature, watch the interactions between your students when you have a moment or two. Watch the interactions between your administrator and the staff. Watch the interactions between your colleagues. Especially take note of the interactions between yourself and others. Then take some time to think about those interactions. Why did she say that? Why did he react that way? What did you feel when someone made that comment to you? How did you react? Why? Do you see any patterns? How do those patterns evolve? How do they affect the current interaction and future interactions between these people?

By gathering and using this information, you can determine what kinds of interactions you want to have with other people, whether they are students or adults, and modify your own words and actions to bring that about. Without asking these kinds of questions and without being a student of human nature, your interactions will continue to be instinctive rather than deliberate.

Help your interactions be positive ones by gaining an understanding of how people work. The more you observe and reflect and look for understanding, the more it will come to you. The better you understand others, the better you will be able to interact with your students, parents, and colleagues. Always remember that a student of human nature seeks first to understand and then to react.

Collaboration

As part of the school community, you are working with other professionals. Collaboration is important not only because it makes your job easier, but also because it benefits the students. Whether you are working as a mentor, with other veteran teachers, a special area instructor, or the office staff, it is beneficial for all to engage in a sharing of ideas and resources.

Once again, Troen and Boles have accurately described the importance of team teaching in the school: "Numerous studies conducted both in the United States and in other countries, notably China and Japan, have shown that teachers become more proficient by continually working on curriculum, demonstration lessons, and assessments together. Research shows that not only does working in teams improve the practice of teaching; it also eliminates the isolation inherent in most teachers' work lives" (2003, p. 150).

Attend School Events to Show Support
Being a part of the school community means being visible at school events. Students and parents want to see you involved. They are invested in their

neighborhood school and want to know that you are part of the community. In addition, students love it when you show up for their art shows, science fairs, sports events, carnivals, and other events.

> As fifth-grade teachers, there were just the two of us and both new to the grade level. In order to help our students and each other, we chose to team-teach the majority of the year. Each week we planned our lessons together and often taught together as well. We gathered the students into one room and presented the lesson as a team. One would be at the front giving information, while the other was monitoring students, providing one-on-one help, and interjecting timely and insightful comments throughout the lesson. In this way, we were both teaching, and students were getting the benefit of two perspectives and experiences. Whenever we covered a topic that was my expertise, I taught the majority of the lesson. Alternatively, my partner taught the topics and concepts that were her forte. Our students really enjoyed the banter between the two of us and often told us it was more exciting to learn this way.

Participate in Vertical Planning Teams

Many schools have implemented vertical planning teams to build consistency from one year to the next. For example, they may have second- and third-grade teachers meet together to determine benchmarks (where students need to be at the end of the year in terms of skills learned) for student progress.

It is also helpful for students when teachers agree on certain terminology to use in different subject areas. For example, students are exposed to the term *prewriting* from kindergarten as a means for brainstorming and gathering ideas. This same term is used throughout their schooling.

Also, be sure to discuss classroom procedures and skills such as paper headings, checking mailboxes, and whether pencil or pen is required at each grade level. This helps the next grade-level teacher know what skills and procedures upcoming students are already familiar with.

Participate on School Committees

Working with others as a team on a committee helps us network with other teachers in the school and build camaraderie. There are times when we may feel that being a part of a committee is just another item added to an already large workload. Instead, think of this as a type of break from the usual routine of retying wet shoelaces, wiping tears, and redirecting behavior. All day you are surrounded by children or adolescents. This gives you an opportunity to be part of an adult group.

Classrooms that Spark!

Working with Special Area Teachers and Paraprofessionals

When planning lessons, be sure to include your special area teachers such as art, music, physical education, special education, and English as a Second Language. They can be valuable for student learning as well as to make connections for students between subject areas. In addition, these teachers are sources of expertise in their field and can provide you with ideas, support, and resources. For example, when studying Africa, you might approach the art teacher to do a unit on African masks, and the music teacher could provide music from the areas in Africa that you are studying.

> " As the parent of a nonsighted child, I have seen the value of teachers working together for the benefit of my son. The classroom teacher plans lessons with the speech teacher and the VI teacher [the teacher for those who are visually impaired] to make sure that my son can take part in the fun and exciting lessons going on in the classroom. Although the regular teacher is wonderful, the special education teachers can offer specific ideas to make the lessons more meaningful for my son. For example, while in preschool my son's class planted seeds in a garden one day. The VI teacher knew that my son wouldn't like to touch the dirt. Although he still participated, they also did an edible garden as an extension. Pudding and Oreo cookies became the dirt, with jelly beans as the seeds. He certainly didn't mind touching and using food! This really made the lesson come alive for my son, and the other kids loved it too! As a parent, this type of collaborative effort really impresses me! "

Working as a Mentor

By being a mentor you have a profound impact not only on the new teachers but on the education system as a whole. As a mentor, you have the ability to shape a new educator into an effective teacher over the course of one or more years. This means that you also have an impact on all of their students. Just think of how many lives you can touch each year that you act as a mentor.

This sounds like quite a daunting task, but supporting new teachers is not as challenging as you may think. The key is to take everything step by step rather than all at once. By offering advice and training in small spurts throughout the year, the beginning educator is better able to absorb and apply this new knowledge. For example, it is better to discuss report cards sometime during the fourth week of school rather than overwhelming the new teacher with this information right before school starts.

Your role as a mentor is important. Most new teachers feel overwhelmed by the reality facing them when they enter their own classroom. They have not been trained in the practical day-to-day operations and may flounder at the first sign of trouble. As the experienced educator, you have the opportunity to create a confident successful teacher.

According to the National Mentoring Partnership, most of what a mentor provides falls into the four areas mentioned below. Keep these in mind, and communicate this information to your mentee.

Advice: Mentors can offer advice to help new teachers evaluate their options and make better choices.

Access: Mentors can give new teachers access to a world of ideas and experiences. They can include their mentee in their own network of friends and colleagues.

Advocacy: Depending on your relationship, the mentor can work as an advocate. That is, you can speak up for their mentee in important situations.

Accountability: Mentors help new teachers stay true to their goals by holding them accountable. They can check and evaluate the progress made by the new teacher and give helpful feedback.

Guidelines for Mentors

- Refrain from being judgmental in your actions and comments to the new teacher.
- Ask guiding and specific questions rather than umbrella questions such as, "How is your week going?" or "How are you doing?" Specific kinds of questions might include:
  - What did you like about the first day?
  - Have you had any contact with parents?
  - Are your students meeting your classroom expectations?
  - Do you feel you are maintaining control with your class?
- Do not be afraid to offer suggestions, but don't be offended if they are not used immediately. It may not be that the new teacher thinks your ideas are bad, but he or she may be too overwhelmed to make any changes at that point.
- Being a buddy is fine, but it shouldn't be your only goal as a mentor.
- Give information and ideas in small amounts and at appropriate times.
- When observing new teachers, be ready to provide an immediate positive comment and one area that needs improvement. Save the rest for your debriefing session.
- Allow the new teacher to listen to some of your initial parent phone calls and sit in on one of your parent conferences. This allows him or

her to see how you handle different situations and builds this person's comfort level.

- When going over paperwork, be ready to fill out an example with the new teacher.
- Offer a time for the new teacher to observe you on a regular day or class period. Talk to the principal about setting up someone to cover the new teacher's class during that time.
- Take your role seriously. Use the time with your mentee in a constructive manner. Don't give in to the temptation to simply gossip.
- Be ready to provide constructive criticism when necessary. And always start out with a positive comment first.
- Help the new teacher get acquainted and involved with other faculty members.

For additional information about mentoring, go to the National Mentoring Partnership's Web site: www.mentoring.org.

Moment of Reflection

Think about the way you relate to others. What are some positive and negative reactions you've experienced when working with other people? What kinds of changes might you make to your interpersonal skills to receive more positive reactions than negative? Do you think collaboration among teachers is important? Do you collaborate with others in the school?

Practice Reflection

The concept of journaling is something we stress to our students. We use the journal as a way to help them become better writers. But for years, journals or diaries have been used as a way of recording daily thoughts. These diaries, while sometimes a simple recollection of what was done each day, are often a self-reflection. This is evident in those diaries of famous persons who have been published into books. They offer us a way to understand how a particular person thought. We are able to see their stream of consciousness in print. What about us? As teachers, is reflection an important part of teaching? In fact, you are probably reflecting each day. Do you mentally make a note of what works and what doesn't in each class? Do you try to implement a change to your plans for the next class? At the end of each class period, do you briefly think back over what worked and what didn't in that particular class as a whole? Do you then use that information to mentally adjust your attitude, plans, and approach for the next class? Informal reflecting like this is a continual process for many teachers. But what happens at the end of the day when school is over and everyone has gone home? How can you make full use of the reflections we do each day?

Catch yourself thinking. Whenever you have a thought about the way your lesson or activity is proceeding, jot it down on your lesson plan or on a separate sheet of paper. At the end of the day, label the paper for easy identification later, and staple it to your original lesson plan.

If you work on a team, where you and one or more teachers work together teaching the same or related lessons, be sure to do some reflection together each day or each week. Find out how the lesson went for the other teachers. Did they approach it differently than you did? Was their approach more or less successful than yours? The purpose is not to compare teaching styles in order to judge, but to determine the most successful way to help your group of students. This will often change from year to year.

Keep a journal. When you write down your thoughts and feelings, you are better able to analyze them. Dyan: I know that when I write about a situation or problem I face in the classroom, I am better able to think through it. Later I can go back and follow the flow of my thoughts. This especially helps when I feel frustrated but cannot identify the problem. Often I am better able to pinpoint the exact issue through writing. Writing can also help you clarify your thoughts and feelings on different topics. We work from nebulous thoughts to a concrete statement of what we believe. Once these ideas are solidified in your own head, then you are able to clearly communicate them to others.

If you are not in the habit of keeping a journal, try to write for five or ten minutes right after your students have left while everything is still fresh in your mind. Make it part of your daily schedule so that it becomes a habit. A blog is another format for daily reflection that may also help other teachers. Reflection, both informal and formal, helps us to both understand and improve our teaching practice. This is vital for effective teaching and learning to take place in the classroom.

Here are some topics and questions to help you reflect on your teaching practices:

- *The classroom.* Is your classroom arranged in a welcoming way that encourages student learning? Does the flow of the room help or hinder learning? Are the decorations distracting, or do they encourage learning and motivate students? Do you and your students feel comfortable in the classroom?

- *Classroom routines.* What routines did you use that you feel were effective this semester? Which ones need an overhaul? How can you change them so that they are more effective for you and for the students? What new routines would you like to put in place for the new semester? Think about the ideal flow of daily activities and events in the classroom.

- *Parent communication.* What level of parent communication did you encourage this semester? Were parents actively involved in the classroom?

Do you feel you kept them adequately informed of what was happening in the classroom? What made you the most nervous about calling and talking with parents? What can you do to ease that nervousness? What can you do to encourage more parent involvement? Did you find yourself calling parents when it was necessary, or did you put off the phone calls? How has the parent response been to you in the classroom? What can you do to help parent response be positive?

- *End of the semester.* What are your thoughts at the end of this grading period? What worked well in terms of lessons and units? What needs to be changed? How were your interactions with students, parents, and colleagues? What challenges are you facing? What are your thoughts on these? How might you overcome or solve the issues facing you at this time? What new ideas do you plan to implement at the start of the new grading period?

These are just a few overarching topics to consider at the end of the semester as you reflect and plan for the future. Our hope is that these questions will lead to further reflection over all areas of your teaching. Keep a journal, and jot down your thoughts and ideas to help you put them into a better frame of reference. You'll find that this type of reflection not only helps you put away past baggage but also helps you reenergize.

Professional Development

It is important for teachers to continually increase their knowledge about effective teaching practices. This new knowledge is often gained through staff development within the school or from outside sources. For those of us who have been in the profession for a while, we come to think of staff development as torture equal to any medieval stretching machine. While some districts may excel at providing stimulating and useful workshops, others are not so great. Nevertheless, professional development should be a time of professional growth and continuing education. Here are some ways for making sure all training attended is a valuable learning experience.

Take the Learning into Your Own Hands

Remember that you are the one who needs to benefit from this information. Come to the session with an open mind and a willingness to learn. Just as our students need to be open to what we teach them, so should we be open to what others have to teach us. You never know what jewel of an idea or strategy you may discover.

Do Not Bring Anything Else to Do

Although you run the risk of being bored, take a chance and be proactive in your learning. If you don't bring any other tasks with you to the workshop, you won't be tempted to start working on them when the presenter is speaking. It is difficult to listen and learn when your mind is focused on other tasks. While others may be grading papers, looking over lesson plans, or some other task, ask yourself, "Are they missing out on potential ideas for their classroom?"

Request Meaningful Activities and Information

Before the workshop begins, speak with the presenter and request that he or she give practical ways to apply and implement the information throughout their presentation rather than all at the end or only in a handout. If you let the person in charge know what you are looking for ahead of time, he or she may be able to adapt the presentation to meet your requests.

Don't Be Afraid to Ask Questions

Speak up. If something is confusing to you, raise your hand and ask for clarification. The workshop will not do you any good if you sit through part of it confused. Most likely if you are confused, several others are too. Also, ask for examples of how strategies presented would work in the classroom. Don't wait until the end to ask your questions; ask when the question is pertinent.

Go with a Positive Attitude

We are always saying this to our students, and it applies to us as well. If you walk into a staff development with a poor attitude and no intention of learning anything, you will have a wasted day. If you walk in with an open mind and positive attitude, you may get several great ideas to use during the school year. Sometimes ideas come not only from the workshop itself but also from casual conversations at the workshop.

Encourage Others to Maintain a Positive Outlook

We all know teachers who prefer to sit in the back and complain about the workshop before it even begins. This negative attitude can infect everyone around that person, causing a chain reaction through the room. Instead of responding to a negative comment with a negative comment of your own, try to infect that person with your positive attitude. You might try pointing out something positive for each negative comment that is said. If all else fails, move to another seat so that you are not distracted.

Provide Constructive Feedback to Presenters

If the workshop ends up making it on your "worst" list, let those in charge know why it was a complete bust. Don't forget to start out with one or two positive comments. Be sure to offer a couple of suggestions for correcting the problems. Sometimes those who are presenting staff development forget how to be good teachers. Your comments may help someone else have a great staff development in the future. And perhaps one day you'll find yourself presenting to a group of teachers and will appreciate helpful feedback from them.

Use Additional Sources for Professional Development

Many organizations provide shorter training sessions online through webinars, blog or chat sessions, and video streaming. Universities offer online courses for continuing education as well. Don't forget about these useful online resources as you strive to be a lifelong learner.

Idea Share

If you have questions during a presentation but don't feel it is appropriate to interrupt the speaker, write them down on an index card. Then when the time is right, you will have not forgotten what you were planning to ask.

This strategy can also be used with comments or ideas of your own that you wish to share with others. Write them down, and then at a break in the presentation, feel free to share.

Moment of Reflection

What is your attitude toward professional development workshops? How does this attitude affect your ability to learn and apply new information? What are some ways you can be sure to get the most out of a professional development workshop?

Resourcefulness and Flexibility

Teaching is a profession of constant change and movement. At a moment's notice, a schoolwide assembly may be called, interrupting an important lesson. Students are often unpredictable in their thoughts and actions, which means that you need to be prepared to handle all sorts of situations. Being flexible also means being able to use resources on hand when necessary. For example, if the art teacher is ten minutes late letting your class in her room, what are you going to do with them standing out in the hallway? What quiet instructional activity can you do to keep students occupied? Also, how are you going to spend your planning period now that you have ten minutes less of it? If a pep rally or other type of assembly is called at the last minute, how will that affect your lesson plans? What will you require of your students to make up for this loss? Will you rearrange your plans to compensate?

Situations like these ones can cause serious frustration and stress. In fact, a teacher's professional life is full of stressful events. We recently attended a professional workshop where the presenter stated, "Stress makes you stupid." What he meant was that when you are working in stress mode, you are not performing at your optimum level. Below are some stress busters and other strategies to help you along.

Take Time-Outs

We give our students time-outs when they need a break to cool off and get back on task. Why not give yourself one every now and then? When you are feeling a little hot under the collar, that's the moment you need to take a time-out. Turn away from the situation, go out into the hallway, and collect yourself. You'll find that even with a small amount of distance, your blood pressure will fall, and you will have a fresh look at the situation.

Take Time for You

Life is not meant to be spent inside grading papers all the time. You need to take some time for yourself. Leave those papers at school at least one night a week, and treat yourself to something fun. Go to a movie, attend a happy hour, cruise the mall, or get to the gym. There is more to life than teaching, and there will always be more papers to grade.

Set a Goal; Then Pamper Yourself

Set a goal for yourself such as, "I'll plan lessons for next week." When you've reached your goal, pamper yourself: treat yourself to a relaxing bath, a nice dinner out, or a great dessert. Although these are things you should be doing for yourself every now and again anyway, you might feel better about doing them if you know you've accomplished at least one goal.

> "I've always made it a priority to take one day off a week from my usual after-school, into-the-night, working-like-a-dog routine. Most of the time I go to the local movie theater and watch a bargain matinee. As a movie buff, this is a real treat for me and helps me remember that there is life in the world outside of school."

Five-Minute Exercises

If you are feeling exceptionally stressed, try some of these exercises:

- Count slowly to ten. Breathe deeply in on the odd numbers and out on the even numbers.

- Tighten your body from head to toe. Then slowly relax the muscles in your body starting with the toes and working your way up the neck and shoulder muscles.
- Do a few small circular muscle stretches with your wrists, ankles, and neck.
- Close your eyes and imagine a place where you feel happy and relaxed. Keep that image in your mind when you are stressed.
- A moment of meditation goes a long way toward serenity.

Working in Difficult Situations

There may be times where you face a difficult situation at work. Whether it is a personality conflict or differing attitudes about teaching practices, it is in your best interest to maintain a professional demeanor. Here are some ideas:

- Be diplomatic. Your mother was right that you can catch more flies with honey than vinegar.
- Work to solve problems through mediation and compromise.
- Respect the experience and knowledge of other teachers or the administrator even if you don't agree with their strategies.
- Be humble when approaching and working with others.
- Keep lines of communication with that person open. Don't let assumptions build to damage the situation further. In other words, don't let a spark of anger turn into a raging inferno.

Power of the Positive

We enter the profession looking through rose-colored glasses, but it often doesn't take long for those glasses to come off. Most new teachers hit a period of disillusionment with teaching between November and March or April of their first year. As the year progresses, more and more time is spent on paperwork requirements, meeting district policies, endless meetings, test preparation, and other duties that seem to have little or nothing to do with the actual teaching of children.

Disillusionment also comes in the form of colleagues or administrators who do not live up to our expectations. Either way, this can spiral into self-doubt and a questioning of being in the profession. This disillusionment can happen to veteran teachers as well who are frustrated with the system and the requirements added year after year. Our first comment to those of you who may be feeling this way is, "You are making a difference!"

When you are feeling low or blue and wonder why you are giving up so much of your time and energy, just remember that child who looks up to you or that teenager who finally started participating in class. These kids need you! They need someone who is steady and consistent and who will care for them no matter what. They need teachers like you who care enough to spend their personal time looking for strategies to improve, refine, or bring new ideas into the classroom. Don't give in to your feelings of frustration and helplessness. You are not helpless. You are able to make a difference daily, even if the results aren't immediately apparent.

Not only can you make a difference in the lives of the students in your own classroom, but you can make a difference in the lives of your colleagues, administrator, and all of the students in your school. When you face a difficult situation, always do what is right. Are you not being supported? Then find someone in the school who needs help and support that person as you are able. Be a good role model. Show others what support looks like.

Does your administrator keep piling on extra duties? Do those duties with a cheerful attitude, and then go above and beyond when you are able. Giving cheerfully helps our heart and spreads like wildfire. Be a model for others. Do you have a negative colleague? Come up with one positive comment for every negative comment this person makes. By being a positive influence in the lives of our colleagues, we also become a positive influence in the lives of the students they encounter. Will you see an immediate change? Probably not. Will you ever see a change? Definitely.

While we may have no control over the attitudes of others, we do have control over our own attitudes. Keep a laminated card on your overhead cart, filing cabinet, the visor of your car, the bathroom mirror, and everywhere else you think you may see it. This card should read: "I am making a difference in the lives of thousands of children. I choose to be a positive influence to everyone around me. I will greet the day, tasks, and challenges with a cheerful heart." When in a bad mood and reading this, remember that you do matter. You can choose to be a negative influence in this world or a positive influence. We personally choose to be positive influences as much as possible. These cards help us to remember this goal to keep our priorities straight. Once you do, you'll be amazed at how the little and big things that annoyed you in the past no longer have power over your life.

Is this easy? No. Just like teaching, it takes hard work and consistency. However, for us, the rewards are well worth it. You must decide for yourself whether the potential rewards of a positive working environment and learning environment are worth the work it takes to approach all situations with a cheerful heart. Before long, it is a habit and is no longer a difficult task to be cheerful each day. You'll also notice others around you being cheerful and the negativity fading.

As an experiment, take a look at what is frustrating you right now, and ask yourself how much of that is happening because of your own attitude. It is not an easy question to ask. How much of it is a cycle of negativity in the school that no one seems able to stop? Are you going to continue to allow other people's attitudes to control your own attitude and outlook on life and on teaching? These are important questions to ask yourself.

Steven Covey's (2004) book, *Seven Habits of Highly Effective People*, discusses the circle of influence each person has in his or her life. It is an excellent book and one that we highly recommend every teacher to read because we not only influence those in our family or a few colleagues, but hundreds and thousands of students over the course of our career. In turn, those students influence others in a circle that is ever growing.

To Sum Up

We'll say it again: you are making a difference in the lives of those you encounter. It is up to you whether that difference will be positive or negative. We have faith that you will join us in working to show the power of the positive.

> ## Moment of Reflection
>
> What are you doing for yourself during the school year? How do you take time to relax and get away from the demands of school, if at all? If you are not, why? What can you do to make relaxation time a priority in your life?

The Outstanding Teacher

There are many good teachers who work very hard at their job. But we need to ask the question: What sets an outstanding teacher apart? We end this book with a few thoughts on the qualities and actions that make a teacher outstanding:

- Flexibility
- Determination
- Persistence
- Humor
- Confidence
- Leadership
- Positive interpersonal skills

A good teacher can take anything from a book and teach it. An outstanding teacher teaches students how to learn, making lifelong learners out of each and every individual in the classroom.

An outstanding teacher

- Builds relationships with students, parents, and other teachers
- Is a student of human behavior and uses experiences to learn more about what makes people tick

- Focuses on the student rather than the content so that the content makes sense to the student
- Knows that he or she has as much to learn from the students as they have to learn from him or her
- Puts each student in the driver's seat rather than the passenger seat
- Is memorable to his or her students long after they've left the classroom

Emma: I can think of three truly outstanding teachers from my own school days: Miss Cowart in second grade, who took the time to listen to my stories; Mr. Morris in sixth grade, who made history come alive; and Mrs. Ray, my high school English teacher, who fired my passion for writing and teaching.

We all have teachers who have stood out in our minds as being outstanding. We remember that person who supported us with an encouraging word, who took a chance and believed in us when others didn't, who took the time to make what we were learning meaningful.

Teaching is much more than passing along facts and basic skills. It is the opportunity to open new vistas for others, share a passion for learning, reach the unreachable, and see the look of true understanding appear. This is why we're here.

Think about the kind of teacher you strive to be. Are you there yet? Like everything else in life, it is a journey. Some are further along than others, but we are all working toward the goal of being an outstanding teacher in the lives of the children who enter our classroom. We encourage you to take some time to think of at least one way you can continue on your journey toward this goal. In the end you will have a classroom that sparks, lighting the fire of learning.

Moment of Reflection

What makes an outstanding teacher in your mind? Who in your past was an outstanding teacher for you?

Conclusion

Teaching is a stressful, intense, unpredictable, and difficult job. It carries a heavy burden. However, when you have the right attitude, level of dedication, and coping strategies at your fingertips, teaching is also the most rewarding career in the world. For the same reasons that make it hard, it is also exciting, challenging, and fun. It certainly is never dull. It is a wonderful career made all the better with a positive attitude.

In addition, when we act as education professionals, we change the public's view of teaching. Since the early 1900s, teachers have often been viewed as nothing more than glorified babysitters. It is time to change this perception, and it is up to us to change it. Remember, the more we act like professionals, the more we will be treated as such by others.

References

Covey, Steven. *Seven Habits of Highly Effective People*. New York: Free Press, 2004.

Troen, Vivian, and Boles, Katherine C. *Who's Teaching Your Children?* New Haven, Conn.: Yale University Press, 2003.

Web Site Resources

25 Stress Relievers, http://stress.about.com/od/tensiontamers/a/25_relievers.htm

Education World: Teacher Mentoring, http://www.education-world.com/preservice/classroom/mentoring.shtml

Interpersonal/Human Skills, http://managementhelp.org/intrpsnl/intrpsnl.htm

Suggested Reading

Chapter One

Feldman, Jean. *Wonderful Rooms Where Children Can Bloom.* Peterborough, N.H.: Crystal Springs Books, 1997.

Kaufeldt, Martha. *Begin with the Brain: Orchestrating the Learner-Centered Classroom.* Tucson, Ariz.: Zephyr, 1999.

Nations, Susan, Boyett, Suzie, and Dragon, Steve. *So Much Stuff, So Little Space: Creating and Managing the Learner Centered Classroom.* Gainesville, Fla.: Maupin House, 2002.

Waddill, Kathy. *The Organizing Sourcebook: Nine Strategies for Simplifying Your Life.* New York: McGraw-Hill, 2001.

Chapter Two

Beane, Allan. *The Bully Free Classroom: Over 100 Tips and Strategies for Teachers K–8.* Minneapolis, Minn.: Free Spirit Publishing, 2005.

Fay, Jim, and Funk, Dave. *Discipline with Love and Logic.* Golden, Colo.: Love and Logic Press, 2001.

Glasser, William. *Choice Theory in the Classroom.* New York: HarperCollins, 1988.

Marshall, Marvin. *Discipline Without Stress, Punishments, or Rewards.* Los Alamitos, Calif.: Piper Press, 2007.

Chapter Three

Kralovec, E., and Buell, J. *The End of Homework: How Homework Disrupts Families, Overburdens Children, and Limits Learning.* Boston: Beacon Press, 2000.

Price, Kay, and Nelson, Karna. *Daily Planning for Today's Classroom: A Guide to Writing Lesson and Activity Plans.* Belmont, Calif.: Wadsworth, 1998.

Chapter Four

Lewin, Larry, and Shoemaker, Betty Jean. *Great Performances: Creating Classroom Based Assessment Tasks.* Alexandria, Va.: ASCD, 1998.

Osborne, Nancy. *Rubrics for Elementary Assessment: Classroom Ready Blackline Masters for K–6.* Livonia, Mich.: Osborne Press, 1998.

Popham, W. James. *Classroom Assessment: What Teachers Need to Know.* Needham Heights, Mass.: Allyn & Bacon, 2007.

Spinelli, Cathleen. *Classroom Assessment for Students with Special Needs in Inclusive Settings.* Upper Saddle River, N.J.: Prentice Hall, 2001.

Chapter Five

Jones, Alanna. *Team Building Activities for Every Group.* Richland, Wash.: Rec Room Publishing, 1999.

Chapter Six

Gardner, Howard. *Multiple Intelligences: Theory into Practice.* New York: Basic Books, 1993.

Gardner, Howard. *The Unschooled Mind.* New York: Basic Books, 2004.

Jensen, Eric. *Brain Based Learning.* Thousand Oaks, Calif.: Corwin Press, 2008.
Kovalik, Susan. *Integrated Thematic Instruction: The Model.* (3rd ed.) Village of Oak Creek, Ariz.: Susan Kovalik and Associates, 2003.

Chapter Seven

AIMS Education Foundation. *Math and Science: A Solution.* Fresno, Calif.: 1991.
Delta Education. *Delta Science Readers.* Nashua, N.H.: Delta Education, 2004.
Jensen, Eric. *Teaching with the Brain in Mind.* Alexandria, Va.: ASCD, 2005.
Kagan, Spencer, Kagan, Laurie, and Kagan, Miguel. *Cooperative Learning Structures for Teambuilding.* San Clemente, Calif.: Kagan Cooperative Learning, 1997.
Olsen, Karen. *Synergy.* Village of Oak Creek, Ariz.: Susan Kovalik & Associates, 1995.

Chapter Eight

Cunningham, Patricia, and Allington, R. L. *Classrooms that Work: They Can All Read and Write.* Needham Heights, Mass.: Allyn & Bacon, 2006.
Nations, Susan, and Alonso, Mellissa. *Primary Literacy Centers: Making Reading and Writing Stick.* Gainesville, Fla.: Maupin House, 2001.
Johnson, Bea. *Never Too Early to Write: Adventures in the K–1 Writing Workshop.* Gainesville, Fla.: Maupin House, 1999.
Harvey, Stephanie. *Nonfiction Matters: Reading, Writing, and Research in Grades 3–8.* Portland, Me.: Stenhouse, 1998.
Richardson, Will. *Blogs, Wikis, Podcasts, and Other Powerful Web Tools for Classrooms.* Thousand Oaks, Calif.: Corwin, 2006.

Chapter Nine

Burns, Marilyn, and Ohanian, Susan. *Writing in Math Class: A Resource for Grades 2–8.* Sausalito, Calif.: Math Solutions Publications, 1995.
Carratello, Patty. *Maps, Charts, Graphs, and Diagrams.* Huntington Beach, Calif.: Teacher Created Materials, 2004.

Chapter Ten

Gibbons, Maurice. "Walkabout: Ten Years Later Searching for a Renewed Vision of Education." *Phi Delta Kappan,* May 1984, pp. 591–600.
McCarty, Hanoch, and Siccone, Frank. *Motivating Your Students: Before You Can Teach Them, You Have to Reach Them.* Needham Heights, Mass.: Allyn & Bacon, 2000.
Peregoy, Suzanne, and Boyle, Owen. *Reading, Writing, and Learning in ESL.* (2nd ed.) Upper Saddle River, N.J.: Addison-Wesley, 2000.
Turnbull, Ann, and others. *Exceptional Lives: Special Education in Today's Schools.* (3rd ed.) Upper Saddle River, N.J.: Prentice Hall, 2001.

Chapter Eleven

Lynch, E. W., and Hason, M. J. *Developing Cross-Cultural Competence: A Guide for Working with Children and Their Families.* (2nd ed.) Baltimore, Md.: Brookes Publishing, 2004.
Barden, Robert, and Hacker, Michael. *Living with Technology.* Albany, N.Y.: Delmar, 1988.
Hershman, Dyan, and McDonald, Emma. *ABC's of Effective Parent Communication.* Allen, Texas: Inspiring Teachers, 2000.
Hildebrand, V. *Knowing and Serving Diverse Families.* Columbus, Ohio: Merrill, 1996.
McDonald, Marie, and Ruggieri, Katherine. *Teachers' Messages for Report Cards.* Grand Rapids, Mich.: Frank Schaffer, 2002.

McEwan, Elaine. *How to Deal with Parents Who Are Angry, Troubled, Afraid, or Just Plain Crazy.* Thousand Oaks, Calif.: Corwin, 2005.

Chapter Twelve

Carter, Carol. "Mentoring Magic: Helping Women Flourish," *The Key,* Spring 2002, *119,* 10.

Saphier, Jonathon. *Bonfires and Magic Bullets. Making Teaching a True Profession: The Step Without Which Other Reforms Will Neither Take Nor Endure.* Carlisle, Mass.: Research for Better Teaching, 1994.

Index

E

Elementary students. *See* Intermediate students; Primary students

E-mail, 9–11, 306–307

The End of Homework (Kralovec and Buell), 98

English as a Second Language (ESL) students, 177, 328–331, 346

Enrichment centers, 206–207

Enthusiasm, 321

Erikson, Erik, developmental stages, 158–161

Essays: compare-and-contrast, 250–251, 264; descriptive, 250, 253–254, 266; how-to, 250, 254–255, 267; persuasive, 250, 251–252, 265

Evaluation. *See* Assessment

Expectations: classroom, 56–60; for cooperative learning, 179–180; for journals, 246

Experiences, past school, 162, 338

Experiential learning, 186–189

Experiments, 188, 302

Expert advice, 180, 182, 187, 302

F

Families, characteristics of, 339–342

Feedback: on journals, 246–247; to professional development presenters, 396–397. *See also* Grading

Field trips, 211–213, 216–217

Files, organizing teacher's, 4–11

First day of school: checklist on preparing for, 148; importance of, 129–130, 143–144; lesson plans for, 132–135; opening activities for, 136–137; random seating ideas for, 130–131; student supplies considered before, 135–136; welcome packets for, 131–132, 145–147, 345–346

First week of school: get-to-know activities for, 137–140, 149–152; setting goals in, 135; team-building activities for, 140–141

Flash drives, 5, 6, 8

FlyLady.com, 10–11

Focus assignments, 79–80, 136–137

Formative assessments, 105, 106

Fuller, M. L., 336, 370

G

Games: cooperative learning, 141–143, 153–154; to motivate students, 302–303; spelling, 236, 303; to teach math skills, 271–272

Gardner, Howard, 166

Getting to know your students: activities for, first week of school, 137–140, 149–152; to create nonthreatening environment, 47; importance of, 158; to motivate students, 303

Gibbons, Maurice, 319, 331

Gifted and talented students, 177–178, 179, 327–328

Glasser, William, 180, 214, 291, 331

Goals: of homework, 351; pampering yourself after accomplishing, 398; of portfolios, 110; setting, in first week of school, 135. *See also* Objectives

Going outside, to motivate students, 309

Good behavior, recording, 67, 69–73

Grading: essays, 252, 254, 255; homework, 97–98; journals, 246; modified scales for, 326, 332–333; with rubrics, 113–114; student reading, 247–248, 259–260; writing assignments, 114–115, 122. *See also* Assessment; Progress reports

Graphic organizers: for essays, 251, 264, 265, 266, 267; to incorporate reading into any subject, 239–240

Greeting: parents, 362, 367; students, 45, 47, 350; teaching students procedure for, 61–62

Group work. *See* Cooperative learning

Guardians, 341. *See also* Parents

Gurian, Michael, 164, 170

H

Hacker, Michael, 186, 214

Handouts: in absent folder, 15; binders for storing, 6–7, 8; in day-of-the-week folders, 18; electronic storage of, 4, 5, 87

Happy sack activity, 304

Hart, Leslie, 166, 167

Helping others, to motivate students, 304

High school students. *See* Secondary students

Highlighting, to motivate students, 304

Holidays, integrating math with, 272

Home life, of students, 161–162

Home-School Relations (Fuller and Olsen), 336

Homework, 93–98; communication about, 96; grading, 97–98; parents' complaints about, 358–360; procedures for, 95–96; pros and cons of, 93–94, 98; teaching organization skills for, 94–95; tips on, 97, 98

The Homework Myth (Kohn), 98, 359

Humor, 46, 82, 304

Hunger, and brain functioning, 168, 169

Hunter, Madeline, 77, 99

I

"I learned.." statements, 107

"I wonder" questions, 187–188, 305

"If you were.."questions, 140, 304

Implementing new strategies, 17

The Important Book (Brown), 310